Unwilling To Know

Since the 1970s, historians have claimed that an insatiable 'will to know' has powered the growing concern with male homosexuality across Europe and the West, especially from the late nineteenth century onwards. *Unwilling To Know* challenges this dominant narrative by demonstrating how, unlike in neighboring France, Germany, and Britain, a mixture of silence and code surrounded homosexuality in Belgium until well after the Second World War. Whereas hundreds of scientific monographs on homosexuality were published across Europe during the *fin de siècle*, the lack of publishing in Belgium was combined with a marked lack of interest from the police, psychiatrists, and wider society. Through internationally comparative analyses, and with particular reference to the importance of religion, Wannes Dupont complicates overly monolithic views of European developments based on a handful of familiar national cases. In doing so, this study lays bare the many cultural, institutional, legal, and religious differences that have shaped the scrutiny of homosexuality in diverging ways.

WANNES DUPONT is a lecturer in the history of sexuality at the University of Edinburgh. His research focuses on queer history, reproductive politics, and the intersections of biopolitics and religion. Dupont has previously published articles in journals including the *History Workshop Journal* and the *Journal of the History of Sexuality*.

Unwilling To Know

Male Homosexuality at the Crossroads of Europe, 1870–1965

Wannes Dupont
University of Edinburgh

Shaftesbury Road, Cambridge CB2 8EA, United Kingdom

One Liberty Plaza, 20th Floor, New York, NY 10006, USA

477 Williamstown Road, Port Melbourne, VIC 3207, Australia

314–321, 3rd Floor, Plot 3, Splendor Forum, Jasola District Centre, New Delhi – 110025, India

103 Penang Road, #05–06/07, Visioncrest Commercial, Singapore 238467

Cambridge University Press is part of Cambridge University Press & Assessment, a department of the University of Cambridge.

We share the University's mission to contribute to society through the pursuit of education, learning and research at the highest international levels of excellence.

www.cambridge.org
Information on this title: www.cambridge.org/9781009570145

DOI: 10.1017/9781009570169

© Wannes Dupont 2026

This publication is in copyright. Subject to statutory exception and to the provisions of relevant collective licensing agreements, no reproduction of any part may take place without the written permission of Cambridge University Press & Assessment.

When citing this work, please include a reference to the DOI 10.1017/9781009570169

First published 2026

A catalogue record for this publication is available from the British Library

A Cataloging-in-Publication data record for this book is available from the Library of Congress

ISBN 978-1-009-57012-1 Hardback
ISBN 978-1-009-57014-5 Paperback

Cambridge University Press & Assessment has no responsibility for the persistence or accuracy of URLs for external or third-party internet websites referred to in this publication and does not guarantee that any content on such websites is, or will remain, accurate or appropriate.

For EU product safety concerns, contact us at Calle de José Abascal, 56, 1°, 28003 Madrid, Spain, or email eugpsr@cambridge.org

Voor duif en muis.

Contents

Acknowledgments		*page* viii
List of Abbreviations		x
	Introduction: Small Countries and Grand Narratives	1
1	Cruising through a Crossroads of Europe	15
2	The Problems and Priorities of Surveillance	31
3	The Legal Irrelevance of Sexual Specifics	45
4	Psychiatric Resistance to the Medicalization of Sin	57
5	Free Will Politics and the Avoidance of Inversion	70
6	Demographic Anxieties and Catholic Code	88
7	Literary Activism on Behalf of a Strange Love	105
	Coda: Pink Perils and Postwar Blues	121
Notes		135
Bibliography		196
Index		237

Acknowledgments

This book has been a long time in the making. It has been with me on a trek through three continents and five countries. Along the way, there have been many reasons to temporarily step away from it. Serially packing and unpacking was one of them. Another was climbing the learning curve of each new academic system. Some of these experiences have been bruising, chief among them the sudden and tragic announcement that Yale-NUS College would be discontinued. Fortunately, many others have been simultaneously a pleasure and a privilege, and I owe my heartfelt thanks to all those who have offered their kindness and support along the way.

My academic odyssey began at the University of Antwerp. I am indebted to the entire history department there for the opportunities it provided me with, and I owe special thanks to Peter Stabel for his early encouragement. I am also grateful to the Research Foundation Flanders for supporting the doctoral project that resulted in this book. A considerable chunk of the research would not have been possible without the wide access which Procurator-General de le Court granted me to the court records of Brussels. It was also made possible by the countless librarians and archivists who assisted me during my pilgrimage from one archival shrine to another. Particular thanks are owed to the staff of the wonderful Hendrik Conscience Heritage Library and of the (now defunct) repository of the State Archives of Brussels at Anderlecht for so kindly facilitating my work.

After finishing my dissertation, I was honored to receive a grant from the Belgian American Educational Foundation to spend a year conducting research at Yale University. I am also beholden to the Research Foundation Flanders for offering me a postdoctoral grant to continue my research upon returning to Belgium. Life, though, is full of unexpected twists and turns, and before I knew it, I found myself teaching at Yale-NUS College in Singapore. Few experiences have been as delightful or as formative as the next four years in Southeast Asia. A liberal arts education is something truly special, and so was the unforgettable community of students and colleagues who gathered there from all over the world. I will always remain a proud Kingfisher. Special thanks are due to Pericles Lewis and Naoko Shimazu for making this experience possible. I also want to thank the college for the various grants it offered to support student–teacher synergies and to fund the start of my new research project.

I am similarly grateful to the colleagues at the history department of Utrecht University for the months I spent teaching among them, to Katie Sutton and the Research School of Humanities and the Arts at Australian National University for the delightful fellowship they sponsored, and to David Paternotte and the Maison des Sciences Humaines at the Free University of Brussels for my time as a visiting professor there. The historians at the University of Edinburgh have been kind enough to take me on as their colleague and I thank the School of History, Classics and Archaeology for supporting the publication of this book.

We all need a few lucky breaks in life, and they often come in the form of meeting generous people. One of my luckiest was when Henk de Smaele took me on as his doctoral student. Few combine a warm heart and a sharp mind like he does, and I owe a great deal to his lasting mentorship and friendship. George Chauncey's continuous support and guidance have also been a major blessing, as have the kindness and advice of Dagmar Herzog, Chris Waters, Robert Nye, Kaat Wils, Alana Harris, and Bart Hellinck. Being a co-chair of the European Social Science History Conference's Sexuality Network has been a wonderfully enriching experience, and I am indebted to Jens Rydström and Jullie Gammon for bringing me on board.

Too many friends and colleagues have, in various ways, contributed to this book to name them all here. Dries Raeymaekers and Houssine Alloul deserve special praise. So does my family, especially my mother and my uncle Leo, whose hospitality gives every visit to Lichtaart that preciously familiar sense of being home. I am also grateful that everyone, including Goele, Nele, my father, and their families, are doing well, which makes living abroad not feel quite so far away.

Finally, I owe no one more than Katrien. We have traveled far together, never knowing what lay ahead. Without her, I would be lost. Some seven years ago, a new companion joined us on our travels. Part-Belgian, part-Singaporean, and now part-Scottish, Amélie is the light of our lives and a constant reminder that the journey is the destination.

Abbreviations

ACB	Assize Court of Brabant (Hof van Assisen van Brabant – Cour d'Assises du Brabant)
AML	Archives and Museum of Literature, Brussels (Archives et Musée de la Littérature)
BCA	Brussels City Archives (Stadsarchief Brussel – Archives de la Ville de Bruxelles)
BSMM	Belgian Society of Mental Medicine (Société de médecine mentale de Belgique)
CAB	Court of Appeal of Brussels (Hof van Beroep in Brussel – Cour d'Appel de Bruxelles)
CFIB	Court of First Instance of Brussels (Rechtbank van Eerste Aanleg in Brussel – Cour de Première Instance à Bruxelles)
CFIB-JC	Court of First Instance of Brussels, Juvenile Chamber (Rechtbank van Eerste Aanleg in Brussel, Kinderrechtbank – Cour de Première Instance à Bruxelles, Tribunal des Enfants)
COC	Center for Culture and Leisure (Cultuur en Ontspannings Centrum)
GSA	General State Archives (Algemeen Rijksarchief – Archives Générales du Royaume)
ICPC	*International Criminal Police Review* (*Revue internationale de police criminelle*)
PGCAB	Procurator-General's office attached to the Court of Appeal of Brussels (Parket-Generaal bij het Hof van Beroep van Brussel – Parquet-général près de la Cour d'Appel de Bruxelles)
port.	portfolio
reg.	registry number (griffienummer – numéro de greffe)
SABF	State Archives of Brussels at Forest (Rijksarchief Brussel te Vorst – Archives de l'État de Bruxelles à Forest)
SABr	State Archives of Bruges (Rijksarchief Brugge – Archives de l'État à Bruges)

Introduction
Small Countries and Grand Narratives

In 1967, the middle-aged Belgian sex reformer Jos Van Ussel successfully defended his doctoral dissertation on the history of bourgeois sexual morality.[1] The viva took place at the University of Amsterdam because Van Ussel had been unable to find a supervisor willing to take on such a daring subject in his native Flanders.[2] The Dutch-speaking north of Belgium was a historical bulwark of Catholicism. It delivered the bulk of the votes that, with very few interruptions, sustained continuous Catholic political dominance from 1870 to 1999.[3] Culturally too, Catholicism's influence was profound. So difficult was it to broach sexual matters in Flanders during these years that they are collectively remembered as *de jaren stillekes*: the silent years, when such things were mentioned only in hushed embarrassment. Van Ussel had spent his early career as a high school ethics teacher after graduating from the Catholic University of Leuven in 1944.[4] It did not take long before the ignorance and distress of his pupils led him to become part of the small circle of activists who pushed for change in the way Flemish society kept a lid on all things sexual.

Van Ussel worked with the still young Belgian Society for Sexual Education during the 1960s and he co-authored a small but controversial Kinsey-inspired study of sexual behavior among university students in 1962.[5] Troubled by the anguish everywhere around him, he began working on a PhD project about sex negativity's historical roots. His study took on the form of a whodunit: Who had been responsible for the "antisexual syndrome" that sickened Western societies like his own?[6] To Van Ussel's surprise, the church had not been primarily to blame. At the outset, he later confessed during an interview, "I really wanted to kick away at the church and take some revenge for all the misery that it had caused myself and many of my friends." But "as a historian I just discovered other things."[7] Capitalism, it turned out, was the main culprit.

In making his case, Van Ussel drew heavily on the writings of the German-Jewish sociologist Norbert Elias. European society, Elias had first explained back in 1939 while building on Freud, was the product of an increasing "conversion of shame into self-restraint" since the late Middle Ages.[8] Growing sexual restraint had been a necessary condition for and a key instrument of a wider civilizing process. More of a synthesist than an original thinker by his own admission, Van Ussel now blended Elias' historical analysis with the philosophical activism of another German-Jewish émigré, the critical theorist Herbert Marcuse.[9] Based in the United States, the latter had published *Eros and Civilization* in 1955 before becoming an intellectual guru of New Left student politics and the push for a transformative socio-sexual revolution a decade later.[10] Marcuse's liberationist mixture of Freud and Marx explained how sexual shame had been imposed onto Western society by its bourgeois leaders as the development of capitalism demanded the near-total sublimation of the workforce's sexual energy into economically productive labor power. Van Ussel agreed with Marcuse that a series of successive revolutions would be necessary to liberate the West from this 500-year-old trend towards sexuality's subdual. Summarizing the main thesis of his dissertation, the Belgian wrote: "If it is true that Christianity is not the cause of the hostility towards the sexual but that this is the unsought consequence of socio-economic changes, namely the increasing bourgeoisification of our society, then this also means that the emancipation of the sexual is only possible when the basic conditions of that society, which prevent emancipation, are altered."[11]

Beyond the Repressive Hypothesis

Van Ussel's thesis chimed extremely well with the heady climate of contestation when, in 1968, it was published as a *History of the Sexual Problem*.[12] The book flew off the shelves and its instant-celebrity author toured the Low Countries to give lectures and to pontificate about the impending sexual revolution and its provenance.[13] The book was so successful in providing Marcuse's prescriptive analysis with historical grounding that it was soon translated into several major languages. A German version appeared in 1970, followed by editions in Italian, French, Spanish, Portuguese, and Danish.[14] (The work was never translated into English, which is why Van Ussel has been almost entirely ignored in the Anglosphere.) All of these translations modified the original title to better capture what everyone agreed was the main subject of the book. On the European continent and across Latin America, the volume gained a huge readership as a *History of Sexual Repression*. But the French philosopher Michel Foucault had strong reservations about Van Ussel's bestseller.[15] His objections went beyond the fact that the Belgian's views were all too "hastily drawn from Marcuse."[16] During Foucault's lectures at the École des Hautes Études in early 1975, he criticized *L'Histoire de la répression sexuelle* as the quintessential example of a problematic analytical tradition. In it, he noted, "there is an implicit reference to a power whose major function is repression, ... and whose mechanisms are essentially linked to ignorance and blindness."[17]

In Van Ussel's work – as in that of Marx, Freud, and Marcuse before him – power took the form of denial and suppression; a system of censorship and concealment that drove sex underground. Foucault felt that such a one-sided focus on power as prohibition ignored the fact that there was much more to history than the instrumental repression of sex from the top down. He would take on what he dubbed Van Ussel's 'repressive hypothesis' in a revisionist series of studies of his own on *The History of Sexuality*, the programmatic first volume of which appeared a year later, in 1976. That introduction famously argued how, rather than an ever more strictly enforced embargo on sex, the past few centuries had actually witnessed the rise of an intense 'will to know' everything about it. Certainly, the language that gave expression to this analytical desire had been forbidding in tone, but it had nevertheless produced "a veritable discursive explosion" that pushed sex onto the very tip of society's tongue, where it has remained ever since.[18] Always at once analytical and prescriptive, the sprawling discourse on sex showed how the creation of normative knowledge had historically shaped social relations, individual behavior, and understandings of the self. In other words, the history of sexuality showcased how much more subtle power operated in society than the hegemonic but reductive materialism of (Freudo-)Marxism allowed for.

So Copernican was this insight, and so abundant the evidence, that Foucault's claims fundamentally changed the historiography of sexuality. Historians now pored over the abundance of pedagogical pamphlets, medical guidebooks, psychiatric case studies, sexological typologies, sociological surveys, demographic statistics, criminological evaluations, police reports, court files, and newspaper reports in support of the claim that the West had indeed become thoroughly preoccupied with sex in modern times. Often driven by anxiety, this preoccupation had produced a number of symbolical figures who embodied the fear of sex's power to lead astray. The masturbating child became a metaphor of innocence's irreversible corruption. The couple using birth control put the pursuit of pleasure before the duty of procreation. The hysterical woman personified the opposite of the submissive spouse and committed mother she was supposed to be, and the 'pervert' incorporated gender and sexual 'deviance' in its pathological extremes: the lecherous beast within, unchained and out of control. All of this turned that *will* into a burning *need* to know.

No subspecies of these modern icons of sexuality's subversion has appealed more to historians than has the homosexual. In the 1980s, male homosexuality emerged as the quintessential example of how, during the second half of the nineteenth century especially, a sexual ontology and identity emerged from the pathologization of sodomy, which had previously been discredited primarily in moral rather than medical terms.[19] As a particular 'being,' the homosexual was held up as a modern invention of the scientific knowledge about sex so eagerly pursued in the West. Although ideas about the social construction of modern sexual identities had been pioneered in the Anglosphere before Foucault's *History of Sexuality*, his name would henceforth be invoked time and again to buttress the common claim that homosexuality – like sexuality more generally – was shaped by historical change and therefore not an immutable psychobiological constant.[20] A large body of literature is now available on the advent of homosexuality as a key marker of 'sexual modernity.' There were disagreements about the chronology, about the specific factors driving homosexuality's construction, and about the concept's coherence, but the consensus view held, as in many ways it still does, that the late nineteenth century saw an unprecedented discursive preoccupation with same-sex eroticism across the West.[21]

The Belgian Paradox

Van Ussel never had the chance to respond to Foucault's criticism. Aged fifty-eight, he died several months before *The History of Sexuality* first appeared in print. With his untimely passing, the history of sexuality in Belgium fell into neglect.[22] When I began my research, no history of homosexuality in the country on the period before the Second World War had yet been written.[23] Belgium was a conspicuous blind spot on the otherwise well-explored map of male homosexual history in northwestern Europe, lying smack in the middle of those countries on which much of the existing scholarship had been based: the Netherlands, Germany, France, and Britain. My task, therefore, seemed straightforward enough at the outset. It would merely be a matter of retrieving and recording the Belgian variation on the well-versed theme of homosexuality's construction in the late nineteenth-century West. There were, after all, plenty of examples from abroad to show the way. What could possibly go wrong?

One rather crucial thing proved lacking, however. The sources were nowhere to be found. In stark contrast to the situation abroad, not a single monograph devoted to 'perversion' appeared in Belgium before the Second World War, let alone one on homosexuality specifically. If the issue was not entirely absent in the dozens of medical and forensic journals I perused with growing unease, it was extremely marginal at best. There was no denying the increasingly obvious: No concern with homosexuality even remotely comparable to that in neighboring countries emerged in the country prior to the 1950s.[24] After gaining independence from the Netherlands in 1830, Belgium neither undertook nor ever actively considered the recriminalization of sodomy, which had been scrapped during the French Revolution when all of the Low Countries temporarily came under French rule.[25] Sure enough, homosexual 'deviance' did feature in a number of case files from Brussels that needed filtering from among thousands of records pertaining to broader offenses like public indecency. But these files were typically brief, and they almost never displayed any particular interest in the homosexual nature of the offenses under investigation. Medico-legal assessments of so-called pederasty were few and far between, and they never ventured into the domain of psychiatry. The Brussels police archives made it painfully clear just how little material there was to work with. One thin folder containing a ragbag of incoherent documents was all that remained on the subject of 'pederasty' for the entire period before 1940. Nothing portrayed my predicament better than that single folder lying next to the huge piles of police documentation on regulated heterosexual prostitution in prewar Brussels.[26]

Naturally, I assumed the fault was mine. One had to simply look harder and dig deeper to turn up the sources that simply *had* to be there. After all, Belgium was hardly a remote island. Both geographically, economically, culturally, and intellectually it was a genuine crossroads of Europe (see Map I.1). It seemed improbable, incredible even, that the *fin de siècle*'s abundant concern with homosexuality abroad would not have spilled over the border from neighboring nations where it was busily discussed. Yet, slowly but surely, little signs emerged that Belgians had effectively failed to share this concern. One such sign was an article from 1900 in the world's first scientific journal devoted to

Map I.1 Map of modern Belgium. After 1839, Belgium's borders have remained stable, except for the small East Cantons, which were ceded to Belgium by Germany after the First World War.
© Peter Hermes Furian, Alamy.

sexual otherness, the German *Yearbook for Intermediate Sexual Stages*. In it, a priest was asked if Catholic influence was not a key reason for homosexuality's active persecution in Germany. He answered the question by pointing to nearby Belgium: "There, power resides in the hands of a firm Catholic majority that could easily outlaw homosexuality if it chose to. Yet no bishop, no priest, no Catholic journal, no member of parliament, nor anyone else in the country calls for such a thing. No one would even think of it."[27] Why no Belgian would even consider these things the priest did not care to explain. But his assessment only amplified the paradox presented by the country's unlikely and unexplained silence on the subject of homosexuality amid the discursive explosion with regard to the issue elsewhere. Belgium seemed to be the exception to the rule that homosexuality was 'invented' or 'constructed' throughout the West at the close of the nineteenth century. But in contrast to conventional wisdom, exceptions do not prove rules. They disprove them.

The Mythology of Modernity

On closer examination, the narrative about the emergence of homosexuality has generally been extrapolated on the basis of evidence from only a few well-studied countries. Mirroring a much wider and persistent tendency in the historiography of modern Europe, Britain, France, and Germany often get to tell the story of the continent as a whole. Where the period before the Second World War is concerned, the 'big three' frequently even get to stand in for the entire West. One need only browse the shelves of male homosexual histories going back to the 1980s to come away with the distinct impression that modern homosexual identity germinated primarily in the molly houses and medical circles of Paris, London, and Berlin. There is some truth to this impression insofar as unmistakable parallels can be observed between the developments in various European and American countries between the eighteenth and the early twentieth century. But to assume that all 'Western' countries followed the same trajectory by reference to the situation in only a handful of the most familiar ones is to mistake similarity for homogeneity.[28]

This homogenization of the West for the sake of argument is an old historiographical habit that dies hard. Both Van Ussel and Foucault were principally concerned with an attempt to account for the presupposed singularity and simultaneity of historical developments in an exceptional West: the growth of a Western anti-sexual syndrome in Van Ussel's case and the rise of a Western science of sex or *scientia sexualis* in Foucault's.[29] The latter's tour de force in challenging Van Ussel's and others' repressive hypothesis masked the fact that Foucault relied almost exclusively on French and German sources in making sweeping claims about 'the West' as a whole.[30] The inherent orientalism of such claims – Foucault opposed the rise of *scientia sexualis* in a dynamic

West to the ageless *ars erotica* of an unexamined an supposedly inert Rest – has rightly come under attack from postcolonial scholars and queer theorists.[31] While historical analyses of male homosexuality were mostly preoccupied with the birth of 'the' modern homosexual in the 1980s, a sophisticated debate ensued in the 1990s about the intellectual validity and conceptual cogency of such a project.[32] Queer theory suggested that sexual desires and identities were fluid rather than fixed. To argue that a single sexual identity gained ascendancy at any one point in Western history, in the words of one early commentator, was "to maintain the unlikely in the face of substantial evidence to the contrary."[33]

With John Howard's analysis of queer sex between men in the southern United States leading the way, debunking the mythology of modernity in an exceptional West has become a staple of queer histories since the start of the new millennium.[34] Their principal concern is mostly with the messiness, complexity, and multiplicity of queer histories and identities in the plural rather than with dating the threshold of a single universal modernity in an ill-defined West.[35] The building of a grand narrative about linear sequence has given way to an emphasis on historical contingency and on the particular rather than the general.[36] In 2013, Laura Doan called for historians of (homo)sexuality to appreciate more fully how much their approach is informed by present conditions and categories that should not be casually projected onto a past on which these categories may have had little bearing.[37] Swapping the search for recognition for an approach that stresses discontinuity and difference, queer histories have since spun off in various directions. This has done much to enrich, complicate, and diversify the field.[38] But that field is now also more scattered than was once the case, making its overarching aims, if any, more difficult to discern.

It is certainly not obvious where these profound shifts in perspective have left the queer history of Europe.[39] One positive tendency is that the old privileging of Western Europe has increasingly given way to an exciting wave of new scholarship about the countries of East-Central and Eastern Europe.[40] Many of these and those on other parts of the continent have also shifted the once dominant focus on the nineteenth century onto the second half of the twentieth.[41] Much less new work, however, challenges the vestigial grand narrative on how 'perversion' in general and male homosexuality more particularly became prime topics of concern in the later decades of the nineteenth and the first half of the twentieth century across the European continent.[42] This book does revisit that period and that narrative, both so central to a body of scholarship now nearly half a century in the making. It does so by using the case study of a small and overlooked country to illustrate that modernity is in the selective eye of the beholder. More empirically, it asks that if Belgium was at the heart of 'modern' Europe in a geographical sense as well as any other, then why did it not develop a similarly intense concern with 'homosexuality' between 1870 and 1940?[43]

The Meanings of Silence

Historians put a premium on profusion. Both by necessity and by preference, they home in on a past that speaks to us at length from plentiful archives. Few things were more foundational to the historiography of sexuality than the observation that where it comes to sex the archives speak verbosely of their own silence.[44] Time and again, it has been shown how the grave tones of medical scrutiny and forensic analysis warranted an eager engagement with sex and its perversions, especially from the later decades of the nineteenth century onwards. But what if the archives barely speak at all? Is their silence an aberration or something to be taken seriously?[45] Silence, after all, "is less the absolute limit of discourse, the other side from which it is separated by a strict boundary, than an element that functions alongside the things said."[46] Silence, in other words, could be the product of simple omission or constitute a discursive strategy in its own right. I argue that in Belgium it was a bit of both. Partly on purpose and partly by accident, homosexuality was a topic omitted by Belgians to a remarkable degree when compared to neighboring countries. While more than 1,000 scientific books on homosexuality are said to have been published in Europe between 1898 and 1908 alone, none of them appeared in Belgium.[47] No psychiatrist specialized in the matter, while many did abroad. No great homosexual scandal, like the Eulenburg affair in Germany or the Wilde trial in Britain, set tongues wagging. Parliament never addressed the matter directly, and the legal and forensic literature ignored it. The first serious scholarly article on homosexuality did not appear in a Belgian journal until 1955.

There are no simple answers to account for this deafening silence. If one pays due attention to national difference and transnational spillovers, as few books do but this one aspires to, it becomes readily apparent how the concern with homosexuality actually arose at very different times and for highly divergent reasons in much-studied countries like France and Germany. By comparing some of the key drivers of homosexuality's *mise en discours* abroad with the situation in Belgium, I will show how national specificity did much more to differentiate the discourse of sexual deviance than the existing scholarship on Europe often recognizes.[48] Rather than cast this in the teleological terms of a truncated or incomplete development, it is more helpful to speak, with Regina Kunzel, of sexual histories' "unevenness" and heterogeneity.[49] If 'modernity,' that hackneyed and empty signifier, was characterized by the eager scrutiny of homosexuality as a social problem in many countries, a counterintuitive unwillingness to know marked Belgium's.

Some of this unwillingness was baked into the country's institutions, but religion informed the most deliberate forms of silence and the most evasive ways of speaking. To an extent far outstripping its neighbors, Belgium was politically and culturally shaped by Catholicism.[50] Long before Foucault pointed this out to the rest of us, Catholics were acutely aware of language's power to shape ideas and identities. The church, after all, had purposely treated sodomy as the *crimen nefandum* (the unmentionable vice) for hundreds of years.[51] Catholics were therefore sharply averse to the explicit discourse of 'perversion' circulated by the growing medicalization of sex abroad during the late nineteenth and the early twentieth century. With remarkable success, Catholics resisted that discourse's proliferation in Belgium, partly by smothering the issue in silence and partly by couching it in a veiling language of their own devising. Van Ussel, then, had arguably been right when he initially saw the church as the main inhibitor of an open discussion of sex in his country. It is a testament to the enormous influence of Marxism in European academia during the decades following the Second World War that he and so many others with him came to claim that the secular forces behind capitalism were primarily to blame. Foucault, who opposed the materialist reductionism of Marxism among his contemporaries, attributed great importance to religion. To him, the Catholic practice of confession was at the root of how European societies produced knowledge about sex and the self.[52]

It is ironic that the flurry of sexual histories to draw on Foucault's in one way or another have devoted comparatively little attention to religion. This is particularly the case in the many histories of (male) homosexuality that have focused on the formative late nineteenth century, except perhaps to note religious opposition to the indomitable forces of secular change.[53] Beyond Marxist frameworks, the fact that many pioneering historians of homosexuality were also activists disaffected by the religious conservatism of the Moral Majority and Pope John Paul II probably had something to do with this. But the interest in religion has also been surprisingly slow to pick up in the queer histories following the cultural turn, especially where Europe is concerned.[54] That is why this book pays due attention to religion.[55] It will show how religion played a crucial role in Belgium's history of homosexuality, and it argues that Catholicism's approach to the discourse of sex and perversion was self-consciously different from that of Protestant denominations, which formed the majority in Northwestern Europe and the Anglosphere. In so doing, this study also calls for religion to feature more centrally in future sexual and queer histories of Europe and beyond.

The Challenge of Silence

How to write a study of silence, one might ask. I certainly did. The sobering answer is: with considerable difficulty. Furthermore, one must accept, as I hope the reader will too, that such a story cannot take the same shape as others based on a more generous archive do. Because of the wealth of sources to draw on, the latter are always in danger of zooming in so closely on sex itself that the analysis becomes detached from the broader social context, as if the debate about sex was conducted in relative isolation from other issues and considered as a separate matter altogether.⁵⁶ Here, however, I will argue the opposite, namely that homosexuality, when discussed at all, was a mere extension of much wider ideological themes that preoccupied Belgian intellectuals. It was, in other words, always and inevitably inflected by wider concerns and, indeed, often a topic wholly determined by them.

Combined with the lack of legal or other institutional incentives to scrutinize the issue, this set of historical circumstances shapes the analysis to follow in two important ways. Firstly, the comparative dearth of evidence forces me to prove a negative. The main difficulty in doing so is that in making my case I have to rely on those rare traces of same-sex eroticism in the archive I did come across. Doing so may inadvertently give the impression that Belgian intellectuals and authorities took the matter to heart after all. Yet I hope the reader will permanently recall how short in supply those fragments really were. They have been culled from among thousands of court files, and from piles of parliamentary papers, government reports, city council minutes, social studies, scientific journals, conference proceedings, official statistics, pedagogical writings, legal compendia, forensic treatises, police records, organizational archives, press coverage, and many other documents.

The second way silence shapes my narrative is by regularly forcing me to zoom out and examine a broader set of circumstances that help to account for the marked lack of explicit concern with homosexuality in Belgium. As several colleagues have noted with a grin, this produces a history of sexuality with less sex in it than is usually the case. If that feels counterintuitive to some, it does provide an opportunity to explore how sex fitted into society more broadly.⁵⁷ It also allows for comparative analyses of how particular circumstances induced the discourse of homosexuality elsewhere while slightly different ones inhibited the same thing from happening in Belgium. Such comparisons, in turn, help us overcome the limitations of a literature that both has long been overly constrained by national silos and has recently centered so heavily on the particular and the contingent as to raise the question what kind of claims historians of sexuality are still able to make that venture beyond affirming the otherness of the past or the singularity of events and identities. This book aims to further break up a long-homogenized Europe (and West) but also to reconnect it through comparisons that recognize both divergence and correspondence.⁵⁸

Archival constraints do come at a cost. While my research is informed by queer history in a larger sense, it proved impracticable to do justice to the diversity a fully queer and trans* perspective requires. The amount of material to sift through was so vast and the relevant residue so thin that I had to confine the analysis to the one issue that did feature enough in the sources to make for a coherent narrative, namely male homosexuality.⁵⁹ I can only hope that this limitation will serve to encourage future histories of Belgium that map out a fuller range of gender and sexuality's many permutations.⁶⁰ Terminology presents another problem. While 'queer' can sometimes be too indeterminate and protean a label to apply accurately to the people – the men – discussed in my sources, 'homosexual' is often both too narrow and anachronistic. Yet contemporary terms like 'gay' or LGBTQI+ are more anachronistic and inappropriate still. The police and wider public in my sources mostly used the muddled invective *pédéraste* to describe men who had sex with men, alongside colloquial monikers such as the French and Flemish equivalents of 'sodomite,' 'bugger,' and the like. 'Invert' was the most common technical term used – when used at all – by Belgian intellectuals until the early twentieth century, when 'homosexual' began making a very occasional appearance too. In the absence of a more elegant solution, I will be relying on the terms used at the time for the most part. Where that proved difficult, I have attempted not to become overly wedded to any one term in recognition of the fact, as David Halperin put it, that "no feat of scholarly rigor" can do full justice to the historical complexity of acts and identities.[61] Going forwards, I will also often dispense with the scare quotes in the use of historical and other terms, such as perversion or deviance, which should not be taken as an endorsement of their casual use in the present.[62]

Finally, this book has the aim to also be accessible to those who are relatively new to the history of (homo)sexuality. Having taught undergraduates for some years now, it can be a challenge to find scholarship that does not assume a great familiarity with several decades' worth of historiographical debates, a working knowledge of the field's complex theoretical underpinnings, and the mastery of a jargon that can be daunting not just to the uninitiated alone. I have therefore tried to write this study with a relatively broad audience in mind and for the benefit of students in particular, although I hope that more seasoned colleagues will also find value in the claims it makes.

The Road Ahead

Unwilling to Know consists of seven chapters, each of which centers on a key site commonly associated with the growing discursive concern with homosexuality during the late nineteenth century. Chapter 1 sets the stage by contrasting the lively queer scene of Belgium's capital with the country's striking silence on homoerotic deviance. It makes clear that this silence cannot be explained away by the lack of a visible queer presence. In fact, Brussels compared favorably to other sprawling *fin-de-siècle* cities in this regard. Due to its central location and lack of direct criminalization of homosexual acts, the city was a popular destination for sex tourists from countries such as Germany and Britain. In several ways, the absence of discursive and institutional concern with homosexuality in Belgium appears to have actually facilitated non-heteronormative lifestyles rather than impaired them.

Chapter 2 focuses on law enforcement. It shows that, more so than in Paris, London, or Berlin, the police in Brussels lacked both the mandate and the means to focus on something they clearly deemed a minor nuisance. Poorly trained, underpaid, overworked, and ill-disciplined, its officers were thinly stretched and primarily preoccupied with other matters. In fact, no unit better exemplified the shortcomings of law enforcement than the controversial vice brigade. Still, those men cottaging in public could and did get arrested on charges of public indecency. Even then, however, solid evidence often proved hard to come by and public prosecutors were averse to scandal and wary of wrongful convictions.

While the forensic scrutiny of homosexual deviance was a key source of concern with the issue in Germany and Britain, Belgium's legal system was deliberately unconcerned with the specifics of indecency. Chapter 3's comparison of Belgian and German jurisprudence in this regard will establish how much importance the latter attributed to aim and intent, which fostered the involvement of psychiatrists in the legal process and their active probing into the nature of perversion. This not only complicated legal proceedings but was expensive, time-consuming, and often controversial to boot. For those reasons, Belgian criminal law deliberately disregarded intent when dealing with indecency and concentrated exclusively on the facts of the matter. By consequence, there was no institutional incentive for Belgian magistrates and judges to devote any special attention to homosexual transgressions. Unlike elsewhere, they tended to pass through the system without notice and without recourse to psychiatric expertise.

Like Belgium, France also did not have a sodomy statute such as Britain's or Germany's. There, however, the rise of a militantly secular psychiatric profession closely allied with the state did much to stimulate the pathologization of perversion. Chapter 4 compares French psychiatry's development to Belgium's. It establishes that the latter was seriously hampered by commercial interests and, above all, by the Catholic Church, which ran the bulk of the country's insane asylum system. Catholic psychiatrists also dominated the profession and they actively resisted foreign ideas about sexual inversion because such ideas downplayed the role of free will in resisting temptation. Sexual inclinations, of whatever sort, were to be held in check by the power of reason and by the strength of moral character. The notion of an inborn and irresistible homosexual condition was therefore considered offensive and unacceptable.

Chapter 5 contextualizes the wider entrenchment of ideological resistance to the pathologization of perversion in Belgium. As nearby France leaned ever further left during the late nineteenth century, firm and continuous Catholic control marked Belgian politics. While socialist protests were being quelled in the streets, the socio-intellectual establishment of Catholics and conservative liberals joined forces to subdue progressive radicals on the intellectual front. That establishment abhorred the materialism and the determinism rampant among a minority of positivist scientists whose French- and Italian-made ideas on congenital social deviance – including innate inversion – constituted an attack on the hallowed belief in free will. This belief underpinned the two institutions at the helm of Belgian society: the judiciary and the church. In 1892, during the Third International Conference on Criminal Anthropology in Brussels, Belgian conservatives and progressives struck a pragmatic deal to enable criminal justice reform. That deal included the future avoidance of unhelpfully divisive issues, like inversion. Because of this, the conference was the first and the last time Belgian intellectuals openly discussed homosexuality before the 1950s.

How Catholics developed a discourse on sex that purposely omitted naming its specifics and perversions explicitly forms the subject of Chapter 6. This happened in response to falling fertility rates and the spread of contraceptive knowledge. France went through this process first. There, the crushing military defeat against a rising Germany triggered a panicked response as the birth rate dropped precipitously. The patriotic campaign against birth control to follow railed against all perversions and inversions of the reproductive norm, nurturing a strong and hostile interest in homosexuality. Belgium's fertility decline came considerably later, and when it did the Catholic Church formulated the country's response. Unwilling to call sexual sins by their names and thereby let the cat out of the bag, as was happening in the Protestant Netherlands and elsewhere, the church elected to smother the subject of perversion in the language of onanism.

Chapter 7 turns to literature and to the one Belgian who did briefly pierce the country's protracted silence on inversion. In 1899, Georges Eekhoud published a daring novel about queer love. The artistic community rallied in support when the celebrated novelist was accused of spreading filth, but Eekhoud's subsequent triumph in court proved short-lived. His friends on the left had been willing to defend the principle of free speech, but they were quick to distance themselves from the substance of the book. While celebrated as a hero of homosexual activism abroad, Eekhoud grew isolated and unhappy at home. For a fleeting moment, he had constituted something of a one-man movement, but he soon returned to silence and secrecy.

When homosexuality finally did become a topic of debate in Belgium during the 1950s, the country played an incongruously prominent role in raising the matter internationally. The book's Coda shows how a change in policing on the very streets of Brussels where homosexuality had raised little concern for decades now fueled Interpol's interest in the issue. By 1958, this interest informed a UN recommendation to countries around the world for the adoption of youth protection measures along with the liberalization of consensual homosexual acts in private. Within a decade, most Western European countries turned this recommendation into official policy by partially decriminalizing homosexuality. Belgium was an outlier once again, since alignment with the new consensus caused it to partially recriminalize homosexual acts for the first time in 160 years. One year later, in 1966, the first and remarkably sympathetic documentary on homosexuality was broadcast on Belgian national television.[63] It featured a series of talking heads whose cigarettes and solemn tone were meant to help an anxious society overcome its historical avoidance. Among them, a nervous Van Ussel bravely explained that homosexuality was a human condition like any other, and that there were no reasonable grounds on the basis of which to condemn it.

1   Cruising through a Crossroads of Europe

To this day, the skyline of Brussels is dominated by the colossal Palace of Justice, which towers over the city. Built at enormous expense between 1860 and 1883, it was meant as a didactic symbol of public order and judicial power. For all its panoptic pomp, however, the maze of streets and alleyways below still housed the full array of unruly urban creatures that so preoccupied the nineteenth-century bourgeois mind. On a rainy November night in 1893, a lawyer embarked on an excursion into the underworld of Brussels. With a seasoned police officer as his guide, he descended the steps that led downwards from the Palace of Justice to the shabby working-class Marolles neighborhood stretching north from the foot of Gallows Hill. "The spectacle," as the lawyer's later account of this slumming tour noted invitingly, "is about to commence."[1]

The pair visited the dance halls where the poor waltzed away their leisurely hours, and where gangs of pickpockets operated under a cloak of cigarette smoke and drunken stupor. They explored "the labyrinth of sordid little streets" where paupers and crooks lived in dingy houses, and they also visited the crammed shelters where vagrants and day laborers found a bed in return for the money not spent on gin.[2] Beyond the Marolles lay the city center that housed Brussels' vast and varied sex industry. Here, sex was for sale in licensed brothels, in the backrooms of shophouses, and in the countless bars on the grand boulevards connecting the busy Gare du Nord with the downtown area. There were ten such bars on a stretch only fifty yards long of the Boulevard de la Senne alone, not even counting the high-end taverns and café-concerts where those with deeper pockets could find whatever they were looking for.

Just a stone's throw from Brussels' famous Grand-Place, in a byway of one of the city's most fashionable shopping streets, the lawyer and his guide also called at "an establishment frequented by pederasts." Their arrival drove off "two amorous couples, trimmed and dressed with elegance."[3] Such references to the queer world of *fin-de-siècle* Brussels are extremely rare. Even this one is agonizingly brief. But its casual appearance in a description of the city's seedy side reveals that such a world existed all the same. Moreover, it goes to show that queer bars operated and were well-known to operate in the historical and commercial heart of the city. Why they nevertheless failed to attract more attention to themselves will be analyzed in the chapters to follow. In this first one, I rely on a wide array of court files, police records, and other sources to show that the striking absence of discussions about homosexuality in *fin-de-siècle* Belgium cannot be explained by the absence of something to discuss. In fact, Brussels, like many other booming cities at the time, was home to a thriving queer subculture.

The Big Sprout

Homosexuality has long been closely associated with cities, but even more particularly with the metropolis.[4] Most histories of male homosexuality in the late nineteenth and the early twentieth century have concentrated on the era's largest urban giants, like New York, London, Paris, and Berlin.[5] The latter two numbered some 2.5 million inhabitants by 1900. New York already had 3.4 million, and London a whopping 6.4 million.[6] These demographic heavyweights have been identified as the places where conditions were most favorable for the emergence of non-heteronormative lifestyles and communities. Size, in other words, mattered. But historians' emphasis on this handful of unrivaled mammoths tends to obscure the fact that many of the same forces conducive to the formation of queer subcultures were operative in medium-sized cities too. Steven Maynard, for example, has demonstrated that a dynamic one existed in Toronto in the 1890s, at a time when its population barely exceeded 200,000.[7] Clearly then, queer urban subcultures were not limited to the megacities mentioned. In fact, the study of their emergence should focus on the process rather than merely on the level of urbanization.

On closer examination, the historiographical overrepresentation of only the very largest cities creates the false impression that others were small. Most European cities certainly were considerably smaller, but many were nevertheless of substantial size. Brussels was a good example of this midrange majority. At the turn of the century, its population was well below that of Vienna (1.6 million) or some of the industrial hubs of northern England. But with 625,000 inhabitants, the sprawling conurbation was not substantially behind Warsaw (765,400), Budapest (716,500), or Hamburg (705,700). The Belgian capital was also more populous than Amsterdam (524,000), Munich (500,000), Milan (491,500), Marseille (491,000), Copenhagen (476,800), and Rome (462,800). Brussels, in other words, was a fine specimen of the era's predominating 'large' city, much bigger than provincial towns, and only small by comparison to a few enormous ones. Moreover, cities like Brussels were far more numerous and therefore more typical of urban size and urban growth than Paris or London.[8]

Like many cities of its kind, Brussels experienced a transformative boom from the 1840s onwards, prompted by Belgium's rapid industrialization process that was second only to Britain's. The city lay smack in the middle of the country, with Ghent's textile production and Antwerp's seaport to the north and the large centers of the coal and steel industries to the south. Because of its political and geographical centrality, the kingdom's capital was also the navel of the nation in many other ways. The canal that connected the heavily industrialized hinterland of Charleroi with Antwerp's port ran straight through Brussels, where factories and transshipment companies huddled together on its banks. Belgium's concentrically laid out railway network converged on the capital, making it the country's busiest traffic hub with direct lines to every other major town.[9] Brussels also served as the main intersection in a railway junction that linked the Dutch economy to that of northern France, and the German Ruhr region with Britain via Ostend or Antwerp. Cologne and Paris were both no more than three hours away, and London only eight, including the ferry. Consequently, transit and trade both added greatly to Brussels' rapid growth, which was further fueled by the large banking and investment firms that settled there after the Franco-Prussian War, appreciative of Belgium's political stability, international neutrality, and economic laissez-faire.[10]

Along with capital, industry, and trade, Brussels' gravitational pull also drew in thousands of migrant workers. The skilled ones sought employment in the many small shops and workshops of butchers, bakers, brewers, printers, glovemakers, and shoemakers that still operated within the so-called Pentagon: the characteristic shape of the inner city lined by the broad avenues where the town's medieval ramparts once stood (Map 1.1). Others lived in the boroughs of Schaarbeek and Sint-Joost-ten-Noode to the north of Brussels along with much of the petty bourgeoisie for whom they often worked as domestic servants, or in Sint-Gillis on the opposite side of town. Unskilled immigrants put up – often temporarily – in the poor neighborhood of the Marolles that filled the Pentagon's southern tip, or they settled west of the busy central avenues that cut through the inner city to connect the Gare du Nord with the Gare du Midi.

Increasingly, demographic growth, the saturation of the inner city's housing market, and rising rent prices pushed many of the poorer blue-collar workers towards the sprawling suburbs directly west of Brussels, where the canal and its docks stimulated industrial expansion like a pulsating vein. Although the manufacturing industry was important in the capital, the bustling service economy employed more people. Thousands worked as servants in the wealthy boroughs of the city's east and southeast.[11] Laundry and ironing provided many women with an income, and all genders could find a job in the thousands of hotels, bars, and restaurants of the downtown area and near both main stations. As elsewhere in Europe, demographic growth depended heavily on the constant influx of newcomers. From the 1880s onwards especially, the importation of cheap American grain pushed impoverished farmhands to the city in droves.[12] For those looking to replace the precariousness of seasonal

Map 1.1 Baedeker map of Brussels and surroundings from 1905. The urban sprawl of the city, which had been historically confined to its pentagonal-shaped ramparts, is clearly visible. Karl Baedeker, *Belgique et Hollande: Manuel du voyageur*, Anstalt von Wagner and Debes, Leipzig, 1905. https://commons.wikimedia.org/wiki/File:Brussel_en_omgeving_1905.jpg.

employment in rural areas for a more permanent income, Belgium's beating heart was as a place of promise and opportunity. With a wage, after all, came relative independence from a more traditional way of life.

A Brave New Bachelor World

Most migrants did not come to Brussels as a family and singles abounded before long. By 1890, over half the men and women between the ages of fifteen and fifty-five who lived in greater Brussels were unmarried.[13] Many of these bachelors, more than 54,000 of them, lived in the inner city.[14] Proportionately, male singles flocked to the industrial west of the agglomeration whereas their female counterparts settled more commonly in the residential suburbs of the city's east, where many of them worked as housemaids. These women tended to live with their employers, while male bachelors usually rented rooms in houses across town. By 1910, on average 20 percent of all households in the capital's nearest suburbs consisted of people living alone. That number rose to more than a quarter in Brussels proper. The bulk of these singles occupied one-room tenements.[15] They were typically situated on the upper floors of the old two-story houses above a shop, workshop, or bar on the ground floor. The higher up, and the farther removed from the street side, the lower rent prices were, but rents were constantly going up as old houses made room for large department stores and office buildings. A hunger for prestigious large-scale redevelopment projects *à la Parisienne* also caused the demolition of entire working-class neighborhoods. The concentration of singles living downtown was therefore likely well over 26.5 percent before 1910, even though earlier censuses do not provide the necessary data to be more precise.

By consequence, Brussels became home to a distinct bachelor culture in the closing decades of the nineteenth century. "The city," in George Chauncey's words, "was a logical destination for men [and women] intent on freeing themselves from the constraints of the family, because of its relatively cheap accommodations and the availability of commercial domestic services."[16] The latter were especially useful to single men, who traditionally depended on the unpaid household labor of women. These men took their meals outside the house in affordable mussel houses or in cafés where faro beer accompanied the *plat du jour*. They also spent a part of their income on the services of charwomen and laundresses for cleaning their rooms, and for washing, mending, and ironing their clothes. Bathing often took place in public bathhouses, and with little to come home to after work, they sought company in bars, sex with prostitutes, and amusement in the growing range of establishments that offered every kind of entertainment. This characteristically urban infrastructure, tailored to the consumption of domestic and other services, made it possible to lead a life outside the bonds of marriage and the traditional family unit.

In similar fashion, the rapid growth of an urban bachelor culture also facilitated queer lives. Many of the queer men who featured in Brussels' police records and court files were working-class, wage-earning singles. In one case, involving forty-one men known to have sex with men and whose profession could be identified, two of them were soldiers and six others ran their own small businesses as grocers, poultry salesmen, and so on. The rest of them, that is four out of every five, worked for wages. They were employed in the city's iron, glass, and textile industries or served as waiters, shop assistants, clerks, and coachmen.[17] Twelve of them were married, eighteen were unmarried, and in eleven cases their civil status was unclear. Another case file notes the full details of eight men between the ages of eighteen and forty-four. They included a domestic servant, an unemployed paperer, a flower vendor, a bell-ringer, a soldier, a waiter, and two barkeepers. None of them was married, and six of them lived alone in the city center.[18] Larger numbers only became available when the Brussels police first began cracking down on the capital's queer community in the 1950s. Between January 1955 and March 1957, they identified 1,359 "homosexual" men. Only a third of them turned out to be married, whereas 65.4 percent of the nation's adult population was.[19] Almost seven out of every ten of these men lived in the city, and 38 percent lived alone. Although no information is provided about the classification method, 54 percent of the people registered as homosexual, and 57 percent of those included in a sample of 200 court cases from the period were listed as manual laborers.[20]

Some of these men were originally from the capital, but most of them were immigrants. No more than eighteen from a set of fifty-eight queer men who lived in the metropolitan area at the end of the nineteenth century and whose place of birth could be ascertained had lived in the city all their lives.[21] The other forty had come to Brussels from across and outside the country. But one did not necessarily have to live in the city to enjoy the anonymity and sexual opportunities it provided. Even in 1864, Belgium's sprawling railway system and compact size allowed the mayor of an Antwerp suburb to pursue homosexual pleasures in the capital twenty-seven miles away and return the same evening.[22] Before long, such mobility was available to the working class as well. In 1895, an unmarried steelworker from the small industrial town of Tubeke, twelve miles south of Brussels, was arrested while soliciting a plain-clothes policeman. It soon transpired that he regularly commuted to the capital in the evening to cruise there all night and catch the first train back.[23] In fact, many thousands of Belgians commuted between city and countryside on a daily or weekly basis, encouraged by low fares and the constant expansion of rail and narrow-gauge lines specifically designed to mobilize the rural workforce for an industrializing economy.

Writing in 1910, the French sociologist Henri Joly was deeply impressed by the fact that it seemed "necessary or perfectly natural to work 50 kilometers away from home" in Belgium, which gave Brussels' train stations the air "of a general mobilization" from the earliest hours in the morning.[24] In a country of roughly 3.7 million inhabitants of working age, the government issued nearly 6.7 million subsidized rail passes in 1907.[25] The system was meant to strike a good balance between fueling urban industries with sufficient labor while maintaining the rustic model of traditional life in the country as the cornerstone of society and social stability.[26] There was, after all, no question that "contact with the city is harmful to many workers," Minister of Railways Liebaert explained to parliament in 1905. The choice was between this considerable expense and "a worker condemned to writhing in the slums of the capital."[27] Still, many such workers only returned home for Sundays and lived in cheap boarding houses during the week, where beds were permanently occupied in shifts and often shared. Alarmist reports on the lodging houses for bachelor workers railed against the 'promiscuity' of such close quarters and the rampant alcohol abuse in the bars above which they were usually situated.[28]

Such conditions were hardly unconducive to social and sexual 'deviance.' In his book on sexual inversion of 1893, the French physician Julien Chevalier warned that any "crowding together of men begets the sin against nature in the same way that it does typhoid fever."[29] All homosocial environments had the same contagious effect, whether they were of a "penitentiary, military, religious, medical, industrial [or] educational" kind, but this was particularly obvious in *les grandes agglomérations* and among their armies of male bachelor workers. The "promiscuities of communal sleeping," Chevalier noted, induced a "pederasty of necessity." So too did "the washing and relieving that inevitably takes place for all to see," as well as the "age difference" among the boarders, the pressure to join in, or even "threats and violence." As Chevalier saw it, this "endemo-epidemic perversion of the masses" was a simple fact of experience.[30] While Belgian commentators were less explicit about urbanity's (homo)sexual debauchery, they too considered the growing urban bachelor culture as a dangerously destabilizing phenomenon. Policy efforts against this "disorganization of the family"[31] were steadily ramped up.[32]

Seizing the City

To argue that the booming city served as a magnet for those in search of or forced into a life less ordinary is not to suggest that said city was a homogeneous space. Different parts of Brussels facilitated different kinds of homosexual acts. This created a geography of opportunity, which, as Matt Houlbrook has found with reference to London, was "never unequivocally affirmative."[33] It was always enabling and impeding at the same time, constituting a queer world with its own map, its own know-how, and a distinctive mixture of pleasures and perils. It was, moreover, a changing map and a changing world, the shape of which was constantly being redrawn by a cityscape in rapid transformation. Public space in particular was undergoing an uneven but radical conversion. While traces remained of the old provincial town Brussels had been before the Belgian Revolution of 1830, much of it was hastily being redeveloped, either to fit the needs of the young capital of a fast-industrializing nation or to reflect King Leopold II's imperialist delusions of grandeur.[34]

One notable example of how public works shaped queer space was the fight against cholera. A series of devastating outbreaks brought about large-scale sewage works and sanitary improvements from the late 1860s onwards.[35] The construction spree included a wild proliferation of public toilets and urinals, tucked away in back alleys and cul-de-sacs for the sake of propriety. There they soon became hotbeds of immorality, as one of the city's aldermen recalled in horror during a council meeting in 1881.[36] In them, "the congeners of Mr. de Germiny," a French right-wing politician disgraced when caught fondling a youngster in a Parisian urinal a few years earlier, would give "free rein to their abhorrent inclinations."[37] A new design was to prevent such abuse in future with the help of bright gas lights and easier surveillance, and a few dozen such urinals were commissioned, but they too were prone to creative appropriation while older ones remained in use. Strewn across the city, one estimate puts their total number at about 200 by the mid 1880s.[38]

These semi-private retreats created an erotic potential where nudity was necessary and where subtle overtures could always be explained away as unintentional. Freely accessible to all due to a lack of private latrines, public urinals were a place where social and sexual worlds overlapped. Men whose mingling with other men would raise eyebrows elsewhere all crossed paths here: straight and queer, young and old, rich and poor. Married men and others without access to more private spaces sought them out in particular, often plying between popular urinals to check for fellow cruisers. Some were widely known as homosexual rendezvous, like the one behind the Stock Exchange downtown. During the day, it was frequented by "des boursiers et des gens d'affaires" (stockbrokers and businessmen), and after midnight also by "des gens des affaires de derrière" (backdoor businessmen), a little *Guide to the Urinals of Brussels* knowingly indicated.[39] Here and elsewhere, perfect strangers hooked up briefly through meaningful looks and suggestive remarks or gestures, often followed by the question: "How much?"[40]

With strict public decency laws on the books and plain-clothes police officers on the beat, cruising in urinals carried obvious risks, which is why transient couples often sought out more secluded places after getting in touch. Undeveloped urban wastelands served that purpose. Construction sites, railroad yards, and canal banks offered refuge at night. One example was the area around Tour and Taxis, a large transshipment hub in the northwest of Brussels, and only a mile's walk from the city center. In the early hours of one morning in 1898, a police officer stumbled upon an ostensibly abandoned taxi coach there, only to find its driver and his customer masturbating each other inside. In search of some privacy, they had made the short drive there from the twenty-four-hour bustle surrounding the Gare du Nord.[41] Across the canal from Tour and Taxis lay the Allée verte, a leafy promenade connecting the city with the Park of Laken, a forty-minute stroll from the city center. Both the park and the bench-lined Allée verte were cruising hotspots, as was the Bois de la Cambre park on the opposite side of town, in the wealthy southeastern suburb of Ixelles. The principal parading ground of bourgeois virtue until the end of *l'heure chic* at around six o'clock, its crowd and its function quickly changed after dark.

Rather than seek seclusion, male couples sometimes opted for the riskier option of hiding in plain sight and sticking closer to the downtown area. During the early 1880s, a twenty-seven-year-old bachelor known as Joe the bugger (Jef den enculeur) was a familiar face at those auction rooms known as cruising sites.[42] Some even went so far as to fondle each other amid a crowd, as two men did on the second-floor balcony of one such auction room situated on the central Boulevard d'Anspach.[43] Others enjoyed furtive pleasures under the cover of darkness of popular musical halls and vaudeville theaters. In 1893, for instance, a corpulent salesman took advantage of the distraction provided by a female contortionist on the stage of the Alcazar variety hall to feel up the soldier standing next to him.[44] The same thing also took place in much smarter venues, like the Royal Mint opera house, and in the many cinemas that became all the rage just before the First World War. Meanwhile, busy train stations and their anomic surroundings were good cruising areas too, as were the overcrowded trams on which strangers were squeezed tightly together and where exploratory strokes could be blamed on the carriage's movements as it wound its way through town.

Although clearly spread across the city, cruising was most intense in its historical heart. All of Brussels' inhabitants regularly gravitated towards these narrow medieval streets between the Boulevard d'Anspach and the Royal Park. Here, a wide variety of stores, bars, and restaurants catered – as they still do today – to an equally diverse range of audiences. The very density and diversity of the neighborhood were its key attractions. Wealthy shoppers and foreign tourists mixed with blue- and white-collar workers amid the shouts of hawkers. Nowhere was this urban spectacle more colorfully on display than in the Royal Saint-Hubert Gallery. This much beloved and majestic temple of modern consumer culture had been erected in the mid 1840s. The rich flocked there to buy luxury items in posh little boutiques, while office clerks enjoyed a drink after work and the poor gazed at shop windows as they sheltered from the rain under the Gallery's glass ceiling. At night, male and female hustlers alike plied their trade in the Gallery under the yellow glow of gaslight. In 1864, one twenty-five-year-old bachelor admitted to the police that he had been picking up customers there in the evening ever since he was seventeen.[45] Much later, in 1897, another rent boy was reported lounging about the Gallery from six until midnight on a daily basis.[46] Clearly, this was common practice. The Gallery topped a list of known queer meeting places in a case file from the early 1890s.[47]

Little codes and conventions were an important part of cruising in plain view. The rent boys would parade up and down the shop windows before halting to admire the goods on display in one of them to give interested parties an opportunity to approach. The latter would then come and stand alongside the boy, feigning a similar interest in what often were tobacco shops with various kinds of pipes on display – 'making a pipe' (*tailler une pipe*) and 'piping' (*pijpen*) being slang terms for fellatio in French and Dutch respectively. Some discrete touching would then follow to make one's intentions known before a few words were exchanged to determine where to go next. Weather allowing, similar hook-ups could also take place in the surrounding streets. The busy shopping arteries connecting the Gallery to the stately Place Royale were particularly in vogue. From here, a turn left provided entrance to the Park of Brussels between parliament and the royal palace. Equipped with a urinal, this park formed the easternmost corner of the city's main queer cruising area. In 1871, a sixty-year-old priest was known to loop through the area three times a day, giving young men piercing looks and searching for sex in several urinals along his carefully calibrated route.[48] As the examined court files clearly show, many others were similarly opportunistic in their appropriation of public urban space and its modern infrastructure.

Privacy, Community, and Money

As in other cities across Europe, the risks of sex in public encouraged the creation of safe spaces that functioned as the hubs of a growing urban queer community. In the 1880s and possibly sooner, there were several rooming houses in downtown Brussels where all lodgers were queer men. A middle-aged man known as 'the brewer' ran one such rooming house above his bar in the touristy Rue des Bouchers within a stone's throw from the Gallery.[49] One of the brewer's typical tenants was a twenty-four-year-old waiter called René Demulder, who had migrated to the city from the provincial town of Geraardsbergen, some twenty miles west of the capital. This young bachelor mostly lived off sex work. He was often seen in the vicinity of the Park of Brussels where he found his clientele, and where he was also believed to be blackmailing an elderly English gentleman. Demulder and others took their clients to assignation houses such as the one on the nearby Rue du Marais. It had a little salon on the first floor where guests could enjoy a drink before retiring to one of the bedrooms. Just around the corner from the brewer's place, there was also another such a venue that catered specifically to those with a taste for teenage rent boys.

Rooming houses like these offered shelter and a sense of community to those who lived and worked in them. But most of queer community life in late nineteenth-century Brussels, like community life in general, took place in the city's countless bars. In 1890, there was one bar for every fifty inhabitants inside the Pentagon, and while it is impossible to say how many of them catered to a queer clientele, there was no shortage of such venues.[50] Some queer dives were located in the vicinity of large railway stations, while others were tucked away in the backstreets of relatively underpoliced working-class neighborhoods like the Marolles and Sainte-Catherine. Others still were to be found downtown, in the seedy popular quarters of the Putterie and Saint-Roch that separated the historical center from the elevated government quarters, and which were later razed for urban renewal projects precisely because of their dubious reputations. Here, illegal brothels and drinking dens where "the devotees of the sin that once sent Oscar Wilde to prison" gathered were to be found in concentrations unmatched elsewhere, as a survey of the city's underworld reported in 1908.[51]

The Alsatian homosexual activist Eugen Wilhelm regularly visited the Belgian capital from 1895 onwards.[52] In his comparison of what major European cities had to offer in terms of homosexual infrastructure, written in 1902, he noted that Brussels lacked the private bathhouses that were available in Berlin and Paris. "[O]n the other hand," he continued, "Brussels has the largest number of homosexual taverns of any European city."[53] Although probably an overstatement, it was a telling one. By the early 1930s Brussels was reported to house "dozens of establishments ... where the shameful sin is openly committed with revolting cynicism."[54] Christopher Isherwood spent several months in the Belgian capital in 1935. "Brussels seems lively after Copenhagen," he wrote cheerily to a friend. A notorious sexual slummer, he found the city "raffish and shabby, with dark monkeyish errand boys and great slow Flamands with faces like bits of raw meat." And, he added, there were plenty of "queer dives."[55]

Colloquially known as 'yellow foundries' (*geelgieterijen* in Dutch or *fonderies jaunes* in French), such dives were the places where regulars could take off the masks many of them wore at work or at home.[56] Police reports noted how a number of their customers spent practically every night in their favorite haunts.[57] They came primarily in order to enjoy the company of kindred spirits and to find friendship, love, or casual sex. But if sociability was key, money was always in the mix. Economic relations complicated social ones in an environment of stark inequality where sex commonly served as a form of currency. Court files and police records often paint a grim picture of extortion, exploitation, prostitution, and child abuse. Such a picture is obviously one-sided and obscures the strong connections and sense of community fostered by the bars. But as one adolescent testified to the police in 1883 about the beerhouse where he had earned his keep for a year, such establishments really had only "two kinds of customers: those who paid dearly and those who did not have the means to pay for anything other than their drinks."[58]

The former kind were mostly middle-class men who could afford to spend a couple of francs or small gifts on the good-looking youth they fancied most. Sometimes upper-class types came slumming too. One bar owner liked to brag about the patronage of a rich aristocrat who spent lavish sums on champagne during his occasional visits, when he would also have sex with several young men in the backroom.[59] There was no lack of working-class partners if the money was good. Those looking for 'trade' – straight young men open to sex with other men for a price – could easily find them among the many soldiers garrisoned in Brussels eager to supplement their meager pay. Like many hard-up working-class youths, soldiers were a familiar sight in queer dives, and their availability for "the trick" was common knowledge.[60] Showy queens or "tapettes" catered to a different taste and they were often professional sex workers, but for most sex work was a temporary survival strategy.[61] When asked by a woman in the market if he was unemployed, one boy answered prosaically: "Yes, but that's alright, because I hang around with the buggers and I can make money there when I don't have any."[62]

Shame, Honor, and Identity

The transgenerational, transactional, and cross-class dynamics of the queer community did a lot to discredit it in the eyes of the public. The term *pédérastie* had originally referred only to the love for boys in antiquity.[63] By the late nineteenth and early twentieth century, however, *pédéraste* had become the common and confused moniker in French to describe all men who engaged in homosexual acts of whatever kind, and to reduce this secretive "freemasonry" to the ways in which its members outraged inviolable social norms.[64] The urban underworld's shadow economy of vice and exploitation closely associated the pederast with other paragons of modern urban anomie. Like the swelling mass of vagrants, pederasts were perceived as work-shy riffraff. Rather than make an honest living, they would sell sex for money like female prostitutes, or, worse still, blackmail bona fide citizens with false accusations. Most unforgiveable of all, pederasts were reviled as pimps who debauched the young and innocent in a ruthless and immoral pursuit of profit.[65]

If homosexual acts did not constitute a violation of law per se (see Chapters 2 and 3), the pederast's inversions did offend the informally policed boundaries of respectable masculinity.[66] The notorious "house of sodomy" run by Auguste Mesens in the working-class docklands of Sainte-Catherine, for example, was repeatedly raided by bands of drink-fueled local men who threw in windows and who loudly chastised the *"enculeurs"* (buggers) in a charivari-like public shaming ritual. Young bachelors might get away with a scolding, but fathers and husbands found inside could expect a remedial beating. "[A] married man cannot submit himself to such disgraceful things," one raiding party bellowed pedagogically, while dragging a man back to his family.[67] In fact, a married man's homosexual habits could be deemed so dishonoring that they were admitted as a ground for divorce. Acts of pederasty "constitute one of the gravest injuries possible to a legitimate wife," a Brussels judge ruled in 1899.[68] "Little does it matter," another commented, "that in order to avoid scandal legislators only punish these acts when committed in public [since] divorce requires the gravity and not the publicity of the injury."[69] In practice, then, pederasty was more than a pardonable extramarital sin, like adultery.[70] It was a violation of entrenched social and gendered norms, the unceremonious enforcement of which went without saying.

The importance of honor and the fear of shame could make homosexual acts extremely consequential. For the middle classes, discovery meant social ostracization. When caught fondling a youth in the 1860s, the above-mentioned mayor of an Antwerp suburb chose death over a life in infamy by hanging himself in his cell mere hours after being arrested.[71] The novelist Georges Eekhoud (see Chapter 7) envied the working-class men he yearned for because they supposedly "suffer[ed] the tyranny of form, of platitude, of ready-made opinion, of fashion and of education far less" than did the middle classes to which he belonged.[72] In practice, however, working-class men were highly protective of their performative rough manliness. They could react with violent outrage to 'emasculating' propositions, as one day laborer did in 1899 when asked by another man "to serve him as a woman."[73] Indeed, many of the examined court cases began with such miscalculated affronts to men's gender. But in certain poorer parts of the city, where the concentration of social outsiders was highest, a climate of conditional tolerance existed, providing that sufficient care was taken not to threaten the masculinity of 'real' men.[74] On a visit to Brussels in 1904, the German sexologist and homosexual activist Magnus Hirschfeld was most enamored by the Marolles for this reason. "Here," he later recalled, "one finds that rather rare popular atmosphere that I have witnessed in the Sankt Pauli district of Hamburg, in the former Santa Lucia neighborhood of Naples, along New York's Bowery, on the Zeedijk of Amsterdam, as well as in many of the so-called 'fair grounds' of Berlin."[75]

It was towards these kinds of proletarian surroundings that queer men gravitated. The main thoroughfare of the Marolles, the Rue Haute, housed by far the largest concentration of bachelor tenements in the entire city.[76] Hirschfeld chatted with the pairs of men he witnessed dancing "cheek to cheek" in the Rue Haute's dancehalls, and he observed how such men formed tight "communities of blood brothers."[77] Those with little else left to lose found refuge in these communities. In the 1890s, one sixteen-year-old boy had been shown the door by his mother when she had found out about his homosexual habits. Since then, he had become a fixture of the queer hustlers sauntering up and down the Gallery in search of clients.[78] Some of them adopted a flamboyant style of dress that served as both an emblem of their trade and a self-assertive expression of nonconformity. One of the Gallery's familiar faces in the early 1880s was that of Charles Vanderwouden, who always wore a trademark jockey cap and telltale red tie, and whose "presentation and behavior [was] entirely that of a woman," according to the police.[79] A legally male seventeen-year-old also known to work the area went through life as Georgette and always wore pearl-gray gloves to match an ornate (though unspecified) outfit.[80] As Jules Gill-Peterson points out, feminine-presenting youths like them had very few options other than sex work, and while their gender catered to a clear demand, their visibility made them especially vulnerable to aggressive reassertions of hetero- and cisnormativity.[81] One newspaper article mentioned in passing how the police took "pleasure" in physically shoving aside "the young men with curly hair, lily-white and rosy complexions, covered in jewelry and dressed in tight-fitting clothes, who talk in hushed voices and parade around like women."[82]

Effeminacy set men 'like that' apart.[83] In 1897, the girlfriend of a cisgender soldier who also had sex with other men saw gender inversion as the defining marker of difference. Her boyfriend, she insisted, would allow others to pleasure him for money, but he was not like them. "All those men adopt women's names, and they try to imitate our lingo and our ways," she indicated.[84] But a more textured sense of self among the youths and men who feature in the examined archives is hard to make out from the single-sentence appearances they make. These were certainly complex and layered identities, of which sexual inclination was a part, but into which also factored a variety of other elements, such as the kinds of sex acts one would engage in and one's gender expression (which could be consistent or situationally changing), one's role in the sexual economy, as well as things such as class and marital status, age, attractiveness, and so on. While the rising tide of medical and criminological concepts of homosexuality began to percolate into the minds of some well-read middle-class men, such theories appear to have exerted minimal influence on the thriving working-class queer communities in cities like Brussels well into the twentieth century.[85] No neat categorization applied, but that did not stand in the way of growing signs of self-affirmation. In 1922, for example, a forty-one-year-old man who had tried to feel up a plainclothes policeman on a tram in Brussels did not deny that he had made overtures towards the officer. "I confess it willingly," he later said. "I like that kind of thing. I fancied him."[86]

Conclusion

All proportions considered, the queer world of late nineteenth- and early twentieth-century Brussels resembled those of London, Paris, and other European cities in many respects.[87] In Brussels too, a fast-changing economy stimulated the growth of an urban bachelor culture that unmoored more people than ever before from the dominant heteronormative nuclear family model. While, of course, homosexual acts also occurred in the countryside, as court files from beyond Brussels show, it was in the bigger cities that the combination of this bachelor culture, an appropriable cityscape, relative anonymity, and the emergence of specialized social spaces first generated a distinctive sociotope. Located at the heart of the nation, it simultaneously existed at the geographical center and on the moral fringes of society. The transgressive and transactional dynamics that sustained many in the queer community closely associated queer men with other creatures of a distinctly urban 'underworld,' which public and policymakers alike loved to loathe. Descriptions like the one with which this chapter began clearly indicate that *les pédérastes* were a visible and recognizable feature of this 'underworld,' but references to its existence are rare, and the legal record regarding homosexual acts is comparatively thin.

The roughly ten dozen relevant case files that inform my reconstruction of Brussels' male queer world had to be pieced together from a much wider set of largely uncatalogued court records stretching over 200 running meters of archives. This paucity of sources reflects the wider lack of active institutional and discursive interest in homosexuality in prewar Belgium, which contrasts sharply with the relative wealth of similar archives and the intensity of such interest in neighboring countries. The remaining chapters will examine the divergent reasons for Belgium's ostensible anomaly in this regard. This first one, however, serves to underline the salient fact that the authorities' comparative unconcern with the issue was not simply due to an absence of queer creatures to be concerned about. By implication, it also begs the question if historians' common insistence on the importance of legal, medical, and other discourses for the emergence of modern queer identities has not unduly overshadowed the driving role in this regard of more structural changes pertaining to, among others, the economy, mass transport, urbanization, and housing arrangements in enabling alternative genders and sexualities.[88] At any rate, a queer subculture and sense of community could certainly thrive in prewar Brussels regardless of much institutional or regulatory attention paid to it.

Moreover, there are indications that Brussels' queer culture partly flourished not *despite* but precisely *because* it operated under the radar for a long time. In cities like Paris, Berlin, and London, it was in no small part because the police kept a close watch on the queer community that homosexuality became a subject of public debate. But there are few indications that the authorities did the same in Brussels. The same policeman who accompanied the lawyer on the 1893 slumming tour of the capital with which this chapter began acknowledged the presence of "a rather large number of pederasts" in 1931, but he also emphasized their general discretion.[89] By then a senior police commissioner attached to the public prosecutor's office, he explicitly warned against any excessive zeal on the part of the police. Such reticence already existed in the late nineteenth century, and Chapter 2 will explain why the police, who were so instrumental in flagging homosexuality as a pressing problem elsewhere, failed to do the same in Belgium.

2 The Problems and Priorities of Surveillance

A major contributor to the growing attention for male homosexual 'deviance' in the late nineteenth century was the intensification of its policing in some of Europe's major cities. Despite the abolition of sodomy laws during the French Revolution, the Paris prefecture maintained and increased its surveillance of 'pederasts.'[1] "The police," the head of Paris' vice squad wrote in the 1860s, "which has no legal means to act against unnatural love, nevertheless seizes upon every opportunity to put a check on its outward manifestations."[2] The 1870s saw the creation of a dedicated unit and a special ledger with the details of more than 1,800 known 'pederasts.'[3] Even though those years may have been the heyday of repression, police vigilance certainly continued afterwards.[4] Both Jens Dobler and Robert Beachy have described at length how mounting queer visibility and growing police scrutiny went hand in hand in Berlin as well from the 1880s onwards through the creation of a separate Department of Homosexuals.[5] Active surveillance of queer men by London's Metropolitan Police increased from the 1840s onwards, and the law expanded the scope for police action towards the end of the century.[6]

In Belgium, by contrast, signs of police concern with homosexual acts and their 'perpetrators' are scant and scattered. Not until the 1950s is there clear evidence that the issue was considered a growing problem, requiring careful scrutiny (see the Coda).[7] This is not to say that Belgian law enforcement authorities were simply ignorant of the queer subculture that existed in cities like Brussels. Rather, as this chapter explains, the Belgian police lacked both the mandate and the means to focus on something they clearly deemed a minor nuisance by comparison to more pressing matters. Unlike in Britain and Germany, homosexual relations between consenting adults in private were not illegal. More so than in France, where the legal situation was similar, Belgium's highly decentralized design impeded the formation of effective and efficient law enforcement authorities.[8] Moreover, policing homosexual acts was difficult, unpleasant, and often frustratingly unrewarding. While Brussels' authorities were unforgiving where it came to flagrant public indecencies of any kind, their efforts to curb queer 'deviance' beyond that were generally lukewarm if not downright lackadaisical. The investigation into the sensational *crime de la Place Royale* on the eve of the twentieth century nicely illustrates the limited extent of the police's knowledge of and concern with the queer world described in Chapter 1.[9]

A Murder Mystery

In June of 1899, the concierge of Baron Osy de Zegwaert's townhouse on Brussels' stately Place Royale went missing while the family was out in the country. When the watchful servant of a neighboring nobleman used a ladder to glance through the concierge's upper floor bedroom, he found it in disarray. That night, Baron Osy received a telegram from the police at his estate, urging him to return to the city. Arriving on the first morning train, the baron immediately made his way to the grand eighteenth-century mansion, the entrance of which now provides access to the Museum of Fine Arts. The chilling sight of bloody footsteps greeted him from the moment the door swung open. They led the way from the lobby, over red-splattered white marble steps upstairs. Shortly thereafter, a brief message landed on the public prosecutor's desk at his cabinet in the nearby Palace of Justice: "Isidore Bruyère, concierge of Baron Osy, Place Royale No. 3 found murdered at 9 o'clock this morning."[10] In the middle of a drawing room, Bruyère's lacerated body had been discovered lying face down in a pool of dried-up blood.

When investigators rolled the heavyset corpse on its back, it was hard to miss the victim's undone trousers. Inquiries among the sentries standing guard on the Place Royale soon learned that Bruyère had had "the reputation of being a pederast" and "a bugger" among the soldiers of their regiment.[11] He had often beckoned them in, offering cakes, cigars, or a drink in exchange for 'company.' "He never left me alone," the milkman complained about the prurient man, who regularly paid for sex with the male guests he received in his absent master's house. "He paid some of them for their visits," the milkman further testified to the police, "but he preferred those who did not require payment."[12] The press covered every step of the investigation into this gory uptown murder, printing detailed plans and drawings of the crime scene.[13] But newspapers remained remarkably silent about the unpalatable direction in which the evidence clearly pointed. "Theft," one journalist concluded, "has not been the crime's motive, which, it seems, has been committed for reasons that are unnecessary to dwell upon."[14] A strained mixture of eager sensationalism and scrupulous reserve marked the extensive reporting on the *crime de la Place Royale*.

Pragmatism rather than mere prudery explains this reticence. Belgium's newspapers were uncensored, but the archives clearly show that the police actively scanned them for any violations of public decency in print. Belgian law gave magistrates broad leeway in defining ad hoc what constituted such a violation, and the law was enforced with growing zeal during the late nineteenth century and through the interwar period (see Chapter 3). Accompanying the democratization of readership that followed the end of stamp duties after 1848, this rising tide of repression induced a strong tendency towards self-censorship where it came to matters of the flesh in an otherwise free press.[15] While a more sensationalist 'new journalism' germinated in Belgium as it did elsewhere in the late nineteenth century, the investigative alarmism over sexual issues that became a distinct feature of the British press never developed to the same extent, nor did the scale or political clout of British tabloid culture in the twentieth century.[16] In fact, Belgian legislators and police were very keen to avoid all public scandal, especially the smutty kind, for fear of its contagious effects. Moreover, the continuous political hegemony of the Catholic Party from 1884 to 1914 ensured that newspapers toed the line of sexual propriety.[17]

The single newspaper that ventured further than others dared to was *La Gazette*, a key exponent of the budding commercial attempts to move beyond Belgium's high-brow press by focusing more on infotainment.[18] It was the only one to mention Bruyère's undone flies and it professed outrage when a young soldier was arrested after a few days, unable to account for a fresh cut in his hand. To provide for his pregnant fiancée, Arthur Wallemacq "had not flinched from selling himself to the odious Bruyère," *La Gazette* spat in disgust.[19] By withholding desperately needed payments, the jealous concierge had sought to bind the young man to him and to prevent his attachment to other patrons in the underworld "to which Bruyère had introduced him." The last time the pair had met, Wallemacq had brought a knife to enforce his claims, and things had gotten out of hand. Now that the truth had come to light, the paper decided that there had been "enough wading through the mire: for seven days now, we have been immersed in this ghastly circle of vicious creatures, all too numerous, alas, in Brussels! The time has come to breathe some fresh air."

Three days later, the anonymous journalist returned to the matter once more. With the classic paralipsis the subject required, as the case "only serve[d] to excite salacious interest," he claimed to do so because it was "not possible to close one's eyes to the evil [this case] call[ed] attention to," and which seemed marked by "an alarming growth."[20] This "vile sin" was hardly the rare aberration of an unfortunate few. "The evil now has its dilettantes, its own abominable and pernicious literature, its shameless eulogists, and something like its own celebrities," the article lamented; and yet the authorities were "powerless" to act in the absence of a law forbidding such 'indecencies' in private. "Vigorous measures," the journalist insisted, "should be taken so that the loathsome characters who spread their filth can be removed from society and be denied the possibility to cause harm." Summing up the rant entitled "Crime à punir" (crime to be punished), the reporter granted that it would be a difficult law to enact but an indispensable one to be sure.

That Unknown Quantity

A carefully annotated clipping of "Crime à punir" survives in the Brussels police records. The article's alarmist explicitness could well have been enough to draw the authorities' attention. But what ensured that the clipping landed on the chief commissioner's desk was its claim that the police disposed of "precise and revealing information" on "this filth." Another clipping claimed that detailed police "statistics" clearly demonstrated the problem to have been a fast-growing one in recent years, and that "a special brigade" had been created to quell it. This seems to have taken the chief commissioner by surprise. He promptly sent a memo to the head of the vice squad, requesting a report on "all special indications … regarding the question of pederasty, especially those obtained by the surveillance his service has allegedly had to carry out in this regard (frequentation of certain urinals, etc.)."[21] The report came back a week later. It began by confirming that "[t]he vice of pederasty is definitely taking root in the capital in an alarming way."[22] It also made clear, however, that actual intelligence on the matter was patchy at best.

Most of what the short report listed was either anecdotal or based on hearsay. It mentioned, for example, how one man who induced young street urchins into prostitution had been successfully convicted back in 1896. There was also an unsubstantiated claim that soldiers were "often found in the cloacae where pederasts gather." It further noted that the "bestial passion of these degenerates" drove some of them into the city's public urinals in search of sex. However, here too few details could be provided. "Since the closing of the one situated on the pavement behind the Stock Exchange, we have had no further indication about any other urinals where these corrupters are known to lounge about," the report admitted surprisingly, even though court records clearly show that a great many more urinals served as queer cruising hotspots. Female prostitutes "quite often" redirected male clients who asked to be serviced by other men, as the head of the vice squad knew through the grapevine. "I have made multiple inspections in this regard," he continued, "which have not produced any result."

As to queer dives, the report indicated that they were "few in number." The police knew about only four them. Half of these, it turns out, they only learned about through the ongoing investigation into the *crime de la Place Royale*. "There are bound to be quite a few more," the report admitted in affirmation of its manifest ignorance about the city's lively queer scene. Indeed there certainly were quite a few more. I was able to identify at least eighteen places in *fin-de-siècle* Brussels that catered to a queer clientele. The only bar the report could elaborate on had first come to the attention of the police not through careful surveillance but through spontaneous testimony; and this despite the bar's location in a blind alley just off one of the capital's most prestigious shopping streets and its well-established bad reputation in the neighborhood. About half of the report drew on this single case. Attached was a list of "the principal pederasts identified in recent years."[23] It contained a mere twenty-two names, and at least nine of them were known through the investigation into that same bar.

Clearly, the report hardly contained the "precise" information or detailed "statistics" newspapers had alluded to. In fact, combined with the wider record it raises serious questions about the extent to which homosexual acts and the queer community were actively policed at all. Court files and police records suggest that certain urinals did at times receive closer monitoring. At least in the early 1890s a ledger – now lost – with the names of some 440 'PDs' (short for *pédérastes*) also seems to have existed, even though it features only twice in all the case files I have examined.[24] Remarkably, it is never mentioned in the report to the police commissioner. More than anything else, and like the Brussels police records more generally, the report reflects how very fragmentary, disjointed, and impressionistic the authorities' awareness of queer life in the city seems to have been. The single police file on 'pederasts,' only half an inch thick, pales by comparison to the huge piles of documents that the vice squad compiled in the execution of its principal task of managing regulated heterosexual prostitution.[25]

The 'pederasts' file contains a ragbag of short notes and letters dated anywhere between the mid 1880s and the mid 1930s. They show no discernible coherence and many of them actually relate to heterosexual prostitution, instances of exhibitionism, and so on. Where these documents do pertain to homosexual acts, they are generally drafted in response to complaints that were made by the public about the 'indecencies' that continued unabated throughout this period in the city's urinals, and they indicate that little in the way of systematic surveillance of this particular kind of 'indecency' was ever put into place before the Second World War. Only one of the file's documents considered 'pederasty' a distinct phenomenon with its own commercial infrastructure and prostitution practices: the report drafted in response to the hyperbolic newspaper articles that appeared in the wake of the *crime de la Place Royale* from 1899. I have found nothing to suggest that homosexual acts were ever scrutinized in a manner similar to the painstakingly bureaucratic way in which the authorities policed heterosexual prostitution before the Second World War. Indeed, by comparison to its mounting surveillance in cities like London, Paris, and Berlin, the policing of 'pederasty' in Brussels seems to have been lackluster at best. But why?

Police Priorities

Brussels' police force continuously faced more pressing problems than 'pederasty,' many of which were of an organizational kind. One of the key reasons for Belgium's secession from the United Kingdom of the Netherlands in 1830 had been authoritarian Dutch impositions on the Southern Low Countries' centuries-old tradition of local autonomy.[26] The new country's constitution, at the time the most liberal in Europe, enshrined the subsidiarity principle to curtail the executive powers of the central state (which laid the basis for the country's complex federal structure today). A foundational law of 1836 charged municipalities – rather than the national government – with the task of maintaining public order.[27] From a financial and organizational perspective, this soon turned out to be a very heavy burden for local authorities to bear. Small villages lacked the means to deploy more than a token police presence, while towns and cities could not keep up with the demographic expansion triggered by the country's industrial revolution beginning in the 1840s. Especially in sprawling cities like Brussels, police capacity and professionalism persistently lagged behind what was required to keep a lid on the tensions created by the growing density, complexity, and social polarization of a booming population.[28]

"The police force of Brussels is relatively small and unimportant," observed the American Raymond Fosdick in his international comparison of European policing systems from 1915, "for the reason that no advantage is taken of the opportunity to organize a single department for the greater city."[29] As Brussels had swallowed up ten surrounding towns by the end of the nineteenth century, the Municipalities Acts of 1836 ordained that the conurbation numbered an equal number of mutually independent police forces "responsible to its own burgomaster, and operating under its own rules." Fosdick concluded that "the net result of this arrangement" had been "confusion and ineffectiveness."[30] Economies of scale were missed out on, while certain types of crime would opportunistically move between boroughs, looking for the weakest link. Fosdick noted that the city would have been "more efficiently and less expensively policed" under a unified metropolitan system like that of London or Paris. But even in the twenty-first century, the same jurisdictional fragmentation and organizational problems persist.

Making matters worse was the fact that most policemen were hardly educated, badly trained, and often illiterate. They had to work long hours – up to fourteen a day in 1900 – and were poorly paid.[31] In light of this, it is not surprising that Brussels' policemen were notoriously ill-disciplined, known for leaving their posts or for jawing away with idle coachmen and soliciting prostitutes.[32] Handicapped by the continuous lack of sufficient financial means, the path towards professionalization was slow.[33] Only after 1902, when the national government finally awarded the city a much-needed annual grant for this purpose, did things gradually begin to change. But not until 1911 were new recruits first required to take basic courses in math, spelling, and pronunciation; and only then too did the all-important language skills first become part of the training program in a city where most people spoke either exclusively Dutch or French or the blended Brussels patois.[34]

The vice squad epitomized just about everything that was wrong with the city's police force. The unit's main task, which monopolized virtually all its dedicated men and means, had long been to monitor the system of regulated prostitution.[35] This system took the hard-to-control 'nature' of male virility for granted. It saw heterosexual prostitution as a necessary safety valve that prevented worse evils from spreading, such as masturbation, adultery, illegitimacy, and the spread of venereal disease.[36] In theory, it included a hierarchically organized network of licensed brothels, regular police controls, and the compulsory registration of prostitutes who had to undergo a medical examination twice every week. In practice, however, the system was increasingly ineffective, and it coexisted with a much larger industry of illegal brothels and street prostitution that reduced the official system to a futile fig leaf. An internationally comparative report from 1914 for the Rockefeller Foundation found that while the vice squads of Berlin and Paris numbered 200 and 240 officers respectively, only six policemen staffed that of Brussels.[37] After dark, even the capital's poshest parts were rife with "veritable hordes of night flowers," as a newspaper complained in 1886.[38]

Just a few years earlier, a major scandal had made it painfully obvious that Brussels' vice squad was not just impotent but also riddled with corruption.[39] The so-called White Slave Trade Affair began in 1880 when an article in the London *Standard* inveighed against the trafficking of underage English girls into the brothels of Brussels.[40] It was part of a decades-long international campaign, led by British evangelical Protestants, to abolish the system of regulated prostitution they deemed immoral across Europe and its empires.[41] The protracted Brussels scandal exposed connivance and financial ties between the city's vice brigade and the very brothel keepers they were supposed to police. The stench of corruption reached all the way to the top, forcing both the chief commissioner and the city mayor to resign in shame. The new mayor, Charles Buls, immediately launched a campaign to flush out the worst elements and to raise the bar for new recruits, but his and later attempts at reform were curtailed by the usual structural problems, and the dysfunctional system continued to operate under the discredited vice squad until 1948.[42]

Meanwhile, growing sociopolitical tensions consumed much of the capital's law enforcement. The bourgeois establishment was increasingly gripped by a red scare when a Belgian Workers Party was founded in 1885 (in the same café on the Brussels Grand-Place that had been the stomping ground of Karl Marx while he wrote *The Communist Manifesto*), and then a violent national strike erupted the following year after a commemoration of the Paris Commune.[43] From then on, mass demonstrations regularly descended on Brussels, demanding the vote and forcing the authorities to channel large amounts of manpower and resources into the day-to-day maintenance of public order, which, as Luc Keunings has argued, happened manifestly "to the detriment of detective services."[44] Under pressure, the insolvent city had to axe its successful criminal investigation taskforce in 1880.[45] By 1905, this led to outraged claims that 70 percent of all criminal inquiries had to be dropped for want of police capacity and "patently obvious impotence."[46] Not until 1919 was a legislative framework put in place for the creation of a dedicated *police judiciaire*, but more mundane and more urgent priorities still took precedence over investigative police work afterwards.[47]

Case Dismissed

The men and means devoted to solving high-profile murder cases like the *crime de la Place Royale* were very much the exception. My experience with a wide range of court files on all manner of crimes suggests that a minimum amount of resources were usually spent on cases not brought before the Assize Courts, which only ruled on crimes punishable by a minimum of five years' imprisonment.[48] With the exception of instances involving young children and those in which the perpetrators (parents, priests, or teachers, for example) had abused their position of authority over their victims in committing the act, the vast majority of vice cases were brought before the lower 'correctional' courts. There they were ruled over not by juries but by professional judges. These trials were typically processed swiftly, bureaucratically, and without much ado. Cases concerning violations of public decency, the main statute used to prosecute homosexual acts, were nearly always brief, highly technical, and surprisingly uninquisitive. They mostly relied on witness testimony and, from the public prosecutor's perspective, ideally involved people caught in the act by at least two policemen who could corroborate each other's statements.

Historians' common reliance on sentenced case files can give the impression of a vigilant police force, of an efficient judiciary, and, more generally, of a profound will to know on the part of the authorities. However, if one includes the abundance of dismissed cases in the analysis, the picture that emerges is a very different one. Magistrates generally allowed only the most clear-cut cases to be brought to trial, making acquittals rare and adding to a sense that the machinery was as effective as it was unforgiving. But behind closed doors and at their discretion, magistrates threw out the bulk of less promising cases for want of evidence, and these case files make for interesting reading.[49] They show that building a case could be riddled with problems in the absence of unambiguous and corroborated police testimony about flagrant breaches of propriety. Moreover, they demonstrate how the many operational problems that plagued the police provided the accused with a variety of strategies that would get them off the hook.

One obvious but highly effective way of avoiding punishment was to make a run for it. In 1891, for example, a policeman who surprised two men fondling each other in a urinal was left clutching only the jacket of one of them after having been bashed over the head with an umbrella.[50] More commonly, though, suspects had ample time to flee in a less dramatic fashion. Belgium, after all, was a small transit country and its borders were never far away, something foreigners especially made good use of. In 1899, it took the Brussels police twelve days to act on the public prosecutor's orders to find a German accused of sexually assaulting his roommate.[51] Naturally, he was long gone. That same year, another German had a late-night run-in with a group of blackmailers in the Royal Galleries downtown. Mere hours after his interrogation by the Brussels police, the man protested his innocence in a letter to the examining magistrate, which he wrote from a hotel opposite the train station of Liège, a city sixty miles east of the capital and a stone's throw away from the border with Germany.[52] Similarly, a Swedish businessman had plenty of time to catch the train to Paris after making an ill-fated pass at a young aristocrat he had met in a posh tavern.[53] Among blue-collar offenders too, it was common practice to avoid justice by dashing off to France or the Netherlands for a while.

Money, of course, could do wonders in the form of bribery, although instances thereof usually went unreported for obvious reasons. In a remarkable show of integrity, one policeman refused the staggering sum of 2,000 Belgian francs after apprehending a wealthy man with a young Russian sailor in a urinal near the Antwerp docks in 1927.[54] Another police officer was fined a week's wages when it transpired that he had taken hush money from three gentlemen found petting in a box of the Théâtre des Galléries during a play. Only an anonymous line in the newspaper had alerted his superiors to the matter, but they never caught the men in question.[55] Nor was the occasional sanction likely to deter poorly paid cops from allowing their palms to be greased. A letter to the mayor of Brussels from 1931 complained that patrolmen turned a blind eye to the blackmailing 'buggers' loitering around the urinals of the Place de la Brouckère. This, the letter charged, had been taking place on one of the city's busiest squares "for over twenty years."[56] The vice squad was ordered to stake out the square and confirmed that the idling guard at least "indirectly facilitate[d] the to and fro of these pederasts" by never once descending into the urinal.[57]

Clearly, corruption and negligence were still a problem during the interwar period, but even determined surveillance proved a challenge. Another report by the vice squad from 1931 emphasized how "very difficult" it was to catch men looking for sex in urinals "because they recognize us." Three months after another pair of agents was assigned to take over, they too were forced to admit that they had "not a single result" to show for all their efforts.[58] After spending some time in the urinal, men looking for casual sex would simply leave in pairs to seek out the safety of a private home or a locked hotel room. Clearly then, trying to catch pederasts in the act often was a frustratingly futile business. Those charged with the unrewarding task believed it was better to simply shoo them away and be done with it. "We are convinced," one surveillant's report suggested, "that to put an end to the stirrings of this obnoxious bunch, it would be sufficient for the guards to descend down into the urinal from time to time to chase off the many pederasts who regularly visit it."[59] He deemed anything more ambitious to be more trouble than it was worth.

Themis Tantalized

If corruption, incapacity, and ineffectiveness were annoying, few things were more frustrating to law enforcement than being hoodwinked into helping settle personal scores. This was hardly uncommon, and a case from 1898 in which two women were accused by their neighbors of indecency and running a disorderly house may serve as a good example.[60] Catherine Malissart and Elisabeth Fynet ran a dive in a narrow back alley just off the Royal Gallery in the bustling center of Brussels. It was the stomping ground of hard-up single and divorced women, many of whom scraped a living by working the streets of the downtown area. According to the neighbors who lived across the one-yard-wide alley, the dive's main clientele were "a dirty kind of women" who spent their time drinking, arguing, singing filthy songs, as well as "kissing and licking each other on the mouth."[61] The police staked out the place and had no problems confirming that it was "a house of ill repute." Nor did it help that Malissart had previously served three months in Liège for adultery, and that Fynet's criminal record listed nine prior convictions for assault and battery. To make matters worse, Malissart's underage daughter shared a bed with these two women. Still, an outright violation of public decency could not readily be ascertained.

As inquires continued, it transpired that François Lafont, the neighbor who had filed the complaint against the women, was "the most seasoned pimp in the entire city of Brussels," who procured his own wife, as well as a live-in concubine.[62] Pimps were an especially reviled breed in those days, and in 1891 a new vagrancy law was amended to counter their corrupting influence. Meanwhile, the landlady of the accused confirmed her tenants' bad reputation, but she also indicated never having witnessed anything untoward herself. She was convinced that jealousy was likely Lafont's underlying motive. After all, the dive he ran was considerably less profitable than that of Malissart and

Fynet. In fact, Lafont had even approached the landlady about taking over the lease of the two women's business, promising to pay a higher rent in return. When questioned, Malissart also maintained that she was merely envied by her competitors "because I attract more business than they do."[63] As also happened in relation to other types of cases, whether of a straight or queer kind, the authorities soon realized they had gotten tangled up in some inextricable neighborhood quarrel and dropped the matter without wasting any more time or resources on it.

In fact, most cases involving mutual accusations – which were very common – proved problematic to investigate. Instances of blackmail were particularly thorny in this regard, and often vexing to the police.[64] In 1848, for example, an elderly British resident of Brussels was accused of soliciting sex by three youngsters, who in turn claimed he was being extorted. Inquiries soon learned that he was indeed a known pederast, with previous convictions on record. But the reputation of his accusers left a great deal to be desired as well, one of them having been dismissed from the army "for sodomy" and another seen masturbating a man on the Place Royale.[65] Unlike most similar cases, this one was taken to court, but it never should have been, and it ended in an acquittal. More than seventy years later, a file from 1921 showed that instances of blackmail still frustrated the authorities, who commonly could not tell if gangs of extortionists were praying on innocent victims or, as was doubtless often the case too, some conflict among queer cruisers had led to the familiar, unverifiable mutual accusations.[66]

Magistrates were loath to be instrumentalized by blackmailers and to risk bringing charges against innocent citizens. That is why, in 1892, a circular letter from the Crown Prosecutor of Brussels impressed upon law enforcers that, however important it was to crack down hard on the "despicable characters" who lounged about the city's urinals, it was equally if not even more important "that observations in such matters are made with the most scrupulous exactitude and the greatest conscience."[67] At all cost were "honest men" to be spared "the shame of having to appear in court on such a disgraceful charge." These directives were issued in response to a note from the procurator-general demanding that "[e]very excess of zeal on the part of the police in delicate matters of this kind" would "immediately be reported" to his office.[68] The result was that policing pederasty became more difficult still. Working in pairs, policemen occasionally had to allow themselves to be felt up by men in a urinal to make sure they had enough grounds for an arrest.[69]

Sometimes a basic understanding of the law was enough for queer men to frustrate the authorities, as when a forty-four-year-old glazier faced accusations of molesting seven adolescent boys in 1895. All of them claimed they had been threatened with violence into sexual acts at the man's home. The authorities were skeptical because money had clearly changed hands and most boys had visited the man's home several times. Moreover, by the boys' own admission, the accused had asked for their age before inviting them back, and all of them were over the legal age of consent of sixteen. The accused had also always taken care to lock his door, and so any homosexual acts that did take place in the house were technically legal if the use of violence or threats could not be proved beyond a reasonable doubt. When one of the boys had first threatened to turn to the police, the man had countered that he might well end up getting himself into legal jeopardy. After all, "you are of age," he had warned the youth.[70] After a short inquiry, public prosecutors reluctantly dropped the case. Clearly, as others did too, the glazier realized both the limits and the leeway of the law.

A Wall of Silence

Securing convictions depended heavily on having the police catch perpetrators in the act.[71] This seriously compromised all investigations in which such conclusive evidence could not be depended on. Quite a few inquiries, for example, were prompted by anonymous complaints. One such letter from 1897 reported on "an unnatural venereal act" witnessed in a dodgy downtown dive. It also decried the fact that "such things were taking place in the center of the city."[72] The adjoining police memo admitted that the place was known as a den of pederasts run by "[o]ne of the most fervent devotees of this sect" but also that no incriminating facts had yet been established despite all efforts to that effect. In fact, nine months of close surveillance failed to turn up the evidence required to close the place down. Police were also aware that the owner, known to his friends as *la belle Indienne* (the pretty Indian), had previously run similar bars elsewhere in the city, and that he had been in business for about a decade without getting caught. During the 1880s, the queer bar run by Auguste Mesens in the busy docklands of Sainte-Catherine was similarly well-known in the neighborhood, and the police had received several letters of complaint concerning it. In a rare show of determination, they even had an officer and his wife move into the building for a while to gather evidence, but to no avail. As one policeman explained to an outraged neighbor: "A reputation is not enough, I require proof, and I don't have any."[73]

Although cruising men were vulnerable to surveillance in public spaces, the close-mouthed solidarity that held it together provided relative safety to those inhabiting the "special little world" of pederasts, as it was called in relation to the *crime de la Place Royale*.[74] When investigators had visited the queer bars the murdered concierge Bruyère was known to have visited, they had learned nothing from their tight-lipped owners whose livelihoods depended on their discretion. The officer in charge of the investigation into Auguste Mesens' bar testified how he had ordered plain-clothes policemen to go and have drinks there several times without any result. Whenever an outsider entered the place, someone would invariably make a loud remark about the weather, "which meant one had to shut up" and sit apart.[75] A frustrated policeman noted that regulars "proceed[ed] with the greatest caution and talk[ed] in low voices as soon as they notice[d] someone unfamiliar to them."[76] As one of them testified, even the more familiar faces of straight customers were treated with vigilant suspicion and regulars would stop talking in the middle of a sentence and nudge at them in a warning to be careful.[77]

Insiders would also cover for each other. In 1882, one nineteen-year-old called in for questioning frustrated the authorities by assertively refusing all cooperation. "My testimony will not change," he told the police. "Do not contact me again, because I will not answer your letters."[78] His annoyed interrogator noted that the young man was "fearless," that his statement "was wholly prepared in advance," and that he answered all questions with pugnacious "impudence." In the end, not "the slightest piece of information or any confession" could be extracted from him. Other clients of Mesens' bar similarly kept their mouths shut. "It is obvious that this man has been prepped," the police complained about another regular. "He has given his statement in the same way a pupil recites his lessons." Where camaraderie fell short, threats and hush money helped. Mesens reminded people of their outstanding debts to keep quiet, and he offered presents and cash to neighbors in exchange for silence.

Considering all the above, it is unsurprising that by far the most detailed accounts of Brussels' *fin-de-siècle* queer subculture have come to us not through inquisitive and effective policework but through the spontaneous testimonies of insiders who bore a grudge. In the case of Mesens, a penniless young rent boy was promised money and a new suit by Mesens' landlords in exchange for testifying in a civil suit they had lodged against him. Mesens' business had cost the house its reputation and its owners several tenants. Similarly, the investigation into *la belle Indienne*'s bar began when its owner threw his much younger brother out of the house after a big row. Broke and disgruntled, the sixteen-year-old went to the police and gave damaging statements in a rash act of revenge. In the end, however, the two brothers reconciled and the younger one retracted his testimony. The case collapsed and the investigation was called off. *La belle Indienne* (his real name was Xavier Henry) continued running his business until the police were finally able to pin a minor licensing offense on him more than a year later. Typifying the many limitations of law enforcement at the time, Henry easily eluded the sentence of seven days' imprisonment and the fine of twenty-five francs by moving just across the border to the French town of Lille.

Conclusion

There is little to suggest that the Brussels police clamped down much harder on queer men during the interwar period, although evidence from these years is scant because retreating German troops set the Palace of Justice alight in 1944.[79] A surviving case file from 1935 seems telling, however, when an anonymous tip-off led to the raiding of a queer bar near the Gare du Midi.[80] No indecencies could be established, nor was there any evidence that the upstairs rooms were being let out for the purposes of prostitution, as the anonymous letter had claimed. Nothing could be made to stick. Nobody talked and the public prosecutor's office was forced to drop the inquiry. Presumably because they knew the case was unlikely to produce any indictment, the police had made the most of their descent on the bar. In an unmistakable effort at intimidation, eleven policemen had burst into the place with their pistols drawn, and the details of all the thirty men present were taken down. But for all the anxiety such a raid doubtlessly induced among those who feared public exposure, occasional harassment seems to have been the limit of what the police's mandate allowed for.

No doubt, as elsewhere, the authorities had recourse to licensing and vagrancy laws to render queer lives difficult when they had occasion to.[81] Clearly, the police were aware of queer men's presence in the city, but the *crime de la Place Royale* confirms the wider impression suggested by the evidence that this awareness was vague. At any rate, it did not translate into an energetic persecution of homosexual acts or even much sustained institutional interest for them. Plagued as law enforcement was by all kinds of problems, its priorities lay elsewhere and the elusive issue of *la pédérastie* was never high on the agenda. In part this was due to the lack of a clear legal mandate. But more so than their colleagues in Paris, who similarly lacked such a mandate, the Brussels police (and the Belgian police more generally) had to contend with problematic levels of organizational fragmentation, and with the capacity issues perpetuated by a hyperlocal and woefully inadequate funding model. As Chapter 3 will show, Belgium's strong culture of legal liberalism further prevented homosexuality from becoming a public matter. Moreover, legal specificities also put a check on the pathologization of perversion through forensic medicine, which did so much to fuel the discussion of homosexuality abroad.

3   The Legal Irrelevance of Sexual Specifics

One of the most compelling developments in the history of sexuality has been the progressive medicalization and pathologization of 'perversion' during the late nineteenth and early twentieth centuries. Historians have pored over the wellspring of medico-legal and sexological writings that were produced with fast-growing intensity from the 1870s onwards. The judiciary increasingly relied on forensic physicians and psychiatrists to explain the irrational motives driving compulsive sexual offenders, especially those partial to nonnormative sex acts. If, as moralists and scientists claimed, 'natural' sexual desire was geared towards procreation through coitus, this raised the question if 'unnatural' desires were the consequence of either immoral choices or inborn pathological instincts, as certain examples seemed to suggest. In the latter case, were such people legally responsible for the acts they committed?

In other words, the question of moral and legal responsibility was of paramount importance in the production of forensic and medical discourse on the so-called perversions, among which homosexuality took pride of place during the *fin de siècle*. It did so in a range of countries and arguably most profusely in Germany and France. This makes it all the more remarkable that in Belgium, huddled between its two larger neighbors to the east and south, such a forensic concern with homosexual 'inversion' was almost entirely absent. While the forensic literature on the subject flowered abroad, Belgians hardly contributed to it. They did not produce a single significant study on the issue until the mid 1950s, eighty years after it first became a hot topic elsewhere. Certainly, Belgians read foreign works, but that does not explain why they failed to engage with the matter themselves, as they did do on so many other topics. Part of the explanation for this lack of concern is provided by the dynamics of the country's psychiatric profession and the specificities of the nation's political culture, as will be shown in Chapters 4 and 5. For example, while France very much resembled Belgium in that it did not specifically criminalize homosexual acts, the much more marked French preoccupation with sexual 'perversion' was partly due to the institutional and political clout of psychiatry there, which Belgium lacked. Before turning to Belgium's differences with France, however, this chapter first compares Belgium to Germany by zooming in on the importance of legal theory and practice to explain why the medicalized concept of homosexuality as a recognizable 'condition' did not feature in Belgian court files until well into the twentieth century.

The most sophisticated forensic psychiatry pertaining to sexual perversion in general and to homosexuality more specifically emanated from the German-speaking lands of Central Europe and from Germany itself especially. This was in no small part because Wilhelmine Germany explicitly prohibited male same-sex sexual acts under paragraph 175 of the imperial penal code. Beginning as early as the 1860s with the writings of Karl Heinrich Ulrichs, this raised the forensic question of legal responsibility and a debate about the fairness of such a law.[1] In Belgium, as in France and several other countries whose criminal law drew heavily on the Napoleon-era penal code of 1810, the absence of any specific prohibition of homosexual acts automatically diminished the incentive for a similar debate. On closer examination, however, the way Germany's legal culture nurtured medical and psychiatric discussions about inversion while Belgium's inhibited them went beyond mere statutory differences. While German law was deeply concerned with an offender's psychological motives, Belgium's was not as a matter of principle.[2] A discussion of both legal cultures' approach to indecency more generally will explain why a medicalized concept of homosexuality as a distinctive entity or ontology did not feature in the examined court files from late nineteenth- and early twentieth-century Brussels.

The Obscurity of Obscenity

Between the periods of Austrian (1715–1795) and Dutch rule (1815–1830), the area that became the independent country of Belgium in 1830 was part of revolutionary and Napoleonic France (1795–1815). As such, it underwent extensive administrative and legal reforms, including the introduction of the French penal codes of 1791 and 1810, which did not maintain the *ancien régime*'s sodomy statutes.[3] Sodomy statutes were rooted in the Christian condemnation of 'unnatural' sexual relations. Revolutionary Enlightenment secularism deliberately stripped such Christian notions from the exported French penal code. By consequence, sexual transgressions would henceforth only be punishable if they involved minors, infringed on adults' personal integrity, or outraged public decency. By implication, homosexual acts between consenting adults in private were henceforth legal in Belgium as they would also be in other parts of Europe and the world that were influenced by French criminal law.[4] The reasoning behind this decriminalization was that prosecuting homosexual acts was not in the public interest, because, as leading Belgian legal theorists explained soon after independence, "carried out in secret," such acts did "not openly trouble a society oblivious to them."[5] Since prosecution would stir public scandal, the repression of homosexual acts did more harm than good. This line of reasoning was maintained in independent Belgium's revised penal code of 1867. Consequently, the country's late nineteenth-century legal situation pertaining to same-sex eroticism contrasted sharply with that of the German and Austro-Hungarian empires, the Nordic countries, and the British Isles.

This glaring difference in criminalization created an important and strangely underexplored international divergence in the history of homosexuality. The existence of a statute like Germany's paragraph 175 galvanized forensic debate on homosexual acts and political resistance to their repression. Germany was the first country where an organized movement seeking decriminalization emerged in the 1890s.[6] Homosexuality's partial (re)criminalization in the Netherlands in 1911 similarly triggered the creation of a Dutch chapter of Germany's so-called Scientific-Humanitarian Committee.[7] But the presence or absence of a legal ban on male homosexual acts, while important, shrouds another consequential legal difference between countries like Germany and Belgium and the way they respectively nurtured or hindered medico-legal concern with homosexuality as a pathological or an ontological condition. When Belgium's first criminological article on homosexuality finally appeared in 1955, it rightly noted that the issue of intent in cases of indecency more broadly constituted "a fundamental difference" between Belgian and German criminal law.[8] Intentionality, in other words, was key.

How is made clear by comparing the application of both countries' very similar statutes prohibiting public indecency, that is, *öffentliche Ärgerniss* (paragraph 183 of the German penal code) and *outrage aux mœurs publics* (article 385 of the Belgian one).[9] In either case, the offense consisted of an objective element on the one hand, being the material facts of the matter or *actus reus*, and a subjective element pertaining to the perpetrator's intentions or *mens rea* on the other. As in other Napoleonic jurisdictions, however, Belgian law effectively disregarded intentionality. "The general principles that govern our criminal law," the authors of the 1955 article on homosexuality wrote, "do not permit the judge to probe into the motives that have driven the offender to his actions."[10] An authoritative article entitled "The Evolution of Belgian Jurisprudence in Matters of Public Indecency" from 1927 explained paradoxically that "the offense exists regardless of any special intent to commit it, by the sole fact of voluntarily causing a public scandal."[11] What this meant was that Belgian law assumed that all those of sound mind always acted willfully, and that as such they could have known or should have known that the acts they engaged in outraged decency.[12] Perpetrators who were not manifestly insane were thus automatically found guilty. Criminal intent often being something very difficult to prove in court, this was a pragmatic assumption: It served to prevent most prosecutions for indecency from being dismissed for want of evidence.[13]

But this deliberate abstraction also led to the kind of legal chicanery that sometimes bordered on the absurd. In 1890, for example, it led to a clash between the (Catholic) minister of justice and the (liberal) mayor of Brussels. The former was appalled that many of the public urinals in the working-class areas of the capital had been constructed in such a way that "the public cannot make use of them without offending public decency," instructing public prosecutors to rigidly apply the law so as to pressure local authorities into making (and paying for) improvements.[14] "Damn it," a leading (liberal) newspaper exclaimed indignantly, "one does not commit an offense against public decency without doing so on purpose!"[15] But in fact the law assumed that one did, and when magistrates obliged the minister by stepping up prosecutions, Mayor Buls asked sarcastically if, by allowing continued use of the urinals in question by the public, he should not be charged with incitement.[16] Indeed, the jurisprudence around this issue more often reveals the common tensions between legal abstractions and real-life situations.[17] Despite these aporetic problems and occasional objections, however, this reductive interpretation of intentionality persisted until after the Second World War.

Moreover, Belgian law did not define public decency and deliberately left the interpretation of what constituted a breach thereof entirely up to the presiding judge.[18] In practice, any uncovering of genitals was deemed obscene. During the late nineteenth and early twentieth century, therefore, even something as harmless as summertime skinny-dipping carried jail sentences. In August 1898, for example, a poor, illiterate, and unskilled worker was arrested while swimming in a Brussels canal without a bathing suit. Convicted for public indecency, he served eight days in prison and had to pay a fine of twenty-six francs; a correctional sentence that could have cost anyone their livelihood.[19] His case was hardly an exception, and similar ones were common enough among the examined court files.[20] In fact, the unforgiving application of article 385 became even more expansive over time. In 1909, a man was convicted not for committing but for merely referring to indecent acts committed by others in public. As part of a carnival procession, he had staged a school scene. In it, the 'teacher,' dressed in a clergyman's cassock, had dipped a small baton in a bowl of syrup and let the students lick it. Meanwhile, the baton was also used to point at the number 69 on a blackboard and at the letter q (pronounced similarly to *cul* or bottom in French). As the scene bore the name Maltebrugge and the students had all the while been singing the lullaby "Frère Jacques" (Friar James), the entire display was an unmistakable reference to well-known instances of sexual abuse at the Maltebrugge school for boys run by Catholic clerics.[21] "Repression has the wind in its sails," wrote a Brussels judge, "and it is helped along by the loosely drafted letter of the law."[22]

Germany's Indecency

An important book on morality offenses by the German jurist Rudolf Quanter paints a very different picture.[23] It shows how, in his country, public indecency was enforced with the greatest caution. If, for example, someone should accidentally expose him- or herself while urinating, German magistrates would not, unlike their Belgian counterparts, automatically consider that an offense against public decency. Whether or not they would depended on circumstance. "Where it comes to this," Quanter explained, "we Germans are generally a little more discerning than the French and the Italians," and indeed the Belgians.[24] Under German law, which applied an elaborate and highly sophisticated concept of *mens rea*, not the act itself but the offender's specific aims and intentions in committing it served as the main legal criterion for conviction.[25] A German judge wanted to know why the person in question had exposed him- or herself in public and if he or she had "really 'only' acted" in order to answer a call of nature. "The perpetrator's deliberate aim [*Absicht*] to commit an indecent act" was thus considered of paramount importance.[26]

In practice, this emphasis on deliberation and intentionality made the German courts proceed with far more reticence than their Belgian counterparts did where it came to public indecency.[27] For one thing, legal practice had established "that the concept of an indecent act, aside from the effect of grossly offending the sense of shame and decency, requires a sexual connotation [*geschlechtlige Beziehung*] of sorts."[28] Put another way, "an indecent act that has no bearing on sexuality whatsoever, [could] never fall under § 183," Quanter explained.[29] Nonerotic improprieties could take on a sexual meaning in particular circumstances, but as a general rule "washing up and changing cannot be regarded as indecent acts." Any "seemly" witness to a scene of this kind, Quanter added, would never consider this an outrage. Such an involuntary witness would simply point out the fact that one was exposed to view, and only if the indecently exposed person brushed aside such advice would there be evidence of "malicious intent [*böswillige Absicht*]." Moreover, even if acts committed in public were sexual in nature they did not necessarily cause offense. If a man and a woman had forgotten to close the curtains before having sex, it was "a matter of course" that they should not be prosecuted. Only "the kind of acts, committed solely for the purpose of exciting or shocking other people" were to be prosecuted under paragraph 183, since only in cases like these were people "knowingly and willingly" breaking the law.[30]

From a Belgian perspective, where even an accidental exposure of genitals was prohibited, the German application of paragraph 183 was so limited as to make the offense difficult to commit, especially since German law also wielded a much more restrictive definition of publicity. For example, in late nineteenth-century Belgium a traveling salesman and a female prostitute were tried for public indecency after they had had sex atop a 154-foot-tall monument overlooking downtown Brussels. Even though nobody had seen them at it, the unfortunate pair was arrested when a policeman overheard the two arguing about the price afterwards. Following precedent, the court later ruled that the fact that the two *could* have been seen was more than enough for a conviction.[31] By contrast, a German judge acquitted a heterosexual couple who had been surprised by a policeman while having sex on a bench in a remote part of Berlin's famous Tiergarten park. As Quanter explains, to charge the pair for acts "which no law can forbid" would have constituted an "absolute departure" of the legislator's intended objective.[32] A park was indeed a public space, he granted, but this hardly applied at night, and certainly not to those who had retired into an obscure corner with the obvious aim "not to be seen by others." The arresting policeman was deemed to have been overzealous and the case was thrown out.

Clearly, the policing of public decency was worlds apart in Belgium and Germany. Belgian magistrates not only operated a much more intolerant definition of indecency but their understanding of publicity was also much more extensive and stretched far deeper into the private sphere.[33] Where morality was concerned, the liberalism of Belgium's penal code and lack of criminalization of specific types of sexual behavior (like homosexuality) had been compensated for by the severity of article 385's elastic and expansive application. At the same time, Belgian courts' effective disregard of the perpetrator's specific aims and intentions that were so pivotal to German judges in weighing both public indecency and homosexual acts engendered another major difference between both countries. While Belgian courts neglected the nature of aims or desires driving morality offenders, "German doctrine goes through great lengths to establish the existence or the nature of such elements."[34] Such was the importance German law attached to the precise 'mindset' of offenders that the juridical process tended to venture into the realm of psychology by commonly having recourse to the expert opinion of forensic psychiatrists in such matters. It needed to, much more so than was the case in Belgium.

The narrowness of the German concept of public indecency had the effect that many of the cases retained for prosecution were the more blatant and baffling examples of lechery. Where it came to exhibitionists, who clearly derived sexual pleasure from exposing themselves to passersby, Quanter noted that "one should definitely ask oneself if such … shameless thug[s] can really be mentally fit, since a normal person would scarcely consider ever doing something like that."[35] He wondered why no one was openly advocating the nullification of paragraph 183 on the basis that these people were mentally unfit to stand trial. He believed that this "would be no less justified than in the case of § 175, against which such a fierce campaign is presently being mounted." Paragraph 175 on 'unnatural fornication' (*widernatürliche Unzucht*) had indeed come under fire from activists and sexologists who argued that 'homosexuality' was actually an inborn affliction, and that, as such, those who practiced it did so because of an instinctive drive and not out of free will. While Quanter did not buy into the argument that basically declared all homosexual men irresponsible for their actions, he was nevertheless unopposed to the strong current of psychiatrization that ran through Germany's forensic world.[36] In his opinion, it was "urgently imperative" that the mental fitness and therefore the legal responsibility of those who committed morality offenses was more closely considered. It was high time, at least in Germany, for physicians to step in.[37]

Belgian Sexpertise

Calls for a similar psychiatric intervention in the legal process were much fainter in Belgium, where physicians' role in the courtroom was limited. Any appeal to medical expertise in criminal matters was left entirely to magistrates' discretion and no counter-expertise was allowed.[38] Only in murder cases was a medical examination legally required. Otherwise, such an examination could only be carried out if offenders were caught in the act or if the examining magistrate (the *juge d'instruction*) obtained special permission from the court.[39] Where such examinations were concerned, a widely used manual pressed mayors and police superintendents "to be slaves of the law, and to observe it scrupulously, even in those cases where they are convinced that the delays caused by this strict observation will be fatal to the inquiry."[40] A person's physical integrity was sacrosanct. That same manual emphasized how "the legislator dreads overzealousness in matters of such great delicacy above all."[41] With regard to cases of public indecency specifically, the country's standard work on legal medicine stated that "there is absolutely no element that can warrant an expert appraisal, nothing that can be deferred to his judgment." Establishing indecency, including that of a homosexual kind, nearly always depended entirely on witness or police testimony and "it should never require the intervention of a medical practitioner," according to the book's author, Ange-Louis Dambre, himself a physician.[42]

Consequently, sexual acts committed between consenting adults were rarely the subject of medical scrutiny.[43] In cases involving sodomy, Dambre briefly pointed out that its physical traces could only be medically established "on persons under 15 years of age, since these depravities, when carried out between adults in secret and with the consent of the patient, fall wholly outside the reach of the law."[44] Would anything be gained, he asked the reader, from "showcasing these scandals, these disgraceful turpitudes and these infamous mysteries before the judge's bench?" Would society and morality benefit from exposing sodomites in court? "Obviously not," he agreed with the legislator. In 1882, Crown Prosecutor Théophile Bormans replaced Dambre's aging work on legal medicine with his own. It contained no entry on public indecency. The enumerated questions to be answered by an expert physician in cases of rape all related to the technical discernment of physical signs of sexual violence on the clothes or body of the victim.[45] None of them pertained to the mental condition of the perpetrator. They might vary somewhat according to particular circumstances, it was added, but when dealing with sexual assault the questions put to medical experts were more or less the same as those when rape was concerned. As to pederastic assaults, a single sentence briefly mentioned that they were "rarely the subject of a medico-legal assessment."[46]

Meanwhile, the medico-legal attention for homosexuality in Germany had been growing steadily since the 1850s and it had boomed from the 1870s onwards.[47] Homosexuality became an openly discussed matter there, further fueled by high-profile scandals and the new nation's concern with geopolitical and reproductive prowess. "The state," wrote Rudolf Quanter, "is ... duly and deeply concerned with seeing to it that the countersexual or homosexual tendency does not become the norm." He was therefore glad to see "the leading names of medical science devote themselves to this issue with such enthusiasm."[48] Indeed, "to establish whether or not homosexual mania really is a mania" and to verify "if such a thing as a 'third sex' really exists" was considered a matter of considerable urgency.[49] The answer to this question would determine the tenability of paragraph 175, but it would also have great consequences for the moral and juridical notions of liability and responsibility at large. The stakes were high and the stakeholders many, as the abundant literature on the history of homosexuality in Germany clearly shows.[50] More than anything, it reflects how the forensic psychiatrization of homosexuality there was in full swing by the 1880s.

In stark contrast, all available evidence suggests that a similar forensic psychiatrization of homosexuality failed to materialize in Belgium. One reason for this was that homosexual acts were only prosecuted when the conditions in which they had been carried out made them liable to indictment under the statutes on the moral corruption of minors, indecent assault, or, most commonly, offenses against public decency. In such cases, however, the homosexual nature of these acts was of no great legal consequence. Thus, homosexual improprieties were lumped together with all other crimes and felonies against the family and against public decency listed in the penal code. There was nothing special or particular about their prosecution. In a way that was very different from countries where specific laws banning homosexual acts drew scrutiny to their prosecution, such acts passed through the juridical process just like heterosexual indecencies or assaults did in Belgium. (In fact, heterosexual matters had a higher public profile as they were often tried by jury – a rare procedure – and under the separate and highly punitive statute of rape, which homosexual acts never could be.)[51] From accidental exposures to aggravated assault, whatever the specifics of the indicted impropriety, their procedural treatment was the same, as were the formal criteria on the basis of which guilt or innocence were established. Only the material circumstances mattered: if trousers had been undone or skirts uplifted, if and how intimate physical contact had taken place, and if any force had been used or resistance offered. Details about the examined acts only mattered to judges to determine the existence of a punishable offense and, particularly when minors or force were involved, to weigh aggravating circumstances.[52]

Hence, like other offenses against morality, homosexual acts were generally tried in a remarkably prosaic, matter-of-fact, and technical manner.[53] (Since morality offenses were systematically tried behind closed doors, few details about them were known to the public either.) The compendia of published rulings reflect this. In the 160 years between 1814 and 1975, the exhaustive *Decennial Repertory of Belgian Jurisprudence* never once listed facts because of their homosexual nature.[54] Compared to Germany, then, the juridical visibility of homosexual acts was extremely limited and penal procedure did nothing to encourage their psychiatrization. Cases involving such acts were typically brief. They led either to quick convictions or to the charges being summarily dropped. None of the only fourteen cases I found in which forensic physicians were called in to examine men who had sex with other men in Brussels bore any reference to the more psychologically and psychiatrically oriented discourse of inversion and homosexuality that was proliferating abroad, especially in Germany.

Moreover, on the relatively rare occasions when defendants were examined for the purpose of establishing their sexual habits, the designated doctors exercised considerable restraint in either confirming or denying whether the body of the person in question showed any clear traces of 'active' or 'passive' sodomy. Wholly in line with legal theory in this regard, forensic physicians recognized in their expert testimonies that "active pederasts do not bear any distinctive traces that result from their vice."[55] Asked to examine a man well-known to engage regularly in receptive sodomy, a highly experienced expert indicated cagily that while the defendant's anus would have "easily" accommodated penetration, "a sufficient combination of signs" could not be ascertained.[56] Examples like these suggest that, rather than zealous overconfidence and professional assertiveness, even leading Belgian forensic physicians showed reserve when dealing with facts of a homosexual kind.

Leery of Insanity

Crucially, Belgian courts only ordered forensic experts to venture into the realm of psychology when there were strong or obvious reasons to doubt an offender's sanity. In one case, a forty-year-old day laborer was arrested in a village near Brussels for the sexual molestation of two boys aged seven and eight. The police deposition immediately cast doubts about the man's mental fitness after the latter had blamed his young victims for what had happened. A medical examination revealed the 'unmistakable' signs of degeneracy. The examining doctors found the defendant's "mental deficiency" to be "so manifest, the physiognomy so typical of intellectual inferiority, that he ha[d] become the plaything of the community's children."[57] That the facts had been of a homosexual kind arrested no attention whatsoever, and the man was confined to an asylum.

Even though rare, more debatable cases did present themselves too.[58] They indicate that when the court did sporadically call for a psychiatric assessment, it usually respected experts' conclusions. They also demonstrate, however, that none of these assessments focused on the homosexual acts that had led to the trials in the first place. On the contrary, the courts showed themselves leery of any disingenuous appeals to the insanity plea. In 1898, for example, an aging upper-class gentleman was discovered soliciting sex from a fourteen-year-old newsboy in a public urinal. He claimed that he had been too drunk to realize what he was doing, but the man had previously been convicted for a similar offense and he was sentenced to four months in prison. A physician certified that the offender was "a neuropath in whom dietary changes and even a moderately excessive alcohol intake can induce acts for which the responsibility would be greatly diminished if not altogether non-existent."[59] Unswayed by these privately commissioned medical excuses, the presiding magistrate underscored that the man should count himself lucky as the sentence carried had been "a very moderate" one.[60]

The same kind of skepticism on the part of magistrates assured the conviction of François Simonis in 1890. His is the only case I have come across in which a defendant invoked his homosexual desires as a mitigating circumstance. Simonis, aged thirty-eight, stood accused of sexually assaulting a fifteen-year-old boy in a field on the outskirts of Brussels. He did not deny the facts but insisted that the boy had consented. Moreover, in a letter to the judge he claimed to "have committed this act having fallen prey to a feverishly morbid excitement." It resulted, he explained, "from the observational study that I have carried out in order to verify statements made by medical celebrities."[61] A search of his rooms had indeed turned up a considerable number of documents, among which were extensive handwritten excerpts from scientific works on sexual perversion. Simonis alleged that his initial purpose had been "to examine the rampant debauchery among much of the popular classes, the causes of this lasciviousness and the means of subduing it." Unfortunately, he added, "unforeseen temptations have made me swerve from my purely scientific goal." Despite his good intentions and best efforts, he had succumbed to what he clearly felt was an overpowering force.

This explanation appeared like a flimsy attempt to account for the incriminating evidence found in his room. But there was also something unmistakably obsessive about Simonis' desire for teenage boys. Among his belongings were the little trinkets he was known to entice these boys with outside their schools, something which neighbors had recently denounced him for with a charivari (a noisy community shaming ritual) "because they consider him a pederast," the police reported.[62] Simonis also kept notes on his exploits with apparent relish, recording the boys' age as ranging between fourteen and twenty. He made drawings of orgiastic scenes accompanied by raunchy poems and several entries in his log-like notes demonstrated that Simonis had spied on two young boys mutually masturbating. A psychiatrist might well have considered the man an inveterate pathological pervert, especially since he had previously been convicted for facts of a similar nature. Even to the medically untrained eye of a policeman, he seemed "at the mercy of a disgraceful passion."[63] Despite this, the record suggests that the court never entertained the notion of homosexual inclinations as a ground for criminal irresponsibility. It did not request a medical examination of the offender. Instead, the judge unceremoniously sentenced Simonis to three years' imprisonment.

Overall, the court records from Brussels clearly show that magistrates were disinclined to excuse homosexual acts as symptoms of a psychopathological condition. Moreover, the medicalized concept of homosexuality as a distinctive affliction does not feature at all in the examined court files until well into the twentieth century. Policemen would occasionally use terms like 'pederast,' 'sodomite,' or 'bugger' to describe 'men like that,' but it took medical epithets such as 'invert' or 'homosexual' a long time to gain currency. The term 'invert' first appears in 1936 with reference to a teenager whose father had requested the juvenile court to step in because the effeminate boy was having sexual relations with men in the capital's "special milieu." It was determined that he was "afflicted with a serious perversion: sexual inversion."[64] Similarly, it was only by the mid 1930s that the word "homosexuality" appeared to describe a particular state of being in the sources I have consulted, even though a policeman's casual reference to "a homosexual" first pops up in 1921, when a man made an ill-fated pass at a plain-clothes officer.[65] One of the authors of Belgium's first criminological article on homosexuality from 1955, mentioned earlier, was the leading professor in forensic psychiatry, Auguste Ley.[66] That article began by stating: "Homosexuality is anything but a distinctive entity."[67]

Conclusion

From the outset, Belgium's legal system was marked by an enduring indifference towards what compelled people to engage in homosexual acts. Unlike German penal law, with its painstaking attention to *mens rea*, the Belgian rules of evidence in morality offenses made perpetrators' specific intentions and desires irrelevant. By consequence, whereas the German judiciary fostered a medico-legal concern with homosexuality as a psychopathological condition, its Belgian counterpart effectively did the opposite. Belgian criminal law, in other words, stifled rather than nurtured the medicalization of homosexual acts. This institutional indifference was further reinforced by the modest role assigned to forensic medicine more generally in the country, wholly subject as experts were to magistrates' omnipotent discretion in appointing and dismissing them, calling on their services only when they saw fit, and free to ignore their findings in judging a case. Forensic work was poorly paid to boot, so that medico-legal expertise advanced only slowly. In fact, the country's psychiatric profession as a whole was similarly hampered in its development. In Chapter 4, comparing that development with the very different one in France will help to explain why the levels of concern with homosexuality in these two neighboring countries with very similar legal traditions diverged markedly.

This chapter has shown that, legally speaking, it was simply "of little consequence" in Belgium "whether the act ha[d] been committed on a person of the male or the female sex, or whether it ha[d] taken place between persons of the same or the opposite sexes," as noted in an authoritative article "On Rape and Sexual Assault" from 1893, which did not expand on homosexuality further.[68] More than thirty years later, in 1925, a similar article by a different author repeated this observation word for word, and it still had nothing else to say on the subject of homosexual acts.[69] In his 1927 study of sexual delinquency, the most extensive one conducted during the interwar period in Belgium, the inspector general of the prison system mentioned in passing how sexually perverse acts did not concern Belgian law, which ignored them with "deliberate naiveté."[70] Neither his study nor a related one, both based on a sample of some 300 sex offenders, devoted any significant attention to homosexual acts, and neither of their extensive classification models treated such acts as a separate category.[71]

4 Psychiatric Resistance to the Medicalization of Sin

Psychiatry was a prime site from which authoritative discourses on perversion and homosexuality emanated during the late nineteenth century.[1] There have been several pertinent correctives of oversimplifying narratives about psychiatry's role in 'inventing' homosexuality as a new medical category to be internalized by docile patients who thereby supposedly came to think of themselves as homosexuals.[2] After all, most working-class queer identities took shape without reference or exposure to these elite discourses until well into the twentieth century, and they were molded primarily by the pressures and possibilities of changing social structures.[3] Even so, psychiatry certainly did have a profound impact on public and policy discussions about this psychopathological 'condition' it was trying to pin down. It was in no small part because of the classificatory zeal of psychiatry that the very notion of the homosexual as a distinct entity and ontology began to take shape from the 1870s onwards. The necessary conditions for this to occur were twofold. First, psychiatry had to be sufficiently professionalized in order for its expertise to impact public discourse and policy. In other words, the discipline needed to have acquired a certain level of public standing and political clout. Secondly, and relatedly, a good number of psychiatrists needed to have gathered enough independence from the religious congregations that had long dominated the care for the insane to be able to secularize the language of sex.

France serves as the *locus classicus* in this regard. As Jan Goldstein's research has demonstrated, "[e]ver since its emergence in the early nineteenth century, the tendency of the French psychiatric profession had been to gravitate towards an alliance with the French state."[4] Until mid-century, the Catholic Church continued to dominate the growing infrastructure of mental institutions outside of Paris. From the 1860s, when positivist secularism gained traction, and more particularly after the birth of the increasingly anticlerical Third Republic in 1870, the power of French psychiatry soared. It became a marker and an instrument of a secular modernity that saw itself as struggling against the reactionary forces of religion and despotism. Psychiatric knowledge, in other words, was profoundly political. Anticlerical psychiatrists set about explaining the mysteries of human 'nature' with recourse to the physiological language of science, thereby chipping away at the hitherto dominant spiritual hermeneutic of the human 'soul' of the Catholic Church. Psychiatric explanations of sexual deviance became an especially contested battleground in a heated culture war. Sex, after all, had long been the domain of the church. Now, annexationist psychiatrists were claiming jurisdiction over what they declared a purely physical impulse.

In France, many psychiatric explanations of sexual perversion were profoundly ideological, unmistakably anticlerical, and, in their wider designs, remarkably successful. Sexual 'inversion,' the dominant medical term for homosexuality in French-speaking countries, implied a corporeal origin and became a showpiece of secular psychiatry's ascendancy in *fin-de-siècle* France.[5] But similar cultural and ideological tensions were producing different outcomes elsewhere in Europe. The profession's relationship with the state and with academia took on numerous forms, and so too did debates about the moral or physiological causes of social and sexual deviance. Psychiatric professionalization also occurred at various speeds across Europe. Neighboring Belgium offers a case in point. There, as this chapter shows, not only was psychiatry's development hindered by a nationally specific political culture and balance of powers but fierce resistance to public control over the private asylum system kept the state at bay and religious dominance intact far into the twentieth century. Attempts to secularize, physiologize, and demoralize the language of psychiatry were thus curtailed. By consequence, and unlike in France, the 'invert' did not emerge as an emblem of secular psychiatric power in Belgium, and there was strong opposition among the country's psychiatrists to the notion of congenital inversion and to the medicalization of sex at large. Tellingly, during the apogee of the French and German psychiatrization of sex in the final decade of the nineteenth century, it was the focus of only 2.41 percent of contributions to Belgium's leading psychiatric journal.[6]

Psychiatry's Curtailment

A little background is needed to clarify how homosexuality fits into wider developments. Belgium emerged from the wave of liberal revolutions of 1830 in Europe against the restoration monarchies that had been instituted by the Congress of Vienna in 1814 and 1815. After Napoleon's defeat at Waterloo, near Brussels, Europe's Great Powers created the United Kingdom of the Netherlands as a buffer state against future French aggression, thus reuniting the predominantly Protestant northern Low Countries and the largely Catholic southern ones for the first time since the Reformation had ripped them apart in the sixteenth century. Old divisions lingered, however, and new ones soon arose. King William I's autocratic rule favored Protestantism and Dutch as the language of administration. Down south, the Catholic Church resented the former, while French-speaking elites took exception to the latter. Both Catholics and liberals begrudged the south's fiscal exploitation as political power was concentrated in the north. They also loathed the experiences of statist centralism under first French revolutionary (1794–1814) and then Dutch dominion (1815–1830).[7] For centuries, after all, the Southern Low Countries had exchanged loyalty to foreign overlords for high levels of local autonomy. This formed the basis for an unlikely and thus dubbed 'monstrous' political alliance between southern liberals and Catholics. When a revolution ousted the Dutch in 1830, newborn Belgium's constitution favored a decentralized, hands-off state that hallowed private initiative, be it clerical or commercial. Based on a tiny electorate of Catholic aristocrats and urban entrepreneurs, the so-called Union of Opposites relied on the shared aversion to Dutch and French statism.[8]

'Unionist' compromise brought stability and marked all the early legislation through which the country's structures were organized, including the care for the insane and the regulation of mental asylums. France pioneered the legal regulation of insanity in 1838.[9] Belgium's own Law on the Administration of the Insane from 1850 was grafted, as much of its legislation was during the early decades of independence, on the French example; France being the often equivocal yet standard point of reference for Belgium's francophone elites.[10] Reflecting the growing strength of the state, the first article of the French insanity bill had stipulated that every *département* should henceforth dispose of a public institution or contract with a private one that would then serve in an official capacity.[11] In so doing, the law had called into life a state-funded and state-run system of mental hospitals that would compete with privately run ventures and with those under the control of religious congregations, both of which were now to comply with minimum government standards. This public system promised secure employment to a growing group of 'alienists' who became salaried civil servants.[12]

Belgium, by contrast, took a very different path. There, the few psychiatrists in favor of a public asylum system lamented how the country's "decentralist theories" ensured that the insanity bill adopted in 1850 deliberately "inked out" the French law's all-important first article ordering the creation of state-controlled institutions for the care and confinement of the insane.[13] Belgium's Municipalities Act of 1836 required local administrations to pay for the placement of insolvent lunatics in private institutions, but the insanity bill refused any administrative or fiscal responsibilities for the central state, and no more than purposely token regulatory ones. Even after unionism petered out, private interests continued to be sacrosanct and government overreach anathema in liberal Belgium. Insane asylums would continue to be largely the dominion of Catholic congregations and partly that of commercial entrepreneurs. Thus, politicians liked to emphasize in parliament, "the government could avoid a considerable expense."[14] Any form of "centralization" was deemed fiscally indefensible, politically repellent, and altogether "contrary to the public morals of our country."[15]

By consequence, successive reports of the government oversight committee denounced the fact that proper medical care was "neglected nearly everywhere" in Belgium's mental hospitals.[16] Asylum physicians were poorly paid and rarely present. A mere "subaltern agent" to religious or business management, their task was a "thankless" one.[17] Understandably, few were called to the psychiatric profession, which hardly constituted a recognized specialty to begin with. The only course in psychiatry was taught at the Catholic University of Leuven, where it was neither a required nor a popular part of medical training.[18] While academic psychiatry was taking flight in France and Germany, raising the discipline's profile across Europe, a scientific approach to mental illness in Belgium simply did "not exist in the vast majority of our asylums."[19] Because of this dire situation, the Belgian Society of Mental Medicine (BSMM), founded in 1869, was a long overdue initiative towards psychiatry's professionalization.[20] The BSMM, however, was sharply divided between a small but militant minority of secularist and pro-state psychiatrists *à la française* and a firm majority of laissez-faire Catholics and liberals in favor of the status quo. Consequently, the organization's politics were muddled by conflicting agendas. In 1871, a scandal involving fraud, maltreatment, and murder in a commercially run asylum gave momentum to the statists' cause, but after much heated debate, the BSMM's numerical bulk endorsed only limited reforms and public intervention.[21] Thus, at the very moment when the newly created Third Republic opened the door to a further deprivatization and active laicization of the French asylum system, Belgium affirmed its commitment to private initiative. Just fourteen out of fifty-two French departmental asylums were privately run in 1897, with 79 percent of all the mentally ill being treated in public institutions. In Belgium, by contrast, only nine of fifty-one asylums were administered by public authorities at the turn of the century, treating just 28.5 percent of all patients.[22]

This delayed professionalization and academization was mirrored in the lack of interest in sexual psychopathology. Both in France and in Germany this subfield was closely associated with self-asserting and often anticlerical psychiatrists' key claim that human behavior is driven by basic instincts and that mental problems are caused by their distortion through neuro-physiological abnormalities in the brain. Sex thus became a particularly emotive focal point in the growing medicalization of morality. To prove that the moral 'sin' of sexual deviance was actually the involuntary – and thus amoral – consequence of disease was to claim a sphere previously the preserve of religion for the widening orbit of science. But the success of secularist psychiatry's ambitions hinged on the sector's emancipation from commercial and especially religious control. In Belgium, that control persisted. Academic psychiatry's development was slow and its social standing limited. In this context, venturing into sexual psychopathology was ideologically suspect.

Krafft-Ebing's Eminence

In view of the above, it was no coincidence that the key figures of psychiatric professionalization in both France and Germany were concerned with sex and gender. In France, the militantly anticlerical Jean-Martin Charcot gained international acclaim through his psychopathology of female hysteria in the 1870s, which had often been understood as a form of demonic possession in the past. Still in its moderate phase, the Third Republic's leaders refrained from giving the country's first chair in psychiatry to this divisive figure in 1878, but as soon as Charcot's political allies rose to power in 1882 a second chair was created especially for him.[23] That same year, together with Valentin Magnan, Charcot published a study on "The Inversion of the Genital Instinct," establishing it as a congenital pathology, and thus something other than sin.[24] As is apparent from its citations, their study was indebted to the pioneering German works in this regard. Carl Westphal had first described what he called 'contrary sexual feeling' in 1869, the year of his initial academic appointment. He would soon occupy the first full chair of psychiatry in Prussia. A student of Wilhelm Griesinger, the trailblazer of psychiatry's emancipation from Romantic and religious speculations about the nature of madness in Germany, Westphal had been the first psychiatrist to claim that contrary sexual feeling's innateness was "unarguable."[25]

The issues of sexual inversion and perversion entered Belgian psychiatrists' awareness primarily through the pioneering work of the German-born Austrian Richard von Krafft-Ebing, another student of Griesinger. Beginning his career in as an asylum physician in Baden-Baden, near the French border in Germany, Krafft-Ebing was a strong advocate of psychiatry's professionalization and academization. In 1873, he moved to another asylum in Austria where he soon rose to prominence through his widely acclaimed work in forensic psychiatry and was offered the chair in psychiatry at the nearby University of Graz in 1882.[26] Krafft-Ebing's international appeal was partly due to the fact that he synthesized elements from French and German scholarship into a neo-Romantic positivism that appealed far and wide. He embraced the anti-metaphysical positivism advocated by Auguste Comte and Wilhelm Griesinger, yet he also drew on the conceptually indeterminate but metaphorically powerful theory of degeneration developed by the Austro-French Catholic psychiatrist Bénédict Morel in 1857. Degeneration theory held that unwholesome (modern) lifestyles induced a hereditary devolution of the species.[27] It was itself an amalgamation of German Romantic notions of vitality and inner drives, French evolutionism and its Lamarckian belief in the heredity of acquired characteristics, and the moralistically compelling existential choice between redemption and damnation rooted in Christianity.[28] Churning out highly practical works too, it is little wonder that the young BSMM offered Krafft-Ebing an honorary membership in 1875 and lauded his recent *Textbook on Forensic Psychopathology* as "eminently remarkable."[29] The Austro-German eminence sent in his new publications on a regular basis and would soon become the most regularly reviewed author in the BSMM's journal.[30]

Krafft-Ebing did much to harden the hugely elastic moral parable of degeneration into a more solid nosological framework. He generally assumed that neuro-physiological abnormalities in the cerebrospinal system perverted the entire health and character of those affected, including their inclinations and most basic instincts. This supposedly resulted in an excessive irritability of the nervous system, in increased cardiovascular tension, motorial spasms, and hallucinations, and also in "the sexual domain, by the perversion or the precociousness of the genital sense."[31] In the mid 1870s, Krafft-Ebing considered sexual perversion a mere "concomitant" of "moral degeneration" in which "free will is replaced by a morbid obsession," but this would soon start to change.[32] In the newly unified Germany, where harsh Prussian sodomy laws now overruled the previously more lenient legalization of Napoleonic origin in other parts of the country, a growing criminological and public debate on what Westphal had called an involuntary 'contrary sexual feeling' drove Krafft-Ebing's interest. Of particular importance to him was the trailblazing activism of Karl Heinrich Ulrichs, a lawyer who wrote a series of pamphlets during the 1860s and the 1870s in defense of what he called 'Uranism': a congenital attraction to persons of the same sex, the legal punishment of which was therefore a glaring injustice.[33] Beginning in 1877, Krafft-Ebing began to devote his research to the analysis of sexual psychopathology with unprecedented depth and devotion.[34]

In Belgium, the first faint echoes of the growing psychiatric preoccupation with homosexuality abroad became noticeable in the early 1880s. The earliest contribution on sexual deviance to appear in the *Bulletin of the Belgian Society of Mental Medicine* was authored by the same asylum physician whose warm reviews had introduced Krafft-Ebing's work to the Belgian psychiatric community.[35] It was the case study of a sexually compulsive man whose "pathological state" was marked by "a veritable depravation of the genital sense," which had induced "complete irresponsibility."[36] The short piece, however, did not develop any theory of sexual perversion. The following year, in 1882, another Belgian asylum physician reviewed Krafft-Ebing's treatise *On Contrary Sexual Feeling from a Clinical and Forensic Perspective*. He noted that this was a "distinctive perversion of the sexual instinct," still new to science and "of extreme importance" to psychiatry.[37] Krafft-Ebing's distinction between the "immoral vice" of pederasty and the "structural deformity" of contrary sexual feeling as the outcome of hereditary degeneration received particular attention. Its forensic implications, after all, were tremendous. "[E]ven if they know their acts to be punishable, their proclivity often pushes them with such extreme violence that they lack common restraints, and to them their inclination is not an unnatural penchant, but a completely natural one, which excludes the notion of a voluntary offence."[38] This, indeed, was what the ontologizing of homosexuality implied most crucially.

Such forensic implications were also where and why Krafft-Ebing's work met with growing resistance. Dr. Jean Cuylits devoted his inaugural address as president of the BSMM in 1882 to the weighty matter of moral and criminal responsibility. In 1885, he objected to 'professor von Krafft-Ebing's tendency to excuse every misdeed with reference to insanity-induced irresponsibility."[39] Cuylits' review of the Austro-German authority's latest article on the subject pointed out how Krafft-Ebing assumed that neuropaths had less control over their sexual impulses and therefore not only struggled more with abstinence than ordinary people did but would actually see their mental health worsen if these morbid impulses were chronically suppressed. While this might be true in isolated cases, the Belgian argued that it certainly was not as a general rule. Such a line of reasoning set too much store by congenital inclinations, and too little by acquired habits, or indeed the human capacity to resist one's carnal urges. In his view, several factors combined to produce "sexual aberrations," and they "do not impose their fatal effects on those willing to avoid them." To Cuylits, "sexual perversion does not have the irresistible character ascribed to it by von Krafft-Ebing."[40] From the mid 1880s onwards, the permissive fatalism the latter sanctioned came under increasing criticism from Catholics in particular.

The Annoyance of Innateness

In 1886, Krafft-Ebing published the first edition of what would soon be recognized as the international standard reference work on sexual psychopathology. *Psychopathia Sexualis* was a compendium of case studies and an attempt to systematize knowledge about perversion in its many guises.[41] As the study's title clarified from the second edition onwards, it made special reference to contrary sexual feeling.[42] Twelve revised editions and several translations followed each other in quick succession before Krafft-Ebing died in 1902. They firmly established him as the world's leading authority on homosexuality during the 1880s, when French, German, and Russian monographs on homosexual deviance were first starting to appear.[43] The BSMM received a copy of the second edition from Krafft-Ebing in the summer of 1887 and asked Dr. Léon De Rode to review the book on its behalf.[44] De Rode was a generally inconspicuous asylum physician and forensic expert at Leuven where he had studied at the Catholic University and continued to work closely with the country's two heavyweights of Catholic psychiatry, Ernest Masoin and Ferdinand Lefèbvre.[45] (Masoin had taken over Belgium's only course on mental medicine from Lefèbvre in 1869.)

On the one hand, De Rode's review of *Psychopathia Sexualis* demonstrates how clearly Krafft-Ebing's professional activism resonated with the grievances of Belgian psychiatrists. Numbering eleven pages, it was very long by comparison to other reviews. There could be no question, De Rode recognized, that sex crimes were increasing along with the general rise in delinquency. Indeed, only recently Belgian newspapers had mentioned two scandalous court cases involving homosexual prostitution.[46] Among the offenders, De Rode proceeded, there were quite a few cases that were more of a pathological than a criminal nature; their sexual aberration was a clear sign of an underlying degeneration. In some of them, this degenerative condition was congenital, and credit was due to Krafft-Ebing for pointing this out. "Justice" was indeed "overly concerned with criminal acts and not enough with the personalities of those committing them."[47] All too often, those who belonged in an asylum and required medical care ended up in prison. They were a danger to their fellow inmates and later to the society in which they were released again without treatment. Exposed to all manner of pathogenic influences in modern society, it could be no surprise that their number increased. The kind of cultural critique made possible by protean degeneration theory – and soon to be made famous by Max Nordau who knew and collaborated with Krafft-Ebing – echoed in De Rode's listing of modern woes.[48] They included "life in large cities," "alcoholic excess," "intellectual strain," and, in a general sense, "modern life and its overstimulation of the senses."[49]

It is not difficult to see how such cultural pessimism, rendered scientific by degeneration theory, chimed with Catholic resistance to runaway modernization. But while sharing the same concerns about the recognition of psychiatric jurisdiction over psychopathological criminals, De Rode fiercely resisted Krafft-Ebing's tendency to inflate the number of congenital cases. As far as he was concerned, to argue in favor of more psychiatric intervention in the legal process was not to claim that all criminals were certifiably insane. It was crucial, De Rode opined, "that the existence of a psychosis is established beyond a shadow of doubt." He emphasized that irrefutable evidence of a neuropathological affliction was not only mandatory to prevent irresponsible and therefore legally and morally innocent degenerates from being unduly sentenced. After all, psychiatrists' forensic expertise cut both ways. The proof it offered was also indispensable "in preventing the risk of covering simple depravation under the cloak of illness." Clearly, he insisted, sexual immoralities could just as well be committed by "debauchees of sound mind," and these "malefactors [*coupables*]" should not be allowed to escape their proper punishment. Yet such misguided leniency seemed at the heart of what *Psychopathia Sexualis* had to say about contrary sexual feeling: that "most interesting chapter of von Krafft-Ebing's book, the one that contains the most original ideas, but also those most susceptible to debate."

Over the years, Krafft-Ebing would indeed increasingly ontologize homosexuality into a hardwired personality trait to the point that he explicitly began questioning if it were abnormal or pathological at all.[50] By the later 1880s, he was already pleading in favor of social tolerance and legal impunity for the 'condition' he now mostly considered inborn. Krafft-Ebing's shifting position, of course, was heavily informed by the lively debate about the abolition of Germany's sodomy law and by Karl Heinrich Ulrichs' arguments in favor of scrapping the infamous paragraph 175 of the German penal code. Similar arguments were going to be made in Britain and in the countries of Northern, Central, and Eastern Europe where such laws also still existed. In a Belgian context, however, where sodomy laws had been abolished during the French Revolution and were never reinstated, the debate about the legitimacy of sodomy laws abroad was largely irrelevant. In a legal sense, a border ran down continental Europe from the Low Countries, following the Franco-German border, straight through Switzerland and then along the Austro-Italian frontier to the Adriatic.[51] To the west of this border, same-sex 'immoralities' were legal between consenting adults in private on the basis of the rarely questioned liberal principle that the state and the courts had no business interfering in the hallowed private sphere. Because of this, the debate about homosexuality in those countries – lively in France and later in the Netherlands too, but more muted elsewhere and barely existent in Belgium – was more specifically concerned with the boundary between morality and disease than it was with criminal justice.[52]

Like Cuylits before him, De Rode dismissed the expansive pathologization of homosexuality as both a factual and a moral error. With regard to clinical facts, there was evidence that sexual aberrations could be the temporary symptoms of a different mental problem and therefore not a congenital condition in and of themselves. De Rode pointed out that the Russian scholar Benjamin Tarnowsky had recently established that not all cases of inversion were inborn, and that Krafft-Ebing acknowledged this. The Belgian returned to this point in his reviews of later editions of *Psychopathia Sexualis*.[53] More often than not, he insisted, contrary sexual feeling was "the consequence of masturbatory or pederastic habits, contracted by simple depravation or through particular circumstances (boarding schools, prisons, barracks, etc.)."[54] His key point was that many if not most of these supposedly innate inverts were, in fact, moral failures. In his 1891 review of Krafft-Ebing's *New Research in the Field of Sexual Psychopathy*, De Rode emphasized that he had had difficulty reading anything other in the growing series of autobiographic case studies than "a perversion acquired at a young age as the consequence of immoral habits."[55] Inverts were not to be allowed to take moral cover behind a façade of disease or disorder. No one, least of all psychiatrists, should condone any invocation of the born-like-this argument as a false "prétexte": an alibi and a get-out-of-jail-free card.[56] The wicked deserved punishment.

The Ferment of Filth

For those who opposed it, there was no better illustration of the moral hazards of overmedicalization than the growing chorus of homosexual apologists. To De Rode's horror, many of the case studies that filled *Psychopathia Sexualis* were not impassive descriptions of clinical facts but colorful confessions or even the unedited autobiographies which Krafft-Ebing had received by mail. What typified them was their shocking explicitness about the "most intimate and the most repulsive details."[57] Their number growing with every new edition, all of them displayed the same "minuteness," the same "exaggerated" preoccupation with the self, the same "egoism or egotism found at the root of many psychopathies and of hypochondriac affections in particular."[58] Clearly, De Rode took a dim view of what he considered to be the disgusting expressions of misplaced self-pity. Nearly all of these accounts attested to what he felt to be "a singular unscrupulousness."[59] Many inverts now felt so at ease with their pathologized identity that they had even started protesting their social condemnation with a sense of entitlement. Describing their sexual exploits with "extraordinary lyricism," they regretted their aberration itself less than they did the social restrictions imposed upon the satisfaction of their 'unnatural' instincts. "They would even go so far as to pose as the victims of the public's prejudices," De Rode jeered indignantly.[60]

This tendency towards unapologetic self-assertion was deeply troubling to him and to many others. He noted that inverts were known to congregate in every large city. They "have their own stomping grounds, throw parties, etc.," thus forming "a veritable freemasonry" with networks stretching across national borders.[61] This growing evil had to be nipped in the bud and hardly needed further encouragement. That sense was at the heart of De Rode's resistance to Krafft-Ebing's publications. In claiming "that we should be more willing to pity than to scorn or to condemn them," Krafft-Ebing was indulging his sexually abnormal patients, if not even emboldening them to see themselves as the pitiable victims of nature and even of society.[62] Where would all this gratuitous medicalizing lead us, De Rode asked, before answering his own question:

Soon, there will not be a pederast left who does not feel compelled to disclose his 'state of mind' to us and to describe his most intimate feelings. Let us hope that some findings useful to the psychologist or the physician may come of all this, and particularly that the pathological character of many sexual aberrations will not be ignored so often anymore. But it is also to be feared that the pretense of disease will be invoked more than before to justify splurges of vice and that many a debauchee will find in it the excuse for his abjection. From this perspective, it is not without some disquiet that we see the editions of 'psychopathy' [i.e. *Psychopathia Sexualis*] succeed one another and we cannot help suspecting that it is not scientific interest alone which ensures this publication's success.[63]

De Rode did not doubt Krafft-Ebing's integrity, and he maintained his respect for the great psychiatrist and forensic expert who had done so much for the profession. But he dreaded the growing circulation of this "special literature," and for good reason. There can be no question that sexological works like Krafft-Ebing's were read not just by fellow scholars and for purely scientific purposes, as Chapter 7 will make clear. Harry Oosterhuis has shown that their popularity was due in large measure to the revelations they were to those trying to make sense of their socially impermissible desires.[64] As such, and as De Rode suspected, sexological works contributed to the emergence of a language of perversion in neutral or even sympathetic terms, transcending the moralistic framework to which sin and sodomy had traditionally been confined. The medicalization of sexuality unquestionably enabled what Michel Foucault called a "reverse discourse," by which "homosexuality began to speak on its own behalf, to demand that its legitimacy or 'naturality' be acknowledged, often in the same vocabulary, using the same categories by which it was [initially] medically disqualified." What he described with a high level of abstraction and with reference to the "productivity" and the "tactical polyvalence" of discourse was exactly the kind of rhetorical maneuvering enabled by books like *Psychopathia Sexualis*, namely the strategic appropriation of the powerful language of science for socially and morally subversive ends.[65]

Indeed, the pathologization of sexual deviance, while providing a scientific basis for discrimination against the 'abnormal' also justified calls for their exoneration on the basis of the claim that one cannot be held to account for one's congenital disposition. This is precisely the line of reasoning that would come to characterize the most influential exponents of the primarily German early homosexual rights movement from the later 1890s onwards, which Krafft-Ebing supported, and which Ulrichs had pioneered in the 1860s. During the 1870s and the 1880s, Krafft-Ebing's works did much to help clad the 'soft' humanistic language of Ulrichs in the imperial purple of 'hard' scientific truth. De Rode, and other Catholic psychiatrists along with him, rightly anticipated that the medical recognition of an inborn inversion of the sexual instinct not only facilitated a reverse discourse but also hollowed out moral objections to what many still saw as sheer filth. From their perspective, the issues of sexual perversion in general and of sexual inversion in particular epitomized the slippery path of psychiatry that was dangerously tilting towards the abyss of moral relativism by those wielding specious sophistry for leverage. There was therefore much at stake in the psychiatric arena and with regard to the issue of inversion; much more than meets the eye at first glance.

The more fundamental debate was an anthropological one about human nature. Problems of sex and sexual deviance inevitably touched on this hugely divisive larger issue. After all, as Krafft-Ebing observed in the successive introductions to *Psychopathia Sexualis*: "in the voluptuous drive to satisfy his natural instinct, man is equal to animals, but he is capable of raising to a higher level, where he is no longer a passive slave to instinct."[66] In order to reach this higher plane, and to prevent tumbling down from it again, "a never-ceasing duel between instinct and morality [*Sinnlichtkeit und Sittlichtkeit*]" was moral man's solemn duty and inevitable fate. In effect, Krafft-Ebing professed, "[o]nly those with sufficient willpower and strong characters can emancipate themselves entirely from carnality."[67] Himself raised a Catholic, he recognized how religion played an extremely important role in the 'civilization' of both individuals and of society at large. But were his increasingly expansive views about the innocence of inverts not opening the door to a form of moral backsliding? Certainly, an unhappy few might well be the victims of an overpowering pathology, but would the wholesale essentialization of criminal and immoral behavior by overzealous physicians not create a scientifically endorsed domino effect? Would it not open the floodgates to a wave of unrestrained indulgence; a wave so powerful that it might even wash away the inhibitive roots of civilization itself?

Conclusion

Chapter 5 will set the very limited discussion of sexual inversion among Belgian psychiatrists against the wider backdrop of ideological shifts, scientific developments, and their international circulation during the late nineteenth century. It will make clear just how much this discussion was inextricably bound up with a much broader and intensely political clash over human nature, and how this clash was influenced by the shifting balance of power in fast-changing societies. In the Belgian context, I will argue, all these contextual elements further inhibited the public and scientific discussion of homosexuality. In this chapter, the goal has been to set the stage for this broader battle of ideas. Psychiatry was a new profession and a new scientific discipline, striving towards recognition and trying to make its mark on public policy. Psychiatry's professionalization was not an easy or clear-cut development anywhere, but there were marked differences in its speed and success across countries. Recognition came faster for asylum physicians in Britain and France than in Austria or Germany, but even in the latter two countries psychiatry's prestige steadily grew along with its emergence as an academic discipline from the 1860s onwards.[68] The situation in Belgium resembled that of the Netherlands more closely insofar as the academization and professionalization of psychiatry lagged behind in both countries. But the influence of Catholic congregations made Belgium exceptional in the sheer strength and persistence of political resistance to public interference with what had long been a private sector.

Formidable Catholic influence over psychiatry made many Belgian psychiatrists reluctant if not outright averse to any wanton medicalization of sin. Whereas sex and sexual inversion served as instruments of psychiatric secularization in closely monitored France from the 1870s onwards, their exploration was no way to curry favor from Belgium's Catholic establishment by a profession badly in need of its benevolence to make any further progress. The more homosexuality was ascribed to an innate 'condition' in the 1880s, the stronger Catholics like De Rode pushed back against the exculpatory implications of such a claim. Where Krafft-Ebing's calls for social tolerance and decriminalization were informed by the specific medico-legal debate on homosexuality in Austria and Germany, in a Belgian context such calls were unpalatable even to the anticlerical advocates of a French-style public system. François Semal, the BSMM's most militant pro-state psychiatric activist, objected to Krafft-Ebing's *Psychopathia Sexualis* in unison with his Catholic colleagues, because it risked brandishing his respectable professional activism with the unhelpful stain of smut.[69] In Belgium, as in Britain, the mixture of bourgeois respectability, liberal principles, and religious reservations did much to discredit the activist sexology of *fin-de-siècle* France and Germany.[70]

5 Free Will Politics and the Avoidance of Inversion

During the final quarter of the nineteenth century, sweeping claims about the hardwired causes of social and sexual deviance alike gained currency across Europe and beyond the field of psychiatry alone. The Italian criminologist Cesare Lombroso published a highly influential study of *Criminal Man* in 1876, which boldly claimed that all kinds of delinquency were primarily caused by congenital defects.[1] The book did much to launch the new academic discipline of criminal anthropology, which was further shaped by a series of prestigious international conferences held from the mid 1880s onwards. Born from a desire to overhaul the existing legal system, criminal anthropology's inherent determinism provoked an ideologically pregnant debate about the existence and the primacy of free will as the foundation of both moral judgments and social organization. After all, if crime was just the involuntary consequence of biological or social pathologies, then punishment made no sense, and the entire criminal justice system needed to become preventive or curative rather than retributive. Criminal anthropology's radical implications elicited strong opposition from the legal establishment.[2] Ultimately, the movement's influence, while tangible, remained limited and the 'classic' legal system largely intact. Criminal anthropology's attack on free will proved far more ambitious than it was effective.

This chapter explains how sexual inversion touched on the heart of this debate and was therefore intensely controversial. Like the Lombrosian notion of the born criminal, that of the innate invert rallied hardliners on both sides of the ideological divide. On the one hand, the defenders of free will arose in support of institutions like the judiciary and the church, whose very legitimacy depended on the belief in man as a free-choosing, rational, and responsible agent. Accordingly, they also refused to swap the moralization of homosexuality for its exculpatory pathologization. Free will's opponents, on the other hand, demanded that society's key institutions no longer be based on misty metaphysical doctrines but on hard scientific evidence instead. To them, the invert's impulses were instinctive and therefore irresistible, rendering moral judgments obsolete. While only one element of a much wider discussion, the emotive issue of inversion forced stakeholders to nail their colors to the mast whenever it arose, as it did at the Third International Conference on Criminal Anthropology held in Brussels in 1892. Tellingly, it was not only the first but also the only time the issue was ever discussed in a high-profile scientific forum on Belgian soil before the Second World War. Friend and foe alike agreed that the vexing matter was too polarizing to pursue at length. Indeed, the self-declared 'Belgian school' of criminal anthropology would not allow for wedge issues like inversion to scuttle the prospect of a practical compromise between ideological opponents.

On closer examination, the late nineteenth century's quarrel over crime and responsibility was a proxy debate between the defenders of the prevailing political order and a rising left that sought to reform or even to revolutionize it. Naturally, in each country this debate varied with national specifics.[3] In Belgium, it pitted the old establishment of Catholics and laissez-faire liberals against a younger cohort of progressive liberals and socialists. Rather than insist on personal responsibility, as the former traditionally did, the latter emphasized the biological, sociological, and political impediments to people's autonomy, and they were more amenable to wielding state intervention to address social problems. As these problems mounted, however, they also augmented a political sense of urgency to tackle them. In the face of growing social unrest, moderate Catholics and liberals increasingly agreed to use the state's resources towards social and political pacification. In the field of criminal justice, even left-leaning stakeholders' primary concern was often with the maintenance of public order. Moreover, forensic specialists of all political persuasions recognized that neither ideological bickering nor radical proposals would serve their professional interests after moderate Catholics obtained long-lasting control of government in 1884. In this climate, nothing stood to be gained from dwelling on an issue, like inversion, considered both divisive and distasteful.

The Politics of Free Will

In 1875, Dr. François Semal presented a programmatic report at the fourth International Cyclical Conference of the Medical Sciences *On the Moral and Legal Situation and the Internment of the Criminally and Dangerously Insane*.[4] Because the latter belonged neither in a regular prison nor in an ordinary insane asylum, the creation of so-called prison-asylums by the state had recently been proposed in parliament.[5] The debate about this ostensibly sensible measure would nevertheless continue unresolved for almost sixty years.[6] Partly, this was because the creation of new state-run institutions met with the usual fiscal and political objections of the country's liberal–Catholic establishment, which favored private initiative over state interventionism (see Chapter 4). But equally if not more important were the ideological implications of this debate, which centered on the problem of moral and legal responsibility. The report by Semal made that radiantly clear. "Regarding this matter, two antithetical theories exist," he wrote. One of them conceived of the human spirit or soul as having "an immaterial essence endowed with the capacity of self-control and with command over the body." In this view, human beings were responsible for their actions by default. The other theory, by contrast, based on the unity of body and mind, saw "mental phenomena as the consequence of material impulses" and therefore as "simple reactions" or reflexes.[7] As such, free will and responsibility were fundamentally compromised, if they existed at all.

The belief in free will had long dominated Western philosophy.[8] It was central to the Christian tradition's key concepts of sin, remorse, and atonement. René Descartes' dualistic notion of an immaterial consciousness and a material body further bolstered the belief in free will as the dominant philosophical view from the seventeenth century onwards. Human beings' ability to subdue bodily urges in adherence to 'higher' principles was commonly thought of as precisely what set them apart from 'lower' animals. The notion of rational and responsible 'man' became the cornerstone of Enlightened penal codes as well as of virtuous citizenship in early nineteenth-century bourgeois society. The latter's principal institutions, the judiciary and the church, relied on this anthropology for their legitimacy. But while this dualistic 'spiritualism' defined man as a conflicting union of body and soul, it never satisfactorily explained how these two entities causally interacted. Monistic 'materialists' increasingly exploited this weakness to disprove the existence of free will as well as the dominance of the institutions and political system empowered by it. Materialism's momentum grew with the rise of the biomedical sciences. In France, it gradually gained prominence through the controversial writings of militant physicians in the eighteenth and the early nineteenth centuries.[9] In Germany, scientific materialism first emerged with the phrenology of Franz-Joseph Gall and it bloomed in the wake of Ludwig Feuerbach's rebuttal of Hegelian idealism during the 1840s and 1850s.[10]

Forensic psychiatry became a prime site where the primacy of free will was contested as the nineteenth century progressed because psychiatrists were increasingly called upon to explain the ostensibly sane but obsessively compulsive. They labeled these perplexing offenders pathological 'monomaniacs' or 'psychopaths' and declared them dangerously irresponsible.[11] The gray zone between the obviously insane and rationally responsible gradually expanded to include petty repeat offenders like drunks, vagrants, and other *demi-fous* (halfwits) whose grip on themselves and on reality seemed obviously limited. Having established the existence of this "intermediary zone" of "questionable individuals," Semal argued at the same conference mentioned earlier that "it would not be asking too much from societies to set their laws in accordance with these scientific insights." Penal codes based on "the outdated view that the will is something absolute" needed revising.[12] A radical materialist and determinist, Semal scoffed at spiritualists' inability to account for these intermediary types' diminished responsibility. He sneered:

> It is precisely because society and the courts turn to physicians every time the question of free will is raised concretely and not in purely abstract terms that physicians have the right and the obligation to seek their arguments elsewhere than in the moldered arsenal of metaphysics, and to take up arms other than the rust-eaten and abandoned artillery on the battlefields of philosophical debates.[13]

As the psychiatrist and director of one of Belgium's very few publicly run insane asylums at Mons, Semal was the nation's principal advocate of psychiatry's professionalization (see Chapter 4), but his ambitions stretched beyond purely professional matters. Like many who shared his view that science and not metaphysics should form the basis of policy, Semal affirmed his adherence to the Frenchman Auguste Comte's doctrine of positivism. Increasingly influential since its conception in the 1830s and 1840s, positivism held that humanity develops through stages in which truth and politics were initially drawn from theology, then from metaphysics, and finally from positive (i.e. exact or empirical) science. Comtian positivism was a bellicose variety of the nineteenth century's optimistic belief in science-driven progress, marked by deep anti-religious and anti-metaphysical resentment and rooted in utopian socialism.[14] Versions of positivism proliferated across Europe in atheist, republican, left-liberal, and socialist circles. In Britain, it influenced John Stuart Mill and Herbert Spencer, and in Risorgimento Italy Cesare Lombroso drew on positivism for inspiration.[15]

In Belgium too, positivism made headway. In the 1860s, it was popular among a new generation of progressive intellectuals at the masonic Free University of Brussels.[16] They loathed the socially conservative oligarchy of libertarian liberals and Catholics whose political rivalry had become all-consuming after the waning of unionist power-sharing during the late 1850s. In the face of radical ideas, however, this bitterly divided 'Belgeoisie' remained united in its shared aversion to the anti-metaphysical iconoclasm and the political heterodoxy of the young left. The president of the Free University of Brussels denounced his positivist students for espousing "the most dangerous kind of socialism."[17] Even progressive liberals scolded positivism as that "poisonous toadstool of the Second Empire."[18] However much the culture of Belgium's francophone elites was akin to that of its larger southern neighbor, the combination of the growing Gallic appetite for radical ideas on the one hand and Emperor Napoleon III's unconcealed annexationist designs on Belgium on the other made the country's mainstream suspicious of all things French.

Positivism would remain a minority view in Belgium and the dominance of anti-positivism a hallmark of the old elite's defensive intellectual phalanx.[19] Tensions constantly flared during the nineteenth century's closing quarter. A good example was the prolonged tussle over the stigmatic Louise Lateau, whose bouts of religious ecstasy garnered great public attention after their first manifestation in 1868.[20] In a bellicose book from 1875, a positivist physician described Lateau as a "poor monomaniac" and her condition as a demonstrably "pathological phenomenon."[21] To the author, it was beyond farce that Ferdinand Lefèbvre, a leading professor of medicine at the Catholic University of Leuven who then taught the country's only regular course on psychiatry, had affirmed the supernatural causes of her condition. The medicalization of conditions heretofore understood in mystical terms was proving a powerful weapon against the ruling metaphysical philosophies in general, and against religious doctrines and clerical influence more particularly.[22] But a sixteen-month-long discussion of Lateau's stigmata before Belgium's Royal Academy of Medicine in 1874 and 1875 eventually petered out without any general conclusions being formulated. Debates like these divided even physicians along fundamental ideological lines, producing something of a trench war with ongoing skirmishes that never resulted in territorial gains on either side.

The creation of new organizations like the Scientific Society of Brussels in 1875 institutionalized this acrimonious battle of ideas. Its statutes stipulated that members would "never permit any attack, however courteous, on the Catholic religion, or on spiritualist and religious philosophy."[23] In his inaugural address as the society's first president, Ferdinand Lefèbvre observed that "such marvelous discoveries have been made in the world of matter that easily dazzle the mind" and which led many scientists to "surrender to a kind of idolatry of nature and of themselves."[24] But they were wrong to dismiss the compatibility of science and faith. Lefèbvre exalted Saint Thomas Aquinas' thirteenth-century synthesis of Christianity and Aristotelian philosophy as the way forwards. Four years later, in 1879, Pope Leo XIII elevated 'Thomism' as the official epistemological doctrine of the church and he made the Catholic University of Leuven its international intellectual powerhouse.[25] Meanwhile, staunch liberals were also weary of venturing too far into the moral swamp of materialistic determinism. Even the venomously anticlerical and socialist author of the above-mentioned book about Louise Lateau opposed "the exaggerations of the materialist school."[26] Especially in the courts, he wrote elsewhere, "the progress of science and brain anatomy" had "caused confusion." Science had simply not yet advanced far enough to make sweeping claims about responsibility and free will, and overzealous forensic physicians tended worryingly towards "exculpating the vast majority of the accused."[27]

Materialism's momentum was clearly mounting in Belgium as it was throughout Europe, reaching its zenith in debates about free will and the pathologies of responsibility during the 1880s. Grafted on the French example, the newly created Anthropological Society of Brussels brought together the country's most militant materialists from 1882 onwards.[28] Recruiting mainly among faculty, students and alumni of the capital's Free University, several of its notable members later held seats in parliament as progressive liberals and socialists.[29] No fewer than twenty-two of the Anthropological Society's forty-five founding members were physicians. In imitation of the revered Lombroso, who was a corresponding member of the society from the start, one of these members studied the skulls of executed assassins to establish craniometric signs of criminality.[30] Other medically trained members also had a strong interest in criminal anthropology, including the relentless François Semal. By the mid 1880s, their often radical ideas about criminal justice reform were gaining some traction, but these ideas were also tainted by their close association with Parisian psychiatric politics, socialism, and sex.

The Sexual Roots of Radical Materialism

Materialism's verve was clearly on display during the Conference on Phreniatry and Neuropathology of 1885.[31] Hosted by the Belgian Society of Mental Medicine (BSMM) during the world fair at Antwerp, there was no shortage of prominent international attendants. These included the inspectors-general of the French and Dutch asylum systems, the chief physician of the Paris police prefecture, the famous Austrian neurologist Moritz Benedikt, as well as prominent British alienists and representatives from Italy, Germany, Denmark, Russia, and Argentina. In a telling demonstration of the simmering spiritualist/materialist divisions, the conference's two keynote speeches were given by the archenemies Lefèbvre and Semal. Semal's paper on the "Relations Between Criminality and Insanity" had stirred much controversy within the BSMM in the run-up to the conference, with colleagues forcing him to clarify that he would not be speaking on behalf of the society as a whole.[32] Glued together by concepts like heredity, atavism, and degeneration, Semal's activist keynote drew on British social Darwinism to lament that magistrates still commonly based their verdicts on the "obscure arguments of metaphysics" and that, in changing this, "positivism aspires to reign."[33] Semal specified that a recent lecture by Valentin Magnan before the Medical Academy of Paris in January 1885 had provided him with "the possibility of formulating the relations between the criminal and the insane with some accuracy."[34] In his lecture *On the Sexual Anomalies, Aberrations and Perversions*, the eminent French psychiatrist had used sexual perversion to calibrate the entire spectrum of degeneration. "These sexual anomalies," Magnan had argued, "are so numerous, and so varied, that they might lead to confusion if their mutual ties were not clarified by a classification based on anatomy and physiology."[35]

With Magnan present among the Antwerp audience, Semal now applied the profoundly anatomo-deterministic model of sexual perversion to issues of crime and responsibility more broadly. He explained that vertebral drives condemned so-called spinal types to a primitive existence; their actions "imbued with an irresistibility disengaged from all restraint, from all decency, and from any scruple."[36] In the "posterior cerebrals" the instinctive back of the brain overpowered a poorly developed capacity for conscious reasoning. "Here, the tyranny of either insatiable or perverted appetites can be observed, but … it is no longer suffused with passivity." These "mental retards" were still "powerless in governing their whims." The "anterior cerebrals," by contrast, in whom the frontal lobes predominated, were more conscious of and had more control over their actions. From a criminological point of view, these composed the most relevant category of bizarrely inclined but ostensibly normal psychopaths. Semal explained that "[t]his is the domain of illegitimate, incestuous, [and] depraved attachments, of the refinements of debauchery and of the offences that they provoke all too often." In the fourth and final category, that of the "psychics," a certain independence of the frontal lobes from the more primitive system in the rear and towards the spine existed, and thus there was a degree of independence from the unruly instincts. In this category, the perversions were limited to those of the imagination, such as "platonic erotomaniacs," "ecstatics" like Louise Lateau, and even "sectarians, revolutionaries," and "anarchists." Semal's argument, in short, echoing Magnan, was that all sexual and social deviance – even that of an ideological kind – could be explained with reference to anatomo-pathological lesions of the brain and the spinal cord.

To many present, both its pedigree and its tone fundamentally compromised Semal's report. His findings were too sweeping, too materialistic, too deterministic, and too therapeutically fatalistic to be true. But they were also too political and far too French to Belgian ears especially. They smacked of the kind of socialism generally associated with radically positivist ideas, and they reeked more particularly of the militant anticlericalism rampant among a coterie of Parisian psychiatrists, led by Magnan and the illustrious Jean-Martin Charcot, who enthusiastically supported the vindictive secularist policies of the increasingly left-wing French Third Republic.[37] As the moderate Moral Order had come to an end in 1877, sweeping progressive Republicans into power, foreign commentators often branded France a hotbed of godless and dangerously radical ideas.[38] During the early 1880s, the French government embraced Charcot's hard-line positivism by appointing him to a chair in neurology created especially for him at the medical faculty of Paris.[39] Around that very time, in 1882, Charcot and Magnan co-authored the influential paper on "The Inversion of the Genital Instinct" mentioned in Chapter 4, which legitimized the study of homosexuality in France while firmly anchoring the issue to a positivist, materialist, and determinist political agenda.[40] By consequence, anything to do with sexual perversion and inversion was henceforth tainted by this agenda.

At the Antwerp conference, foreign dignitaries took issue with the immoderation of Semal's overly ideological paper. A prominent British psychiatrist noted that Semal attached "so much importance to the claim that criminal acts are the result of congenital cerebral malformations that he seems to deny free will altogether, and all criminal responsibility along with it."[41] The less theoretically inclined British school could not support such a view, nor could a Dutch psychiatrist who insisted that the question of responsibility was one to be settled by judges, not psychiatrists.[42] For his part, the Austrian neurologist Benedikt admitted to being supportive of deterministic ideas to a certain extent, but he nevertheless opined that it was "neither justified nor practical to conflate professional criminals and the insane in a general way."[43] Meanwhile, Belgian physicians kept aloof. Irritated though many were by Semal, they were also fearful of the loss of face that the BSMM would suffer from a public falling-out. After all, Belgium's political developments had recently taken a very different turn from those in France, and they were forcing forensic specialists seeking to advance their professional interests to ditch politics and be pragmatic.

Ostensibly following in the footsteps of France, 1878 saw an aggressive anticlerical government of laissez-faire liberals come into office in Belgium, but its ill-fated attempt to curtail Catholic dominance over primary education rocked the country to its foundations.[44] Catholics rode to power on the major backlash against the so-called School War, successfully holding on to their absolute majority from 1884 to 1914.[45] A liberal bastion at the time of France's conservative Second Empire, Belgium now switched roles to become its southern neighbor's political opposite once again; not just as a bulwark of Catholic power in contrast with the secularist Third Republic but also because of the successive Catholic cabinets' emphasis on moderate centrism as opposed to French partisanship and political hackery. That centrism reaped electoral rewards and ensured political stability at a time when French governments fell in quick succession.[46] In this political climate, those – including psychiatrists and forensic physicians – who sought the backing of the Catholic ship of state stood little to gain from ideological fundamentalism. Amplifying the aversion to irreligious left-wing radicalism in particular was the fact that, sparked by anarchists in Liège, a wave of violent strikes had rippled through the country in 1886.[47] Going forwards, Belgium's bickering elites focused a little less on their mutual differences and a lot more on their joint concern with maintaining social order and their hold on political power.

No one exemplified this new bipartisan centrism better than Jules Lejeune, the liberal–Catholic lawyer who became Minister of Justice in 1887.[48] He championed reforms to the legal system based on the ideas of his former pupil Adolphe Prins, who had recently developed the doctrine of 'social defense' at the Free University of Brussels to emphasize society's right to neutralize 'dangerous' elements through customized punishments and, where necessary, indefinite detention. Prins, a member of the Anthropological Society, flirted with the determinist theories of criminal anthropology, but, like Lejeune, his primary concern was the more practical challenge of social stabilization through the fight against recidivism, petty crime, vagrancy, and public drunkenness.[49] Even so, the BSMM rejoiced at the prospect of finally seeing their roles as arbiters of 'dangerousness' enhanced. Its members noted how Lejeune, who mixed in progressive as well as conservative circles, seemed "strongly inclined to realize our projects" after a delegation of psychiatrists met with the minister shortly after his appointment.[50] However, they "also detected a sense of skepticism" in the man regarding the overzealous tendency among some *médecins-aliénistes* to declare vast swathes of offenders irresponsible based on flimsy evidence.[51] Like much of the political class, Lejeune remained a product of his legal training after all.[52] While they lobbied for reform, therefore, psychiatrists in the BSMM had to be wary not to get lost in "the mists of theory," as one critic warned them.[53] They had to close ranks for tactical reasons. When invited to bring their proposals regarding the creation of prison-asylums before the Royal Academy of Medicine in 1889, a senior psychiatrist reminded his colleagues: "Let us not forget that the problem before us is one of practical organization and that our diverging opinions, inevitably put on display by venturing into any theoretical discussion, would only weaken our cause in the eyes of the Minister."[54]

The Slope Downwards to Sodom

This strategic ceasefire was a fragile one. It would only hold if topics that inflamed the ideological tensions always bubbling under the surface could be avoided. Sexual inversion was one of those emotive topics. That much became crystal clear at the Third International Conference on Criminal Anthropology held in Brussels in the summer of 1892. It was a high-stakes event. The first two of these conferences, held in 1885 (Rome) and 1889 (Paris), had done little to ingratiate the new discipline in the eyes of policymakers. They had seen a fractious falling-out between the hard biologistic Italian school of Lombroso and his Parisian followers on the one hand and the softer, more sociologically inclined French school, headquartered in Lyon, on the other.[55] But the slew of reformist initiatives taken by Lejeune since assuming office – including a proposed bill to build the much-coveted prison-asylums and the creation of a psychiatric prison service in 1891 – generated a sense that this conference would be about concrete policies rather than basic principles and big personalities. Far exceeding attendance at previous conferences, some 400 participants from 28 different countries were present, including King Leopold II.[56] There too were the future archbishop, the leader of the newly created Belgian Workers Party, and, of course, Minister Lejeune himself. Striking a balance, the two main organizing societies of the conference were the deterministic Anthropological Society of Brussels and the spiritualist-dominated BSMM. Mirroring that balance, its chair was Semal, with Lefèbvre as vice-chair.

The program slated a report on sexual inversion on the final day of the conference by Léon De Rode.[57] As we know from Chapter 4, this Belgian psychiatrist was familiar with the topic, even if he had never done any research on it himself. Taking the floor, he granted that sexual inversion was an unpleasant matter, but its discussion proved necessary as recent years had seen fundamental changes in the way the issue was scientifically understood.

Until a short while ago, unnatural love was only considered as a form of debauchery. The sin has been met with public disdain. Legislations have meted out the severest punishments against it. Moralists have condemned it. Satiric poets have stigmatized it in indignant verses. But only lately has the question become the object of closer inspection and of scientific scrutiny.[58]

Before this international audience, De Rode essentially repeated what he had previously argued in his reviews of Richard von Krafft-Ebing's *Psychopathia Sexualis* for the BSMM, namely that the German Carl Westphal's insistence on the innateness of what he, in 1870, had dubbed 'contrary sexual feeling' had since been disproved. The etiological details he provided with reference to the theory of degeneration and to a host of mostly non-German authors were fuzzy and they ran counter to key writings on the issue, but De Rode's main point was clear: Even if the existence of isolated cases of congenital inversion could not be denied, the vast majority of 'pederastic' inclinations were merely the acquired consequence of unchecked hedonism, educational failure, and a weakness of character. In essence, he explained:

It concerns persons who, during adolescence, have been incited by friends to habits of masturbation. Later, they have tried coitus but, failing in their first attempts or only experiencing partial satisfaction, they then reverted to their wicked habits and were soon unable to experience anything other than an insurmountable aversion towards the normal act.[59]

Rather than victims of a cruel nature, inverts' story was usually one of "tragic banality." For the most part, there was no involutionary atavism or degenerative defect whatsoever at play. The simple truth was that "one does not become an invert overnight" and that "one does not give in to unnatural pleasures with impunity" but rather "descends into the depths of degradation step by step."⁶⁰ To De Rode, sexual deviance was pathogenic rather than pathological per se. Genuine psychopathology was typically the consequence of immorality and not the other way around. By implication, the good news was that real perversion could be prevented and often even reversed, "provided that the will has not lost all resilience and the patient has the courage to renounce his immoral habits."⁶¹ But all therapeutic hopes were vested on the summoning of sufficient willpower. In the end, it was all a matter of psychopedagogical prevention.

Here, as in every kind of therapy, it is at the beginning that the evil needs to be nipped in the bud. To prevent is better than to cure. Education must be the great prophylactic against a disease for which no efficient remedy has yet been discovered, and against which all efforts will soon be in vain if it is left to fester. And if there is some innate inclination that drives the subject exclusively towards persons of his own sex, it is still up to education to intervene, not to remove that inclination, which would be impossible, but to prevent, in short, the *invert* from becoming a *pederast*.⁶²

Although a physician, De Rode advocated self-control and strength of character as the categorical imperatives of mental and moral health in the best spiritualist tradition. One had to resist one's sexual inclinations just as one had to resist all excessive and unwarranted temptations of the flesh.

Many examples have shown that this fight can be won. Perhaps it is not much more difficult than the one fought daily by unspoiled youngsters of vigorous temperaments in the struggle for survival. In any case, numerous observations have been published that show those [congenitally] afflicted with genital inversion victoriously resisting the titillations of their unnatural proclivities. These unfortunates deserve to be pitied for their misery, and to be congratulated for their courage; they should also be thanked for demonstrating to us that even to a neuropath or to an invert Responsibility is not a hollow term.⁶³

In placing such emphasis on chastity and self-control, De Rode simply echoed mainstream moral maxims. The leading Belgian Catholic psychiatrist, Xavier Francotte, similarly believed that physicians, as "secular confessors," were not to condone any kind of non-procreative indulgence, since "nothing would justify the encouragement or tolerance of sexual aberration."⁶⁴ In an authoritative book on criminal anthropology published a year before the conference, Francotte had pointed out that all 'men' are born with immoral inclinations. Like De Rode, but in a more general sense, he had insisted that if one does not learn "to restrain one's depraved instincts" from the very beginning, intemperance would inevitably lead to a life of sin and crime.⁶⁵ The striking parallels between De Rode's report and Francotte's writings testify to how representative the opinion they shared was for the entire Catholic community. In a dismissive reference to Lombroso's notion of the born criminal, Francotte had wondered "what to think of the influence such doctrines might exert on the criminals themselves, if they should learn about them?"[66]

But this was hardly a view held by Catholics alone. A renowned prison doctor and belletrist who moved in the capital's most progressive artistic circles similarly believed that "the moralization of sexual life has to form the basis of every preventive action against sexual diseases and disorders."[67] Abstinence and self-control were also at the core of freethinkers' ethics. In 1877, a proselytizing liberal mason had published a purposely low-priced series of educational books *On Self-Government* (*Du gouvernement de soi-même*) for adolescents.[68] The author was closely associated with the deeply anticlerical Belgian League of Education, the membership of which overlapped with that of the Anthropological Society of Brussels.[69] Even though they were actually Francotte's words, many freethinking liberals would have subscribed to the spiritualist adage that "to achieve and to maintain self-control is to achieve moral perfection."[70]

In sum, De Rode's report is not particularly interesting for the limited etiological details it provides, and it is therefore no surprise that it has never received attention before. The conceptual innovations of authors like Krafft-Ebing, Havelock Ellis, Sigmund Freud, and others have guaranteed historians' detailed scrutiny of their work, how it drew on that of their peers, and how they contributed to the emergence of new paradigms over time.[71] But a more ideologically than conceptually interested reading of lesser figures like De Rode can tell us a lot about the strategic investment of discourses concerned with sex.[72] His exposé on inversion was so fundamentally imbued with Belgium's dominant spiritualist outlook on the human condition that it could not be detached from the wider issues which it inevitably raised. This much was nicely illustrated when De Rode finished, and his paper's discussant arose. Eugène Hubert was a respected professor of obstetrics and medical deontology at the Catholic University of Leuven who did not linger in connecting inversion with the tenuous question of free will.[73] "Every time a horse rages underneath its rider," he began metaphorically, "scholars and public alike are divided into opposing camps: those who accuse the animal and those who blame the cavalier." Assessing the causes of such social and criminal "fits of paroxysm" to assist the courts was what criminal anthropology was all about. Hubert granted that there were "vicious horses" as well as "hopeless riders," but he went on to ask whose task it was "to train, to control or to master the steed?"[74] Indeed, what good was education if willpower was a mere word? Free will has been the essence of civilization itself, he opined; the edifice built through centuries of people choosing to rise above their basic instincts. Hard as they had tried, Hubert argued, the positivists and materialists had failed in their misguided attempts to disprove the existence of free will. With growing animus, he continued:

I know from positive science, through the experimental method and all kinds of experience, that while the peripheral impressions nudge me in a particular direction – like good advice or sound argument – they nonetheless do not *command* me. Nothing is more certain to me than knowing that I am the *occupant* of my brain, that I am master in my own house. And my strong sense, which I would call my *common sense*, revolts whenever my brain is reduced to an automatic recorder, offset by sudden reflexes, like a telegraph working without a telegraphist present to operate the machine![75]

To spiritualists like Hubert, the huge implications of deterministic views were beyond endurance. With seething sarcasm he promised his gratitude to any and all "anatomists" who could help him point at the particular spot in the brain "where abstract ideas germinate, where opinions are formed, where memories are kept, where volition begins and where this phenomenon – a contradiction in terms – of self-conscious matter is found!"[76] If humans did not differ from other primates save by their upright position and linguistic ability, he asked disdainfully, "than what have we come here to do?" Surely, if there was no such thing as human liberty, there was no such thing as responsibility or crime either and all conference attendants might as well go home. As to sexual inversion specifically, which he did not waste much time on, Hubert agreed with De Rode that "one becomes an invert in the same way that one becomes a drunk." Any abuse of a natural function induced its perversion, and the effects of such abuse, even when pathological, could never excuse their moral cause. "How," Hubert wondered, "does one willingly place one's hand in a cogwheel only to complain afterwards, as if of something preordained, that the entire arm has been drawn in!" People chose their own paths in life, and those who strayed onto "the slope that descends downward to Sodom" had only themselves to blame.[77]

Keeping the Peace

Inversion's inextricably close connection with the central problem of free will rendered the matter automatically explosive and threatened the conference with collapsing into an embarrassing stand-off between two mutually exclusive views. Lefèbvre, the aging don of Belgium's spiritualist school, poured further fuel onto the fire by intervening to dismiss the presumed "tyranny of the organs" and by extolling the immaterial soul as the engine "at the helm of human life."[78] Rising in response, the prominent determinist Émile Houzé of the Anthropological Society voiced "the most absolute reservations" about Lefèbvre's "profession of faith," before declaring his unwillingness to see one of the last debates of the conference dissolving into a polarizing confrontation between the two schools of thought.[79] He reminded everyone that only the day before a "possible agreement in the field of [criminal anthropology's] practical application" had been proposed, and that the deterministic school had "loyally accepted this deal." It was, after all, an honorable settlement, which did "not compromise anyone's dignity: one side gets to keep its faith, the other its scientific convictions." Please, Houzé implored, "let us try to stay in agreement about questions of application," to which the auditorium burst into prolonged applause.[80] One French attendant later recalled how most of the audience wanted to see both sides make concessions so that some much-needed practical progress could be made.[81]

The pragmatic pressure at Brussels is partly explained by the power of numbers. A rough count shows that whereas almost 78 percent of all French attendees at the previous conference on criminal anthropology of 1889 in Paris had been physicians, Belgian physicians numbered only 46 percent of those present in Brussels. They were, in fact, outnumbered by participants from the legal profession who wanted tangible results. The *Journal des Tribunaux* saw this as "a sign of the times." If not so much the judges, a notoriously conservative elite of whom few were predictably present, a new generation of scientifically interested lawyers was fed up with the "sterile casuistry" that had often paralyzed intellectual and public debates alike.[82] It was also a noted Belgian specificity that, of all people, a young priest had been the one to propose a way out of the looming impasse. This had happened on the second of the six-day conference during a tense debate on a paper concerned with "The Fundamental Principles of The School of Criminal Anthropology" and another, co-authored by Houzé, which asked: "Does the Anatomically Determined Criminal Type Exist?" While praising Lombroso as the discipline's founder, the authors had wavered on the born criminal by also allowing for sociological influences, but they had nevertheless rallied "unconditionally" behind Henry Maudsley's insistence on the "tyranny of the organism" in explaining crime and had declared themselves the enemies of those "adversaries of Mr Lombroso, who fight him in the name of religion and metaphysics."[83]

These deterministic declarations of faith had been received with condescension from senior lawyers in the room. The Belgian public prosecutor Armand Meyers taunted that he was only intervening in response to a sudden reflex. "If then, I offend your views somewhat," he went on, "I hope I may count on your indulgence, because in my attacks you will perceive merely the effect of my organism. (*Laughter.*)"[84] Meyers reminded the attending physicians that the courts already appealed to them when there was serious doubt about a defendant's responsibility, adding that on such occasions it was hardly uncommon for "Hippocrates and Galen [to] find themselves in disagreement," and thereby mocking the lack of medical consensus on these issues and hitting forensic physicians where he knew it would hurt. Meyers granted that the new discipline had helped to reorient the administration of justice towards the personality of the criminal, but he resented the underlying attempt to depose the spiritualist foundations of 'classic' penal law. Everyone expected even more contempt from Maurice De Baets as he took to the stage in his long black cassock. But to general surprise, the young priest beseeched determinists and spiritualists "to reach an understanding" and to each "reconsider what is too absolute in their conclusions. (*Applause*.)" His appeal for moderation resonated with the audience, which welcomed his words with a crescendo of approbation. "I have faith," De Baets admitted, "my cassock makes that clear enough, but I only recognize a single point of departure for science: that is the establishment of facts."[85]

De Baets' surprise appeal for appeasement and collaboration swung the mood completely and others leaped into the opening he created. Albert Nyssens, a young Catholic MP who taught law at the University of Leuven, avowed his adherence to the 'classic' spiritualist school but also summoned his fellow "criminalists" to "take the insights of anthropology into account in the study of criminal law. (*Applause*.)"[86] De Baets (aged twenty-nine) and Nyssens (thirty-seven) represented a new generation of spiritualist scholarship; one that felt less threatened by 'modern' scientific theories than did *éminences grises* like Hubert (fifty-three) and Lefèbvre (seventy-two). They would not allow their reservations about radical determinism and excessive pathologization to stand in the way of sensible reforms.[87] The deterministic chair of the session welcomed these overtures with enthusiasm, stating that "concerning questions of application, we understand each other perfectly. (*Applause*.)"[88] Bringing the increasingly jovial atmosphere to a height, the materialistic hardliner Houzé arose to accept the hand extended by moderate spiritualists, quipping:

While listening to the [hostile] intervention of Mr Procurator-General Zakrewsky, I experienced a defensive reflex. When I heard Mr Meyers speak this reflex overpowered me. (*Hilarity*.) Afterwards, the words of the Reverend De Baets have triggered a tangible relaxation. (*Renewed laughter*.) He has not confined himself exclusively to the issues of free will and responsibility. We find ourselves on opposite banks of a river: he is on the right bank, we are on the left one, but the Reverend De Baets has built a bridge between us. I am greatly pleased and congratulate him for it. This agreement will be one of the principal teachings of this conference and it will be his accomplishment. I am thus perfectly willing to accept a marriage of convenience with the Reverend De Baets, but I must insist that if Mr Meyers were concerned, I would immediately file for divorce. (*Laughter and applause*.)[89]

This marriage of convenience between positivists and spiritualists was indeed celebrated as the basis for the conference's "complete success." The French *Archives of Criminal Anthropology* lauded De Baets' "fine lesson in diplomacy" and the resulting "new era" of reconciliation of not only "free will and determinism" but also "law and biology" and "magistrate and physician."[90] In essence, it was a shotgun marriage required to secure Lejeune's continued support. The minister had earned the loyalty of moderates and radicals alike with his reforms, which included the law on the conditional release of prisoners (1888), the law on the internment of vagrants and beggars (1891), and a range of (ultimately unsuccessful) legislative proposals to tackle recidivism, alcoholism, regulated prostitution, and gambling. The price for his efforts was that incendiary issues and ideological acrimony be omitted by both sides. These included that of the born criminal and the born invert. When Houzé later intervened to prevent the discussion on sexual inversion from breaking a pact that had so promisingly been sealed only days earlier, it was clear that even this committed materialist was willing to pay the price.

Degeneration's Evanescence

The final fifteen years of the nineteenth century saw an unprecedented level of scientific engagement with sexual perversion and inversion across much of Europe. From 1897 onwards, the "Annals of Unisexuality" in the French *Archives of Criminal Anthropology* offered readers a regular digest of all publications concerned with homosexuality.[91] The first scientific review wholly devoted to the subject came into existence with the creation of the *Yearbook of Intermediate Sexual Stages with Special Reference to Homosexuality* in Germany two years later.[92] Monographic studies abounded too. Books by the Russian Benjamin Tarnowsky, the Italian Paolo Mantegazza, and the Austrian Richard von Krafft-Ebing were translated and reprinted or revised many times after they first appeared in the mid 1880s.[93] In Germany, Albert Moll's influential analysis of *Contrary Sexual Feeling* was published in 1891, and in 1896 Magnus Hirschfeld's *Sappho and Socrates* was the first of many works he would go on to write with regard to the subject of homosexuality.[94] Meanwhile, France saw the first edition of Julien Chevalier's analysis of sexual inversion in 1885, followed by similar volumes by Benjamin Ball, Paul Garnier, and many others.[95] Albeit with difficulty, Havelock Ellis published the first edition of *Sexual Inversion* in Britain in 1897, and in 1905 *The Uranian Family* by Lucien von Römer came out in the Netherlands.[96]

Homosexuality was clearly foremost on European scientists' minds, but in Belgium things remained remarkably quiet by comparison. Not a single book-length study of sex or its perversions, let alone inversion, appeared there before the Second World War, and even article-sized contributions were extremely few and far between. The single significant exception was the forty-three-page-long chapter devoted to "The Sexual Psychopathies" by the physician Jules Dallemagne in his magnum opus *The Degenerate and the Unbalanced* from 1894.[97] In it, like Semal before him, Dallemagne borrowed the Parisian psychiatrist Valentin Magnan's materialistic typology of degenerative cerebrospinal defects to explain the entire spectrum of sexual and social deviance all at once. Amid the jargon, his main point was that people were hereditarily driven to deviance and that all attempts to distinguish between immoral perversity and pathological perversion were consequently futile. But by the mid 1890s this radically deterministic view was falling out of favor fast. The London-based

French poet and publicist Marc-André Raffalovich dismissed the theoretical abstractions of self-declared experts, like Dallemagne.[98] Raffalovich, who published copiously on inversion in the *Archives of Criminal Anthropology*, wrote that "Dallemagne discusses inverts as if they were newly imported savages heretofore unknown to Europe."[99] He reproached physicians for a lack of firsthand experience with inverts, and he lambasted their persistent recourse to the panacean theory of degeneration as "antiquated and backward."[100]

Raffalovich favored the more psychosociological approach to (homo)sexuality pioneered by Havelock Ellis in Britain and by Paul Näcke in Germany. He argued that "[e]ducation, moral and physical circumstances, friendships, various influences, indeed anything that might exert a small or a large effect determines, little by little, the form that the growing child's sexuality will take on."[101] During the early 1890s, Näcke had put forward his psychological ideas in Belgium, where he became an honorary member of the BSMM. In 1894, he published an article on "A Case of Footwear Fetishism" in the society's bulletin.[102] Like Raffalovich, Näcke was frustrated by the gratuitous reliance on such indeterminate stopgap notions as heredity, degeneration, and instinct. Desires, he insisted, were formed through associations and intense experiences, and while rooted in physiological reflexes, they could not be reduced to them. This proto-constructivist concept of sexuality in general and of homosexuality more particularly chimed well with Belgian Catholics' moralistic views on the matter. At the same time, it offended those in the country's psychiatric profession who were strategically invested in the materialistic explanation of mental deviance based on degeneration theory.[103]

Apart from a very few summary and hard-to-find digressions on the issue, however, Dallemagne was by far the one to touch most explicitly and extensively on perversion as part of his ill-fated attempt to keep degeneration theory alive. The book with his chapter on "The Sexual Psychopathies" was the outcome of a series of lectures he gave before the Free University of Brussels' Society for Criminological Studies in 1892 and 1893, a key forum for exchanges between the capital's reformist Young Bar Association and the members of the Anthropological Society.[104] But the recent conference on criminal anthropology where pragmatic moderation had proudly been declared the essence of the Belgian school made Dallemagne's rants against such "asexual doctrines" and "middle-of-the-road logic" seem out of touch and all too Parisian.[105] In the *Journal des Tribunaux*, the uncompromising determinism, reductionism, and biologism of Dallemagne's published lectures were condescendingly reviewed as ideas that had recently suffered "an undeniable bankruptcy."[106] "It is the duty of us all," Adolphe Prins, Belgium's intellectual champion of penal reform, argued in 1895, "to counter these tendencies, to reaffirm our commitment to volition, to responsibility, and to liberty."[107] Frustrated, Dallemagne feverishly continued his advocacy on behalf of medical influence in the courts as the head of Brussels' autopsy service, as a highly active member of the Belgian Society of Forensic Medicine, and as the prolific author of eight more books on the inexistence of free will until he burned out around the turn of the century and disappeared into oblivion.[108]

As Raf de Bont has noted, militant criminal anthropology was "as good as dead" in Belgium by the turn of the twentieth century.[109] The closest Dallemagne had to a successor was Louis Vervaeck, an unsystematic thinker who came to oversee the fairly inconsequential anthropological service of the prison system created by Minister Lejeune.[110] Vervaeck was a far cry from the hardliner his mentor had been, and his unremitting lip service to degeneration theory was diluted by his affirmed Catholicism. (He was the personal physician to two archbishops.) Despite a long list of publications, retiring only in 1939, Vervaeck never touched on the issue of sex, let alone its inversion. Consequently, Dallemagne's chapter on sexual perversion stands out as a lonely reminder of just how little Belgian scholars engaged with a subject so intensely taken up abroad.

Conclusion

The specific contexts in which sexual inversion was received varied significantly across Europe. In Belgium, it was received, firstly, by a psychiatric community handicapped by a lack of independence and preoccupied with the efforts to secure the envied legal, institutional, and financial forms of support the profession enjoyed abroad, especially in France. It was also received at a time when the tensions generated by ideological polarization were producing an acrimonious stand-off between opposing epistemological and ontological views, which hardliners held to be mutually exclusive. Finally, it was received as the insufficiencies of penal law and the penitentiary system increasingly called for some pragmatic way of transcending the paralyzing intellectual conflict over human nature, the faculty of volition, and the problem of accountability. Not only did inversion fail to attract much attention from Belgian psychiatrists due to the discipline's much-lamented underdevelopment from an academic point of view. Inversion was also disregarded because the issue formed an impediment to the advancement of professional interests. Closely associated as it was with a deterministic offensive against the prevailing philosophical conception of man as an ethical and rational being, inversion tended to inflame the ideological tensions that cut across the psychiatric and criminological communities and thus prevented it from forming a united front. In practical terms, little could be gained from this constant infighting, especially over an issue no one liked to associate their cause with anyway. After the 1892 conference, no Belgian scholar would devote anything more than fleeting attention to homosexuality until the 1950s.

6   Demographic Anxieties and Catholic Code

With the rise of the nineteenth-century nation-state came mounting concerns about the composition, quantity, and quality of the national body politic.[1] The census was the population's principal tool of administration, providing vast amounts of serial evidence about its health and size.[2] Amid the strengthening economic and geopolitical competition between the nations of Europe, a healthy population was first and foremost a growing one. Despite mechanization, industrial output was still heavily determined by sheer manpower. So too was military might. Naturally, therefore, fecundity was considered a patriotic duty, and fertility rates became a benchmark of the nation's virility. High rates of fertility instilled self-confidence and low ones were the cause of deep anxiety and existential fears. Consequently, the experience of decreasing and differential fertility rates across much of Europe from the mid nineteenth century onwards sparked a great deal of unrest, especially when combined with national crises or lagging economic output. Moreover, they triggered not just a debate about numbers but also inflated fears about moral decline and racial degeneration.

In 1896, for example, Italy's dramatic loss at the Battle of Adwa in Ethiopia not only crippled its colonial ambitions but a White army's loss against a Black one at a time of unquestioned racist imperialism was an unprecedented national embarrassment, causing deep apprehension.[3] Portugal found itself humiliated into calls for national regeneration when, in 1890, the waning power was forced to concede to a British ultimatum regarding colonial expansion in Southern Africa.[4] A decade later, initial defeats at the hands of South African settlers in the Second Boer War (1899–1902) raised the specter of racial degeneration in Britain, especially when reports indicated that up to 60 percent of working-class army recruits were physically unfit for duty.[5] In Spain, the disastrous demise of empire in the war of 1898 against the United States marked massive territorial losses as well as the birth of a mournful push for national revival.[6] In all of these countries, such traumatic events precipitated anxious debates about their causes. They helped to politicize issues of gender and birth control, and often focused on the metaphorically powerful embodiments of national emasculation: childless couples, selfish bachelors, manly feminists, depraved syphilitics, and effeminate inverts. The latter, in whom the gendered and reproductive norms seemed upended, were part of the declinist imaginary across Europe between 1870 and 1914, but they were not everywhere to the same extent.

This chapter shows how the demographic transition to lower fertility levels affected France and Belgium differently. It also argues that while the invert figured among other dreaded outgrowths of national decadence in France, he did not in Belgium for several reasons.[7] The first is that the *fin-de-siècle* experience was markedly dissimilar in both countries. Whereas the decades after defeat in the Franco-Prussian War of 1870–1871 prompted decades of soul-searching and scapegoating in France, Belgium was at the peak of its economic power and international prestige during the same period. Hence, there was less need for someone to blame the woes of the nation on. Secondly, falling fertility rates raised the alarm in France from the mid nineteenth century onwards, but similar worries only surfaced in Belgium during the decade leading up to the First World War.[8] Demographic anxieties thus emerged far later in France's northern neighbor. Moreover, and this is the third reason, when they finally did, the tone in which demographic decline was debated reflected the strong political and cultural clout of Catholicism in Belgium. The Belgian church deliberately used the cryptic, biblical language of 'onanism' to prevent the specification of perversions from spilling into the public sphere and soiling innocent minds, as had recently happened under the impetus of secularist and Protestant forces abroad. In so doing, Belgian Catholics successfully kept the genie of sexual 'abnormality' in the proverbial bottle.

French Fears

Fin-de-siècle France was an anxious country. Its fortunes as the dominant power on the European continent were challenged by the rise of Germany. In 1866, Prussian forces crushed the Austrian armies near Königgrätz, thereby paving the way for the foundation of a North German Federation under Chancellor Otto von Bismarck. Few could doubt his ambition to unite all of Germany. "Whether the unification of Germany into a single state is achieved due to an impassive France or in spite of a beaten France," warned the prominent journalist Lucien-Anatole Prévost-Paradol prophetically soon after the battle, "it would, in one way or another, constitute the irrevocable collapse of French glory."[9] In 1870, war came and a united German Empire was proclaimed in the halls of Versailles and on the ruins of a defeated France. With the shame of Napoleonic conquest avenged, a militarily superior and economically booming Germany was now the rising star in the firmament of Europe, with Britain as its only remaining rival. The French self-image, by contrast, would henceforth be overshadowed by the defeatist sentiment "that France was somehow not what she used to be," as Robert Nye has poignantly observed.[10]

The growing disparity between France and Germany was mirrored by many eagerly compiled statistics; most alarmingly so, by the diverging levels of human fertility and demographic growth.[11] Whereas the natural population growth rate of Germany averaged 12.7 per 1,000 inhabitants between 1870 and 1914, that of France did not exceed a paltry 1.2 per 1,000.[12] In the span of the four and a half decades preceding the First World War, this meant that while Germany's population mushroomed from roughly 40.8 million to 67.8 million, its French counterpart grew only marginally from 38.4 million to 41.7 million. The simple yet alarming truth was that France was producing far fewer factory workers and army conscripts. When the demographic data of the early 1890s revealed that stalling natural growth had turned into actual numerical decline, the growing anxiety over the dangers of depopulation turned into public hysteria. It firmly installed the pro-natal consensus among French policymakers that has marked the country ever since. By 1900, 135 senators signed a petition for the creation of an extra-parliamentary commission to examine all means to fight the looming threat of depopulation.[13]

In a country where the prestigious (bio)medical establishment had become infused with the theory of degeneration since the late 1850s (see Chapters 4 and 5), it was inevitable that the concept's infinite elasticity and huge metaphorical appeal spilled over into the panic-stricken language of social analysis and cultural pessimism.[14] With alcoholism and syphilis taking on epidemic proportions, everything from propaganda for birth control to the spread of pornography, feminism, and the prevalence of prostitution was perceived as indicative of the decadent hedonism that affected the quantity and health of French stock.[15] In his famous novel *Fécondité* (*Fecundity*) from 1899, Émile Zola warned that any abuse and exhaustion of a natural function would inevitably induce psychological and physiological aberration.[16]

Decreasing infant mortality, deferred marriage, and birth control were key causes of falling fertility rates, but critics also liked to point at the more galvanizing embodiments of national decadence. Unwilling mothers and unwomanly women were important targets of apprehensive men's alarmist cultural commentary.[17] Men who ostensibly violated the heavily gendered, familialist, and reproductive sexual order were similarly accused of bad sexual citizenship. A broad category, this included the perennial bachelor as well as the syphilitic frequenter of prostitutes and the depleted sybarite. As Andrew Counter has argued, Zola's *Fécondité* lumped them all together into the "singularly capacious category of the negative."[18] Others agreed. In all such libertines, the dissolution of the natural procreative drive had supposedly reached such extremes as to induce moral indifference, sexual impotence, and at its most extreme even physical androgyny.[19] The quintessential personification of devirilized decadence was arguably the main character of Joris-Karl Huysmans' novel *Against the Grain* from 1884, whose series of perverse pursuits led inevitably to the final stage of decline: an affair with an effete street urchin.[20] This too, in Huysmans' own words, was a consequence "of that singular malady which plays such havoc with races of exhausted vitality."[21]

In most lamentations of France's degeneration and decline, as Judith Surkis points out, men's various 'perversions' of gender and sexuality were only implicitly linked to same-sex vice, but homosexual abandon often loomed in the background as a powerful symbol of immoral sterility.[22] Some commentators were more explicit though. In *The Moral Crisis of Modern Times*, the pro-natal social critic Paul Bureau warned that "when the abuse of physical relations among young people of both sexes is pushed too far it will inevitably engender three forms of wickedness: the sin against nature, abortion and infanticide."[23] Among physicians and forensic specialists, homosexuality's association with a lack of virility was expressed in physical terms. Portrayed as effeminate, enfeebled, anemic, impotent, frail, wimpish, and weak-willed, sexual inverts embodied the 'real' man's binary opposite and negation. In 1893, Dr. Julien Chevalier explained that the sexual invert was a pseudo-female monstrosity marked by "limited muscular strength, soft facial features, thinly sown beards, sparse body hair, sizeable breasts, a broad pelvis, adipose skin, rounded curves and utterly feminine manners."[24] Félix Carlier, a former head of Paris' vice squad, observed that "pederasty, especially when contracted during youth, will corrupt even the most vigorous dispositions, emasculate the most hardy characters, and engender pusillanimity."[25] The physician Charles Féré closely associated effeminacy, homosexuality, and impotence as both the causes and consequences of racial degeneration.[26] Often serving as a protean countertype to the virile sexual citizen, the invert personified a cluster of fears about gender, sexuality, and demography.[27]

Consequently, there was no shortage of damning writings about the male invert. In the foreword to Dr. Georges Saint-Paul's popular study of inversion, Émile Zola cast the invert as "a disorganizer of the family, of the nation, and of all mankind."[28] Against the background of the nation's wavering international position, worsening demographic, and mounting anxieties about gender, the effeminate queer became an often implicit and underdefined but powerful exemplification of all that was wrong with the nation's modernity. The discursive preoccupation with sexual inversion and perversion in France was not only feverish; it was also almost entirely negative, especially when compared to some of the more level-headed expertise and affirmative activism coming out of Germany.[29] Saint-Paul opined "that the tolerance or loathing of inverts is closely linked to fluctuations in the birth rate."[30]

Belgian Self-Confidence

In contrast to France, the sexual invert never figured in discussions of national degeneration and demographic decline in Belgium. One key reason is that such debates were far less pressing than in France to begin with. Certainly, the effects of rapid urbanization, industrialization, proletarianization, technological innovation, and consumerism unnerved analysts in Belgium too. But, overall, the country's outlook was decidedly less gloomy than France's. While the latter was regularly racked with regime change and political turmoil throughout the nineteenth century, Belgian democracy had proved remarkably stable by comparison ever since it was founded in 1830. When a revolutionary wave swept Europe in 1848, Belgium's liberal government quickly restored order.[31] The country had also managed to stay out of the Franco-Prussian War, and while growing tensions between liberals and Catholics produced a political crisis from the late 1870s to the early 1880s, that crisis was democratically resolved, resulting in three decades of Catholic political hegemony, all the way to the First World War. While the French Third Republic's governments often fell after mere months, most Belgian ones lasted for years, and one even almost for a decade. In view of the tremendous political turbulence that continental Europe endured throughout the nineteenth century, and particularly when compared to France, Belgium was a conspicuously tranquil country.[32]

Diplomatically speaking, this tranquility was congenital. With the 1839 Treaty of London, the Concert of Europe had imposed international neutrality upon the new nation, which its politicians scrupulously observed and the Great Powers guaranteed.[33] While this reduced Belgium to observer status in high-stakes international politics, it also kept it out of military conflicts. Importantly, this also meant that Belgium lacked the constant saber rattling of French Germanophobia, even if the danger of being overrun in a renewed Franco-German clash became a growing political theme after the First Moroccan Crisis of 1905.[34] Moreover, the combination of political stability and laissez-faire government paid economic dividends. Belgium was the first country after Britain to rapidly industrialize. Between 1842 and 1872, it was the fastest growing economy in Europe, and it was outpaced only by Germany between 1873 and 1913.[35] By 1860, Walloon mines in Belgium's French-speaking south yielded 9.6 million tons of coal to France's 8.3 million and Belgian foundries overall managed 320,000 tons of pig iron steel, while all of what was soon to become Germany still produced only 529,000 tons.[36] In a quarter of a century, the export of (crude and cast) iron octupled and the successful reconversion to the production of steel and heavy metals enabled continuous growth, even throughout the international economic crisis between 1874 and 1895.[37] The colonization and exploitation of the Congo in the early twentieth century further bolstered the nation's economic prowess.[38]

With 6.7 million inhabitants in 1900, Belgium was also the world's most densely populated and most intensely industrialized nation at the turn of the century. It was the fifth-largest economy worldwide, the fourth-largest exporter, and only the port of New York surpassed that of Antwerp in terms of trade and traffic.[39] An official report on *Modern Belgium*, commissioned by the French government and published in 1910, succinctly captured the small nation's manifestly dynamic aura, writing that: "Belgium is a land of blast-furnaces, of rolling mills, of factories for processing ideas as well as minerals. As such, and all proportions considered, Belgium is the most industrialized, the most enterprising, and the best cultivated country in the entire world: which is to say one of the most affluent."[40]

Culturally and intellectually too, Belgium was thriving. The nation's central location and international neutrality made it a good venue for international fairs and conferences.[41] Between 1885 and the outbreak of the First World War, six world exhibitions took place in Belgian cities.[42] The provincial town of Leuven boasted the world's largest Catholic university. At the masonic Free University of Brussels, Ernest Solvay, founder of a giant chemical company, created a series of internationally prestigious research institutes. Meanwhile, the nation's capital was teeming with artistic activity. At least 103 different art journals were published there between 1860 and 1914, many of them, like the internationally renowned *L'Art Moderne*, reflecting the confidence and the optimism of the country's wealthy elites.[43] Articulating this spirit, the founder of *L'Art Moderne* had no patience for Parisian prophets of doom, as he made clear in a front-page article on New Year's Day of 1891:

I hate the expression so sacramentally, so automatically attached to so many things; this wicked expression: Fin de siècle. Picturesque though it may be, I hate it for its malice, for its overtone of injury and denigration, for its sense of dispirited resignation, its cynical admission of impotence and of steadily worsening degeneration as we draw closer to the centenary's Sibyllic number.[44]

In sharp contrast to France, modernity was "a positive idea" and "something hopeful" in *fin-de-siècle* Belgium.[45] The flourishing country allowed for its art to reflect "a happy modernity" by comparison, at least for the well-off lucky few.[46] To underline its stability, its energy, and its prosperity is not to suggest that Belgium was without serious sociopolitical problems. The growing mass of the urban poor drove the sprawl of cities where living conditions in working-class neighborhoods ranged anywhere from poor to abysmal. The amalgamation of various socialist groups into the Belgian Workers Party in 1885 and that party's bid for universal (male) suffrage ensured that late nineteenth-century politics concentrated on social pacification. During the 1890s, franchise and labor law reforms began to lay the foundations of the welfare state that Belgium would later become.[47]

As elsewhere, this process went accompanied by a growing appeal to the biomedical sciences for solutions to social problems.[48] With regard to social deviance, aside from crime – especially theft, vagrancy, and recidivism – the unholy trio of alcoholism, tuberculosis, and syphilis was a prime focus of concern.[49] Though many of these problems were the consequence of glaring inequality in one way or another, their analysis was commonly framed in moralizing terms. Temperance leagues achieved their first major success in 1887 by seeing public drunkenness outlawed, and in 1905 Belgium banned the sale of absinthe.[50] Parliament enacted legislation against begging and vagrancy in 1891, the same year as a parliamentary commission was put together in an unsuccessful bid to bring the municipal regulation of prostitution under national jurisdiction.[51] Several social reform societies, including the National Belgian League against Tuberculosis, were actively supported by the government in the form of subsidies and official patronage.[52] Their tone, however, was altogether less alarmist than that of their French counterparts. Belgium, after all, was in its prime. There was less need for (homo)sexual scapegoats in particular, since the country faced very similar social problems under very different demographic circumstances.

Diverging Demographics

The demographic transition not only affected Belgium much later than it did France, where the issue became a pressing one after 1850. It also took much longer for dwindling fertility to be perceived as problematic after this transition set in.[53] This decline had begun around 1880 but was compensated by a similar decline in mortality until 1900, after which the number of births began falling rapidly. When the army physician Charles Petithan addressed a report on "The Degeneration of the Belgian Race" to the Royal Society of Public Medicine in 1888, bewailing the rising numbers of tuberculars, alcoholics, and syphilitics, his colleagues dismissed it as hyperbolic and unsubstantiated.[54] One of them countered that if the population was degenerating, surely this should be reflected by a drop in fertility. But a simple glance at the country's demographic statistics suggested no such decline. In fact, Dr. Schrevens adduced, the natural growth rate – which weighs births against deaths – had been steadily increasing for decades, from 6.25 percent in the 1840s to 9.65 percent in the 1870s.[55] "Instead of degenerating," he concluded on the basis of these figures, "we are actually thriving; our vital stamina grows together with the force of reproduction."[56]

In fact, Petithan was fully aware of the fact that Belgium's actual demographic development contradicted him. Rather than too small and too thinly sown a population, as was the problem in France, he therefore asserted that Belgium's was precisely the opposite. The country was simply overcrowded.

Even in 1879, at the sixth International Conference of the Medical Sciences, Petithan had made the counterintuitive case that "[w]e should be long past congratulating ourselves for the growth of the population."[57] The key problem was that "we now have more than 200 Belgian citizens per square kilometer, and they quarrel over both the tiny speck of land they have to live on and the meager salaries they retain from an excessive amount of labor." He argued that the combination of proletarianization and unchecked population growth undermined social stability. According to Petithan, "a people weakened by misery, ignorance and alcohol constitutes a permanent source of danger." Following Germany's recent example, he insisted in 1888, Belgium should urgently acquire colonies and start exporting its surplus population or risk "social disintegration."[58]

Petithan denounced the peril of degeneration precisely at a time when a first wave of violent strikes in 1886 and 1887 had shocked the middle and upper classes into realizing that social issues urgently required their attention. Even so, his eugenic proposals fell on deaf ears. Catholics especially balked at any hint of 'neo-Malthusianism,' that is, the diffuse movement in favor of birth and population control.[59] More so than in Britain, neo-Malthusianism suffered from a strong association with radicalism and libertarian anarchism on the continent. There was, moreover, no external military threat to fan the flames of demographic anxiety. To officers' perpetual frustration, public and politicians alike were also deeply skeptical about the army. As military budgets went up across Europe in the late nineteenth century, neutral Belgium's went down, and while conscription was adopted in many countries, Belgians fiercely resisted it.[60] Besides, as already explained, according to its leadership Belgium was doing just fine. When, in 1904, the socialist minority suggested that the country was lagging behind its neighbors, the leading Catholic MP Charles Woeste sung the nation's praises in parliament:

Tell me, in what respect is Belgium inferior to other nations? Is it in relation to its population density? But this density is higher than anywhere else. After Saxony, it is in Belgium that the population is densest, and no one could dispute the fact that a rising birth rate constitutes an element of strength and prosperity in a nation.

Is it in relation to commerce then that Belgium leaves much to be desired? Though only a small country, we are the sixth trading power in the world.

Are you referring to industry? Does it not grow at a remarkable pace? ...

Is it in terms of the financial situation that we find ourselves in a position of inferiority? Nearly all countries are faced with severe problems in this respect; our budget, however, is a balanced one.

Or does it have to do with our civil liberties? No country enjoys more liberties than Belgium does: anyone can write and think, teach and associate as they please.[61]

With an unholy sense of glee, the same indefatigably anti-socialist and anti-French Woeste – who was born a German – had already pointed out Belgium's and France's diverging demographics three years before. "I would recall," he had remarked on that occasion and in reference to the recently published population figures for 1899, "the fact that while the excess of births in France ... did not exceed 51,384 in that year, it reached 67,505 in Belgium."[62] Considering that Belgium's total population was only one-sixth that of its massive neighbor, this was undeniably an impressive statistic. Among those to whom it was ideologically convenient, which is to say the Catholic majority in particular, numbers like these did nothing to lessen the impression that Belgium was somehow everything that France was not. To them, Petithan's claim that the Belgian 'race' was in an alarming state of degeneration was baseless. There was no need to worry about Belgians' vitality and virility, not yet anyway. Likewise, there was no need to tar and feather the invert as a decadent incarnation of emasculation or infertility in the way this happened in France. Said invert was totally absent from Belgian discussions of degeneration and demography in the late nineteenth century. Moreover, he would continue to be as demographic anxieties quickly mounted in the early years of the twentieth. The dominant Catholic response did not focus on geopolitical prowess but on differential regional fertility levels as a sign of growing irreligion. The church would launch a campaign against birth control that, more pervasively than elsewhere, deliberately encoded all talk of perversion and inversion.

Looming Frenchification

Belgium's own demographic slump was first detected in 1903 by the statistician Camille Jacquart.[63] He noted that the country's overall growth shrouded important and deepening regional differences. In Belgium's Dutch-speaking north, where industrialization was limited and the influence of the Catholic Church pervasive, fertility rates remained very high. In the industrial heartlands of the French-speaking south, however, specifically in the Sambre and Meuse river basin connecting Charleroi to Liège, those same rates were falling fast. Confirmation came in 1906, when Jacquart crunched the numbers in the official *Bulletin of the Central Commission for Statistics*. They showed that the nation averaged 200 births per 1,000 married women of childbearing age. All Flemish *arrondissements* had levels far above this number, and all Walloon ones far below it. The regional averages were 267 and 161 per 1,000 respectively.[64]

Especially in the rural parts of Flanders, fertility rates were impressively high, at around 300 per 1,000. Even the larger Flemish cities of Ghent (218 per 1,000), Antwerp (223 per 1,000), Mechelen (248 per 1,000), and Ostend (272 per 1,000) remained comfortably above the national average. In the largely Catholic woodlands of the Walloon Ardennes they still approached that national average, but the urbanized, industrial, and secularized valleys were a different story. Charleroi's fertility rate had dropped to 137 per 1,000, while Thuin and Philippeville did not surpass 120 and 114 per 1,000 respectively. A color-coded map accompanying Jacquart's figures showed that the closer one got to the French border in the Walloon south, the bleaker the picture looked. Worst of all was the unmistakable fact that the gap between the two parts of the country was growing rapidly. In the southern industrial hubs of Soignies, Charleroi, and Verviers, the average number of births in married women had dropped by fifty-four points in twenty years. During the same period, that number had risen by twenty-four points in the Flemish districts of Roeselare and Turnhout, and even by forty-four in that of Tielt. The differential demographics could hardly be more pronounced.

Jacquart observed that French analysts often referred to the abolition of primogeniture during the French Revolution as the initial push towards ever smaller families, as these sought to keep the family estate intact. Whereas the ties of land, marriage, and kinship had long formed the fabric of society, they had now been replaced by the individualism of landless wage-earners. A change had taken place at the core of culture itself, which no stopgap fiscal measures like those that were being proposed in the French Assemblée were likely to overturn. Belgium, moreover, having similarly seen the dissolution of primogeniture during the French Revolution, supposedly demonstrated that legal changes were less important than cultural and religious ones. "These religious feelings can maintain family cohesion there where it is not imposed by law," Jacquart argued. Religion provided a shared outlook, a shared sense of duty and destiny. "A people dies when it no longer has a reason to live," Jacquart explained. "And pleasure or sensualism is not a reason to live; it is a cause of death."[65] Now, following the example of France, the consequences of dechristianization were supposedly making themselves felt in Belgium too.

Based on this culturalist analysis, the reaction to declining fertility in Belgium was not, as in France, led by a broad and jingoistic coalition of forces, including many staunchly secular ones, but almost entirely by the Catholic Church, with the wholehearted endorsement of the Catholic government. Early in 1907, the newly appointed archbishop and cardinal Désiré-Joseph Mercier called upon Jacquart.[66] Immediately after their meeting, Mercier's confidant, the moral theologian and priest Arthur Vermeersch, began working on "precise instructions" for both the faithful and the clergy concerning "the complete prohibition of practices contrary to the prime goals of marriage."[67] Around the turn of the century, a small neo-Malthusian movement had taken root in Belgium with French assistance in the Walloon south and Dutch support in the Flemish north.[68] However minute, the movement would serve as the villainous face of a structural problem, which Catholics set out to crush, helped by the sharpening enforcement of public decency laws and the power to ban the distribution of 'propaganda' by mail.[69] Early in 1909, Mercier published a pastoral letter on "The Duties of Married Life." It was the first statement on birth control by the primate of a national church. The letter railed against the advancement "in certain parts of our country of the evil from which France so cruelly suffers."[70]

While also aimed against the neo-Malthusian enemies of godless hedonism, the campaign launched by Mercier was first and foremost a moral offensive against the increased tolerance for birth control among Catholics and their confessors. This growing tolerance, particularly associated with France, was a phenomenon that can be traced back to the late eighteenth century, when a doctrinal shift had occurred from Aquinian rigor and legalism to Liguorian tolerance and pragmatism in the field of moral theology, particularly where sexual matters were concerned.[71] Whereas, in the thirteenth century, Thomas Aquinas had equated contraception, even within marriage, with murder, the widespread adoption of Alphonsus de Liguori's more tolerant views on these issues since the late eighteenth century had diluted the spilling of life-giving seed into something less damning, if still serious. What this essentially boiled down to, for the sake of brevity, was Liguori's concrete directive that:

> In things regarding the sixth commandment [i.e. thou shalt not commit adultery] and spouses' duties and rights, the confessor should not make demands nor permit accusations except insofar as the common sentiment of theologians judges it necessary. Thus he should not inquire into aggravating circumstances; and, speaking frankly, it is not even suitable that he permits the accusation. Nor should he lend his ear needlessly to detailed confessions, whether general or particular, in this area. He should not judge sins according to the malice theologians recognize in them, but according to the malice those committing them suppose them to have.[72]

Following Liguori's recommendations, the leading French handbooks for confessors of the nineteenth century had encouraged confessors to be more reticent about probing the sexual habits of their confessants, particularly women, upon whom the church came increasingly to depend as a majority of men stopped practicing their tarnished faith in the wake of the French Revolution.[73] Women, indeed, were very often deemed reluctant participants in their husbands' widespread practice of *coitus interruptus* (i.e. the withdrawal method), so many priests felt it unjust and imprudent to admonish them. In the absence of formal directives from the hierarchy to do otherwise, the pastoral grip on marital sexuality gradually loosened in the confessional. The Vatican was not particularly concerned with such matters yet, and, in John Noonan's words, "as birth control swept France, the church was not yet its active and tireless adversary."[74] That changed with Pope Leo XIII's reaffirmation of the more stringent teachings of Saint Thomas Aquinas as official doctrine. With the promulgation of the encyclical *Arcanum Divinae Sapientiae Consilium* (*The Secret Wisdom of God's Plan*) in 1880, the new pope also reconfirmed the right of the church to prescribe all aspects of married life. Two years later, a prestigious new chair in Thomist philosophy was created at the Catholic University of Leuven, effectively making it the world's most important center of neo-Thomist teachings outside Rome (see Chapter 5). The chair was given to the then thirty-one-year-old prodigy Mercier.

Liguorian tolerance for those acting in good faith now came under increasing attack. As a Belgian theologian observed in 1906, France now faced the ruinous consequences of "the indefinite complacency of tolerant silence" after confessors there had long turned a blind eye to the practice of "conjugal onanism," which had therefore spread like wildfire. The situation "thank God!" was not quite as depressing in Belgium, but to prevent worse confessors should never let their clientele off the hook. Thorough inquiries were necessary until they were satisfied that confessants' observance was not "more ostensive than real," since many of the faithful were suspected of only nominally adhering to the rules.[75] To that effect, in June of 1909, mere months after his pastoral letter had reminded the pious of their marital duties, Mercier also issued stern *Instructions against the Vice of Onanism* for the use of confessors.[76] Combined with his earlier pastoral letter, these two documents would serve as the international blueprint for the Catholic Church's growing concern with sexual sin and birth control. Similar instructions to the faithful were soon issued in Germany (1913), France and Austria (1919), and the United States (1920).[77] Postwar, the move to ban all contraceptive information as neo-Malthusian propaganda was partly due to Catholic influence in nationalist France (1923) and fascist Italy (1926), and wholly so in Belgium (1923), Spain (1928), and the Irish Free State (1929).[78] Meanwhile, Arthur Vermeersch had moved to the Gregorian University in Rome. There he became the world's leading moral theological authority and the architect of *Casti Connubii* (*Chaste Union*), the church's landmark ban on contraception, promulgated in 1930.[79] Thus, in several ways the Vatican's strong engagement with sexual issues throughout the twentieth and into the twenty-first century began in Belgium.

Catholic Code

Much more so than in neighboring countries where various voices could be heard, demographic and sexual debates in Belgium were heavily saturated with the language and logic of Catholicism. The Catholic offensive against neo-Malthusian 'onanism' dwarfed all other pro-natal initiatives. It was once more at the personal instigation of Cardinal Mercier in 1910 that Catholic physicians established a National League against Depopulation. Liberal members of the Royal Society of Public Medicine and Medical Topography proposed the foundation of a separate, ideologically neutral league, which would focus more on demographic decline as a social and economic problem, but it came to naught.[80] Socialists, for their part, showed little enthusiasm for the demographic problem. Since birth rates shriveled first and foremost among the industrial proletarians forming their constituency, party leaders like Émile Vandervelde rejected birth control on the basis that the working class would be ill-served by numerically weakening itself. So although there certainly were staunch supporters of neo-Malthusianism among the socialist, libertarian, and anarchist far left, their inability to mobilize outside a small fringe is reflected in the indifference towards the issue in the mainstream left-wing press.[81] Even so, the full force of the state was brought to bear on the tiny neo-Malthusian movement through the courts and executive orders.[82] With few defenders and under permanent attack from the Catholic establishment, the marginal movement failed to reconstitute itself after the First World War.

This near-hegemony stifled the overt discussion of sexual inversion and perversion since Belgian Catholics' writings purposefully refrained from naming them. Catholic intellectuals were extremely wary of the moral relativism that ensued from the rash pathologization of sin (see Chapters 4 and 5). Moreover, they deemed the very specification of sexual sins to be dangerously ill-advised. Only copulation between husband and wife, for the purpose of conception and without the application of any means of diminishing the chances thereof, was 'natural' and therefore legitimate according to the newly reasserted teachings of Thomism. All others amounted to a sacrilegious waste of life-giving seed; the kind of spilling for which God had mercilessly slain Onan in the book of Genesis. Though some forms were even more onerous than others, all 'onanisms' were essentially the same, and to dwell on their differences would be to inspire immoral thoughts.[83] Such matters, like Vermeersch's authoritative tract on the issue, written in veiling Latin, were best reserved for a learned few and should certainly not be discussed in the open, let alone by the wider public.[84]

A good illustration of this discourse of onanism was the work of Auguste Knoch, a canon who taught pastoral theology at the grand seminary of Liège. His treatise *Conjugal Onanism and the Confessional*, which went through at least six revised editions by 1922 and was swiftly translated into German and Spanish, served as a guide to the implementation of Mercier's instructions.[85] As the title suggests, its primary aim was birth control among married couples, but the term onanism handily condemned all other 'unnatural' forms of sex by muted implication. In his pedagogical vademecum *The Education of Chastity*, the third edition of which appeared in 1914, Knoch argued that while "the number of temptations multiplies from all sides and in so many different forms, there is *far too much* talk, and woefully lightly so" of sexual matters. The right approach was all about avoiding the harmful exposure of the young to impure thoughts. The responsibility of parents and teachers, Knoch's target audience, "should have precisely the effect of repressing unwholesome inquiries, of buttressing the sense of virtue, of speaking chastely, but with precision, of delicate issues in order to be able *to speak of them as little as possible.*"[86]

Of course, silence itself would not suffice in shielding children from the increasing ubiquity of corrupting influences. But the constant moral guidance provided by the confessor would not only prevent youngsters from being led astray. It would also ensure that they gradually mastered the level of disciplined self-control, self-abnegation, and asceticism required of the mature Christian.[87] The direction and discretion of the confessional were Catholicism's greatest asset for which many other denominations lacked an adequate substitute. "It is not surprising," Knoch commiserated:

that Protestants, although well-intentioned, but deprived of the possibility to resort to confession and faced with the daunting problems raised by the crisis of puberty, have had recourse to ... scientific explanations, to books that simultaneously provide a hasty and a very complete solution to questions pertaining to the origins of life, the realistic description of luxury's vices and of their terrible consequences.

In the absence of the disciplining technology of confession, Protestants, Jews, and gentiles alike were forced to render explicit knowledge likely to produce the opposite of the edification it was ostensibly intended for. After all, Knoch insisted, the "primary danger" of that which passed as pedagogical or scientific literature abroad:

resides in describing, before all eyes and without any distinction, the sexual aberrations to which the perverted child and adolescent may succumb. It resides in familiarizing such impulsively natured children, still so weak-willed and capricious, with secrets and perversions whose existence they did not even begin to suspect.[88]

Innocence and virtue, once spoiled, remained tarnished forever. "Nihil volitum, nisi praecognitum," wrote Knoch, summarizing the church's view on the issue of sex and its aberrations. "One cannot want, one cannot practice, in a truly human way, something one is ignorant about."[89] Code was key. Omitted when at all possible, the language of sex was to be expressed in purely moral terms. Beyond that, "extreme vigilance," preventive action, and "inexorable severity" were required to keep the lid on Pandora's box. "Special friendships," for example, required active suspicion. As Knoch explained in a manual on purity in boarding schools:

The fact that two pupils enjoy each other's company, and seize every opportunity to seek each other out, to talk during walks and recreational activities, in class, while studying, in the dormitories; this fact should arouse highly justified misgivings, especially if these pupils tend to retire in complete seclusion, avoiding any witness and ingeniously pursuing regular meetings.[90]

Knoch detailed the ideal height of partitions in school dormitories to optimize "active" and panoptic surveillance as "an indispensable means of control." Such control was most effective when successfully internalized into self-control. "One has to form such conscience," he explained.[91] Clearly then, Catholics were acutely aware of the 'productive' power of discourse. Particularly where it came to matters of the flesh, they were extremely mindful and heedful of discourse's tendency to render (unchaste) thoughts thinkable, to awaken (unnatural) desires, and to provide ontological status to the previously inconceivable. The confessional served as the secluded workshop where pure souls were forged under the hammer of scrutiny, avowal, admonition, repentance, and absolution. The technology of confession required, in Foucault's words, that "sex must not be named imprudently, but its aspects, its correlations, and its effects [had to be] pursued down to their slenderest ramifications: a shadow in a daydream, an image too slowly dispelled, a badly exorcized complicity between the body's mechanisms and the mind's complacency: everything had to be told."[92] But not out in the open. To speak of sex in public was to lose control over its articulation. That had been the mistake of secularists, Protestants, and even Catholics abroad, and now, unchained and out of control, sex was running wild among them.

Conclusion

French Catholics also spoke out against calling sexual sin by its name, but the strength of anticlerical secularists and the more pronounced sense of declinism in France favored a more explicit discussion of various non-procreative 'aberrations' in the public sphere. In Belgium, by contrast, where the demographic problem was of a different kind and where the church was politically and culturally powerful in a way it no longer was in republican France, Catholics succeeded in consciously curbing the public discussion of sex and its so-called perversions. In both countries, the interwar period saw a continuation of previously developed patterns. Both remained staunchly pro-natal, but while deepening French fears of degeneration and depopulation were propelled more than anything by the fear of a resurrecting Germany, Belgian ones continued to be dominated by less geopolitical and more religious overtones. In France, moreover, the invert increasingly figured ever more explicitly as a symptom of emasculation and degeneration.[93] Meanwhile, in Belgian discussions pertaining to demography and the state of the nation such references were absent, and they continued to be dominated by Catholic voices.[94]

It should be clear from this chapter that religion has been more important than often acknowledged in fueling the discourse of sexuality and its perversions, including inversion. In fact, Protestants were among the first to actively inject sex into the public sphere in most Northern European and

Conclusion 103

North American countries during the second half of the nineteenth century. The post-Enlightenment reaction to anthropocentric rationalism had sparked a Great Awakening among Protestants on either side of the Atlantic, many of whom committed to evangelizing efforts towards the establishment of God's kingdom on earth.[95] Anti-slavery was a big part of such efforts in English-speaking countries, and temperance movements were often led by Protestants across the West.[96] In response to the Contagious Diseases Acts of the 1860s, abolitionism was reinvented as an international struggle against the 'rational' European system of regulated prostitution by the religiously inspired British feminist Josephine Butler. The network of contacts she established with continental allies in Denmark, Germany, the Netherlands, Belgium, France, Switzerland, and – less successfully – in Italy to form the International Abolitionist Federation in 1875 consisted primarily of fellow Protestants.[97] Meanwhile, conservative Evangelicals reacted to modernity with the creation of male-dominated morality movements from the 1870s onwards in Protestant-majority countries.[98] In Germany, they coalesced into the highly influential General Conference of German Morality Associations by 1889.[99]

These Protestant morality movements had their internal differences, particularly regarding the role and rights of women, which sowed division between the male-led orthodox and women-led liberals. Combined, however, they were crucial in raising the problem of sexual immorality and placing it on the political agenda. Rather than reserve the matter for the confessional or speak in general terms, as Catholics often preferred, many Protestant morality campaigners believed the evil should be brought into the open for all to see so that it could be more effectively eradicated. As the Berlin Society of Men for the Fight against Indecency put it in 1889, it was because of the "foolish reluctance to call dirty things by their proper names" that the moral problem had gotten out of hand.[100] In the Protestant-majority countries of Europe, these morality movements were key drivers behind the far more explicit politics of sex such countries would see from the end of the century onwards than a more muted Catholic nation like Belgium did. At least in part this was because Catholics feared that immorality would begin speaking in its own name if imprudently spoken about at all.

When the Scientific Humanitarian Committee began to agitate for homosexual rights in Germany in 1897 and a Dutch chapter emerged in 1912, a mixture of horror, exasperation, and *Schadenfreude* ran through Belgian Catholics' comments like Knoch's. A minority within the tiny minority of Protestants, conservative Evangelicals did not influence the morality debate in Belgium. A liberal, Protestant-driven Belgian Society for Public Morality did emerge in 1882 as part of the International Abolitionist Federation, but it remained a single-issue organization, strictly committed to the abolition of regulated prostitution, and pacified by the strong ties it developed with the Catholic establishment through the patronage of the liberal-Catholic minister of justice Jules Lejeune.[101] While critically important in fueling feminism, religious discourse did much more to muffle than to raise the matter of homosexuality in Belgium, and that would not change for decades to come. Previous chapters have shown that religion was not the only factor to either constrain or catalyze talk of perversion, but its importance has often been overlooked by historians of (homo)sexuality, as the Belgian case clearly demonstrates.

7   Literary Activism on Behalf of a Strange Love

As Chapter 1 made clear, "silence and secrecy" allowed for "relatively obscure areas of tolerance," like firmly locked bedrooms and the urinals and back alleys of downtown Brussels.[1] Silence, then, certainly created opportunities. But like the much more explicit discourses on homosexuality abroad, silence and code also had intense disciplining effects and were therefore often an amplifying conduit of power rather than a sign of its weakness or absence. Silence too was 'productive' rather than merely 'repressive.' Written in 1892, the famous characterization of homosexuality by Lord Alfred Douglas as "the love that dare not speak its name" perfectly captured the disciplining power of imposed silence, shame, and euphemism.[2]

In 1976, the same year when Foucault's first volume on *The History of Sexuality* appeared, James Kirkup's controversial poem "The Love That Dares To Speak Its Name" signaled just how much the discourse on homosexuality had changed in the meantime. Even though successful, the charge for blasphemy leveled against this description of a Roman centurion having sex with Christ's crucified body – a mystical meditation on martyrdom, self-assertion, and liberation – seemed like a rearguard action by then.[3] The origins of this shift from a timid towards a brazen homosexuality lay in the fermentation of what Foucault dubbed a 'reverse discourse' (see Chapter 4). Seizing the new language invented for its description as a pathology, this reverse discourse asked how justice could be served by prosecuting people for congenital compulsions in the late nineteenth century. Before long, it ventured a daring step further. At the Fifth International Conference on Criminal Anthropology held in Amsterdam in 1901, the Dutch criminologist Arnold Aletrino argued that uranism was not an aberration but "simply a variation." The homosexual, he boldly claimed, was "the complete equal of the heterosexual."[4]

Needless to say, such claims were not readily accepted, and the path towards their growing currency was hardly a linear one. Nor, it bears emphasizing, did the emergence and elaboration of reverse discourses regarding homosexuality occur simultaneously across national borders. The vanguard of intellectual and artistic activists who pioneered their development certainly did form a loose international network of personal connections in which mutual inspiration and support played an important role.[5] But a shared sense of purpose did not necessarily translate into a shared pace of success. In trailblazing Germany, homosexual activism was more organized and more outspoken than anywhere else.[6] It took until the turn of the twentieth century for more cautious voices to be raised in France and Britain, and only in the Netherlands did a small organized movement, grafted on the German example, emerge shortly before the First World War.[7] In the middle of all this, Belgium maintained its characteristic silence, with, however, one notable and intriguing outlier that merits closer attention.

This chapter will explore the life and work of Georges Eekhoud whose literary defense of homosexuality briefly pierced Belgium's comparative silence on the issue. *Escal-Vigor*, his unusually overt novel about homosexual love, was tried for obscenity in 1900. Eekhoud was a celebrated author and his trial a high-profile affair. It is tempting to interpret Eekhoud's acquittal as a resounding win for the queer cause or, failing that, as the belated start of a more public and explicit discussion of homosexuality in Belgium at the very least. He unquestionably pioneered the reverse discourse regarding homosexuality in Belgium and therefore rightly looms large in the country's collective queer memory. But his prominence also betrays the absence of others who went before or who followed in his footsteps. While Eekhoud's bravado brought him fame abroad, he paradoxically faced mostly scorn at home. Even his artistic and political supporters carefully decontaminated his victory in court from the smut of homosexuality that detracted from it. In growing realization of how hollow that victory had been, Eekhoud became increasingly desperate, isolated, and silent. For all the formative influence of his writings on later generations, Eekhoud stands out as a testament to the potency and the persistence of Belgium's politics of silence on homosexuality.

La Jeune Belgique

Nowadays, Eekhoud is so readily identified with his homosexuality and with his literary activism on homosexuality's behalf that he is in danger of being reduced to this aspect of his personality and of his writings. He was, after all, also an exponent of the intellectual and artistic movement of which he formed a part in the 1880s and the 1890s.[8] Born in 1854 to a middle-class, French-speaking family in the Flemish port city of Antwerp, Eekhoud was orphaned at a young age and raised by first an uncle and then his grandmother.[9] In pursuit of a literary career, he moved to Brussels in 1881 at the age of twenty-seven to join the capital's artistic avant-garde.

Brussels was teeming with esthetic experimentation in those days of political turmoil as the First School War pitted liberals and Catholics against one another, while socialists alarmed elites by occupying the city's streets in demand of universal suffrage with growing regularity. Dozens of new and experimental art journals were founded in Brussels during this period, many of them bearing programmatic and revisionist titles such as *La Renaissance* and *Le Progrès*.[10]

Eekhoud's personal trajectory mirrored the political shifts of the time. He initially joined the bourgeois naturalists and symbolists of *La Jeune Belgique* but came to resent their politically apathetic *l'art pour l'art* and turned towards the committed *art social* of the young left.[11] Progressive liberals and champagne socialists united under the banner of *L'Art Moderne*, the internationally renowned journal that led the esthetic opposition to a political culture of census suffrage and self-serving elites. They saw the all-consuming brawl between liberals and Catholics as a ruse "meant to divert attention away from real reforms," which the Belgian Workers Party was determined to bring about.[12] Giving expression to his anarchist sympathies in well-received short stories and widely acclaimed novels such as *La Nouvelle Carthage* (1888), Eekhoud found himself among the cream of the nation's effervescent art world by 1890 and, as such, in the company of fellow writers like Maurice Maeterlinck (a Nobel laureate for literature) and Émile Verhaeren (Nobel-nominated six times), of painters like Fernand Khnopff and James Ensor, and of architects and designers such us Victor Horta and Henry Van de Velde.[13]

Eekhoud's work invariably articulated a deep affection for the working class. His primitivist exaltation of the noble savage was nurtured by a love for the simple authenticity of peasant life in the Arcadian villages of the Flemish Campine region where he spent his holidays. In 1895, Eekhoud co-founded a new literary journal called *Le Coq rouge* (*The Red Rooster*). Tellingly, its editors did not meet, as did those of most political and artistic societies, in one of the smart cafés housed in the eminent patrician homes on or near Brussels' famous Grand-Place but rather in one of the local dives of Saint Catherine's proletarian docklands.[14] The writer's fondness for the common man went well beyond political convictions. A mixture of esthetic, exotic, and erotic longing always reverberated in his admiring descriptions of the toil-hardened bodies of farmhands and manual laborers. A lot of what Eekhoud wrote can therefore be read as an attempt to align his utopian political views with a personal yearning for those men and boys to whom he was so irresistibly drawn. At the same time, his writings also convey his constant anguish over the contempt with which his middle-class environment would regard such yearnings if they were not sufficiently dignified with lofty references to human brotherhood, class-transcending camaraderie, and social progress.

Splendid Roughs

Eekhoud took care to mask the literary exploration of his homoerotic feelings as naturalistic outings into the boisterous lives of rural youths, urban proles, and social outcasts.[15] His extensive diary reveals how very autobiographic these expeditions were. The following entry from 1902, which he jotted down in veiling English, typifies his many desirous excursions into a blue-collar world, which class and propriety kept tantalizingly outside of reach:

> Half a dozen splendid roughs did play yesterday at the foot of the Palace of Justice, as I went down from the Place Poelaert, towards the high street and that little street of our Lady of Grace. They were the perfect ones, lads of eighteen to twenty. One was beating another, rubbing him on the ground and kicking his bottom; the other attempting to scratch his bully in his parts. And as I was halting one of them talked to me and said: 'What voyous [i.e. rascals] ain't it, Sir, always fighting!' And another said: 'Look how pretty they are now, both their clothes full of dung!' Why did I not answer: 'I love roughs!' Will it be for the next time. In every case, I will take sometimes that way.[16]

Further along in his diary, the mixture of excitement and apprehension that accompanied Eekhoud on his cruising adventures through Brussels is tangible as he followed a young man in hopes of an erotic encounter. "I took a walk around the promenade of the Park of Laken yesterday afternoon," he journaled on May 14, 1903 (in French), before continuing:

> I first met a young worker in Havana-colored velvet trousers, who had stopped, as I had, at the closed railroad crossing of Laken. Following him, I satisfyingly managed to brush the lukewarm cloth covering his legs as the barrier opened. ... I followed him for a long time, stopping occasionally before a house under construction. Several times I had the impression that he had noticed me following him and that he sought to expedite our meeting, since he looked around two or three times, and seemed intent on turning into one of the remote alleyways. But every time he reconsidered. I broke off my pursuit when I saw him take the Strombeek Road [out of the city].[17]

Court files similarly show that this kind of cruising was anything but uncommon at the time. Eekhoud, however, knew from experience how ruinous the consequences of homosexual peccadillos could be for middle- and upper-class men in a society where the boundaries of heteronormativity were ruthlessly policed even more by the threat of social ostracism than by that of criminal prosecution. In 1872, at the age of eighteen, Eekhoud had enrolled in the Royal Military Academy only to be dismissed six months later. Mirande Lucien has credibly advanced that he was expelled for homosexual indecencies, as is indeed suggested by one of his short stories in which an agonized lancer is ejected from the army and ritually dishonored for his "ignominious degradation."[18]

The Lancer's Quadrille (1892) describes the sufferings inflicted by this indelible social stigma with great emotional depth and in typical semi-autobiographical fashion. "Impossible to fall any lower," Eekhoud had the lancer lament, "to be more abject, more odious than this scum of the army."[19] Perpetually stained by this particularly heinous sin, the disgraced soldier "was irreparably rejected by law, society, and family alike!" The traumatic memory of a similar humiliation and the trepidation at its possible recurrence helps us understand why Eekhoud, despite his tacit activism on the invert's behalf, would remain loath to identify himself or be identified as one himself throughout his life. The same story also reveals the crucial effect this shameful experience seems to have had on Eekhoud's private resolve to embrace his sexual otherness. At the height of his despair, the lancer's desperation turns into determination. "What an enormous farce virtue is," he exclaimed in sudden realization. He inhabited a hypocritical world that publicly avowed a strict set of moral precepts often ignored in private; and this world would invariably close ranks against those caught in the act of something unseemly. "My mistake was to get caught," the lancer now understood, "that's all."

To Eekhoud, middle-class morality was nothing but a straitjacket to keep human nature in check. He let his surrogate self become suddenly aware of the fact that "[n]ature scoffs at human laws and social conventions." With Nietzschean disdain for modern mores, Eekhoud deemed it "a travesty" of nature to see the "domesticated" reduce the "raptorial" to "impotence." The lancer had almost believed those who declared him an abomination. "The fool I was to consider myself the exception, the only derogator of my species," he now understood. Like Eekhoud himself, he reviled the society that rejected him, but unlike Eekhoud, the lancer decided to embrace marginality and exclusion if it meant he could do as nature commanded. "If law and order condemn me without remission," the lancer concluded, "I will enlist in the army of rogues and renegades who are true to themselves." With heroic resolution, he embraced his true 'nature' and renounced the world. Recognized at a commoner's ball, the attending women tried to rehabilitate the soldier by seducing him, but the man remained placidly unresponsive to their advances. He even succeeded in awakening in the men "an impulse they had never before discovered under their rugged chests." In the end, the lancer is violently put to death by the women who feared the imminent disaffection of their male suitors.

The lancer's tale testifies to Eekhoud's growing sense of self-awareness and self-affirmation, and its dramatic conclusion expressed the ardent conviction that one should be true to oneself and to one's nature despite the petty restraints of forbidding mores. That same ending, however, also betrays the fear of the inevitable consequences that those daring to put that creed into practice would suffer. The story reflects the frictional distance between Eekhoud's queer desires and the strait-laced society he inhabited. Resisting these pressures, Eekhoud grew increasingly self-assertive throughout the 1890s. By 1893, after all, his reputation as a writer was definitively established when he received the highly prestigious quinquennial state prize for literature. Invigorated by his success, indignant about the misfortune that befell Oscar Wilde and inspired by the budding homosexual activism emanating from Germany and Britain, Eekhoud began working on an overtly homosexually themed novel that would expose him to accusations of indecency.[20]

A Strange Love

Escal-Vigor, later translated into English as *A Strange Love*, was published in 1899 and has been described as "perhaps the most daring gay novel of the period."[21] It contained Eekhoud's characteristic blend of bucolic nostalgia, a celebration of the noble savage's wholesome sensualism, a naturalistic examination of troubled souls who went through life tormented by the constraints of (over)civilization, and a utopian idealization of class-transcending camaraderie. More than anything else, however, it was also a vindication of intergenerational homoerotic love and of the essentialized homosexual condition, as well as an indictment against social intolerance. The book tells the melodramatic story of the young count Henry Kehlmark, returning home after years of studying abroad at a boarding school in Switzerland. Determined to settle down, he began a hopeless relation with the servant girl Blandine to overcome his homosexual inclinations, before falling desperately in love with the young peasant boy Guidon, whose mentor and benefactor Kehlmark became. Between the pair, separated by class, age, and propriety, a platonic romance blossomed, but the secret is discovered. A disconsolate Blandine sobbingly implored why Kehlmark had been so cruel to seduce her. "I wanted to change," the count admitted in tears, "to conquer myself."[22] Yet all attempts to overcome his nature had been in vain.[23]

There were many obvious parallels between Kehlmark's ordeals and Eekhoud's personal ones. Eekhoud too had returned home a young man after years of boarding school in Switzerland. He too, in trying to subdue his feelings, had married a servant girl: his grandmother's kitchen maid Cornélie. All of Eekhoud's female heroines were selflessly loyal, and it is quite likely they resembled his wife in that respect. Eekhoud was devoted to her, but, like that of the fictional count, his true love was for a young working-class youth. Alexander 'Sander' Pierron was the son of a blacksmith and had attended school only until the age of thirteen. When he and Eekhoud first met in 1892, Sander had been the enterprising secretary of the associated Young Socialists from Sint-Jans-Molenbeek, Brussels' poorest suburb. Talented and drawn to art as Pierron was, Eekhoud soon became the nineteen-year-old's loving tutor in very much the same way as Count Kehlmark dedicated himself to the education of the country boy Guidon. Less true to life was *Escal-Vigor*'s dramatic dénouement, with the violent lynching of both protagonists by an angry mob in a scene that evoked the martyrdom of Saint Sebastian, a classic trope of homosexual art and literature. That thespian ending served as a denunciation of the violence that innocent inverts suffered from a viciously intolerant society.[24]

The novel bespeaks the suppressed agony and bitter loneliness Eekhoud always felt, even among his close friends and colleagues. Through Kehlmark, Eekhoud described his peers as "excellent men," and "an indulgent and understanding elite," but if these libertarians would have learned about his homosexuality, even they "would have shunned me like a leper."[25] Indeed, progressive writers, including the otherwise broad-minded Zola, had hastily distanced themselves from Oscar Wilde when he had been convicted for gross indecency in 1895. For all its caution, however, *Escal-Vigor* does epitomize the reverse discourse through which homosexuals began to claim legitimacy for their difference with reference to newly coined biomedical categories. His extensive personal library testifies to Eekhoud's keen familiarity with the burgeoning sexological literature of the *fin de siècle*.[26] He owned copies of all the period's pioneering works on uranism, including those by Edward Carpenter, Havelock Ellis, Magnus Hirschfeld, Albert Moll, and Marc-André Raffalovich. In fact, many of them were sent to him, dedicated and signed, by their authors themselves. The way in which Eekhoud's reading of these works directly informed his own writings is strikingly apparent from his well-thumbed copy of Krafft-Ebing's *Psychopathia Sexualis*.[27] The many blue and red pencil marks in its margins reveal points of agreement or recognition and occasional bursts of asterisked excitement.[28]

Eekhoud was particularly struck by the many autobiographic confessions Krafft-Ebing had gathered over the years.[29] They echoed "the continuous fear of being discovered" and the "many indescribable sufferings" he also experienced, as well as the sense that this "cruel play of nature" was "not our fault." Indeed, some did "not feel unhappy about loving young men," but merely "unfortunate that the consummation of this love should be regarded as inadmissible" and could not be achieved without overcoming "serious obstacles." One confessant's highlighted passage failed to understand "why, or how the love among men should be at odds with morality" while another condemned that morality for forcing "the sexually abnormal to violate arbitrarily created laws."[30] Here one sees lived experience turn into literary script: a path that leads from internalized shame towards self-affirmation via revelation and acceptance.[31] Eekhoud drew precisely on those passages in *Psychopathia Sexualis* which the Belgian psychiatrist Léon De Rode had identified a few years earlier as dangerously subversive.[32] *Escal-Vigor* was therefore a milestone in the popular dissemination of the originally scientific reverse discourse on homosexuality in Belgium, offering consolation and inspiration to generations of men and women to come. Many of his works, for example, featured on the shelves of Suzanne De Pues, the woman who founded Belgium's first lesbian and gay organization in 1953.³³ Moreover, Eekhoud had explicitly intended *Escal-Vigor* to serve this purpose. In a letter to Sander Pierron from 1900 he wrote: "I believe that this book will console and uplift quite a few homogenic lovers and that it will reconcile them with themselves, renew their courage, their sense of dignity and their passionate heroism."³⁴ Conservatives took note of Eekhoud's attempt to call attention to a subject they deemed pernicious. They did not linger in trying to keep *Escal-Vigor* from infecting the public.

The Trial of Bruges

In the summer of 1899, policemen confiscated several books from a librarian in Heist, a small resort town on Belgium's North Sea coast. Among them were Camille Lemonnier's *L'Homme en Amour* and Eekhoud's *Escal-Vigor*.³⁵ The seizure had been ordered by the crown prosecutor of nearby Bruges on a charge that the novels in question outraged public decency. A reactionary aristocratic magistrate from the heartland of Catholic Flanders, Léon Janssens de Bisthoven had already made a name for himself in the period's ongoing culture wars between the progressive left and the religious right. There were even whispers that Janssens had staged the entire thing by allegedly having a friend living in Heist order the books at the librarian's only to have them impounded on arrival.³⁶ Whatever the case may have been, both Lemonnier and Eekhoud were celebrated authors and former laureates of the five-yearly state prize for literature, which they had received from the hands of Catholic ministers no less. This was an orchestrated scandal in the making.

Predictably, the chief prosecutor from liberal Brussels indicated that he had no intention of prosecuting the matter.³⁷ Since cases like these touched on the constitutionally enshrined freedom of speech, they would have to be tried by jury and experience showed that metropolitan juries were extremely unlikely to convict on the basis of such questionable charges. Janssens eventually got his way when Eekhoud and Lemonnier were summoned before the Assize Court of West-Flanders at Bruges, where more provincial and congenial jurors would hear the case. Worried, Eekhoud turned to Edmond Picard for his defense: the nation's star barrister, his personal friend, a fellow champion of *l'art social*, and the country's first socialist senator.³⁸ Picard had nothing but contempt for the prissy Philistine he took Janssens to be. "If it's a spectacle they want, that's precisely what they'll get," he announced pugnaciously in *L'Art Moderne*, adding that it would be a piece of cake to "avenge the writer and the country for the dishonor and the ridicule to which this zealotry [had] expose[d] them."³⁹

Setting the tone for Eekhoud's defense, Picard insisted that the "sad" and "curious" drama of uranism, which *Escal-Vigor* analyzed in naturalistic fashion, was completely lost on the likes of Janssens. The prosecutor, he wrote, was clearly oblivious to the recent study by Raffalovich on "Uranism and Unisexuality" and thus hopelessly out of touch with the latest science on the subject. Raffalovich, after all, had established that uranism was "a congenital instinct" and therefore not "a vice that depends on will." Hence, Count Kehlmark was nothing but a Flemish case of the same condition that had marked "Plato, Socrates, Michelangelo, Shakespeare, Molière, Goethe, Byron," and so many others who had channeled – Freud would have said sublimated – their suppressed passions into the pursuit of beauty. Indeed, Picard argued rather implausibly, "unisexuality" was "platonic per se."[40] Clearly, tactical considerations mandated that a conceptual wedge be driven between immoral practices and a chaste ontology, between perversities and perversion, and between the pervert and the invert.

When the trial began on October 25, 1900, Janssens set great store on the testimony of psychiatric experts, one of whom, Xavier Francotte, was a prominent criminal anthropologist, brother to a Catholic MP, as well as a confirmed Catholic himself.[41] But even though these experts reliably declared uranism an evil to be eradicated and an epidemiological hazard, the approach backfired. Picard ridiculed their examination of fictional characters and made them answer silly questions to prove how very divided medical opinion on the subject really was. Far more impactful was the defense's line-up of many of the nation's most renowned authors intended to wow the small-town jury. They declared in unison that Eekhoud's intention had been to probe into the mind of his troubled protagonist and not to incite impurity among his readership. Janssens countered that this shrewd bit of absolving paralogism would not hold water in court. He reminded the jury – correctly – that whether or not the author had actually meant to offend public decency was beside the point. Under Belgian law, one could just as well be found guilty of indecency *ipso facto*, an important technicality the implications of which I examined in Chapter 3. Legally speaking, Janssens insisted, it sufficed that Eekhoud had been "of sound mind" at the time of writing. By implication, any book that outraged public morals was pornographic, self-declared art included.[42]

The case therefore boiled down to whether or not the jurors found the book indecent. Janssens hit a nerve when he charged that the portrayal of a man who renounced his wife for the love of a young boy "degrades and soils something sacred!"[43] But when he went on to name some of the actual vocabulary that offended him, including words like "bosom" and "nudity," Janssens elicited chuckles instead of outrage from those present. Chuckles turned into jeers when he reproached Eekhoud for singing uranism's praises and Picard interjected: "That's completely false! You're the one singing! (*Prolonged laughter*)." Picard's aide diagnosed the prosecution with a bad case of "incurable artistic color blindness," which made it "the laughingstock of Europe." The grand finale came when, on the last day of the trial, the presiding judge asked

Picard to begin his closing remarks. He had to repeat his request three times before the unresponsive barrister suddenly exclaimed: "I am waiting!" When the startled judge inquired what precisely he was waiting for, Picard, pointing at the prosecutor, roared at the top of his voice: "I am waiting for him to leave! (*Prolonged upheaval*)." Turning to Janssens, he bellowed:

Are you still here? You have finished, haven't you? You have finished insulting the artists of which Belgium is proud, finished pouring yourself with ridicule for the rest of your life! Be gone! Get out! Go home! Go explain to your wife and children what you have come here to do!

Without giving his opponent an opportunity to protest, a theatrically infuriated Picard went on to dismiss Janssens as "the Don Quichotte of morality" before a baffled courtroom that hung on his every word. He insisted that Eekhoud was above any suspicion or reproach and praised his dedication to *l'art social* for more than an hour. Courtroom pleading was considered a form of fine arts in those days. "The barrister is in the prime of his eloquence," an anonymous reporter wrote admiringly. Even though the jury only narrowly acquitted Eekhoud by seven votes to five, the audience burst into cheers and applause. A few days later, Lemonnier, also defended by Picard and a whole range of his fellow belletrists, was similarly acquitted by eight votes to four.[44]

Free Speech

A commemorative plaque in the Walloon town of Verviers depicts a man behind barbed wire wearing the inverted pink triangle in an obvious reference to the persecution of homosexuals by the Nazis. The man looks up at a passage from *Escal-Vigor* in which Count Kehlmark proudly declares: "I am neither sick nor guilty."[45] In this way, Eekhoud has been woven into the narrative of oppression and liberation that was constitutive of the postwar gay and lesbian movement.[46] But while he was the first Belgian to address the matter publicly and sympathetically, the outcome of his famous trial was not perceived as a symbolic victory for homosexuality at the time. This is well illustrated by an article the lauded writer Auguste Dewinne published in the socialist newspaper *Le Peuple* soon after Eekhoud's acquittal. Dewinne echoed the artistic community's satisfaction at the verdict's affirmation of free speech, but he also opined that *Escal-Vigor* was the distasteful "glorification of an odious sin."[47] To him, "pederasty, onanism and sadism [were] not forms of love but of disease; the desecration of love." Eekhoud had even had his protagonist express the wish that one day all these aberrations would be tolerated. "Yuck!" The very idea sickened him.

Writers like Eekhoud might well pay lip service to *l'art social*, according to Dewinne, but instead of portraying the heroic beauty of the proletarian struggle against exploitation, their chosen themes were often those of extravagant decadence. Pederasts were just the latest to join a long line of fêted degenerates. "Now [decadent] bourgeois literature is complete," Dewinne lamented. He urged that it was every socialist's "solemn duty to reject the literary tendencies manifested in this book and others like it." The Workers Party heavyweight Émile Vandervelde declared himself in total agreement with Dewinne, and Jules Destrée, later minister of the arts and sciences, also deemed *Escal-Vigor* "unwholesome."[48] In an interview, Eekhoud admitted that Dewinne's article had "saddened" him and that he felt misunderstood.[49] Mere weeks after his triumph in court, he found himself once more under attack, and now from his own corner. At one point, Eekhoud interrupted the interview to fetch his copy of Albert Moll's *Contrary Sexual Feeling* in an anxious effort to establish his purely analytical credentials and intentions. But when pressed on the latter, he retreated behind the constitutional argument that had won him his trial. "I defend the absolute freedom of the artist," he stated.[50] On that point, and that alone, he could count on broad support from progressives.

After all, to most observers, the trials of Bruges – including Lemonnier's, which had nothing to do with homosexuality – were just another skirmish in the ongoing war against Catholic censorship. Naturalist writers had been fending off charges of 'indirect' – that is, printed – offenses against public decency since the artistic renaissance of the early 1880s. Lemonnier, for example, had already stood trial several times before, most notably in 1893 for *L'Homme qui tue les femmes* (*The Man Who Kills Women*), a story that probed into the mind of Jack the Ripper.[51] To the government's growing embarrassment, Belgium had become an international turntable for pornography since the 1860s. Already on the rise in the later 1870s, prosecutions were stepped up dramatically after Catholics seized power in 1884 and the deeply conservative Charles Woeste became minister of justice.[52] Entire print runs were impounded, specific publications banned from railway transport or mailing through the post, and a long series of trials followed.[53] Henry Kistemaeckers, an indefatigable publisher of naturalistic novels, including several of Eekhoud's, was prosecuted before the Assize Court of Brussels no fewer than eighteen times between 1880 and 1902.[54]

Of course, the defense invariably screamed blue murder over violations of the constitutional right to free speech, and the jury system often frustrated prosecutors' designs. Kistemaeckers, for instance, was acquitted every single time in the Assizes.[55] In the five cases they managed to bring against him in a lower criminal court where professional judges ruled on guilt, he was convicted twice. The fact that so many avant-garde writers were trained or practicing lawyers themselves, including Lemonnier, certainly proved useful in avoiding conviction.[56] A book on *L'Art en cour d'assises* from 1893 testifies to the heavy overlap between Brussels' milieus of avant-garde artists, left-leaning intellectuals, and progressive lawyers, and to their shared distaste for the stale artistic academism and for the prudish conservatism of the senescent bench. The book denounced the legal system as an "unworthy parody of Justice," fabricated as it was, "by census voters for their own benefit and overseen by judges with bourgeois ideas and conservative instincts."[57] *L'Art Moderne* monitored the courts through a "Legal Chronicle of the Arts." Clearly, art was a profoundly politicized matter in the *fin de siècle*, and the courts were a battleground between the establishment and those looking to overthrow it.[58]

From the outset then, it had been obvious that the confiscation of *Escal-Vigor* would once again mobilize the artistic community in protest against another spasm of censorship in the name of public decency. Joining Picard's indignation, writers both at home and abroad rose in support of Eekhoud and Lemonnier with a petition on behalf of "the freedom of Art and Ideas," signed, among others, by no lesser men than André Gide, Félix Fénéon, Octave Mirbeau, Maurice Barrès, Stuart Merrill, Albert Mockel, Anatole France, Jules Elslander, and Émile Zola.[59] This would be "a trendsetting trial, of which the wider ramifications are such that the book and its author disappear before the [higher] principle," a liberal newspaper wrote, before continuing: "It is therein that the significance of the affair resides and it is that which explains the great wave of emotion that has washed over the literary and artistic community."[60] Edmond Picard agreed that the trial had really been just another assault "on the freedom of Art by magistrates who were still liable to mistake Literature ... for vile and lowly Pornography." An "excess of scruples, morality and religion" haunted the dying old world of *Bruges-la-Morte*, as Eekhoud's friend Georges Rodenbach immortalized the sleepy medieval town.[61] *La Jeune Belgique* was to be a very different place.

The Quiet after the Storm

For a fleeting moment, the trials of Bruges brought the issue of homosexuality to the fore; quite literally even, when Picard published an unprecedented front-page piece on "*L'Uranisme*" in *Le Peuple* on November 19, 1900.[62] Despite the fact that he could only defend and distort it as a purely platonic form of loving camaraderie, unsoiled by the "wickedness" of "sexual interversion [*sic*]," it briefly got Eekhoud's hopes up. When he learned that the great Zola supported his cause, Eekhoud exclaimed "Hip Hip Hurray!" in a letter to Pierron.[63] Always short on money, he now looked forward to the day he would no longer have to tutor rich ladies, expecting that the sale of his books was about to soar.[64] A piece he wrote for the libertarian journal *L'Effort éclectique* shortly after the trial testifies to this newfound confidence. It argued that while homosexuals were no longer punishable in Belgium as they still were in Germany, *Escal-Vigor* had sought to combat the lingering public prejudice against them, which was proving far more difficult to eradicate.[65] Such prejudice, Eekhoud pointed out, ran deep and was still widely shared across the political spectrum, from the "the priest-like fanatic" to the "ignorant collectivist."

In activist circles abroad, Eekhoud's cause célèbre gained him fame and recognition. The leading German activist Magnus Hirschfeld deemed *Escal-Vigor* a "moving novel" and an article about the trial of Bruges appeared in the *Yearbook for Intermediate Sexual Stages*, which Hirschfeld had recently launched in Berlin.[66] Eekhoud contributed to the *Yearbook* and became a member of Hirschfeld's Scientific Humanitarian Committee in defense of homosexuals, which had sent in a scientific endorsement of *Escal-Vigor* to help with the trial.[67] In 1903, the novel appeared in German and the following year Hirschfeld paid the writer a visit in Brussels.[68] Eekhoud also corresponded with the poet and activist Edward Carpenter in Britain, and with the exiled French novelist Jacques d'Ädelsward-Fersen in Capri, whose homoerotic journal *Akadémos* the Belgian writer contributed to.[69] Closer to home, he collaborated with two Dutchmen on the Flemish anarchist journal *Awakening*: the physician Lucien von Römer, who co-founded the Dutch branch of the Scientific Humanitarian Committee in 1912, and the homosexual novelist Jacob Israel De Haan, who admiringly called Eekhoud his "master."[70] Clearly, in the first few years of the twentieth century Eekhoud became the Belgian node in an international network of homosexual activists.

This makes it all the more striking that Eekhoud maintained a very low profile at home by comparison. He certainly never became a Belgian Hirschfeld, nor did he ever play the outspoken role that Aletrino and von Römer did in the Netherlands. "If he engaged in advocacy at all," Cathérine Gravet and Emile Van Balberghe have duly noted, "he would appear to have been more active abroad."[71] Eekhoud did go on to publish a second queer-themed novel in 1904. However, *L'Autre vue* (tentatively: *Another Perspective*) was a far cry from the unambiguous messaging that had marked *Escal-Vigor*.[72] It may have been Eekhoud's most autobiographic novel, drawing heavily on his longing forays into the working-class districts of Brussels on the trail of *voyous de velours* (velvet street urchins), and it definitely was his personal favorite.[73] But a detailed examination of the book's genesis has revealed the author's unmistakable "will to erase anything that might shock the right-minded reader."[74] It lacked a clear storyline or focus and dissolved into a mystical meditation about love and death towards the end. A lukewarm review in the *Yearbook* noted Eekhoud's tactical ambiguity and astutely pointed out that only a profound sense of suffering torment tied the disparate whole together.[75]

Eekhoud's relief and optimism had indeed been short-lived. Less than a year after his triumph in court he faced financial ruin. He was forced to go through the humiliating ordeal of borrowing money from close friends and fellow writers.[76] His letters to Pierron reveal growing feelings of solitude and despondency. "I often pass weeks without going out other than in order to run errands," he wrote to his former lover, who was now thirty-two, doing well for himself, and no longer in need of a mentor.[77] Eekhoud also hated being "forced to keep company" with the many he knew to whisper behind his back. "I feel very lonely, very misunderstood," he noted in his personal diary at one point, adding that he yearned "to be surrounded by friends who fully understand me, and who are not just being civil."[78] In December 1901, he wrote to Pierron: "Ah, how I would like to vomit on life!"[79]

By then a man in his fifties, Eekhoud roamed the streets in search of sex like many other middle-class men his age; paying for the privilege and exposing themselves to blackmail and irredeemable disgrace as many court files demonstrate. For all the furtive pleasure such adventures provided, they also exposed anyone who embarked on them to the huge risks involved. Eekhoud seems to have had regular contacts with a working-class boy – his "Velvetian" – in 1902 and 1903.[80] Nearing sixty, his fling with "Stan" in 1910, whom he also referred to as "my peasant butcher," involved considerable sums of money.[81] One of the diary entries about Stan is followed by another that notes a newspaper report about the conviction of two young men caught in the act.[82] The way Eekhoud scanned the papers for such news clearly captures his awareness of the chances he was taking, and the brief cuttings about ruined lives and reputations he sometimes glued in his journal must have sharpened a permanent sense of anxiety.[83] In a talk he gave around the time *L'Autre vue* came out, Eekhoud lamented that legal restrictions were not what confined people most: "we suffer primarily from narrow-minded prejudices and from the tyranny of the thousands of tiny straps that keep our desires in check."[84]

He would never openly embrace the role of an activist or his identity as a uranist or a homosexual. The prospect of committing social suicide in so doing must have simply appeared too daunting. When, in 1909, the German sexologist Iwan Bloch mentioned Eekhoud's name in a list of prominent uranists, and the Dutch writer Hubertus Johannes Schouten asked him to openly avow his homosexuality, Eekhoud sent a stern letter of protest that was published in the journal *Sexual-Probleme*. "I have not authorized anyone to assimilate me with my fictional characters," it stated unambiguously, "nor has my conduct provided any proof or arguments to those who would do so."[85] One can only speculate as to what extent the memory of his own expulsion from the military continued to play a role in his fear of being labeled a *bougre* (bugger). Adding to his fears was the way many leading writers had dissociated themselves from Oscar Wilde when he had been exposed and convicted as a sodomite in 1895. Eekhoud, by contrast, received a signed copy of *The Ballad of Reading Gaol* from the disgraced writer he so ardently admired after dedicating one of his own stories from 1898 "to Mister Oscar Wilde, Poet and Heathen Martyr, tortured in the name of Justice and of Protestant Virtue."[86]

In 1922, the writer Maurice Bladel wrote a portrait of Eekhoud in which he depicted *L'Autre vue* as a magnanimous novel about the way society's outcasts lifted themselves up through the immaculacy of their feelings. He also presented *Escal-Vigor* as a woefully misinterpreted allegory of the Flemish "race," which captured "the spiritual power of a people" by laying bare the purest sentiments of love and mutual devotion. To those who might suggest that the novel had been an autobiographical one, Bladel replied: "Certainly not!"[87] More than two decades after the book had first appeared he was still trying to scrape the homosexual layers from the author's work, just as any compromising passages were later scraped from Eekhoud's diary in a frustratingly successful attempt at censorship.

Conclusion

In many European countries a series of scandalous trials propelled the 'problem' of homosexuality into the limelight around the turn of the twentieth century.[88] Oscar Wilde's conviction was probably this long series' most internationally resonant one, but there were many others.[89] In 1902, Germany's hugely influential steel and weapons industry tycoon Alfred Friedrich Krupp died in mysterious circumstances following his exposure as a sodomite.[90] The British general Hector MacDonald, known as Fighting Mac, committed suicide in a Paris hotel in 1903 after damning allegations of buggery had been made against him.[91] Later that same year, the above-mentioned Baron Jacques d'Adelswärd-Fersen was tried and convicted for similar charges, while, in 1906, a Great Morality Scandal rocked Denmark over the problem of male prostitution.[92] Shortly thereafter, tongues wagged all over Europe when the notorious Eulenburg affair erupted, which centered around a number of the German emperor's closest courtiers.[93] The climate of scandal blew across the border into Austria-Hungary too.[94] Time and time again, homosexual scandals proved both salaciously savory and politically useful.

In the Netherlands, meanwhile, the conference paper by Arnold Aletrino from 1901 in support of uranists, which I referenced at the start of this chapter, had seriously backfired.[95] In a matter of months, it had incentivized the Calvinistic prime minister and moral entrepreneur Abraham Kuyper to call for legislative action against homosexuality. The liberal minority government that followed his conservative one fended off further attempts by the Catholic MP Robert Regout to pass such legislation, but the 1908 elections swept another religiously conservative cabinet of Catholics and Calvinists into power, which made Regout minister of justice two year later. Eager to make their mark after half a century of liberal dominance, this cross-denominational alliance of religious conservatives passed the so-called Morality Law of 1911, which cracked down on gambling, public indecency, abortion, prostitution, and homosexuality. The new article 248bis of the revised penal code raised the legal age of consent for homosexual relations to twenty-one, while leaving that for heterosexual ones at sixteen. With it, the Netherlands had partially abandoned the decriminalization of homosexuality from 1811. Both the debates that preceded the article's enactment and those that followed firmly established homosexuality as a matter of public and political concern in the Netherlands.

In Belgium, by contrast, no such debate emerged and homosexuality's recriminalization was never actively considered. A penal statute very similar to its Dutch counterpart was only adopted in 1965, and even then it passed through parliament without any debate worth mentioning.[96] It is almost ironic that Eekhoud's sensational trial, one of the very few of its kind with a happy ending, failed to give the issue a higher profile. In the end, his would remain a one-man movement if it was a movement at all. Partly because of the acquittal and consequent lack of martyrdom, and partly because Belgium's religious conservatives refused to take the bait for fear that it would only fan the flames of public debate, the trial could not inspire the kind of indignation that the active repression of homosexuality was busy galvanizing elsewhere, above all in Germany, but in the Netherlands and Denmark too. Without detracting from the significance of Eekhoud's work, the famous 'trial of Bruges' and its outcome did little to put the issue of sexual inversion onto the public or the scientific agenda in Belgium. If it was to homosexual activists abroad, at home the trial was hardly perceived as a resounding victory for homosexuality. Eekhoud's impact was less on legal and political history directly but very real and enduring for those readers of his with whom his writings resonated.

Coda
Pink Perils and Postwar Blues

In many ways, the First World War marked the end of an era and the beginning of a new one. The map of Europe was redrawn, and the politics of extremes replaced the long nineteenth century's liberal consensus. Belgium was no exception. The country was devastated by four years of violence and German occupation. Its economy struggled to recover while its political system became fickler as fragile coalition governments replaced the Catholic Party's prewar hegemony. But there was continuity too. Like the Netherlands, Belgium remained a remarkably stable place compared to neighboring France and Germany, where the interwar years were marked by the wild swerves of social and political turmoil.[1] If fascism and communism had a distinctive presence, their appeal remained limited among a population fiercely loyal to its ideological identities as either socialists, liberals, or Catholics. On the sexual front too, continuities were significant. Catholic morals still prevailed, and in those urban and industrial areas where they did not, anything that smacked of free love libertarianism was a fringe phenomenon at best.[2] Even among that fringe, homosexuality was anathema.[3] After Eekhoud, there was insufficient latitude in Belgium for the open queer activism of interwar Germany and the Netherlands or even the more coded literary kind coming out of France and Britain.[4] Belgian silence, it seems, subsisted.

There is much we still do not know about this period though. As mentioned in Chapter 4, sources are scant because, in 1944, the retreating *Wehrmacht* set fire to Brussels' Palace of Justice after another four years of occupation, destroying much of the juridical record of the preceding quarter century. Still, the little that survived strongly suggests that homosexual life in the capital after 1918 much resembled that of the decades preceding 1914. Court files testify to a vibrant queer culture centered on the historical heart of the city. Newspapers occasionally grumbled that there were a great many haunts in Brussels "where the vile sin is openly committed with revolting cynicism."[5] Male sex workers could be picked up in shady round-the-clock bars downtown, while the same public urinals and parks were still well-known to serve as night-time cruising hotspots. Jonathan Fryer, Christopher Isherwood's biographer who spent much time in Brussels himself, has noted how "few Belgians are aware of what great attraction their country exerted on English gays during the 1930s."[6] Like Isherwood, E. M. Forster and W. H. Auden were similarly drawn to the country, as had been so many of the wealthy German and British sex tourists who feature in court records before them.[7]

Indeed, little changed in terms of homosexuality's repression in Belgium during the interwar period. As in the late nineteenth century, there were sporadic complaints that the authorities still stood idly by. For too long the prudish Belgian legislator had deliberately played "Mr know-nothing," complained *La Nation belge* in 1931, adding that "one cannot quell an evil by denying its existence."[8] *L'Étoile belge* added that "young rogues dressed and made up like lowly working girls shamelessly offer themselves to passers-by" and no longer made "the least effort to conceal themselves."[9] The newspaper decried how the police did "nothing to diminish their number." That was not entirely correct though. There certainly were occasional raids on queer bars or stakeouts of known cruising areas as there had been for decades. But they were meant to intimidate rather than weed out the 'problem.' "Sure," noted a seasoned police officer who had monitored Brussels' underworld since the late nineteenth century, "we have some of those unfortunate wretches in our large cities." He agreed that they had to be contained. But he also downplayed the issue's importance. Brussels' queers generally "stayed well within the shadows" and went about their business "without much ostentation." Moreover, he warned against "excessive severity" on the part of the police "in this special domain." It would only cause a stir.

The available evidence does not suggest that this policy changed significantly later in the 1930s. Even during the Second World War there was no clear sign of tightening, let alone of any systematic persecution. Dimitri Roden's extensive research of prosecutorial practice in Belgium under Nazi rule clearly demonstrates that charges brought under paragraph 175 of the German penal code were extremely rare there. At least in part this was because Belgium and northern France remained under military control. Unlike the Netherlands or Poland, where civil administrations were installed, this meant that police tasks were generally handled by the *Wehrmacht* rather than the ideologically more fanatical *SS*, whose unchecked and murderous carnage in Poland irked German military command.[10] The *Wehrmacht* relied mostly on the Belgian police and gendarmerie for the day-to-day maintenance of public order. It also allowed Belgian magistrates to try cases that did not affect German interests, including vice matters. By consequence, the only three instances of persecution under paragraph 175 in occupied Belgium that Roden has come across all pertained to Belgian men who had sex with German men or who were in German employ while committing homosexual acts.[11] Thus, the direct persecution of homosexuals paled by comparison even to that in the Netherlands or the German-annexed parts of eastern France, where it also was far less pronounced than in the Third Reich itself.[12]

Moral Reconstruction

If Belgium's liberation in September 1944 brought great joy, there was also great sorrow.[13] Amid acute scarcity, the wealth of Allied troops inflated the prices of basic goods, while the destructions of war had produced a severe housing shortage.[14] When winter came and German retaliatory V-rockets flew overhead, hunger, hardship, and an abundance of weaponry "transform[ed] men into wolves," a Belgian sociologist observed in 1945.[15] Meanwhile, widespread wartime collaboration led to brutal score-settling.[16] The authoritarian sympathies of King Leopold III prevented his return from exile in Switzerland and produced a deeply divisive six-year controversy of mass protest, street violence, and riotous strikes. Meanwhile, the heroic bloodlettings of the USSR and of far-left partisans closer to home had invested communism with a newfound prestige which translated into the kinds of electoral gains that raised serious questions about the prospects of democracy's survival. In the late 1940s, Belgium was a far cry from the pacified and prosperous country it would be once again a decade later. Like the rest of postwar Europe, as Tony Judt has observed, "it was the insecure child of anxiety."[17]

Property crimes, the economy, and politics aside, there was a deeply felt sense that the most profound damage had been done to the social and moral fabric of society. One of the clearest and most worrying indicators thereof was the enormous spike in juvenile delinquency. "The morality of our youths is in peril," began a report titled *The Criminal Law Confronted with the Corruption of Youths and Incitement to Immorality*. It went on to lament how the young had been transformed by war. They were the children "of the frenzied hours of liberation with its armies of young soldiers, equally passionate in combat as in pleasure; the youths of dislodged families, of deported and recently or still imprisoned fathers; the youths, moreover, of [extravagantly priced] silken stockings at 200 francs a pair, of 20-franc movies and 15-franc ice creams."[18] Deprivation had made them unruly, indulgent, and materialistic. A two-pronged approach was required to bring the nation's future back into the fold. First, a restoration of the traditional family was urgently required. In January 1947, a front-page "Declaration of the Rights of the Family" noted how mounting divorce and illegitimacy rates, together with slumping fertility, had borne witness to the family's decline throughout the interwar period.[19] Shortly after liberation, a 300-page plan of action was published that focused primarily on legal and fiscal incentives to bolster marriage and childbirth.[20] But where carrots failed, sticks were in order. In December 1946, the moral restoration campaign's second leg was announced in the form of a comprehensive overhaul of youth protection measures.[21]

The sexual connotation of calls for such measures was unmistakable, at least where women were concerned. Women who had engaged in so-called horizontal collaboration with the German occupier were brutally shamed and ostracized upon liberation.[22] Moreover, it had not taken long before the way young Belgian women took to allied soldiers became a source of resentment among civilian men, all the more so because some of these soldiers were Black.[23] As early as October 1944, allied command expressed alarm at the surge in venereal infections and it pressured the Belgian government into a humiliating track-and-trace ordinance that focused mainly on women by early 1945. The allies also pushed for the closure of the continent's regulated brothels, and when France obliged in 1946, the onus was on Belgian authorities to follow suit and abolish regulated prostitution, which parliament unanimously did in 1948.[24] As it had previously also done, the law protected persons of either gender (*de l'un ou de l'autre sexe*) against their sexual corruption, but it was aimed overwhelmingly at the safeguarding of young women and the penalization of the much-maligned pimps who led them astray. Throughout the interwar period, adolescent boys had been closely associated with theft and general mischief, while society and the juvenile courts alike considered sexual iniquity a girls' problem as a matter of course.[25]

This, however, was about to change as a growing concern with homosexuality emerged in no small part because of changing police practices in the wake of regulated prostitution's abolition. The old municipal vice brigades tasked with surveilling licensed brothels were abolished by law. Enforcing the legislation that replaced regulated prostitution, however, proved difficult because of the milieu's surreptitiousness and the fact that Belgian law forbade the execution of search warrants between 9 p.m. and dawn.[26] But whereas previously there had been no solid legal mandate to curb soliciting in public, a more workable new one was introduced. Article 380quater of the penal code now made indecent proposals "by verbal means, gestures or signs" broadly punishable and doubled the penalties "in case the offense [was] committed towards minors."[27] Enforcing this new measure still proved difficult as the new vice squads needed to establish clear evidence while always facing stringent denials and allegations of unwarranted accusation.[28] Even so, the article immediately became the most commonly enforced part of the new prostitution law by far. More than ever before, policing sexual vice shifted from inside brothels to outside on the streets and the numbers reflected this. By the early 1950s, prosecutors noted with surprise that alongside female prostitutes, the offense of public soliciting was "being committed by men too," and increasingly so.[29]

Homosexual Seduction

At the same time, courts and criminologists alike were warning that incitement by adults was an important driver of growing juvenile delinquency numbers, especially in vice cases.[30] A key empirical survey from 1935 had argued that prostitution imperiled girls "almost exclusively."[31] The postwar follow-up study, by contrast, observed that homosexuality "should give us pause, because it seems that we are facing a new phenomenon in juvenile delinquency here."[32] Not until 1950 had reports about boy prostitutes from large urban areas and from Brussels in particular reached the juvenile courts. One magistrate now complained that "homosexuality is becoming a real scourge," and that many of these rent boys had been "inducted by those veritable professionals of male prostitution who wreak their havoc in Brussels."[33] Public space was designated as the prime site for adolescents of both genders' moral corruption, and "pedophilia," wrote the capital's youth magistrate, "requires special attention."[34] The spike in homosexual relations with minors was particularly clear to observers and deemed especially alarming where boys were concerned, even if much of what was now first being detected had been prevalent in Brussels since at least the late nineteenth century.

Aside from changing police practices, a further factor that translated the postwar moral panic over youths into homosexual terms was the rising influence of psychoanalysis. The latter had been slow to gain currency in Belgium, where Freud's perceived pansexualism had long been met with scorn from Catholics.[35] Only the careful desexualization of psychoanalysis made it gradually more palatable to Belgian intellectuals. In philosophical and theological circles, these revised psychoanalytic ideas became popular at the Catholic University of Leuven during the late 1950s and the 1960s, especially under the influence of Jacques Lacan. Paving the way, however, were early enthusiasts like the Leuven criminologist Etienne De Greeff who had been bringing Freudian teachings in line with Catholic sensitivities from the late 1930s onwards by developing a carefully desexualized theory of instinctive drives and by insisting on the possibility of their subordination to the rational intellect.[36] Meanwhile, however, a more recognizably Freudian but less intellectual version of psychoanalysis was fast becoming widely influential among the country's forensic community.[37] Written and first published during the war, the study *Psychologie et criminalité* by Florent Louwage deliberately aimed to bring about "a transformation in the conception of [deviant] acts and their perpetrators" among young police recruits.[38]

As the head of the nation's investigative police during the interwar period, Louwage was closely involved in the gradual professionalization of Belgian law enforcement during those years, teaching key courses at the newly created police academy. His biographer notes that "the books Louwage authored alone and in collaboration with others have essentially constituted the bulk of all police literature for three decades – from the 1930s to the 1960s."[39] Among them, *Psychologie et criminalité* familiarized several generations of Belgian policemen with Freudian ideas and impressed upon them the driving importance of the sexual instinct in human behavior. Following Freud,

Louwage argued how children pass through a critical period of sexual ambivalence in puberty, during which exposure to perversion may fixate youngsters into a permanent homosexual condition. Combined with the general concern over wayward youths and the growing detection of underage boys prostituting themselves on the streets of Brussels and other Belgian cities, a psychoanalytically informed idea of 'homosexual seduction' allowed for the 'pederast' – never clearly distinguished from the homosexual – to embody the various anxieties of the early postwar years, not least in the eyes of the law enforcement community.[40]

Consequently, policing homosexuality suddenly became a police concern in a way it never had been previously. While the number of interventions regarding heterosexual prostitution in Brussels peaked in 1954 and tapered off thereafter, those pertaining to homosexual 'deviance' increased spectacularly. Whereas the capital's vice squad listed only 22 such interventions in 1953, they rose to 159 the following year, to 393 in 1955, and to no fewer than 988 in 1956; a forty-fold increase in just three years' time.[41] This finally got the discursive ball rolling. In October 1955, the first-ever criminological article on homosexuality appeared in Belgium's leading criminal law review. It observed how the common "tendency towards proselytization" was "what ma[de] the homosexual dangerous." Because of this, "measures to protect male youths [were] imperative."[42] The Brussels prosecutor Raymond Charles ordered an extensive study of the problem. It was published in December 1957 and based on the analysis of the 1,374 male homosexuals identified in the span of two years in the capital's downtown area alone. (The numbers pertaining to female homosexuality – only 71 cases identified since 1951 – paled by comparison, and lesbianism was still not considered a problem worth dwelling on.)[43]

Both pioneering studies called for the protection of youths against homosexual seduction by raising the age of consent for homosexual relations from sixteen to eighteen. By the summer of 1960, a bill was adopted in parliament on the moral preservation of youths, forbidding minors entrance to corrupting establishments, like brothels, dance halls, racetracks, and so on. But this bill only paved the way for a more comprehensive reform of existing youth protection measures.[44] Buried deep withing this major piece of legislation, which parliament enacted in 1965, was the creation of the new penal statute 372bis. Validating homosexual seduction theory, it partially recriminalized homosexual acts for the first time since 1792 and along the lines suggested by the criminological articles mentioned earlier. There had been no substantive parliamentary debate on the measure and its introduction caught the budding gay and lesbian movement by surprise.[45] As Raymond Charles had suggested, the measure simply and uncontroversially brought Belgium in line with international trends. Paradoxically, this was a trend Belgium had had a hand in setting.

The Franco-Danish Model

The pattern of postwar anxieties generally focused on youths and often specifically on the supposed threat of moral contagion posed by homosexuality. Across Europe, the concern with and policing of homosexuality increased sharply, and while there were spillover effects from the politically infused persecution of homosexuals in the United States (known as the Lavender Scare), much of this fretful homophobia was homegrown.[46] Homosexuality was often implicitly perceived as the most abominable excrescence of wartime disruption. As Florent Louwage tellingly wrote in the 1951 article "Delinquency in Europe after World War II" for the American *Journal of Criminal Law and Criminology*:

> The detention, deportation and execution of a considerable mass of people, broke up ... families. The father was absent, the mother was compelled to work, the children were temporarily abandoned. The youth were in a constant state of vagrancy. Boys from 12 to 16 years of age were especially inclined to crime. They felt the impulse to take the place of the father, to be hostile towards their mother; ... to wander away and to possess money by any means, especially by larceny and black-marketing ... Women were not able to work or to earn a sufficient wage to support their children. Many resorted to adultery, prostitution, abortion and larceny. ... Besides the crimes mentioned, homosexuality was rife.[47]

Louwage, moreover, played an outsized role in international police cooperation in the wake of the Second World War. Since the mid 1920s he had been the Belgian representative at the International Criminal Police Commission, better known by its telegraphic abbreviation Interpol. Interpol disintegrated along with much of the interwar international community as Nazism expanded, and after the war Louwage took the initiative in reviving it, serving as the organization's influential president from 1946 to 1956. Moreover, Louwage was the main editor and book reviewer of Interpol's new journal, the *International Criminal Police Review* (*ICPC*), which appeared in several languages and influenced senior law enforcement officers around the world.[48] Reflecting the time's unease, the *ICPC* regularly published contributions on predatory child molesters, often homosexual ones, during its early years. Louwage circulated excerpts like "Perversions and Neuroses" from his book on *Psychologie et criminalité* in the journal, and he tirelessly wrote warm reviews of books like the American Joseph Paul de River's *The Sexual Criminal*, which dripped with the psychoanalytic language of homosexual seduction, and which fueled the strong concern with sexual psychopathy in the early Cold War United States.[49]

A reader of several languages, Louwage collated criminological works from an array of countries and noted a rise in sex crimes across national borders after the war. He had Interpol conduct and discuss an international survey on the issue in 1952.[50] Under Louwage's chairmanship, further reports were presented at the annual general assemblies of the increasingly global organization on pornography (1953), juvenile delinquency (1953, 1955), psychopathology (1955), and prostitution (1956), the latter one at his personal insistence. Amid the growing concern with homosexuality in Belgium, Louwage's successor as head of first Brussels' and then Belgium's investigative police, Firmin Franssen, took over as the Belgian delegate to Interpol. At the general assembly of 1957 in Lisbon, Franssen formally requested a global report by the organization on homosexuality and crime.[51] Questionnaire HOSEX-4731 was sent out to all member states.[52] The following year, two major conclusions were drawn in the report based on the responses received to it from forty countries. The first was a marked trend towards the decriminalization of homosexual acts among consenting adults; the other a simultaneous shift towards the so-called Franco-Danish model of a raised aged of consent for homosexual relations.[53] This model had been pioneered in the Netherlands in 1911, but it had been adopted in France in 1942 and had recently been proposed in Denmark. Moreover, in September 1957 it had also been recommended by the British Departmental Committee on Homosexual Offences and Prostitution, better known as the Wolfenden Committee.[54]

Interpol's conclusions confirmed and reinforced a liberalizing trend within the international criminal law community. With regard to homosexuality, this trend was informed by an analytical shift away from psychopathology (i.e. extrapolations on the basis of small incarcerated populations of sex offenders) and towards sociology; a shift in which the large-scale empirical studies of human sexual behavior by the American biologist Alfred Kinsey played an influential role.[55] These analyses demonstrated that the vast majority of homosexual acts were consensual and harmless. In a matter of years, all of the world's criminological associations were calling for partial decriminalization: the United Nations' European Consultative Group on the Prevention of Crime and the Treatment of Offenders (1958), the International Society of Criminology (1960), and the International Association for Penal Law (1964).[56] Following this recommendation, Western European countries aligned their laws with the Franco-Danish model in the course of the 1960s and 1970s. For some of them, like West-Germany, England, and Wales, this took the logical form of partial decriminalization. Belgium, by odd contrast, needed to partially recriminalize in order to comply. Raising the age for homosexual relations to eighteen while the age of consent for heterosexual acts remained at sixteen, the addition of article 372bis to the penal code in 1965 did exactly that.

Between Liberation and Institutionalization

The emergence of a vocal homosexual movement had been spurred on early by the existence of discriminating laws in countries like Germany and the

Netherlands. Belatedly, article 372bis similarly rallied resistance from an increasingly organized movement in Belgium. The first such organization to emerge was founded in 1953 by the lesbian Suzanne de Pues in imitation of the Dutch example.[57] However, the generically named Belgian Cultural Center (Centre Culturel Belge-Cultuur Centrum België) was primarily a discreet social circle, politically restrained like homophile groups abroad, but arguably even more timid and certainly smaller still. There was some cautious cooperation with academics and sex reformers from the mid 1960s onwards, but the student revolutions of 1968 were a turning point. Particularly emotive in Belgium, where they preceded events in Paris, these student revolts initially centered on the linguistic tensions between Dutch-speaking Flemings and French-speaking Walloons at the Catholic University of Leuven. Belgium was the only country where the riots toppled a government and triggered a still-ongoing series of constitutional reforms.[58] The protests radicalized the generation of baby boomers and, in its wake, gay and lesbian liberation politics trickled through from New York via Paris, where the Front Homosexuel d'Action Révolutionnaire was formed in 1971.

Radical gay and lesbian liberation spin-offs made a splash during the early 1970s in Belgium too.[59] But groups like the Mouvement Homosexuel d'Action Révolutionnaire in Wallonia, Rode Hond (Red Dog) in Flanders, and the lesbian Biches Sauvages (Wild Hinds) in Brussels proved short-lived due to internal ideological bickering and a lack of organizational structure. Their quick evaporation left Wallonia without much of a movement for years to come, but meanwhile in Flanders a string of more moderate and accommodationist initiatives had been thriving since the late 1960s. Springing up in cities and on university campuses, they were primarily geared towards building a community and providing care in imitation of similarly successful initiatives in the Netherlands. In a country historically dominated by French-speaking elites and culturally oriented towards France, linguistic and political friction increasingly led Flanders to embrace Dutch culture and organizational methods; something helped along by a shared language and the growing Flemish habit of tuning into Dutch radio and television.[60] With more than 3,800 members across the country by 1965, the Dutch homosexual organization COC (short for Center for Culture and Leisure) was the world's largest and served as an example abroad, especially in nearby Flanders.[61] Attempts to build a national umbrella organization like the COC faltered in Belgium because of the usual linguistic tensions, but in 1972 one did emerge at the Flemish level.[62]

Meanwhile, homosexuality was slowly seeping into public discourse. The Introduction has already mentioned the first documentary devoted to homosexuality broadcast on public television in 1966.[63] Several introductory radio broadcasts followed as did more Flemish TV programs in 1970 and the first francophone one in 1973. Liberation groups increased visibility by small events like gay public park picnics, and Belgian queers first took to the streets as part of the feminist marches for the decriminalization of abortion in 1973. Increasingly inspired by movements and intellectuals abroad, not least of which Guy Hocquenghem's pioneering work of queer theory in *Homosexual Desire* (1972), a second wave of uncompromising and genderbending liberationist militancy availed itself of playful shock tactics on behalf of the queer cause during the second half of the 1970s.[64] Its loudest exponent, Rooie Vlinder (Red Butterfly), organized a Faggot Film Festival and a first celebratory Gay Day in 1978. Dutch attendants expressed surprise at the lack of a political platform, and in response Red Butterfly put together the first public demonstration against article 372bis a year later in Antwerp. Enamored by its unexpected success, the guarded Flemish gay and lesbian umbrella organization now agreed to support future marches.

Aside from growing the community's visibility, arguably the most significant result of the gay and lesbian movement during the 1970s was its institutional integration into Belgium's subsidized civil society. Like the Netherlands, twentieth-century Belgium's political culture was marked by the system of consociationalism, also known as pillarization.[65] This meant that Belgian society's three main constituent groups – Catholics, socialists, and liberals – each formed their own comprehensive set of organizations and institutions called 'pillars' in the lap of which their respective members' entire lives took place, from the cradle to the grave. From health insurance and unions to schools and social and leisure organizations, Belgian society was heavily segregated along ideological lines, with socialism dominating in Wallonia and Catholicism in Flanders, and with collaboration only happening through compromise and proportionate power-sharing at the political level. This system, created to pacify mounting political tensions at the start of the century, worked through the principle of *la liberté subsidiée*: the state subsidization of private initiatives that provided useful social services to a specific constituency. By 1978, the ideologically neutral Flemish homosexual umbrella organization, of which the main aim was to provide such services to gay men and lesbian women, began receiving structural subsidies so that it could support and further expand its operations. This laid the foundations of the firmly established, state-integrated, and later often renamed Federation of Homophile Working Groups, which still dominates Flemish LGBTQI+ politics today.[66]

From Contrition to Abolition

Even though little is known about the scale of its enforcement, amid the flowering of Belgium's gay and lesbian organizations article 372bis still partially criminalized homosexuality. Calling for its abolition was one of the few things that brought together an otherwise disparate movement, heavily divided along linguistic lines, operational structures, core activities, and political approach; with the water between the radical liberationist left and the moderate integrationist mainstream especially deep. The 1979 march for the scrapping of 372bis was a landmark event, demonstrating the possibility of coming together around a common cause. One year later, a lesbian high school teacher from Wallonia named Eliane Morissens was summarily fired after coming out on television and stating that her sexual orientation prevented her from becoming headmistress. She fought her sacking tooth and nail, and its injustice sparked public outrage among gays and lesbians both at home and abroad, embarrassing the francophone socialist trade union and party of which Morissens was an active member. Then, in 1984, another major discrimination scandal began when police raided two gay saunas on suspicion of inciting prostitution and debauchery amid the budding identification of the gay community with the spread of a mysterious and lethal disease. Among the arrested owners later acquitted for lack of evidence was Michel Vincineau, a professor of law at the Free University of Brussels who published a series of damning and widely acclaimed legal analyses of the case.[67]

While these high-profile scandals eroded public support for further discrimination, some activists had been quietly and patiently lobbying the political class for years. Jackie Boeykens, an early leader of the Flemish umbrella organization, set up a political task force with the prime aim of seeing 372bis scrapped.[68] Individual members of parliament from various parties were keen to oblige, but Belgium's system of rigid party discipline – the so-called *particratie* – required a careful balancing act of political calculus and momentum. Moreover, Belgium's coalition governments were invariably dominated by the Flemish Christian People's Party, the postwar successor to the Catholic Party, which remained staunchly conservative on moral issues. Boeykens realized that real change would only come if key experts and authorities recommended it. One early ally was the Leuven professor of criminology Steven de Batselier, but he was controversial in conservative circles, including law enforcement.[69] A tipping point came in 1977, when Boeykens met with Raymond Charles via the clergyman Piet de Haene, who liaised between the gay and lesbian movement and the Christian People's Party. Since publishing the study that led to the enactment of article 372bis twenty years earlier, Charles had risen to become attorney-general at the Court of Cassation, the country's highest court of appeal, vesting him with great influence. Charles agreed to be a keynote speaker at a colloquium co-organized by the Federation of Homophile Working Groups later that year. As a result, a who's who of the Belgian legal, criminological, and law enforcement community attended. They concluded that article 372bis was ready for repeal.[70]

Key to this change of heart was the repudiation of homosexual seduction theory. Ironically, it was once again an article by Charles that became the main point of reference for legal change. In a scholarly piece from 1982, he noted how the so-called Speijer Committee working on behalf of the Dutch government had forcefully argued back in 1969 that the most recent scientific findings showed how "minors of sixteen or older cannot be rendered homosexual by exposure to homosexual acts."[71] On that basis, the raised age of consent for such acts had been repealed there in 1971. Meanwhile, France too had very recently done so after the issue had been picked in the run-up to presidential elections.[72] The two statutes on which the Belgian one had been directly based were now gone, and, Charles concluded, "maintaining article 372bis ... no longer seems to rely on a valid scientific basis."[73] He also noted how Ernest Glinne, an MP for the francophone Socialist Party who had voted in favor of article 372bis in 1965, had similarly reversed his position and submitted private bill proposals to see it abolished in 1977 and 1979.[74] By 1981, a landmark ruling by the European Court of Human Rights made clear that homosexuality's criminalization was on its way out, even if it explicitly left the age of consent for countries themselves to determine.[75]

Amid the discrimination scandals of the early 1980s, the slow machinery of parliament set to work. The preparatory committee made much of Charles' reversal, and on June 25, 1983, the Chamber of Representatives overwhelmingly voted in favor of repeal.[76] The Christian-Democratic chair of the Justice Committee took two years to table the bill in the Senate, but when he finally did, in June of 1985, 372bis was overturned unanimously and without any debate, wrapped into a larger package together with unrelated measures as something wholly insignificant.[77] With a noiseless anticlimax, decriminalization occurred a time when the gay and lesbian movement was going through internal difficulties and while the queer community was facing the devastation beginning to be wrought by HIV/AIDS.[78]

Inclusion and Performative Secularism

Throughout the late 1980s and the 1990s, there were failed attempts to enact anti-discrimination legislation. Moreover, the AIDS epidemic had laid bare how there was no civil law framework in place when a same-sex partner became ill or died. As the movement rebounded, it picked up increasing media and political support from the mid 1990s onwards. Then, in 1999, a food health scare suddenly ended a political era when it pushed the Christian Democrats out of government for the first time in more than four decades. (With only three brief interruptions from 1878 to 1884, 1945 to 1947, and 1954 to 1958, Catholics had permanently held power in Belgium since 1870.) An unprecedented coalition of liberal, socialist, and green parties took over. Eager to establish its progressive credentials and mark the beginning of a new political culture, the coalition jumped headlong into a series of reforms pertaining to moral and sexual issues. In 2000, same-sex life partnerships could officially be registered. Three years later, a bill protecting against discrimination on the basis of sex and sexual orientation followed. Also in 2003, another bill made Belgium the second country in the world to legalize same-sex marriage. By 2006, same-sex couples acquired the same adoption rights as heterosexual ones.[79] Legally changing gender was first rendered easier by a law of 2007, and in 2018 the requirement of physical or surgical alignment with one's gender identity was dropped. In 2014, the existing anti-discrimination law had also been extended to include protections for gender identity and expression.[80]

In the twenty-first century, then, Belgium quickly became one of the most LGBTQ-friendly nations in the world and a staunch defender of queer people's rights internationally.[81] Barring the Flemish far right's resistance, which has never yet amounted to much because other parties have so far refused to collaborate with it on principle, this unlikely development took place without a huge amount of debate or social tension. LGBTQI+ rights have so far never been a major electoral issue and nothing even remotely like the American culture wars exists in the country to this day, with the moderate parties right of center vocally in support of those rights. Like other Western countries, Belgium has certainly seen the flipside of secularist triumphalism in the form of gay friendliness' weaponization against a supposedly backward Islam in the wake of 9/11; a phenomenon known as pinkwashing and homonationalism.[82] It is also not unimaginable that the enormous symbolism of LGBTQI+ rights in the growing clash between world views at both the global and the European levels nowadays may lead to their increased politicization in Belgium going forwards.[83] That said, it is still significant that Belgians were dumbstruck by the huge demonstrations against the legalization of same-sex marriage in Paris in 2013. Back then, Belgium was led by an openly gay prime minister and until recently one of the country's widely respected deputy prime ministers was a trans woman.[84] LGBTQI+ rights have so far simply not been that contentious among the bulk of Belgian society.

This relative unconcern forms an odd continuity with the past. While there is no question that queer issues and homosexuality in particular have become much more salient in public discourse and policymaking than they used to be, especially from the 1990s onwards, such matters have never stirred the wider population in the way that they have abroad. Belgian LGBTQI+ politics are (still) far less emotive than they are in France or the United States. They are also not as publicly prominent as in the Netherlands or as strongly politicized as in the United Kingdom. Partly, no doubt, this has to do with a widely felt need to move beyond the old Catholic hegemony and morality that many experienced as oppressive. A similar sense of urgency to 'catch up' with international trends and leaders has helped to build momentum for queer rights in Catholic-dominated countries such as Portugal, Spain, Malta, and Ireland.[85] But, as this book has shown, the reasons for Belgium's peculiar history of homosexuality are complex and historically specific. That history is not reducible to Catholicism's influence but certainly heavily inflected by it. This underscores the relative lack of attention for the formative power of religion in existing histories of homosexuality in 'modern' Europe, which have more commonly emphasized the role of the biomedical sciences, of the law, of activists, and of changing cityscapes. While these were contributing factors in Belgium too, the international comparisons drawn in this book highlight that causes, chronologies, and trajectories varied considerably, and that there is no monochromatic picture of queer history in the West, in Europe, or even in Western Europe to be painted. If, where it came to homosexuality, Belgians were for a long time not entirely unwilling to know, they were often reluctant to, actively prevented from knowing too much, or encouraged to speak its name in a certain tongue. This counterintuitive insight may hopefully contribute to a more kaleidoscopic approach to the queer past; an approach that should help to give us pause amid the political temptations of the present to force messy histories into overly polished and therefore all too useful narratives.

Notes

Introduction

1. Jos M. W. VAN USSEL, "Sociogenese en evolutie van het probleem der seksuele propaedeuse tussen de 16de en de 18de eeuw, vooral in Frankrijk en Duitsland: Bijdrage tot de studie van de burgerlijke seksuele moraal," unpublished doctoral dissertation, 2 vols., University of Amsterdam, 1967.
2. The Jewish historian Jacques Presser from the University of Amsterdam in the Netherlands proved more amenable and was prepared to supervise the research project. See Michel OUKHOW, "Herinneringen," in: Jacques KRUITHOF and Ignace GEURTS (eds.), *De seksualiteit herzien: Het werk van Jos van Ussel*, Deventer: Van Loghum Slaterus, 1979, 154–162, 159–160.
3. The CVP or Christelijke Volkspartij (Christian People's Party) was never out of office between 1958 and 1999. From 1947 to 1954, it had also been part of government until a coalition of liberals and socialists took over for four tumultuous years during which the Second School War erupted between profoundly divided pro- and anticlerical forces. See Wouter BEKE, *De ziel van een zuil: De Christelijke Volkspartij 1945–1968*, Leuven: Leuven University Press, 2005.
4. On Van Ussel, see Jaap KRUITHOF and Ignace GEURTS (eds.), *De seksualiteit herzien: Het werk van Jos Van Ussel*, Deventer: Van Loghum Slaterus, 1979; Lex VAN NAERSSEN, *Zoeken naar warmte: De werken van Jos van Ussel*, Deventer: Van Loghum Slaterus, 1978.
5. Jaap KRUITHOF and Jos VAN USSEL, *Jeugd voor de muur: Vlaamse studenten over hun seksuele problematiek*, Antwerp: Ontwikkeling, 1962. The study was of limited scope. The new foreword to its second edition made clear how the authors assumed that the figures supplied by Kinsey for the United States roughly applied to Belgium as well. On Kinsey's reception in Europe, see Dagmar HERZOG, "The Reception of the Kinsey Reports in Europe," *Sexuality and Culture*, 10/1, 2006, 39–48.
6. Jos M. W. VAN USSEL, *Geschiedenis van het seksuele probleem*, Meppel: Boom, 1968, 13. This pathologizing language was more explicit and abundant in the published version of Van Ussel's dissertation than it was in the less political original.
7. Herman DE CONINCK, "Humo sprak met Jos Van Ussel," *Humo*, 2858, 1976, 28–41, 39.
8. Norbert ELIAS, *Het civilisatieproces: Sociogenetische en psychogenetische onderzoekingen*, Utrecht: Het Spectrum, 1990, 247. The influence of Freud's theory of the id, ego, and superego on Elias' thinking is as obvious as it is ubiquitous. On Elias, see Robert VAN KRIEKEN, *Norbert Elias*, London: Routledge, 1998.

9. For Van Ussel's comments on his own limitations, see Jaap KRUITHOF, "Leven, persoon en werk van Jos Van Ussel," in: Jaap KRUITHOF and Ignace GEURTS (eds.), *De seksualiteit herzien: Het werk van Jos Van Ussel*, Deventer: Van Loghum Slaterus, 1979, 9–37, 23.
10. Herbert MARCUSE, *Eros and Civilization*, New York: Springer Nature, 1955.
11. Jos VAN USSEL, *Afscheid van de seksualiteit*, 5th ed., Deventer: Van Loghum Slaterus, 1978 [1970], 107.
12. On this climate, see Wannes DUPONT, "Catholics and Sexual Change in Flanders," in: Gert HEKMA and Alain GIAMI (eds.), *Sexual Revolutions*, Basingstoke: Palgrave Macmillan, 2014, 81–98.
13. VAN USSEL, *Geschiedenis van het seksuele probleem*.
14. Jos VAN USSEL, *Sexualunterdrückung: Geschichte der Sexualfeindschaft*, translated by Hubertus MARTIN, Reinbeck bei Hamburg: Rowohlt, 1970; Jos VAN USSEL, *La repressione sessuale: Storia e cause del condizionamento borghese*, translated by Milli GRAFFI, Milan: Bompiani, 1971; Jos VAN USSEL, *Histoire de la répression sexuelle*, translated by Catherine CHEVALOT, Paris: Laffont, 1972; Jos VAN USSEL, *La represion sexual*, Mexico City: Roca, 1974; Jos VAN USSEL, *História da repressão sexual*, translated by Ramiro DA FONSECA, Lisbon: Europa-América, 1975; Jos VAN USSEL, *Seksualundertrykkelsens historie*, translated by Inge BERTHELSEN, Copenhagen: Medusa, 1978.
15. There are nevertheless considerable overlaps between Foucault's views and those of Norbert Elias. On these overlaps, see Robert VAN KRIEKEN, "The Organization of the Soul: Elias and Foucault on Discipline and the Self," *Archives européennes de sociologie – European Journal of Sociology – Europäisches Archiv für Soziologie*, 31, 1990, 353–371; Dennis SMITH, "The 'Civilizing Process' and 'The History of Sexuality': Comparing Norbert Elias and Michel Foucault," *Theory and Society*, 28/1, 1999, 79–100. See also Sam BINKLEY, Paddy DOLAN, Stefanie ERNST et al., "The Planned and the Unplanned: A Roundtable Discussion on the Legacies of Michel Foucault and Norbert Elias," *Foucault Studies*, 8, 2010, 53–77.
16. Michel FOUCAULT, Valerio MARCHETTI, and Antonella SALOMONI (eds.), *Abnormal: Lectures at the Collège de France, 1974–1975*, New York: Picador, 2003, 236.
17. Ibid., 43.
18. Michel FOUCAULT, *The History of Sexuality, Volume 1: An Introduction*, translated by Robert HURLEY, New York: Pantheon Books, 1978, 17.
19. Among many other works, a foundational one was Kenneth PLUMMER (ed.), *The Making of the Modern Homosexual*, London: Hutchinson, 1981.
20. For example, Mary MCINTOSH, "The Homosexual Role," *Social Problems*, 16/2, 1968, 182–192; Jeffrey WEEKS, "The 'Homosexual Role' after 30 Years: An Appreciation of the Work of Mary McIntosh," *Sexualities*, 1/2, 1998, 131–152. For all its fruitfulness, the term 'social constructionism' is often loosely used as a procrustean panacea that papers over important methodological differences and causal distinctions. Whereas social historians may insist on the importance of changing socioeconomic conditions, cultural historians are more likely to emphasize ideational and discursive shifts. A stable consensus on the meanings and limits of constructionism does not appear to exist. On the complexity of this issue and its (normative) implications, see Ian HACKING, *The Social Construction of What?* Cambridge, MA: Harvard University Press, 1999.

21. That body is now too vast to be listed here in full. It is usefully summarized in Benjamin KAHAN, *The Book of Minor Perverts: Sexology, Etiology, and the Emergences of Sexuality*, Chicago: University of Chicago Press, 2019, afterword; Howard H. CHIANG, "Liberating Sex, Knowing Desire: 'Scientia Sexualis' and Epistemic Turning Points in the History of Sexuality," *History of the Human Sciences*, 23/5, 2010, 42–69; William B. TURNER, *A Genealogy of Queer Theory*, Philadelphia: Temple University Press, 2000, chap. 2.
22. For an overview that needs updating, see Wannes DUPONT and Henk DE SMAELE, "Orakelen over de heimelijkheid: Seksualiteit in de Belgische historiografie," *Belgisch Tijdschrift voor Nieuwste Geschiedenis – Revue Belge d'Histoire Contemporaine*, 38/3–4, 2008, 273–296.
23. An unpublished master's thesis based on court files from Brussels pertaining to homosexual indecencies initially gave rise to my project. See Nicolas CHARTIER, "De onderbuik van Brussel: De mannelijke homoseksuele subcultuur in Brussel tijdens de negentiende eeuw," *Belgisch Tijdschrift voor Nieuwste Geschiedenis – Revue Belge d'Histoire Contemporaine*, 38/3–4, 2008, 407–435.
24. I am not claiming, however, that there was no growing discourse of sex in Belgium with regard to other issues. There manifestly was, for example, regarding regulated heterosexual prostitution, the spread of venereal disease, pornography, and birth control, as will become clear further along. Even so, far more historical work is necessary to assess how Belgium's concern with sex in a broader sense compared to that elsewhere in substance, scope, and tone.
25. In fact, the prosecution of same-sex sexual acts was already rare by comparison in the pre-independence Southern Low Countries. See Elwin HOFMAN, "The End of Sodomy: Law, Prosecution Patterns, and the Evanescent Will to Knowledge in Belgium, France, and the Netherlands, 1770–1830," *Journal of Social History*, 54/2, 2020, 480–502.
26. On the large-scale production of statistics and information about heterosexual prostitution in Brussels (and Belgium more broadly), see, among others, Aurore FRANÇOIS and Christine MACHIELS, "Une guerre de chiffres: L'Usage des statistiques par les discours abolitionniste et réglementariste sur la prostitution à Bruxelles (1844–1948)," *Histoire & mesure*, 22/2, 2007, https://doi.org/10.4000/histoiremesure.2523, last accessed on August 12, 2024, 103–134.
27. Magnus HIRSCHFELD, "Urteile römisch-katholischer Priester über die Stellung des Christentums zur staatl. Bestrafung der gleichgeschlechtlichen Liebe," *Jahrbuch für sexuelle Zwischenstufen mit besonderer Berücksichtigung der Homosexualität*, 2, 1900, 161–203, 189.
28. Regina Kunzel has called this "the false coherence ... granted to modern sexuality." Regina KUNZEL, *Criminal Intimacy: Prison and the Uneven History of Modern American Sexuality*, Chicago: University of Chicago Press, 2008, 7. Also see Helmut PUFF, "After the History of (Male) Homosexuality," in: Scott SPECTOR, Helmut PUFF, and Dagmar HERZOG (eds.), *After the History of Sexuality: German Genealogies with and beyond Foucault*, New York: Berghahn Books, 2012, 18–30.
29. Wannes DUPONT, "Modernités et homosexualités belges," *Cahiers d'histoire: Revue d'histoire critique*, 119, 2012, 19–34.
30. Foucault made thirty-four such claims in the introductory volume on *The History of Sexuality*.

31. Among others, see Jasbir PUAR, *Terrorist Assemblages: Homonationalism in Queer Times*, Durham, NC: Duke University Press, 2007; Janet AFARY and Kevin B. ANDERSON, *Foucault and the Iranian Revolution: Gender and the Seductions of Islam*, London: University of Chicago Press, 2005; Mitchell DEAN, "Foucault's Obsession with Western Modernity," in: Barry SMART (ed.), *Michel Foucault. Critical Assessments*, 7 vols., vol. 5, London: Routledge, 1994–1995, 285–299; Edward W. SAID, *Orientalism*, New York: Vintage Books, 1979.
32. While there were many more contributors to the 1980s debate that often focused on the differences between constructionist and essentialist approaches, one influential volume was Martin DUBERMAN, Martha VINCUS, and George CHAUNCEY (eds.), *Hidden from History: Reclaiming the Gay and Lesbian Past*, New York: Meridian, 1990. A key work responding to the growing emphasis of queer theorists such as Eve Kosofsky Sedgwick on the fluidity of sexual identity was David M. HALPERIN, *How to Do the History of Homosexuality*, Chicago: University of Chicago Press, 2002.
33. John BOSWELL, "Revolutions, Universals, and Sexual Categories," in: Martin DUBERMAN, Martha VICINUS, and George CHAUNCEY (eds.), *Hidden from History: Reclaiming the Gay and Lesbian Past*, New York: Meridian, 1990, 17–36, 35.
34. John HOWARD, *Men Like That: A Southern Queer History*, Chicago: University of Chicago Press, 1999. It was immediately praised as a methodological and perspectival breakthrough in Lisa DUGGAN, "Down There: The Queer South and the Future of History Writing," *GLQ: A Journal of Lesbian and Gay Studies*, 8/3, 2002, 379–387.
35. A good example of the queer turn towards indeterminacy is Carolyn DINSHAW, *Getting Medieval: Sexualities and Communities, Pre- and Postmodern*, Durham, NC: Duke University Press, 1999.
36. While I endorse the widespread criticism of teleological assumptions, I share Valerie Traub's reservations about a wholesale abandonment of periodization and genealogy. Valerie TRAUB, *Thinking Sex with the Early Moderns*, Philadelphia: University of Pennsylvania Press, 2016, chap. 3; Valerie TRAUB, "The New Unhistoricism in Queer Studies," *PMLA*, 128/1, 2013, 21–39. In Europe, this shift towards contingency was notable in the criticisms formulated by a new generation of British queer historians of their pioneering predecessors. See Harry G. COCKS, *Nameless Offences: Homosexual Desire in the Nineteenth Century*, 2nd ed., London: I.B. Tauris, 2010 [2003]; Sean BRADY, *Masculinity and Male Homosexuality in Britain, 1861–1913*, London: Palgrave Macmillan, 2005; Matt HOULBROOK, *Queer London: Perils and Pleasures in the Sexual Metropolis, 1918–1957*, Chicago: University of Chicago Press, 2005; Matt COOK, *London and the Culture of Homosexuality, 1885–1914*, Cambridge: Cambridge University Press, 2003. While the pioneering generation praised these new works, it also felt strawmanned by them. See, for example, Jeffrey WEEKS, "Queer(y)ing the 'Modern Homosexual,'" *The Journal of British Studies*, 51/3, 2012, 523–539; Chris WATERS, "Distance and Desire in the New British Queer History," *GLQ: A Journal of Lesbian and Gay Studies*, 14/1, 2008, 139–155; Joseph BRISTOW, "Remapping the Sites of Modern Gay History: Legal Reform, Medico-Legal Thought, Homosexual Scandal, Erotic Geography," *Journal of British Studies*, 46/1, 2007, 116–142.

37. Laura DOAN, *Disturbing Practices: History, Sexuality, and Women's Experience of Modern War*, Chicago: University of Chicago Press, 2013.
38. Among the many gains is more attention to previously overlooked issues such as trans* and intersex histories, the intersections of sex, gender, race, coloniality and class, and queer and LGBTQI+ histories of the Global South. For an overview that centers on the United States, see Regina KUNZEL, "The Power of Queer History," *American Historical Review*, 123/5, 2018, 1560–1582.
39. Although growing in many places, the bulk of queer history is still being written in North America, where institutional support for queer and sexual history is far better established than anywhere else. In terms of its focus and priorities, the field reflects this imbalance in many ways.
40. Held in Budapest in October 2015, an interdisciplinary conference on *Sex and Sexuality in East-Central Europe: Past and Present* signaled this shift, which is also clearly reflected in the changing program of the biennial European Social Sciences History Conference's Sexuality Network over the past decade. On the conference, see Łukasz SZULC, "Histories of Sexualities in Central and Eastern Europe," *Notches*, November 24, 2015, https://notchesblog.com/2015/11/24/histories-of-sexualities-in-central-and-eastern-europe, last accessed on July 18, 2023. Among many exciting recent studies on East and East-Central Europe are Agnieszka KOŚIAŃSKA, Kateřina LIŠKOVÁ, and Hadley Z. RENKIN (eds.), *The Routledge Handbook of Sexuality in East Central Europe*, London: Routledge, 2025; Rustam ALEXANDER, *Regulating Homosexuality in Soviet Russia, 1956–91: A Different History*, Manchester: Manchester University Press, 2021; Agnieszka KOŚCIAŃSKA, *Gender, Pleasure and Violence: The Construction of Expert Knowledge of Sexuality in Poland*, Bloomington: Indiana University Press, 2021; Agnieszka KOŚCIAŃSKA, *To See a Moose: The History of Polish Sex Education*, New York: Berghahn Books, 2021; Anita KURIMAY, *Queer Budapest, 1873–1961*, Chicago: University of Chicago Press, 2020; Richard C. M. MOLE (ed.), *Soviet and Post-Soviet Sexualities*, Abingdon: Routledge, 2019; Łukasz SZULC, *Transnational Homosexuals in Communist Poland: Cross-Border Flows in Gay and Lesbian Magazines*, Cham: Springer, 2019; Dan HEALEY, *Russian Homophobia from Stalin to Sochi*, London: Bloomsbury Academic, 2018; Kateřina LIŠKOVÁ, *Sexual Liberation, Socialist Style: Communist Czechoslovakia and the Science of Desire*, Cambridge: Cambridge University Press, 2018; Conor O'DWYER, *Coming Out of Communism: The Emergence of LGBT Activism in Eastern Europe*, New York: New York University Press, 2018; Scott SPECTOR, *Violent Sensations: Sex, Crime, and Utopia in Vienna and Berlin, 1860–1914*, Chicago: University of Chicago Press, 2016; Kārlis VĒRDIŅŠ and Jānis OZOLIŅŠ (eds.), *Queer Stories of Europe*, Newcastle upon Tyne: Cambridge Scholars, 2016; Joise MCLELLAN, *Love in the Time of Communism: Intimacy and Sexuality in the GDR*, Cambridge: Cambridge University Press, 2011.
41. For Eastern and East-Central Europe, see the previous note. On other parts of Europe, see, among others, Christopher EWING, *The Color of Desire: The Queer Politics of Race in the Federal Republic of Germany after 1970*, Ithaca, NY: Cornell University Press, 2024; Javier FERNÁNDEZ GALEANO, *Maricas: Queer Cultures and State Violence in Argentina and Spain, 1942–1982*, Lincoln: University of Nebraska Press, 2024; Katie SUTTON, *Sexuality in Modern German History*, London: Bloomsbury Academic, 2023; Samuel C. HUNEKE, *States of*

Liberation: Gay Men between Dictatorship and Democracy in Cold War Germany, Toronto: University of Toronto Press, 2022; W. Jake NEWSOME, *Pink Triangle Legacies: Coming Out in the Shadow of the Holocaust*, Ithaca, NY: Cornell University Press, 2022; Craig GRIFFITHS, *The Ambivalence of Gay Liberation: Male Homosexual Politics in 1970s West Germany*, Oxford: Oxford University Press, 2021; Janin AFKEN and Bendikt WOLF (eds.), *Sexual Culture in Germany in the 1970s: A Golden Age for Queers?*, Basingstoke: Palgrave Macmillan, 2019; Christine BURNS (ed.), *Trans Britain: Our Journey from the Shadows*, London: Unbound, 2019; Rebecca JENNINGS, *Tomboys and Bachelor Girls: A Lesbian History of Post-War Britain*, Manchester: Manchester University Press, 2017; Todd SHEPPARD, *Sex, France, and Arab Men, 1962–1979*, Chicago: University of Chicago Press, 2017; Jennifer EVANS, *Life among the Ruins: Cityscape and Sexuality in Cold War Berlin*, Basingstoke: Palgrave Macmillan, 2016; Brian LEWIS, *Wolfenden's Witnesses: Homosexuality in Postwar Britain*, Basingstoke: Palgrave Macmillan, 2016; Jennifer EVANS and Matt COOK (eds.), *Queer Cities, Queer Cultures: Europe since 1945*, London: Bloomsbury Academic, 2014; Geoffroy HUARD, *Los antisociales: Historia de la homosexualidad en Barcelona y París, 1945–1975*, Madrid: Marcial Pons, 2014; Massimo PRAERO, *Le moment politique de l'homosexualité: Mouvements, identités et communautés en France*, Lyon: Presses universitaires de Lyon, 2014; Antoine IDIER, *Les alinéas au placard: L'Abrogation du délit d'homosexualité, 1977–1982*, Paris: Cartouche, 2013; Heike BAUER and Matt COOK (eds.), *Queer 1950s: Rethinking Sexuality in the Postwar Years*, Basingstoke: Palgrave Macmillan, 2012; Andreas PRETZEL and Volker WEISS (eds.), *Rosa Radikale: Die Schwulenbewegung der 70er Jahre*, Hamburg: Männerschwarm, 2012; Clayton J. WHISNANT, *Male Homosexuality in West Germany: Between Persecution and Freedom, 1945–1969*, Basingstoke: Palgrave Macmillan, 2012; Andreas PRETZEL, *Homosexuellenpolitik in der frühen Bundesrepublik*, Hamburg: Männerschwarm, 2010; Scott GUNTHER, *The Elastic Closet: A History of Homosexuality in France, 1942–present*, Basingstoke: Palgrave Macmillan, 2009; Julian JACKSON, *Living in Arcadia: Homosexuality, Politics, and Morality in France from the Liberation to Aids*, Chicago: University of Chicago Press, 2009; Lucy ROBINSON, *Gay Men and the Left in Post-War Britain: How the Personal Got Political*, Manchester: Manchester University Press, 2007.

42. For example: "Around the turn of the 20th century, European sex scientists produced an unprecedented scope of literature on the subject of [same-sex desire]." CHIANG, "Liberating Sex, Knowing Desire," 44.
43. I draw on the works of Laura Doan and Valerie Traub in letting my approach be informed by the problematic nature of the archive. Whereas similarly perplexing archives have led them to venture beyond questions of identity, subjectivity, and modernity, I choose to revisit such questions in order to show how problematic assumptions about their historical relevance or centrality can be. DOAN, *Disturbing Practices*, chap. 1; TRAUB, *Thinking Sex*, 12–13.
44. FOUCAULT, *The History of Sexuality*, 8.
45. In the words of Anjali Arondekar: "can an empty archive also be full?" Anjali ARONDEKAR, *For the Record: On Sexuality and the Colonial Archive in India*, Durham, NC: Duke University Press, 2009, 1. Archival silences and the historical

connections between silencing (in whatever form it takes) and subordination have often been analyzed most powerfully with reference to (post)colonial contexts. See, among others, Kevin OLSON, *Subaltern Silence: A Postcolonial Genealogy*, New York: Columbia University Press, 2024; Michael MOSS and David THOMAS (eds.), *Archival Silences: Missing, Lost and, Uncreated Archives*, London: Routledge, 2021; David THOMAS, Simon FOWLER, and Valerie JOHNSON, *The Silence of the Archive*, London: Facet, 2017; Michel-Rolph TROUILLOT, *Silencing the Past: Power and the Production of History*, Boston: Beacon, 2015 [1995].

46. FOUCAULT, *The History of Sexuality*, 27.
47. Robert D. TOBIN, *Peripheral Desires: The German Discovery of Sex*, Philadelphia: University of Philadelphia Press, 2015, 4. Tobin is relying here on a claim by the German sexologist Magnus Hirschfeld.
48. My perspective owes much to Robert A. NYE, "The History of Sexuality in Context: National Sexological Traditions," *Science in Context*, 4/2, 1991, 387–406.
49. Regina KUNZEL, "The Uneven History of Modern American Sexuality," *Modern American History*, 1/1, 2018, 97–100, 98. Also see KUNZEL, *Criminal Intimacy*, 6.
50. A thorough comparison with other majority Catholic countries, like Poland, Ireland, Austro-Hungary, Italy, and those on the Iberian Peninsula would no doubt yield interesting results. The Polish case remains largely understudied. In Ireland anti-imperial resentment helped to cast sodomy as a British vice, and Wilde's recuperation as a martyr of Protestant prudery overshadowed his sexual 'sins' until the establishment of Catholic hegemony after independence in 1922 smothered the issue in silence. The situation in the Austro-Hungarian empire was heavily inflected by the criminalization of homosexual acts, the cultural and intellectual ties with Germany, a series of widely reported scandals, and a sensationalist press, which Belgium did not have. Chiara Beccalossi has demonstrated that sexual 'perversions' were debated very actively among a powerful medical profession, much of which identified strongly with radical positivism and with the new secular Italian state in opposition to a reactionary Vatican hostile to Italian unification. Anticlericalism also played a role in nurturing the discourse of perversion in Spain, where it was further fueled by anxieties over geopolitical decline understood in the gendered terms of emasculation. Research on Portugal is still limited, but scandals and literature seem to have pushed the issue of homosexuality into the open during the late nineteenth century and French influence was significant. See Averill E. EARLS, "Unnatural Offenses of English Import: The Political Association of Englishness and Same-Sex Desire in Nineteenth-Century Irish Nationalist Media," *Journal of the History of Sexuality*, 28/3, 2019, 396–424; Eibhear WALSHE, *Oscar's Shadow: Wilde, Homosexuality and Modern Ireland*, Cork: Cork University Press, 2011, chaps. 1–3; Diarmaid FERRITER, *Occasions of Sin: Sex and Society in Modern Ireland*, London: Profile, 2010, 60–65; Scott SPECTOR, *Violent Sensations*, chap. 3; Chiara BECCALOSSI, *Female Sexual Inversion: Same-Sex Desires in Italian and British Sexology, ca. 1870–1920*, Basingstoke: Palgrave Macmillan, 2012, chap. 2; Richard M. CLEMINSON and Francisco VÁZQUEZ GARCÍA, *'Los Invisibles': A History of Male Homosexuality in Spain, 1850–1940*, Cardiff: University of Wales Press, 2007, chap. 5; Fernando CUROPOS, *L'Émergence de l'homosexualité dans la littérature portugaise (1875–1910)*, Paris: L'Harmattan, 2016.

51. Before the Reformation, sodomy had been an elastic theological and juridical category, the multiple meanings of which varied. By the eighteenth century, however, notably in England and the Dutch Republic, it had become a much-discussed ideological and eschatological concept in Protestant anti-Catholic rhetoric, and it was firmly connected to homoeroticism, which, in the process, began crystallizing into a thing in itself. Harry G. Cocks, *Visions of Sodom: Religion, Homoerotic Desire, and the End of the World in England, c. 1550–1850*, Chicago: University of Chicago Press, 2017; Theo van der Meer, "Sodomy and Its Discontents: Discourse, Desire, and the Rise of a Same-Sex Proto-Something in the Early Modern Republic," *Historical Reflections/Réflexions Historiques*, 33/1, 2007, 41–67; Theo van der Meer, *Sodoms zaad in Nederland: Het ontstaan van homoseksualiteit in de vroegmoderne tijd*, Nijmegen: SUN, 1995. On the emergence of sodomy as a category in the Middle Ages, see Mark D. Jordan, *The Invention of Sodomy*, Chicago: University of Chicago Press, 1997. On sodomy in the Southern Low Countries from the Middle Ages to 1700, see Jonas Roelens, *Citizens and Sodomites: Persecution and Perception of Sodomy in the Southern Low Countries (1400–1700)*, Leiden: Brill, 2024.
52. Paradoxically, however, as Jeremy Carrette has noted, Foucault's central concern with religion in his analyses of the history of sexuality and the self (i.e. Christianity and Catholicism in particular) remained ambivalent, undertheorized, and even essentialist. Jeremy R. Carrette, *Foucault and Religion: Spiritual Corporality and Political Spirituality*, Routledge: London, 2000, esp. chap. 2.
53. I agree with Harry Cocks, where he writes: "Because historians of sexuality have often been in search of a secularizing modernity, they have frequently tended to overlook religious pronouncements as merely conventional. I argue instead that these notions only gained power by virtue of being continually repeated." Cocks, *Visions of Sodom*, 11. Compare with Laura M. Ramsay, *Sexuality and the Church of England, 1918–1980*, Cham: Palgrave Macmillan, 2024, 5–8.
54. Exceptions, though with approaches different from my own, include Timothy Verhoeven, *Sexual Crime, Religion and Masculinity in Fin-de-siècle France: The Flamidien Affair*, Basingstoke: Palgrave Macmillan, 2019; Lowell Gallagher, Frederick S. Roden, and Patricia J. Smith (eds.), *Catholic Figures, Queer Narratives*, Basingstoke: Palgrave Macmillan, 2006; Frederick S. Roden, *Same-Sex Desire in Victorian Religious Culture*, Basingstoke: Palgrave Macmillan, 2002. The lack of emphasis on religion is all the more remarkable because of its importance in stimulating the concern with sexual deviance and sodomy prior to the nineteenth century. See, for example, Cocks, *Visions of Sodom*; Katherine Crawford, *European sexualities, 1400–1800*, Cambridge: Cambridge University Press, 2007; James A. Brundage, *Law, Sex, and Christian Society in Medieval Europe*, Chicago: University of Chicago Press, 1987; Edward J. Bristow, *Vice and Vigilance: Purity Movements in Britain since 1700*, Dublin: Gill-Macmillan and Rowman and Littlefield, 1977. Religion was a driving force behind the purity movements of the nineteenth and early twentieth centuries too. See Edward R. Dickinson, *Sex, Freedom and Power in Imperial Germany 1880–1914*, Cambridge: Cambridge University Press, 2014; Allan C. Carlson, *Godly Seed: American Evangelicals Confront Birth Control, 1873–1973*, New Brunswick, NJ: Transaction, 2012; Jenny Daggers and Diana Neal (eds.), *Sex, Gender, and Religion: Josephine Butler*

Revisited, New York: Peter Lang, 2006; Isabell LISBERG-HAAG, *'Die Unzucht – das Grab der Völker': Die Evangelische Sittlichkeitsbewegung und die 'sexuelle Moderne' (1870–1918)*, Münster: Lit, 2002; Harry OOSTERHUIS, *De smalle marges van de katholieke moraal: Homoseksualiteit in katholiek Nederland 1900–1970*, Amsterdam: s.e., 1992.

55. It does so in the growing recognition that what constitutes 'religion' is neither obvious nor stable from a conceptual, experiential, historical, or methodological point of view. As Kathryn Lofton writes: "Tackling religion as a subject of historical inquiry is difficult for some of the same reasons tackling race and gender [and indeed sexuality] is so challenging: because the tools we use to study these subjects are the very same tools that have comprised their formulation as hierarchical distinctions between human beings." Because of this, she opines that historians must reckon with themselves "as interpretive actors, especially as we search." This book is a part of this reckoning process and, as such, only one unsteady step along the way of a path of continual exploration as my work turns increasingly towards religion. Kathryn LOFTON, "Why Religion Is Hard for Historians (and How It Can Be Easier)," *Modern American History*, 3/1, 2020, 69–86, 85. Work I have previously done on religion includes Wannes DUPONT, "Global Catholicism and the Population Bomb," in: Barbara KLICH-KLUCZEWSKA, Joachim VON PUTTKAMER, and Immo REBITSCHEK (eds.), *Biopolitics in Central and Eastern Europe in the 20th Century: Fearing for the Nation*, Abingdon: Routledge, 2023, 121–134; Wannes DUPONT, "Of Human Love: Catholics Campaigning for Sexual Aggiornamento in Postwar Belgium," in: Alana HARRIS (ed.), *The Schism of '68: Catholicism, Contraception and 'Humanae Vitae' in Europe, 1945–1975*, Basingstoke: Palgrave Macmillan, 2018, 49–71; Wannes DUPONT, "The Case for Contraception. Medicine, Morality and Sexology at the Catholic University of Leuven (1930–1968)," *Histoire, médecine et santé*, 13, 2018, 49–65; Wannes DUPONT, "In Good Faith: Belgian Catholics' Attempts to Overturn the Ban on Contraception (1945–1968)," in: Cécile VANDERPELEN and Caroline SÄGESSER (eds.), *La Sainte Famille: Sexualité et parentalité dans l'Église catholique*, Brussels: Éditions de l'Université de Bruxelles, 2017, 67–76; DUPONT, "Catholics and Sexual Change."

56. Compare with Helen SMITH, *Masculinity, Class and Same-Sex Desire in Industrial England, 1895–1957*, Basingstoke: Palgrave Macmillan, 2015, 4.

57. In this sense, my approach is close to what Foucault has called a 'problematization,' which, in the words of Jeremy Carette, is "a way of identifying how and why issues are positioned in a particular matrix of concern in different historical periods." See CARRETTE, *Foucault and Religion*, 130; Michel FOUCAULT, "Polemics, Politics, and Problematizations," in: Paul RABINOW (ed.), *Michel Foucault: Ethics, Subjectivity and Truth*, translated by Robert HURLEY, New York: The New Press, 1994, 111–119.

58. My research is inspired by Foucault's concept and Joan Scott's defense of 'effective history.' At the same time, and at the risk of drawing on "the vocabulary of theory in the service of its domestication" in the way Scott warns against (p. 22), my approach tries to combine critique with due attention to context and continuity as proposed by David Halperin in his careful response to Eve Sedgwick. Meanwhile, George Chauncey's work remains a paragon of blending insight with evidence

and accessibility worth emulating. Michel FOUCAULT, "Nietzsche, Genealogy, History," in: Donald F. BOUCHARD (ed.), *Language, Couter-Memory, Practice: Selected Essays and Interviews*, Ithaca, NY: Cornell University Press, 1977, 139–164; Joan W. SCOTT, "History-Writing as Critique," in: Keith JENKINS, Sue MORGAN, and Alun MUNSLOW (eds.), *Manifestos for History*, London: Routledge, 2007, 19–38; HALPERIN, *How to Do the History of Homosexuality*; Eve KOSOFSKY SEDGWICK, *Epistemology of the Closet*, Berkeley: University of California Press, 1990; George CHAUNCEY, *Gay New York: Gender, Urban Culture and the Making of the Gay Male World, 1890–1940*, New York: Basic Books, 1994.

59. As Jennifer Terry once aptly put it: "While many aspects of the 'hidden from history' hypothesis pertain to gay men as well as lesbians, lesbian and male homosexuality [and indeed other sex/gender minorities] are shaped by different kinds of historical elision, different conditions of visibility, and different strategies of resistance." Jennifer TERRY, "Theorizing Deviant Historiography," *Differences: A Journal of Feminist Cultural Studies*, 3/2, 1991, 55–73, 68. The problem of male homosexuality's prevalence over other minorities in historiography is an old one. For valuable critiques thereof, see Linda GARBER, "Where in the World Are the Lesbians?," *Journal of the History of Sexuality*, 14/1–2, 2005, 28–50; Susan S. LANSER, *The Sexuality of History: Modernity and the Sapphic, 1565–1830*, Chicago: University of Chicago Press, 2014.

60. There is still preciously little historical work about modern Belgium to draw on. One exception is Tommy DE GANCK, *Le sexe, une invention moderne? Réactions face aux anomalies sexuelles et à l'hermaphrodisme en Belgique contemporaine, 1830–1914*, Brussels: Université des Femmes, 2013.

61. HALPERIN, *How to Do the History of Homosexuality*, 107.

62. With Judith Bennett, I believe that "introducing into historical research a productive uncertainty born of likeness and resemblance, not identity," offers a pragmatic solution to terminological problems. I also take on board Jack Halberstam's call for a 'perverse presentism' in that there is little point assuming that sexual and gender identities were ever straightforward and monomorphous in the past when they clearly are not in the present either. As Laura Doan has put it: "The problem for the historian of sexuality is how to explore the sexual past ... without falling back on ... seductively simple labels." I have thus used male homosexual acts heuristically, but it is clear from the evidence that contemporaries associated a cluster of often contradictory things with the men they were talking about, who only had in common that they had sex with other men or were suspected thereof on the basis of gendered behavior. This study focuses primarily on the historical discourse of homosexuality in a broad and elastic sense. It makes only limited claims (in Chapter 1) about the emergence and the nature of identities associated with that discourse. See Judith M. BENNETT, "'Lesbian-Like' and the Social History of Lesbians," *Journal of the History of Sexuality*, 9/1–2, 2000, 1–24, 14; Jack HALBERSTAM, *Female Masculinity*, Durham, NC: Duke University Press, 1998, chap. 2; DOAN, *Disturbing Practices*, 52.

63. *Diagnose van het anders-zijn*, TV-documentary directed by Piet De Valkeneer, first broadcast by Belgische Radio- en Televisieomroep on December 1, 1966. A copy is preserved in the Fonds Suzan Daniel at the Institute for Social History in Ghent.

1 Cruising through a Crossroads of Europe

1. Berthold AUERBACH, "Dans les bas-fonds de Bruxelles: Choses vues," *Journal des Tribunaux*, 12/1019, 1893, 1457–1468, 1460. On the culture of slumming and its influence on journalism, see Seth KOVEN, *Slumming: Sexual and Social Politics in Victorian London*, Princeton: Princeton University Press, 2004.
2. Berthold AUERBACH, "Dans les bas-fonds de Bruxelles," 1459.
3. Ibid., 1468.
4. See, for example, Julie ABRAHAM, *Metropolitan Lovers: The Homosexuality of Cities*, Minneapolis: University of Minnesota Press, 2009; Phil HUBBARD, "Queering the City: Homosociality and Homosexuality in the Modern Metropolis," *Journal of Urban History*, 33/2, 2007, 310–319; Matt COOK, "Urban Desires," *History Workshop Journal*, 62/1, 2006, 292–300; Robert ALDRICH, "Homosexuality and the City: An Historical Overview," *Urban Studies*, 41/9, 2004, 1719–1737.
5. To name only a few: Andrew I. ROSS, *Public City/Public Sex: Homosexuality, Prostitution, and Urban Culture in Nineteenth-Century Paris*, Philadelphia: Temple University Press, 2019; Robert BEACHY, *Gay Berlin: Birthplace of a Modern Identity*, New York: Knopf, 2014; François BUOT, *Gay Paris: Une histoire du Paris interlope entre 1900 et 1940*, Paris: Fayard, 2013; HOULBROOK, *Queer London*; Régis REVENIN, *Homosexualité et prostitution masculines à Paris 1870–1918*, Paris: L'Harmattan, 2005; COOK, *London and the Culture of Homosexuality, 1885–1914*; CHAUNCEY, *Gay New York*.
6. These and further figures have originally been drawn from the *Almanach de Gotha* and/or *Ritter's geographisch-statistisches Lexikon*. They have been made available in a systematized manner through www.populstat.info. Also see Appendix A of Andrew LEES and Lynn H. LEES, *Cities and the Making of Modern Europe, 1750–1914*, Cambridge: Cambridge University Press, 2010, 287–288.
7. Steven MAYNARD, "Through a Hole in the Lavatory Wall: Homosexual Subcultures, Police Surveillance, and the Dialectics of Discovery, Toronto, 1890–1930," *Journal of the History of Sexuality*, 5/2, 1994, 207–242.
8. For an analysis of European urbanity that decenters the common focus on London, Paris, and Berlin, see Rosemary WAKEMAN, *A Modern History of European Cities, 1815 to the Present*, London: Bloomsbury Academic, 2020.
9. For a European overview, see Rainer FREMDLING, "De Europese spoorwegen 1825–2001, een overzicht," in: Bart VAN DER HERTEN, Michelangelo VAN MEERTEN, and Greta VERBEURGT (eds.), *Sporen in België: 175 jaar spoorwegen, 75 jaar NMBS*, Leuven: Leuven University Press, 2001, 20–63. On Belgium, see Bart VAN DER HERTEN, *België onder stoom: Transport en communicatie tijdens de 19de eeuw*, Leuven: Leuven University Press, 2004, 289–375.
10. Ginette KURGAN-VAN HENTENRYK, "Economie en vervoer," in: Jean STENGERS (ed.), *Brussel: Groei van een hoofdstad*, Antwerp: Mercatorfonds, 1986, 216–226, 222.
11. On domestic servants, see Valérie PIETTE, *Domestiques et servantes: Des vies sous condition. Essai sur le travail domestique en Belgique au 19e siècle*, Brussels: Académie royale de Belgique, 2000.
12. Émile VANDERVELDE, *L'Exode rural et le retour aux champs*, Paris: Alcan, 1903, 94–115; Yves SEGERS and Leen VAN MOLLE, *Leven van het land: Boeren in België, 1750–2000*, Leuven: Davidsfonds, 2004, 50–51.

13. Singles constituted 52.5 percent of the population in the wider administrative arrondissement and 55 percent in the municipality of Brussels itself. *Statistique de la Belgique: Population. Recensement général du 31 décembre 1890*, 2 vols., Brussels: Lesigne, 1893, vol. 2, 30–53.
14. Ibid., 31.
15. *Ville de Bruxelles: Les recensements de 1910*, Brussels: Guyot, 1912, 248–249; *Statistique de la Belgique: Population. Recensement général du 31 décembre 1910*, 5 vols., Brussels: Weissenbruch, 1915, vol. 4, 81.
16. CHAUNCEY, *Gay New York*, 135. Compare with John D'EMILIO, "Capitalism and Gay Identity," in: Ann SNITOW, Christine STANSELL, and Sharon THOMPSON (eds.), *Powers of Desire: The Politics of Sexuality*, New York: Monthly Review Press, 1983, 100–113.
17. Compiled on the basis of SABF, CAB, Series II: Sentenced Correctional Case Files 1811–1884, year 1883, file 3182, reg. 764–765.
18. SABF, CFIB, Series II: Sentenced Correctional Case Files 1893–1899, year 1897, port. 1147, reg. 159.
19. Léon MASSION-VERNIORY and Raymond CHARLES, "Les aspects médico-psychologiques, sociaux et juridiques de l'homophilie," *Revue de droit pénal et de criminologie*, 38/3, 1957, 241–327, 306–307, and 317.
20. Ibid., 309 and 312.
21. This set has been compiled on the basis of BCA, Police records, Twentieth century, Series D, no. D59-104: 'Pédérastes'; SABF, CAB, Series II: Sentenced Correctional Case Files 1811–1884, year 1883, file 3182, reg. 764–765; SABF, CFIB, Series I: Sentenced Correctional Case Files 1795 (year IV)-1896, year 1848, file 669, reg. 40; ibid., year 1864, file 696, reg. 280; ibid., year 1871, file 706, reg. 1126; SABF, CFIB, Series II: Sentenced Correctional Case Files 1893–1899, year 1897, port. 1147, reg. 159.
22. SABF, CFIB, Series I: Sentenced Correctional Case Files 1795 (year IV)-1896, year 1864, file 696, reg. 280.
23. SABF, CFIB, Series II: Sentenced Correctional Case Files 1893–1899, year 1895, port. 376, reg. 5577.
24. Henri JOLY, *La Belgique criminelle*, Paris: Lecoffre, 1907, 159–160.
25. Ernest MAHAIM, *Les abonnements d'ouvriers sur les lignes des chemins de fer belges et leurs effets sociaux*, Brussels: Misch and Thron, 1910, 33. On Belgium's internationally pioneering development of railway commuting through subsidized fares, see Donald WEBER, "Werkmanstreinen en de geboorte van de moderne pendelaar, 1870–1914," *Brood & Rozen*, 15/4, 2009, https://doi.org/10.21825/br.v14i5.3406, last accessed on August 12, 2024, 131–148.
26. Janet L. POLASKY, *Reforming Urban Labor: Routes to the City, Roots in the Country*, Ithaca, NY: Cornell University Press, 2010, 162–181.
27. *Parlementaire Handelingen: Kamer van Volksvertegenwoordigers*, November 29, 1905, 49. Compare with KOVEN, *Slumming*, 42–43.
28. Edmond DEFFERNEZ, *Des maisons de logement pour ouvriers célibataires: Rapport présenté au Congrès contre l'alcoolisme, tenu à Bruxelles en septembre 1897*, Brecht: Braeckmans, 1898. Compare with Nicolas KENNY, *The Feel of the City: Experiences of Urban Transformation*, Toronto: University of Toronto Press, 2014, 137–141.

29. Julien CHEVALIER, *Une maladie de la personnalité: L'Inversion sexuelle*, Lyon: Storck and Masson, 1893, 202.
30. Ibid., 199–203.
31. JOLY, *La Belgique criminelle*, 359.
32. On the politics of working-class housing, see POLASKY, *Reforming Urban Labor*. On vagrancy, see Rik VERCAMMEN and Vicky VANRUYSSEVELDT, "Van centraal beleid naar lokale praktijk: Het 'probleem' van landloperij in België (1890–1910)," *Journal of Belgian History*, 45/1, 2015, 120–161.
33. HOULBROOK, *Queer London*, 42.
34. On urban planning and urbanization in Brussels, see *Brussel, geplande geschiedenis: Stedenbouw in de 19e en 20e eeuw*, Brussels: Meert, 2017.
35. Ibid., chap. 1.
36. On urinals in Paris, see ROSS, *Public City/Public Sex*, chap. 3.
37. *Ville de Bruxelles: Bulletin communal. Année 1881*, 2 vols., Brussels: Baertsoen, 1881, vol. 1, 480. On the count de Germiny, see William A. PENISTON, "A Public Offense against Decency: The Trial of the Count de Germiny and the 'Moral Order' of the Third Republic," in: George ROBB and Nancy ERBER (eds.), *Disorder in the Court: Trials and Sexual Conflict at the Turn of the Century*, London: MacMillan, 1999, 12–32.
38. Claire BILLEN and Jean-Michel DECROLY, *De kleinste kamertjes in de grootstad: Openbaar sanitair in Brussel van de Middeleeuwen tot vandaag*, Brussels: Musea van de Stad Brussel, 2003, 39.
39. It is plausible that this booklet was used as an early kind of cruising guide. *Indicateur des urinoirs de Bruxelles contenant un Tableau officiel des Urinoirs et des chroniques, articles et nouvelles littéraires se rapportant à l'urinoir et à son histoire ainsi qu'à l'Art de bien uriner*, Brussels: s.e., s.a.
40. For example, SABF, CFIB, Series II: Sentenced Correctional Case Files 1893–1899, year 1898, port. 723, reg. 5243 (affidavit dated September 17, 1898, document 4).
41. SABF, CFIB, Series II: Sentenced Correctional Case Files 1893–1899, year 1898, port. 700, reg. 4053.
42. SABF, CAB, Series II: Sentenced Correctional Case Files 1811–1884, year 1883, file 3182, reg. 764–765 (police report dated June 20, 1882, document 20).
43. SABF, CFIB, Series II: Sentenced Correctional Case Files 1893–1899, year 1898, port. 678, reg. 3131.
44. SABF, CFIB, Series II: Sentenced Correctional Case Files 1893–1899, year 1893, port. 909, reg. 314. On Brussels' recreational infrastructure, see Daniel BERGER, Didier COLARD, Michel DE REYMAEKER et al., *Nachtraven*, s.l.: Gemeentekrediet, 1987.
45. SABF, CAB, Series II: Sentenced Correctional Case Files 1811–1884, year 1883, file 3182, reg. 764–765 (recalled in a police report dated June 20, 1882, document 20).
46. SABF, CFIB, Series I: Sentenced Correctional Case Files 1795 (year IV)-1896, year 1871, file 706, reg. 1126 (affidavit dated January 9, 1872, document 13). See also 1147 159 (police report dated April 8, 1897, document 11).
47. SABF, CFIB, Series II: Sentenced Correctional Case Files 1893–1899, year 1891, port. 902, reg. 122 (police report dated December 4, 1891, unnumbered document).

48. SABF, CFIB, Series I: Sentenced Correctional Case Files 1795 (year IV)-1896 year 1871, file 706, reg. 1126 (affidavit dated January 10, 1872, document 17).
49. SABF, CAB, Series II: Sentenced Correctional Case Files 1811–1884, year 1883, file 3182, reg. 764–765 (police report dated June 20, 1882, document 20).
50. Calculated on the basis of Charles LAGASSSE and Charles DE QUÉKER, *Enquête sur les habitations ouvrières en 1890: Rapport présenté au Comité de Patronage de la Ville de Bruxelles*, Brussels: De Bremaeker-Wauts, 1890.
51. Maurice SAEY, *Les dessous de Bruxelles*, Brussels: Dujardin, 1908, 94.
52. On Wilhelm, see Kevin DUBOUT, *Der Richter und Sein Tagebuch: Eugen Wilhelm als Elsässer und homosexueller Aktivist im Deutschen Kaiserreich*, Frankfurt am Main: Campus, 2018, 178.
53. NUMA PRAETORIUS, "Die Bibliographie der Homosexualität für das Jahr 1901 mit Ausschluss der Belletristik," *Jahrbuch für sexuelle Zwischenstufen mit besonderer Berücksichtigung der Homosexualität*, 4, 1902, 775–920, 800.
54. Gaston-L. HUYSMANS, "À propos du monstrueux crime de la Citadelle de Liège," *L'Étoile belge*, August 19, 1931. A clipping of this article has been preserved in GSA, Ministry of Justice, Administration of Public Security, Aliens department, General files, file 1433 'Pédérastie 1930–1960.'
55. Quoted in Jonathan FRYER, *Isherwood*, London: New English Library, 1977, 159.
56. The origin of this term remains unclear.
57. See, for instance, the testimony given by Corneille Dierckx in SABF, CAB, Series II: Sentenced Correctional Case Files 1811–1884, year 1883, file 3182, reg. 764–765 (affidavit dated April 2, 1882, document 14 – excerpts from testimony given in a civil suit).
58. Ibid. (affidavit dated June 2, 1883, document 20).
59. SABF, CFIB, Series II: Sentenced Correctional Case Files 1893–1899, year 1897, port. 1147, reg. 159 (affidavit dated January 23, 1897, number 2).
60. SABF, CFIB, Series II: Sentenced Correctional Case Files 1893–1899, year 1899, port. 868, reg. 1899 (affidavit dated June 19, 1899, unnumbered document).
61. Current in France too, the term *tapette* was surprisingly rare in the examined court files. For examples, see SABF, CFIB, Series II: Sentenced Correctional Case Files 1893–1899, year 1897, port. 1147, reg. 159 (affidavit dated January 23, 1897, documents 2 and 3); SABF, CFIB, Juvenile Court, Sentenced Case Files 1917–1920 and 1954–1959, year 1917, reg. 932.
62. SABF, CAB, Series II: Sentenced Correctional Case Files 1811–1884, year 1883, file 3182, reg. 764–765 (affidavit dated April 2, 1882, document 14 – excerpts from testimony given in a civil suit).
63. Jean-Claude FÉRAY, *Grecques, les mœurs du hanneton? Histoire du mot pédéraste et de ses dérivés en langue française*, Paris: Quintes-feuilles, 2004.
64. Félix CARLIER, *Les deux prostitutions*, Paris: Dentu, 1887, 283.
65. Though this is unsubstantiated by my evidence or by that of Régis Revenin, French observers opined that male queers often acted as the pimps of female prostitutes. Ibid., 372–373; CHEVALIER, *Une maladie de la personnalité*, 185–186; REVENIN, *Homosexualité et prostitution*, 76.
66. On Belgian masculinities, see Josephine HOEGAERTS, *Masculinity and Nationhood, 1830–1910: Constructions of Identity and Citizenship in Belgium*, Basingstoke: Palgrave Macmillan, 2014.

67. SABF, CAB, Series II: Sentenced Correctional Case Files 1811–1884, year 1883, file 3182, reg. 764–765 (affidavit dated February 7, 1882, document 2 – witness 10).
68. SABF, CFIB, Civil Chambers, Minutes of court sessions and rulings 1871–1939, volume 214, no. 456 (October 20, 1900 – Daumière v. Félix).
69. "Tribunal civil d'Anvers (1re ch.): Présidence de M. Op de Beeck. 26 mai 1888. Droit civil. Divorce. Injures graves. Pédérastie. Adultère hors du domicile conjugal. Recevabilité," *Journal des Tribunaux*, 7/538, 1888, 840–842, 840–841. See also "Civ. Anvers (1er ch.), 26 mai 1888: Divorce. Injures graves. Pédérastie. Adultère hors du domicile conjugal. Recevabilité," *Pandectes périodiques: Recueil de jurisprudence, de législation et de doctrine*, 1, 1888, 1544–1545.
70. For men, unlike women, adultery was only illegal if their mistresses lived under the same roof as their spouses. See Josephine HOEGAERTS, "Trust and Temptation: Adultery and Masculinity in the Nineteenth-Century Divorce Court," *Sextant: Revue du groupe interdisciplinaire d'études sur les femmes et le genre*, 27, 2009, 15–28.
71. SABF, CFIB, Series I: Sentenced Correctional Case Files 1795 (year IV)-1896, year 1864, file 696, reg. 280 (affidavit dated November 20, 1864, document 595).
72. Georges EEKHOUD, "De Oorsprong en de Evolutie van een Werk," *Ontwaking*, 4, 1904, 15–31, 30.
73. SABF, CFIB, Series II: Sentenced Correctional Case Files 1893–1899, year 1899, port. 868, reg. 5598 (affidavit dated June 19, 1899, unnumbered document).
74. Such conditional tolerance has also been noted in SMITH, *Masculinity, Class and Same-Sex Desire in Industrial England, 1895–1957*, chap. 5.
75. Magnus HIRSCHFELD, *Von einst bis jetzt: Geschichte einer homosexuellen Bewegung 1897–1922. Herausgegeben und mit einem Nachwort versehen von Manfred Herzer und James Steakley*, Berlin: Rosa Winkel, 1986 [1922–1923], 69. Compare my translation with Magnus HIRSCHFELD, *Memoir Celebrating 25 Years of the First LGBT Organization*, translated by Michael A. LOMBARDI-NASH, s.l.: Urania Manuscripts, 2019, unpaged ebook.
76. In 1910, a total of 388 persons lived on their own in the Rue Haute. No other street in Brussels had even half that many. Several other roads where a lot of singles lived also lay in the Marolles neighborhood, including the Rue Blaes (179), the Rue du Miroir (146), the Rue des Tanneurs (148), and the Rue de Terre Neuve (158). See *Ville de Bruxelles: Les recensements de 1910*, 223–1039 (Recensement spécial des logements).
77. Magnus HIRSCHFELD, *Die Homosexualität des Mannes und des Weibes*, Berlin: Marcus, 1914, 570.
78. SABF, CFIB, Series II: Sentenced Correctional Case Files 1893–1899, year 1897, port. 1147, reg. 159 (affidavit dated April 14, 1897, document 12).
79. SABF, CAB, Series II: Sentenced Correctional Case Files 1811–1884, year 1883, file 3182, reg. 764–765 (police report dated June 20, 1882, document 20).
80. Ibid.
81. Jules GILL-PETERSON, *A Short History of Trans Misogyny*, London: Verso, 2024, chaps. 1 and 2.
82. "Un Crime mystérieux de la place Royale," *La Gazette*, June 13, 1899.
83. This has been richly documented for New York. See CHAUNCEY, *Gay New York*.

84. SABF, CFIB, Series II: Sentenced Correctional Case Files 1893–1899, year 1897, port. 1147, reg. 159 (affidavit dated January 23, 1897, document 2).
85. Compare with SMITH, *Masculinity, Class and Same-Sex Desire in Industrial England, 1895–1957*, 2; Charles UPCHURCH, *Before Wilde: Sex between Men in Britain's Age of Reform*, Berkeley: University of California Press, 2009, chap. 7; George CHAUNCEY, "From Sexual Inversion to Homosexuality: Medicine and the Changing Conceptualization of Female Deviance," *Salmagundi: A Quarterly of the Humanities and Social Sciences*, 58–59, 1982–1983, 114–146; George CHAUNCEY, "Christian Brotherhood or Sexual Perversion? Homosexual Identity and the Construction of Sexual Boundaries in the World War One Era," *Journal of Social History*, 19/2, 1985, 189–211.
86. SABF, CFIB, Unsorted Series of Correctional Case Files from the Interwar Period, year 1922, reg. 758 (affidavit dated October 5, 1921, unnumbered document).
87. Beyond those already cited, also see William A. PENISTON, *Pederasts and Others: Urban Culture and Sexual Identity in Nineteenth-Century Paris*, New York: Routledge, 2004; Jens RYDSTRÖM, *Sinners and Citizens: Bestiality and Homosexuality in Sweden, 1880–1950*, Chicago: University of Chicago Press, 2003; COOK, *London and the Culture of Homosexuality, 1885–1914*; Dan HEALEY, *Homosexual Desire in Revolutionary Russia: The Regulation of Sexual and Gender Dissent*, Chicago: University of Chicago Press, 2001; David HIGGS, *Queer Sites: Gay Urban Histories since 1600*, London: Routledge, 1999.
88. This is hardly a new point and perhaps even a somewhat old-fashioned one. However, the important distinctions between 'social' and 'discursive' constructivism often receive too little attention, a development that has accompanied the generally waning influence of social history and the rising popularity of more discursive approaches in recent decades, which is particularly distinct in the history of sexuality. See Steven MAYNARD, "'Without Working?' Capitalism, Urban Culture, and Gay History," *Journal of Urban History*, 30/3, 2004, 378–398.
89. Victor TAYART DE BORMS, "La prostitution masculine: Les homosexuels devant la loi," *Revue belge de la police administrative et judiciaire*, 52/136, 1931, 50–77, 53.

2 The Problems and Priorities of Surveillance

1. On the policing of homosexual acts in late eighteenth- and early nineteenth-century France, see Jeffrey MERRICK, "'Nocturnal Birds' in the Champs-Elysées: Police and Pederasty in Prerevolutionary Paris," *GLQ: A Journal of Lesbian and Gay Studies*, 8/3, 2001, 425–432; Thierry PASTORELLO, *Sodome à Paris, fin XVIIIème-milieu XIXème: L'Homosexualité masculine en construction*, Paris: Creaphis, 2011; Michael D. SIBALIS, "The Regulation of Male Homosexuality in Revolutionary and Napoleonic France, 1789–1815," in: Jeffrey MERRICK and Bryant T. RAGAN Jr. (eds.), *Homosexuality in Modern France*, New York: Oxford University Press, 1996, 80–101.
2. CARLIER, *Les deux prostitutions*, 571.
3. PENISTON, *Pederasts and Others*.

4. Régis REVENIN, "L'Émergence d'un monde homosexuel moderne dans le Paris de la Belle Époque," *Revue d'histoire moderne et contemporaine*, 53/4, 2006, 74–86; REVENIN, *Homosexualité et prostitution*.
5. See Robert BEACHY, "To Police and Protect: The Surveillance of Homosexuality in Imperial Berlin," in: Scott SPECTOR, Helmut PUFF, and Dagmar HERZOG (eds.), *After the History of Sexuality: German Genealogies with and beyond Foucault*, New York: Berghahn Books, 2012, 109–123; BEACHY, *Gay Berlin*, particularly chap. 2; Jens DOBLER, *Zwischen Duldungspolitik und Verbrechensbekämpfung: Homosexuellenverfolgung durch die Berliner Polizei von 1848 bis 1933*, Frankfurt am Main: Verlag für Polizeiwissenschaft, 2008.
6. COCKS, *Nameless Offences*, 40, 43, 50, and 53.
7. The same has been found with regard to the cities of northern England. See SMITH, *Masculinity, Class and Same-Sex Desire in Industrial England, 1895–1957*, 190.
8. In France too, however, structures were complex and professionalization slow, but the prefecture of Paris was large and well-equipped. See Malcolm ANDERSON, *In Thrall to Political Change: Police and Gendarmerie in France*, Oxford: Oxford University Press, 2011, chap. 4; Jean-Marc BERLIÈRE, "La professionalisation de la police en France: Un phénomène nouveau au début du XXème siècle," *Déviance et société*, 11/1, 1987, 67–104.
9. Also see Wannes DUPONT, "Pederasten op de Place royale: Een fragment uit het vergeten verleden van Brussel," *Leidschrift: Historisch tijdschrift*, 26/1, 2011, 79–91.
10. SABF, CFIB, Series II: Sentenced Correctional Case Files 1893–1899, year 1899, 'Wallemacq Arthur. Caporal 9e de ligne. Assasinat de Bruyère, Isidore. Concierge du baron Osy. Place royale à Bruxelles' (telegram dated June 8, 1899, document number 1bis). Henceforth: SABF, CFIB, Series II, Crime de la Place Royale.
11. Ibid. (from two affidavits both dated June 8, 1899, document numbers 78 and 81 respectively).
12. Ibid.
13. "Le crime de la place Royale à Bruxelles," *Le Petit Belge*, June 9, 10 and 13, 1899; "L'Instruction du crime de la Place royale," *Le Petit Bleu*, June 13, 1899; "Le mystère de l'hôtel Osy," *Le Petit Bleu*, June 14, 1899.
14. SABF, CFIB, Series II, Crime de la Place Royale (undated newspaper clipping, document number 91). Compare with "Le crime de la place Royale," *L'Indépendance belge*, June 11, 1899; "Le crime de la place Royale," *Le Petit Belge*, June 9 and 15, 1899.
15. On the Belgian press, see Bram DELBECKE, *De lange schaduw van de grondwetgever: Perswetgeving en persmisdrijven in België (1831–1914)*, Ghent: Academia Press, 2012; Pierre VAN DEN DUNGEN, *Milieux de presse et journalistes en Belgique (1828–1914)*, Brussels: Académie royale de Belgique, 2005; Els DE BENS, *De pers in België: Het verhaal van de Belgische dagbladpers gisteren, vandaag en morgen*, Tielt: Lannoo, 1997.
16. On the 'new journalism' in the UK, see Judith R. WALKOWITZ, *City of Dreadful Delight: Narratives of Sexual Danger in Late-Victorian London*, Chicago: University of Chicago Press, 1992, 122, 125, and 131; Joel H. WIENER (ed.), *Papers for the Millions: The New Journalism in Britain, 1850s to 1914*, New York: Greenwood Press, 1986; Stephen KOSS, *The Rise and Fall of the Political Press*

in Britain, 2 vols., Chapel Hill: University of North Carolina Press, 1981–1984, vol. 1, 343–349. For the British press' importance in creating public awareness about homosexuality, see KOVEN, *Slumming*, chap. 1. Belgium also had nothing like the sensationalist *Oesterreichische Kriminal-Zeitung*. See SPECTOR, *Violent Sensations*, 146–158.

17. DELBECKE, *De lange schaduw van de grondwetgever*, chap. 8.
18. This type of press was also politically motivated in its attempt to surpass the stale liberal–Catholic debate by a more socially progressive orientation, which it combined with rabid anticlericalism. VAN DEN DUNGEN, *Milieux de presse et journalistes en Belgique (1828–1914)*, 99–108.
19. "Le crime de la place Royale," *La Gazette*, June 15, 1899.
20. "Crime à punir," *La Gazette*, June 18, 1899. The remaining quotes in this paragraph are drawn from the same.
21. BCA, Police records, Twentieth century, Series D, no. D59–104: 'Pédérastes' (memo dated June 20, 1899, number 14996).
22. BCA, Police records, Twentieth century, Series D, no. D59–104: 'Pédérastes' (report from the Bureau des mœurs dated June 27, 1899, number 2206).
23. BCA, Police records, Twentieth century, Series D, no. D59–104: 'Pédérastes' (Tableau récapitulatif des pédérastes qui se sont signalés pendant ces dernières années).
24. This approximate number is deduced from the highest serial number I have come across, which was 437. The elusive ledger is alluded to in SABF, CFIB, Series II: Sentenced Correctional Case Files 1893–1899, year 1891, port. 902, reg. 122 (two letters dated November 18 and 27, 1891, both are unnumbered documents); ibid., year 1893, port. 906, reg. 213 (affidavit dated December 2, 1893).
25. BCA, Police records, Twentieth century, Series D, no. D59–104: 'Pédérastes.' This disproportion was similar in Paris. See ROSS, *Public City/Public Sex*, 97.
26. Marnix BEYEN, Judith POLLMANN, and Henk TE VELDE, *De Lage Landen: Een geschiedenis voor vandaag*, Rekkem and The Hague: Ons Erfdeel, 2021, chap. 14; Bernard A. COOK, *Belgium: A History*, New York: Peter Lang, 2002, chap. 8; Carl STRIKWERDA, *A House Divided: Catholics, Socialists, and Flemish Nationalists in Nineteenth-Century Belgium*, Lanham, MD: Rowman and Littlefield, 1997, 29–30.
27. Luc KEUNINGS, *Des polices si tranquilles: Une histoire de l'appareil policier belge au XIXe siècle*, s.l.: Presses universitaires de Louvain, 2009, 15–17; Lode VAN OUTRIVE, Yves CARTUYVELS, and Paul PONSAERS, *Sire, ik ben ongerust: Geschiedenis van de Belgische politie 1794–1991*, Leuven: Kritak, 1992, 33–34.
28. Luc KEUNINGS, "De geschiedenis van het Brusselse politiekorps (van 1830 tot 1914)," *Gemeentekrediet van België: Driemaandelijks tijdschrift*, 37/145, 1983, 149–184; Luc KEUNINGS, "Du garde-ville à l'agent de police: Les débuts de la professionnalisation de la police en Belgique (1880–1914)," *L'Officier de police – De politieofficier*, 7, 1988, 1–96.
29. Raymond B. FOSDICK, *European Police Systems*, New York: The Century, 1915, 137.
30. Ibid., 138.
31. KEUNINGS, "De geschiedenis van het Brusselse politiekorps," 181–182.
32. Ibid., 171; KEUNINGS, "Du garde-ville à l'agent de police," 9.

33. Other countries suffered similar problems, and police professionalization advanced most rapidly in some of the major metropolises. See Herbert REINKE and Margo DE KOSTER, "History of the Police Profession," in: Gerben BRUINSMA and David WEISBURD (eds.), *Encyclopedia of Criminology and Criminal Justice*, New York: Springer, 2014, 2296–2309.
34. Luc KEUNINGS, "Les 'bras armés' de Thémis: Les policiers bruxellois à la Belle-Époque," *Les Cahiers de la Fonderie: Revue d'Histoire Sociale et Industrielle de la Région Bruxelloise*, 27, 2003, 17–24, 21.
35. On this system, see Hans NEEFS, *Between Sin and Disease: The Social Fight against Syphilis and AIDS in Belgium (1880–2000)*, Saarbrücken: LAP Lambert, 2010, chap. 3; Sophie DE SCHAEPDRIJVER, "De reglementering van prostitutie, 1844–1877: Opkomst en ondergang van een experiment," *Belgisch Tijdschrift voor Nieuwste Geschiedenis – Revue belge d'histoire contemporaine*, 16/3–4, 1985, 476–506; Sophie DE SCHAEPDRIJVER, "Regulering van prostitutie in de negentiende eeuw: Een concreet voorbeeld: Brussel, 1844–1877," in: *Het openbaar initiatief van de gemeenten in België 1795–1940: Handelingen van het 12de internationaal colloquium, Spa 4–7 september 1984*, vol. 2, Brussels: Gemeentekrediet, 1986, 537–558. On the similar French system, see Alain CORBIN, *Women for Hire: Prostitution and Sexuality in France after 1850*, translated by Alan SHERIDAN, Cambridge, MA: Harvard University Press, 1990.
36. The logic underlying the system was blatant in the work of a parliamentary committee set up to evaluate it. Opponents' key criticism was that male continence was morally necessary and practically achievable. When at all, homosexuality was only briefly mentioned in these debates as one likely outgrowth of a ban on prostitution. For example: "We believe that adultery, sodomy and masturbation are evils far worse than that of regulated prostitution, and that abolishing the latter would necessarily encourage the former, to the great detriment of national hygiene." Without eliciting any opposition, the minutes of the committee's work also contain casual remarks such as: "Les hommes ne font pas métier de prostitution" ("Men do not work as prostitutes"). *Commission chargée de préparer un Projet de Loi sur la Police des mœurs instituée par arrêté royal du 13 octobre 1887: Procès-verbaux des séances de la section de législation, des séances de la section d' hygiène et des séances plénières*, Brussels: Joseph Goemaere, 1891, 142 and 167 respectively. A related overview of prostitution in Belgium similarly has next to nothing to say about homosexuality. Louis FIAUX, *La prostitution en Belgique*, Paris: 1892.
37. The number of six cited here concerns only the municipality of Brussels itself, but there is no reason to assume that the other boroughs that made up the conurbation had larger units at their disposal. Abraham FLEXNER, *Prostitution in Europe*, New York: The Century, 1919 [1914], 147.
38. BCA, Police records, Twentieth century, Series D, no. D59-104: 'Pédérastes' (untitled newspaper clipping from *La Nation* attached to a police document dated August 4, 1886, unnumbered document).
39. Similar problems plagued the vice police in Paris. See Jean-Marc BERLIÈRE, *La police des mœurs sous la IIIe république*, Paris: Seuil, 1992; CORBIN, *Women for Hire*.
40. On this scandal, see Jean-Michel CHAUMONT and Christine MACHIELS (eds.), *Du sordide au mythe: L'Affaire de la traite des blanches (Bruxelles, 1880)*, Louvain-la-Neuve: Presses universitaires de Louvain, 2009.

41. On this movement, see Paul KNEPPER, *The Invention of International Crime: A Global Issue in the Making, 1881–1914*, Basingstoke: Palgrave Macmillan, 2010, chap. 4; Stephanie LIMONCELLI, *The Politics of Trafficking: The First International Movement to Combat the Sexual Exploitation of Women*, Stanford: Stanford University Press, 2010; Phillip HOWELL, *Geographies of Regulation: Policing Prostitution in Nineteenth-Century Britain and the Empire*, Cambridge: Cambridge University Press, 2009; Peter BALDWIN (ed.), *Contagion and the State in Europe, 1830–1930*, Cambridge: Cambridge University Press, 2004: Lucy BLAND, *Banishing the Beast: English Feminism and Sexual Morality, 1885–1914*, London: Penguin, 1995; WALKOWITZ, *City of Dreadful Delight*.
42. KEUNINGS, "De geschiedenis van het Brusselse politiekorps," 169–179. Similar scandals compromised the Paris vice police. See BERLIÈRE, *La police des mœurs*.
43. On the Belgian left, see Gita DENECKERE, *Sire, het volk mort: Sociaal protest in België 1831–1918*, Antwerp: Hadewijch and AMSAB, 1997; STRIKWERDA, *A House Divided*; Pascal DELWIT and José GOTOVITCH (eds.), *La peur du rouge*, Brussels: Éditions de l'Université de Bruxelles, 1996; Jan MOULAERT, *Rood en zwart: De anarchistische beweging in België 1880–1914*, Leuven: Davidsfonds, 1995.
44. Luc KEUNINGS, "Ordre public et peur du rouge au XIXème siècle: La police, les socialistes et les anarchistes à Bruxelles (1886–1914)," *Belgisch Tijdschrift voor Nieuwste Geschiedenis – Revue belge d'histoire contemporaine*, 25/3–4, 1994–1995, 329–396, 379. Elsewhere, Keunings writes: "Comme le souligne Goron, un ancien chef de Sûreté parisienne, la police de Bruxelles reste, en effet, avant tout une police administrative focalisée sur le maintien de l'ordre" ("As underlined by Goron, a former head of the law enforcement authority in Paris, the Brussels police effectively remains one of a primarily administrative kind, focused on maintaining public order"). KEUNINGS, "Les 'bras armés' de Thémis," 23.
45. KEUNINGS, "De geschiedenis van het Brusselse politiekorps," 164–167.
46. Louis FRANK, *Le crime de la Rue des Hirondelles: L'Affaire Van Calck à Bruxelles. Étude de police criminelle*, Paris: Frank, 1909, 393 (including note 1).
47. KEUNINGS, "De geschiedenis van het Brusselse politiekorps," 169. The first National School of Criminology was founded in 1921. See KEUNINGS, "Les 'bras armés' de Thémis," 23. On the *police judiciaire*, see François WELTER, "Quand l'intérêt public se heurte aux obstacles institutionnels et matériels: Une police judiciaire près des parquets, solution aux défis de la police judiciaire en Belgique (1830–1922)," *Bijdragen tot de Eigentijdse Geschiedenis*, 24, 2011, 35–63.
48. Excepting major cases of fraud, which often required extensive and expensive expert inquiries into the accounting history of companies.
49. Famke VEKEMAN, "De seponeringspolitiek van gerechtelijke strafdossiers betreffende seksueel geweld doorgelicht: Een bijdrage tot de geschiedenis van de seksuele mentaliteit en het strafrechtelijk discours tijdens de eerste helft van de twintigste eeuw," *Van mensen en dingen*, 3/3, 2005, 269–286.
50. SABF, CAB, Series II: Sentenced Correctional Case Files 1885–1899, year 1892, file 2066, reg. 224.
51. SABF, CFIB, Series II: Sentenced Correctional Case Files 1893–1899, year 1899, port. 1234, reg. 832.

52. SABF, CFIB, Series II: Sentenced Correctional Case Files 1893–1899, year 1899, port. 47, reg. 1143 (letter dated March 27, 1899, document number 6, see document 7 for the French translation).
53. SABF, CFIB, Series II: Sentenced Correctional Case Files 1893–1899, year 1899, port. 1247, reg. 1127.
54. SABF, Prison of Forest, Anthropological service 1918–1940, box 64, file 3378.
55. SABF, CFIB, Series II: Sentenced Correctional Case Files 1893–1899, year 1891, port. 902, reg. 122.
56. BCA, Police records, Twentieth century, Series D, no. D59–104: 'Pédérastes' (letter to the mayor dated June 18, 1931, unnumbered document).
57. Ibid. (police report dated June 16, 1931, unnumbered document).
58. Ibid. (police report dated September 20, 1931, unnumbered document).
59. Ibid. (police report dated June 29, 1931, document 59210).
60. SABF, CFIB, Series II: Sentenced Correctional Case Files 1893–1899, year 1898, port. 1188, reg. 1197 (letter dated June 10, 1898, document 3).
61. Ibid. (affidavit dated May 29, 1898, document 3).
62. Ibid. (affidavit dated October 6, 1898, document 9).
63. Ibid. (affidavit dated October 6, 1898, inv. 12).
64. See Angus McLaren, *Sexual Blackmail: A Modern History*, Cambridge, MA: Harvard University Press, 2002, chaps. 1, 2, and 5.
65. SABF, CFIB, Series I: Sentenced Correctional Case Files 1795 (year IV)-1896, year 1848, file 669, reg. 40.
66. SABF, Prison of Vorst/Forest, Anthropological service 1918–1940, box 42, file 2060.
67. Circular letter nr. 1192 from the Crown Prosecutor's office, dated January 21, 1892. Quoted in "Outrage public aux mœurs," in: Edmond Picard, Napoléon d'Hoffschmidt, and Jules De le Court (eds.), *Pandectes belges*, vol. 72, Brussels: Larcier, 1902, 512–554, 552–553 (paragraph 174).
68. Circular letter nr. 1318 from the Procurator-General's office, dated January 13, 1892. Ibid., 553 (paragraph 175).
69. For example, SABF, CFIB, Series II: Sentenced Correctional Case Files 1893–1899, year 1898, port. 723, reg. 5243 (affidavit dated September 17, 1898, document 4).
70. SABF, CFIB, Series II: Sentenced Correctional Case Files 1893–1899, year 1895, port. 1033, reg. 1000 (affidavit dated September 14, 1895, document 5).
71. Compare with Ross, *Public City/Public Sex*, 103.
72. SABF, CFIB, Series II: Sentenced Correctional Case Files 1893–1899, year 1897, port. 1147, reg. 159 (anonymous letter dated September 24, 1897, annexed to document 19). Note that this case file is enclosed in SABF, CFIB, Series II: Sentenced Correctional Case Files 1893–1899, year 1898, port. 1147, reg. 291.
73. SABF, CAB, Series II: Sentenced Correctional Case Files 1811–1884, year 1883, file 3182, reg. 764–765 (affidavit dated February 7, 1882, document 2).
74. "Le crime de la Place Royale," *La Gazette*, June 15, 1899.
75. SABF, CAB, Series II: Sentenced Correctional Case Files 1811–1884, year 1883, file 3182, reg. 764–765 (affidavit dated February 7, 1882, document 2; see also the affidavit dated February 5, 1883, document 70).
76. SABF, CFIB, Series II: Sentenced Correctional Case Files 1893–1899, year 1897, port. 1147, reg. 159 (police report dated January 17, 1898, document 20).

77. Ibid. (affidavit dated February 7, 1882, document 2).
78. SABF, CAB, Series II: Sentenced Correctional Case Files 1811–1884, year 1883, file 3182, reg. 764–765 (police report dated July 11, 1882, document 37).
79. The same was true of northern English cities, also due to a lack of police capacity. See SMITH, *Masculinity, Class and Same-Sex Desire in Industrial England, 1895–1957*, 57.
80. SABF, CFIB, Unsorted Series of Correctional Case Files from the Interwar Period, year 1935, box 99, reg. 495.
81. This remains to be researched further. The vagrancy law from 1891 explicitly allowed for transient pimps, alcoholics, layabouts, and people of "disordered morals" to be placed in special reformatories at the judge's discretion. J. MERCIER, *De la loi du 27 novembre 1891 sur la répression du vagabondage et de la mendicité*, Brussels: Larcier, 1891, 66 (art. 13). On the importance of the vagrancy law in policing homosexuality, see COCKS, *Nameless Offences*, 55–56; KOVEN, *Slumming*, 73; Angus MCLAREN, *The Trials of Masculinity: Policing Sexual Boundaries, 1870–1930*, Chicago: University of Chicago Press, 1997, 16–18.

3 The Legal Irrelevance of Sexual Specifics

1. On Ulrichs, see the introduction to Douglas O. PRETSELL, *The Correspondence of Karl Heinrich Ulrichs, 1846–1894*, Basingstoke: Palgrave Macmillan, 2020. Also see Ralph M. LECK, *Vita Sexualis: Karl Ulrichs and the Origins of Sexual Science*, Urbana: University of Illinois Press, 2016; TOBIN, *Peripheral Desires*; BEACHY, *Gay Berlin*, chap. 1.
2. Heather Wolffram's research indicates that changes to German criminal procedure in 1879 allowed for a freer consideration of evidence. This led to a diminishing reliance in court on mistrusted witness evidence and a growing recourse to psychological expertise. Heather WOLFFRAM, "Teaching Grossian Criminalistics in Imperial Germany," in: Willemijn RUBERG, Lara BERGERS, Pauline DIRVEN et al. (eds.), *Forensic Cultures in Modern Europe*, Manchester: Manchester University Press, 2023, 92–116, 97. Also see Heather WOLFFRAM, *Forensic Psychology in Germany: Witnessing Crime, 1880–1939*, s.l.: Palgrave Macmillan, 2018.
3. On homosexuality's decriminalization in revolutionary France, see Bryant T. RAGAN Jr., "Same-Sex Sexual Relations and the French Revolution: The Decriminalization of Sodomy in 1791," in: Sean BRADY and Mark SEYMOUR (eds.), *From Sodomy Laws to Same-Sex Marriage: International Perspectives Since 1789*, London: Bloomsbury Academic, 2019, 15–30; Thierry PASTORELLO, "L'Abolition du crime de sodomie en 1791: Un long processus social, répressif et pénal," *Cahiers d'histoire: Revue d'histoire critique*, 112–113, 2010, 197–208; Michael D. SIBALIS, "Homosexuality in Early Modern France," in: Katherine O'DONNELL and Michael O'ROURKE (eds.), *Queer Masculinities*, Basingstoke: Palgrave Macmillan, 2006, 211–231; Michael D. SIBALIS, "Male Homosexuality in the Age of Enlightenment and Revolution, 1680–1850," in: Robert ALDRICH (ed.), *Gay Life and Culture: A World History*, London: Thames and Hudson, 2006, 103–123; SIBALIS, "The Regulation of Male Homosexuality in Revolutionary and Napoleonic France."

4. French influence ushered in the decriminalization of sodomy in the Netherlands, Luxemburg, several German principalities, and those of Northern Italy, Poland, and the French-speaking cantons of Switzerland. Flora LEROY-FORGEOT, *Histoire juridique de l'homosexualité en Europe*, Paris: Presses universitaires de France, 1997, 64–67. For a helpful global overview of decriminalization, see Kees WAALDIJK, *Legal Recognition of Homosexual Orientation in the Countries of the World: A Chronological Overview with Footnotes*, Los Angeles: The Williams Institute (at UCLA), available from Leiden University Scholarly Publications, https://hdl.handle.net/1887/14543, last accessed on August 10, 2022.
5. Adolphe CHAUVEAU and Hélie FAUSTIN, *Théorie du code pénal*, 2 vols., Brussels: Wahlen, 1840, vol. 2, 36–37.
6. John LAURITSEN and David THORSTAD, *The Early Homosexual Rights Movement, 1864–1935*, New York: Times Change Press, 1995; James STEAKLEY, *The Homosexual Emancipation Movement in Germany*, New York: Arno, 1975.
7. Theo VAN DER MEER, *Jonkheer mr. Jacob Anton Schorer (1866–1957): Een biografie van homoseksualiteit*, Amsterdam: Schorer Boeken, 2007.
8. Auguste LEY and André MARCHAL, "L'Homosexualité: Étude médico-juridique," *Revue de droit pénal et de criminologie*, 36/1, 1955, 323–341, 333.
9. The Belgian penal code of 1867 penalized pornographic indecencies, whether expressed in print, imagery, song, or otherwise, through the separate article 383. See Chapter 7.
10. LEY and MARCHAL, "L'Homosexualité," 333–334.
11. Jean-Polydore HAESAERT, "Évolution de la jurisprudence belge en matière d'outrages publics aux mœurs (art. 385 du code Pénal)," *Revue de droit pénal et de criminologie*, 1927, 1155–1173, 1160.
12. "It is enough that by his indifference, by forgetting himself and by disregarding propriety, he has foreseen or could have foreseen and [thereby] accepted the possibility of such an offense." Jean Servais Guillaume NYPELS and Jean SERVAIS, *Le code pénal belge interprété, principalement au point de vue de la pratique*, 2nd ed., 4 vols., Brussels: Bruylant, 1896–1899, vol. 1, 533. As stated in the *Pandectes belges*, one of Belgium's most important collections of jurisprudence: "This doctrine is universally acknowledged in France and Belgium." See "Outrage public aux mœurs," 541. Compare with Marcela IACUB, *Through the Keyhole: A History of Sex, Space and Public Modesty in Modern France*, translated by Vinay SWAMY, Manchester: Manchester University Press, 2016, 31–35.
13. HAESAERT, "Évolution de la jurisprudence belge," 1161.
14. Jules LE JEUNE, "Circulaire ministérielle: Outrage aux mœurs. Intention. Pissoirs. Autorité communale," *La Belgique judiciaire*, 48/68, 1890, 1087.
15. "Un peu gras, ce que nous avons à vous conter," *L'Indépendance belge*, September 3, 1890, 1–2, 2.
16. Dispatch of October 6, 1890, Third Division, nr. 211861. Quoted in: "Outrage public aux mœurs," 550.
17. See, notably, "Double délit: Intention. Juge du fond. Appréciation," in: *Pasicrisie belge: Recueil général de la jurisprudence des cours et tribunaux de Belgique en matière civile, commerciale, criminelle, de droit public et administratif*, 3 vols., Brussels: Bruylant, 1863, vol. 3, 343–346.
18. "Outrage public aux mœurs," 539 (§ 115). Compare with HAESAERT, "Évolution de la jurisprudence belge," 1155.

19. Judges did have some wiggle room through their ability to consider mitigating and aggravating circumstances in sentencing. Consequently, while public nudity automatically led to a conviction, it usually carried the minimum sentence of eight days' imprisonment and a fine of twenty-six francs, but this was a correctional conviction all the same.
20. For example, SABF, CFIB, Series II: Case files of Sentenced and Dismissed Correctional Cases 1893–1899, year 1898, port. 714 and 723, reg. 4746 and 5250. Also see year 1895, port. 330 and 352, reg. numbers 3436 and 4461 from the same series, as well as year 1896, port. 468, reg. 4131.
21. "Gand, 19 mars 1909: Outrages aux mœurs. Articles 383 et 385 du code pénal. Application. Interprétation des faits et gestes. Règles à suivre," in: *Pandectes périodiques*, vol. 22, Brussels: Larcier, 1909, 776–777. Compare with "Cour d'appel de Bruxelles: Huitième chambre. Présidence de M. Hayoit de Termicourt, cons. 26 février 1910. Outrage public aux mœurs. Dessins obscènes. Conférence sur le néo-malthusianisme," *La Belgique judicaire*, 68/45, 1910, 713–719. Indeed, to the extent that (nonconsensual) male same-sex sexual acts were a part of public discourse, it seems to have concerned those cases of sexual abuse, assault, and rape, which liberals and socialists used against the Catholic establishment for political reasons. See Eva MUYS and Karel VELLE, "Seksuele delinquentie in het onderwijsmilieu: Pedofiele onderwijzers in de 19de eeuw," *Belgisch Tijdschrift voor Nieuwste Geschiedenis – Revue belge d'histoire contemporaine*, 18/3–4, 1998, 293–337; Gita DENECKERE, "'Van scholen zoner God verlos ons, Heer': Hoe de liberalen de Schoolstrijd wonnen dankzij een schandaal van kindermisbruik in de kerk," in: Maarten VAN GINDERACHTER, Koen AERTS, and Antoon VRINTS (eds.), *Het land dat nooit was: Een tegenfeitelijke geschiedenis van België*, Antwerp: Bezige Bij, 2014, 126–167.
22. HAESAERT, "Évolution de la jurisprudence belge," 1168.
23. See the chapter on *öffentliche Ärgernis* in Rudolf QUANTER, *Die Sittlichkeitsverbrechen im Laufe der Jahrhundert und ihre strafrechtliche Beurteilung*, 2nd ed., Berlin: Bermühler, 1904, 262–271. First appearing in 1904, the study went through eight revised editions by 1925.
24. Ibid., 264.
25. French law also had a more sophisticated concept of intent (*dol spécial*), even though still not as discerning as Germany's, but it only applied to specific offenses such as murder or defamation. See Mohamed ELEWA BADAR, *The Concept of Mens Rea in International Criminal Law: The Case for a Unified Approach*, Oxford: Hart, 2013, chap. 5.
26. QUANTER, *Die Sittlichkeitsverbrechen*, 264.
27. In Britain, public decency was policed under the interpretively elastic Vagrancy Act of 1824. British courts focused less on defendants' state of mind and more on their general respectability and reputation. See Michal SHAPIRA, "Indecently Exposed: The Male Body and Vagrancy in Metropolitan London before the Fin de Siècle," *Gender & History*, 30/1, 2018, 52–69, 54; UPCHURCH, *Before Wilde*, 188–190.
28. "Nun hat allerdings das Reichsgericht entschieden, daß der Begriff einer unzüchtigen Handlung neben der gegen das Scham- und Sittlichkeitsgefühl gröblich verstoßenden Eigenschaft eine geschlechtliche Beziehung erfordere." QUANTER, *Die Sittlichkeitsverbrechen*, 266.

29. "es kann also danach niemals eine unzüchtige Handlung, die in keiner Weise auf das Geschlechtsleben Bezug hat, unter den § 183 fallen." Ibid. The author did add that some nonerotic acts might take on a sexual meaning they inherently lacked because of particular circumstances.
30. Ibid., 266–267.
31. "Outrage public aux mœurs," 524 (§ 532).
32. Rudolf QUANTER, *Die Sittlichkeitsverbrechen im Laufe der Jahrhundert und ihre strafrechtliche Beurteilung*, 8th ed., Berlin: Scientia, 1970 [1925], 320. This case did not feature yet in the second edition of 1904.
33. The Netherlands may have been somewhere in between the Belgian and German systems. Having also inherited the French penal code, it developed an expansive concept of publicity similar to Belgium's, but Dutch courts required the presence of innocent witnesses for a conviction for public indecency. See Theo VAN DER MEER, "Private Acts, Public Space: Defining Boundaries in Nineteenth-Century Holland," in: William M. LEAP (ed.), *Public Sex, Gay Space*, New York: Columbia University Press, 1999, 223–245.
34. LEY and MARCHAL, "L'Homosexualité," 334.
35. QUANTER, *Die Sittlichkeitsverbrechen*, 267.
36. For Quanter's lengthy remarks on *widernatürliche Unzucht*, see pages 237 to 261 of the second edition from 1904. Franz von Liszt, whose ideas on criminal law reform were highly influential in Germany and its sphere of influence during the late nineteenth century and into the interwar period, similarly believed the role of medical science and psychiatry in the legal process to be indispensable. On that basis, he declared himself in favor of the partial decriminalization of homosexuality in his oft-reprinted *Lehrbuch des Deutschen Strafrechts*. See Kamil KARCZEWSKI, "Transnational Flows of Knowledge and the Legislation of Homosexuality in Interwar Poland," *Contemporary European History*, 2022, https://doi.org/10.1017/S0960777322000108, last accessed on July 29, 2023, 1–18, 5–6.
37. For a good overview of the psychiatrization of homosexuality in Germany, see Philippe WEBER, *Der Trieb zum Erzählen: Sexualpathologie und Homosexualität, 1852–1914*, Bielefeld: transcript, 2008.
38. See article 43 of the Belgian code of criminal inquiry in Gustave BELTJENS, *Le code d'instruction criminelle belge et les lois spéciales annotés d'après 1° Les principes juridiques, 2° La doctrine des auteurs belges et français 3° Les décisions des cours et tribunaux*, 2 vols., Brussels: Bruylant and Maresq, 1903, vol. 1, 218. This situation inhibited the professionalization of forensic medicine. On the comparable situations in France and the Netherlands, see Willemijn RUBERG and Nathanje DIJKSTRA, "De forensische wetenschap in Nederland (1800–1930): Een terreinverkenning," *Studium: Tijdschrift voor Wetenschaps- en Universiteitsgeschiedenis*, 9/3, 2016, 121–143; Willemijn RUBERG, "Travelling Knowledge and Forensic Medicine: Infanticide, Body and Mind in the Netherlands, 1811–1911," *Medical History*, 57/3, 2013, 359–376; Willemijn RUBERG, "Onzekere kennis: De rol van forensische geneeskunde en psychiatrie in Nederlandse verkrachtingszaken (1811–1920)," *Tijdschrift voor sociale en economische geschiedenis*, 9/1, 2012, 87–110; Frédéric CHAUVAUD, *Experts et expertise judiciaire: France, XIXe et XXe siècles*, Rennes: Presses universitaires de Rennes, 2003, chap. 1.
39. Article 25 of the Belgian code of criminal inquiry. BELTJENS, *Le code d'instruction criminelle belge*, 291–292.

40. Emmanuel DESOER, *Code pratique de police judiciaire et administrative à l'usage des bourgmestres, des commissaires et agents de police, des officiers de gendarmerie, des gendarmes et des gardes champêtres*, 2nd ed., Brussels: Larcier and Lauriel, 1882, 81.
41. Ibid.
42. Ange-Louis DAMBRE, *Traité de médecine légale et de jurisprudence de la médecine*, 3 vols., Ghent: Hoste, 1859–1867, vol. 2, 81.
43. Similarly, an analysis of Dutch rape trials has shown that, in the Netherlands too, the appeal to medical expertise was rare until after the Second World War and that such trials nearly always relied on witness testimony. Lara BERGERS, "A Culture of Testimony: The Importance of 'Speaking Witnesses' in Dutch Sexual Crimes Investigations, 1930–1960," in: Willemijn RUBERG, Lara BERGERS, Pauline DIRVEN et al. (eds.), *Forensic Cultures in Modern Europe*, Manchester: Manchester University Press, 2023, 49–70.
44. DAMBRE, *Traité de médecine légale*, vol. 2, 83.
45. For examples involving homosexual acts, see SABF, CFIB, Series II: Case files of Sentenced and Dismissed Correctional Cases 1893–1899, year 1898, map 678, reg. 3131 and year 1899, port. 1247, reg. 1127. These kinds of examinations were common where children under fourteen were concerned. Their testimonies were considered less reliable and therefore had to be backed up by physical evidence. Many of the cases of the sexual abuse of children were tried before the Assize Courts. They dealt with the most serious crimes, were tried by jury, and had their own, more elaborate procedure and a considerably larger budget at their disposal than the lower courts. E.g. SABF, ACB, Series I: 1794–1923, numbers 632–1389, year 1873, file 1043, reg. 1649; and from the same series year 1875, file 1071, reg. 1707. Compare with Geoffroy LE CLERCQ, "La perception des violences sexuelles en Belgique (1830–1867): Construction juridique, pratique répressive et réactions sociales," in: Ginette KURGAN-VAN HENTENRYK (ed.), *Un pays si tranquille: La violence en Belgique au XIXe siècle*, Brussels: Éditions de l'Université de Bruxelles, 1999, 107–129; Geoffroy LE CLERCQ, "Violences sexuelles, scandale et ordre public: Le regard du législateur, de la justice et des autres acteurs sociaux au 19ème siècle," *Belgisch Tijdschrift voor Nieuwste Geschiedenis – Revue Belge d'Histoire Contemporaine*, 28/1–2, 1999, 5–53.
46. Théophile BORMANS, *Répertoire belge de législation, d'instructions, de doctrine et de jurisprudence concernant la médecine légale, l'exercice de l'art de guérir et la police sanitaire*, Brussels: Larcier, 1882, 61.
47. SPECTOR, *Violent Sensations*, chaps. 2 and 3; Jörg HUTTER, *Die gesellschaftliche Kontrolle des homosexuellen Begehrens. Medizinische Definitionen und juristische Sanktionen im 19. Jahrhundert*, Frankfurt am Main: Campus, 1992, 52–60 and 88–103.
48. QUANTER, *Die Sittlichkeitsverbrechen*, 237–238.
49. This is also very clear in the Austrian case. See SPECTOR, *Violent Sensations*, 158–165.
50. For overviews of the historiography of homosexuality in Germany, see BEACHY, *Gay Berlin*; Martin LÜCKE, *Männlichkeit in Unordnung: Homosexualität und männliche Prostitution in Kaiserreich und Weimarer Republik*, Frankfurt am Main: Campus, 2008; WEBER, *Der Trieb zum Erzählen*; Bernd-Ulrich

HERGEMÖLLER, *Einführung in die Historiographie der Homosexualitäten*, Tübingen: Dition Diskord, 1999. On the interwar period, see Javier SAMPER VENDRELL, *The Seduction of Youth: Print Culture and Homosexual Rights in the Weimar Republic*, Toronto: University of Toronto Press, 2020; Laurie MARHOEFER, *Sex and the Weimar Republic: German Homosexual Emancipation and the Rise of the Nazis*, Toronto: University of Toronto Press, 2015.

51. Liesbet STEVENS, *Strafrecht en seksualiteit: De misdrijven inzake aanranding van de eerbaarheid, verkrachting, ontucht, prostitutie, seksreclame, zedenschennis en overspel*, Antwerp: Intersentia, 2002, 49–64 and 183–189.

52. Rulings in criminal cases were not motivated in writing other than by reference to the relevant articles of the penal code and how they formally applied to the acts under scrutiny, which makes it extremely difficult to assess how the nature of these acts played a part in fixing the sentence or in considering aggravating or mitigating circumstances. A quantitative study based on the well-preserved sentencing books might throw some more light on this matter, but since they provide little or no details on cases aside from the relevant articles of the penal code that applied to them, the information to be gleaned from these books is fairly limited in this regard. Moreover, since the files themselves have only been preserved in a highly fragmented way, trying to systematically reconnect the verdicts in the sentencing books with the court files themselves would prove an extremely time-consuming effort with little promise of meaningful results.

53. Harry Cocks has made similar observations on the prosecution of homosexual offenses in mid nineteenth-century England. See COCKS, *Nameless Offences*. Regarding Paris, William Peniston has observed: "With misdemeanor cases, such as those involving public offenses against decency, they [the magistrates] were far more concerned about processing them quickly and efficiently rather than investigating them thoroughly." PENISTON, *Pederasts and Others*, 43.

54. See Lucien JAMAR (ed.), *1814 à 1880: Répertoire général de la jurisprudence belge contenant l'analyse de toutes les décisions rendues en Belgique depuis 1814 jusqu'à 1880 inclusivement en matière civile, commerciale, criminelle, de droit public et administratif*, 11 vols., Brussels: Bruylant-Christophe, 1882–1884, and its successors.

55. SABF, CAB, Series II: Sentenced Correctional Case Files 1885–1899, year 1887, file 898, reg. 437 (minutes of the court proceedings, document 14). With similar prevarication, Bormans wrote that anal penetration only left traces "when repeated a large number of times." BORMANS, *Répertoire belge de législation*, 61.

56. SABF, CAB, Series II: Sentenced Correctional Case Files 1811–1884, year 1883, file 3182, reg. 764–765 (medical report, document 52).

57. SABF, CFIB, Series II: Case files of Sentenced and Dismissed Correctional Cases 1893–1899, year 1898, map 1138, reg. 66 (medical report, document 19B). Compare with year 1896, map 1047, reg. 354.

58. CFIB, Series II: Case files of Sentenced and Dismissed Correctional Cases 1893–1899, year 1895, map 1027, reg. 816; year 1896, map 1047, reg. 354; year 1897, map 617, reg. 186; year 1897, map 622, reg. 414; year 1898, map 1138, reg. 66.

59. SABF, CFIB, Series II: Case files of Sentenced and Dismissed Correctional Cases 1893–1899, year 1898, map 653, reg. 1905 (affidavit, unnumbered document dated May 5, 1898).

60. Ibid. (affidavit, unnumbered document dated July 19, 1898). Compare with SABF, CAB, Series II: Sentenced Correctional Case Files 1885–1899, year 1887, file 898, reg. 437.
61. SABF, CAB, Series II: Sentenced Correctional Case Files 1885–1899, year 1890, file 1836, reg. 313 (letter of the accused, detained at the prison of Saint Gilles, to the magistrate presiding over his case, document 19).
62. Ibid. (police report on the search of Simonis' room, document 4).
63. Ibid. (police affidavit, unnumbered document dated January 26, 1890).
64. SABF, CFIB-JC, Sentenced Case Files 1923–1953, year 1935, reg. 184 (observational report, unnumbered document dated January 13, 1936). My thanks to Aurore François for pointing me to these case files.
65. Respectively, SABF, CFIB-JC, Sentenced Case Files 1923–1953, year 1935, reg. 5 (observational report, unnumbered document dated April 17, 1935) and SABF, CFIB, Unsorted Series Containing the Case Files of Sentenced and Dismissed Correctional Cases 1892–1939, year 1922, reg. 758 (police affidavit, unnumbered document dated October 5, 1921).
66. On Ley, see Brice DE RUYVER and Johan GOETHALS, "Auguste Ley 1873–1956," in: Cyrille FIJNAUT (ed.), *Gestalten uit het verleden: 32 voorgangers in de strafrechtwetenschap, de strafrechtpleging en de criminologie*, Kluwer: Deurne, 1993, 185–193.
67. LEY and MARCHAL, "L'Homosexualité," 323.
68. Alphonse DE BUSSCHERE, "Le viol et l'attentat à la pudeur [part 1]," *Annales de la Société de Médecine légale de Belgique*, 5/1, 1893, 14–31, 21. Further in the article, on page 26, De Busschere also briefly states that "on sait que pour les cas de sodomie, les anciennes législations étaient d'une sévérité outrée" ("we know that regarding sodomy, the old legislations were excessively severe").
69. Norbert BILTRIS, "L'Attentat à la pudeur et le viol," *Revue de droit pénal et de criminologie*, 1925, 1002–1046 and 1161–1199, 1008.
70. Léon BELYM, "Considérations sur la criminalité érotique," *Bulletin de la Société d'anthropologie de Bruxelles*, 41/2, 1927, 132–150, 140. This article was also published in revised and extended form as Léon BELYM, "Aspects actuels de la criminalité sexuelle et perspectives de son traitement pénitentiaire," *Revue de droit pénal et de criminologie et archives internationales de médecine légale*, 1927, 1015–1044 and 1174–1195.
71. O. GALET, "Essai de détermination de quelques caractères de la délinquance contre les mœurs," *Bulletin de la Société d'anthropologie de Bruxelles*, 41/2, 1927, 167–198 and 200–234.

4 Psychiatric Resistance to the Medicalization of Sin

1. Gert HEKMA, *Homoseksualiteit, een medische reputatie: De uitdoktering van de homoseksueel in negentiende-eeuws Nederland*, Amsterdam: Sua, 1987.
2. E.g. CHAUNCEY, "From Sexual Inversion to Homosexuality"; Harry OOSTERHUIS, *Stepchildren of Nature: Krafft-Ebing, Psychiatry and the Making of Sexual Identity*, Chicago: University of Chicago Press, 2000.
3. See Chapter 1.

4. Jan E. GOLDSTEIN, "The Hysteria Diagnosis and the Politics of Anticlericalism in Late Nineteenth-Century France," *The Journal of Modern History*, 54/2, 1982, 209–239, 221. Also see Jessie HEWITT, *Institutionalizing Gender: Madness, the Family, and Psychiatric Power in Nineteenth-Century France*, Ithaca, NY: Cornell University Press, 2020; Ian DOWBIGGIN, *Inheriting Madness: Professionalisation and Psychiatric Knowledge in Nineteenth-Century France*, Berkeley: University of California Press, 1991.
5. The term was originally coined by the Italian Arrigo Tamassia and very much an expression of secularist, materialistic positivism. See BECCALOSSI, *Female Sexual Inversion*, 52.
6. Candido DA AGRA, "Dangerosité et dégénérescence: La médecine mentale en Belgique à la fin du XIXe siècle et au début du XXe siècle," in: Françoise TULKENS (ed.), *Généalogie de la défense sociale en Belgique (1880–1914)*, Brussels: Story-Scientia, 1988, 89–111.
7. On early Belgian history, see Marc REYNEBEAU, *Een geschiedenis van België*, 2nd ed., Tielt: Lannoo, 2009 [2003]; Els WITTE, Jean-Pierre NANDRIN, Eliane GUBIN et al. (eds.), *Nieuwe geschiedenis van België*, 3 vols., Tielt: Lannoo, 2005, vol. 1; Ernst H. KOSSMANN, *The Low Countries, 1870–1940*, Oxford: Clarendon Press and Oxford University Press, 1978.
8. Henk DE SMAELE, "Politieke partijen in de Kamer, 1830–1914," in: Emmanuel GERARD, Els WITTE, Eliane GUBIN et al. (eds.), *Geschiedenis van de Belgische Kamer van Volksvertegenwoordigers 1830–2002*, Brussels: Kamer van Volksvertegenwoordigers, 2003, 131–157; Andrew C. GOULD, *Origins of Liberal Dominance: State, Church, and Party in Nineteenth-Century Europe*, Ann Arbor: University of Michigan Press, 1999, 25–44.
9. France was followed by the Netherlands in 1841 and Britain in 1845.
10. *Loi et règlements sur le régime des aliénés*, Brussels: Deltombe, 1851.
11. Ariste BOUÉ, *Commentaire sur la loi des aliénés du 30 juin 1838*, s.l.: s.e., s.a., 1–3.
12. Jan E. GOLDSTEIN, *Console and Classify: The French Psychiatric Profession in the Nineteenth Century*, 2nd ed., Chicago: University of Chicago Press, 2001, 351; DOWBIGGIN, *Inheriting Madness*, 4. In practice, this law often fell short of its ambitious goals. Hervé Guillemain has shown that the post-revolutionary religious revival of the nineteenth century's first half bolstered Catholic congregations' historical grip on the care for the insane into the 1850s. He also acknowledges, however, that the rise of positivist scientism in the 1860s allowed a Paris-based elite of anticlerical psychiatrists to increasingly expand the public system at the expense of the private one, especially from the 1870s onwards after the emergence of the highly centralist and secularist French Third Republic. Hervé GUILLEMAIN, *Diriger les consciences, guérir les âmes: Une histoire comparée des pratiques thérapeutiques et religieuses (1830–1939)*, Paris: La découverte, 2006.
13. Respectively François SEMAL, "Rapport sur l'organisation du service des aliénés en Belgique," *Bulletin de la Société de médecine mentale de Belgique*, 1/1, 1873, 29–41, 34; François SEMAL, *De la loi sur les aliénés et des réformes à y apporter: Rapport lu en Séance extraordinaire de la Fédération médicale belge le 20 novembre 1872*, Brussels: Manceaux, 1872, 1.

14. *Parlementaire Handelingen: Kamer van Volksvertegenwoordigers*, February 5, 1850, 664. Stripped of any reference to public ownership, the Law on the Administration of the Insane from 1850 was approved by sixty-six of sixty-eight votes, with the only two dissenters claiming that the bill was still not libertarian enough. See *Parlementaire Handelingen: Kamer van Volksvertegenwoordigers*, February 18, 1850, 743 and J. DEMOLDER, "Ontwerp van een juridisch kader," in: Patrick VANDERMEERSCH (ed.), *Psychiatrie, godsdienst en gezag: De ontstaansgeschiedenis van de psychiatrie in België als paradigma*, Leuven: Acco, 1984, 153–160. The single exception, but also a special case, was the home care institution of Geel (also spelled Gheel), which came under public control in 1850. On Geel, see Aude FAUVEL and Wannes DUPONT, "Gheel, la 'ville des fous': Un mythe séculaire, une pratique méconnue (1860–2010)," in: Alexandre KLEIN, Hervé GUILLEMAIN, and Marie-Claude THIFAULT (eds.), *La fin de l'asile? Histoire de la déshospitalisation psychiatrique dans l'espace francophone au XXe siècle*, Rennes: Presses Universitaires de Rennes, 2018, 25–37.
15. "Adresse de la Société au ministre de la Justice, relative aux réformes à inscrire dans la loi sur le régime des aliénés," *Bulletin de la Société de médecine mentale de Belgique*, 1/1, 1872, 79–83, 81.
16. *Rapport de la Commission supérieure d'inspection des établissements d'aliénés instituée par arrêté royale du 18 novembre 1851*, Brussels: Hayez, 1853, 35.
17. *Huitième rapport de la Commission permanente d'inspection des établissements d'aliénés instituée par arrêté royal du 17 mars 1853: 1862*, Brussels: Hayez, 1864, 87; *Neuvième rapport de la Commission permanente d'inspection des établissements d'aliénés instituée par arrêté royale du 18 mars 1853: 1863, 1864 et 1865*, Brussels: Gobbaerts, 1866, xxxiv–xxxv.
18. Only in 1921 would psychiatry become a mandatory part of medical training. Xavier FRANCOTTE, *Aperçu du développement et de l'état actuel de l'enseignement de la médecine mentale en Belgique*, Ghent: Vanderhaeghen, 1894, 7; Zénon GLORIEUX, "La psychiatrie et l'assistance aux malades mentaux (1830–1930)," in: *Cent ans de médecine en Belgique 1830–1930: Numéro spécial publié à l'occasion du centenaire de l'indépendance*, Brussels: Vromans, 1931, 123–145, 136–139.
19. *Treizième rapport sur la situation des asiles d'aliénés du royaume: Années 1883 à 1892*, Brussels: Goemaere, 1895, x.
20. On the early years of the BSMM, see Joris VANDENDRIESSCHE, *Medical Societies and Scientific Culture in Nineteenth-Century Belgium*, Oxford: Oxford University Press, 2018, 253–256. Elsewhere, such professional lobby organizations had emerged considerably earlier. A British one was founded in 1841 and a pan-German one a year later. France effectively had one in 1843 (though it was only formalized in 1852) and the United States in 1844. Only in the Netherlands, where the push for professionalization also lagged behind, did such a society not appear before 1871. Like Belgium, fiscal resistance to an expensive public system of institutional care hindered the medicalization of psychiatric care there, while the Netherlands had become a political bulwark of liberalism and laissez-faire after the constitutional reforms of 1848. Also similar in both Low Countries was the lack of academic interest and proper training. Harry OOSTERHUIS and Jessica SLIJKHUIS, *Verziekte zenuwen en zeden: De opkomst van de psychiatrie in Nederland (1870–1920)*, Rotterdam: Erasmus Publishing, 2012, 31 and 45–46.

21. On this scandal, see Gauthier GODART, *L'Asile en procès: Le scandale d'Evere (1871–1872) et la prise en charge de la folie en Belgique*, Louvain-la-Neuve: Presses universitaires de Louvain, 2019; Gauthier GODART, "'Un drame dans une maison des fous': L'Affaire d'Evere (Bruxelles, 1871–1872), ce qu'elle révèle du régime des aliénés en Belgique, ses effets dans un contexte propice à la réforme," *Journal of Belgian History*, 47/4, 2017, 112–143.
22. Jean CROCQ, *La situation du médecin d'asile en Belgique*, Brussels: Severeyns, 1907, 3; Max BOULENGER, "Quelques appréciations étrangères sur l'assistance des aliénés en Belgique," *Journal médical de Bruxelles*, 14/47, 1909, 737–742, 739.
23. GOLDSTEIN, *Console and Classify*, 368.
24. Jean-Martin CHARCOT and Valentin MAGNAN, "Inversion du sens génital [parts 1–2]," *Archives de neurologie*, 3 and 4/7 and 12, 1882, 53–60 and 296–322.
25. Carl WESTPHAL, "Die conträre Sexualempfindung: Symptom eines neuropatischen (psychopathischen) Zustandes," *Archiv für Psychiatrie und Nervenkrankheiten*, 2, 1869, 83–108, 94. On Griesinger, see Eric. J. ENGSTROM, *Clinical Psychiatry in Imperial Germany: A History of Psychiatric Practice*, Ithaca, NY: Cornell University Press, 2003, chap. 3; Dirk BLASIUS, *'Einfache Seelenstörung': Geschichte der deutschen Psychiatrie 1800–1945*, Frankfurt am Main: Fischer, 1994, 48–51.
26. On Krafft-Ebing, see OOSTERHUIS, *Stepchildren of Nature*, 81–88.
27. Robert A. NYE, *Crime, Madness, and Politics in Modern France: The Medical Concept of National Decline*, Princeton: Princeton University Press, 1984. On degeneration, also see Leck, *Vita Sexualis*, chap. 5.
28. GUILLEMAIN, *Diriger les consciences*, 108–113.
29. François LENTZ, "[Review of] Traité de psycho-pathologie légale [by R. Von Krafft-Ebing]," *Bulletin de la Société de médecine mentale de Belgique*, 4/8, 1876, 67–75, 67.
30. Receipt of the first batch of Krafft-Ebing's works is acknowledged in "Procès-verbal de la séance ordinaire du 4 mai 1875, tenue à Bruxelles au Palais de l'Université," *Bulletin de la Société de médecine mentale de Belgique*, 3/6, 1875, 5–10, 8. Krafft-Ebing acquired Austrian citizenship in 1882 along with his university chair. Renate I. HAUSER, "Sexuality, Neurasthenia and the Law: Richard von Krafft-Ebing (1840–1902)," unpublished doctoral dissertation, University College London, 1992, 51 (note 45).
31. LENTZ, "[Review of] Traité de psycho-pathologie légale [by R. Von Krafft-Ebing]," 73.
32. Richard VON KRAFFT-EBING, *Lehrbuch der gerichtlichen Psychopathologie mit Berücksichtigung der Gesetzgebung von Österreich, Deutschland und Frankreich*, Stuttgart: Enke, 1875, 161.
33. On Ulrichs, see BEACHY, *Gay Berlin*, chap. 1.
34. Richard VON KRAFFT-EBING, "Ueber gewisse Anomalien des Geschlechtstriebs und die klinisch-forensische Verwerthung derselben als eines wahrscheinlich functionellen Degenerationszeichens des centralen Nervensystems," *Archiv für Psychiatrie und Nervenkrankheiten*, 7, 1877, 291–312.
35. François LENTZ, "Attentat aux mœurs: Rapport médico-légal," *Bulletin de la Société de médecine mentale de Belgique*, 9/21, 1881, 67–71. In addition to his

above-cited review, he had also written François LENTZ, "[Review of] Des divers états de trouble intellectuel devant la juridiction civile [by R. Von Krafft-Ebing]," *Bulletin de la Société de médecine mentale de Belgique*, 4/8, 1876, 44–57; François LENTZ, "[Review of] Ueber Geistestörungen durch Zwangvorstellungen [by R. von Krafft-Ebing]," *Bulletin de la Société de médecine mentale de Belgique*, 7/13, 1879, 38–41.

36. LENTZ, "Attentat aux mœurs: Rapport médico-légal," 69.
37. J. A. PEETERS, "[Review of] Zur conträren sexual Empfindung in klinische forensisches Hinsicht [by R. Von Krafft-Ebing]," *Bulletin de la Société de médecine mentale de Belgique*, 10/25, 1882, 68–71, 68.
38. Ibid., 71.
39. "Procès-verbal de la séance ordinaire tenue à Bruxelles, le 31 janvier 1885," *Bulletin de la Société de médecine mentale de Belgique*, 13/36, 1885, 9–12, 11.
40. Jean CUYLITS, "[Review of] Des appétits sexuels contre nature devant le forum ou même devant la justice [by R. von Krafft-Ebing]," *Bulletin de la Société de médecine mentale de Belgique*, 13/39, 1885, 89–90, 90.
41. Richard VON KRAFFT-EBING, *Psychopathia sexualis: Eine klinisch-forensische Studie*, Stuttgart: Enke, 1886.
42. Richard VON KRAFFT-EBING, *Psychopathia sexualis mit besonderer Berücksichtigung der conträren Sexualempfindung: Eine klinisch-forensische Studie*, Stuttgart: Enke, 1887.
43. E.g. Julien CHEVALIER, *De l'inversion de l'instinct sexuel au point de vue médico-légal*, Lyon: Imprimerie nouvelle, 1885; Benjamin TARNOWSKY, *Die krankhaften Erscheinungen des Geschlechtsinnes: Eine forensisch-psychiatrische Studie*, Berlin: Hirschwald, 1886. The latter was originally published as Veniamin M. TARNOVSKII, *Izvrashchenie polovogo chuvstva: Sudebno-psikhiatricheskii ocherk dlia vrachei i iuristov*, Saint Petersburg: s.e., 1885.
44. "Procès-verbal de la séance ordinaire tenue au Palais de l'Université à Bruxelles, le samedi 30 juillet 1887," *Bulletin de la Société de médecine mentale de Belgique*, 15/47, 1887, 3–5, 4.
45. Ernest MASOIN, "Le docteur Léon De Rode," *Bulletin de la Société de médecine mentale de Belgique*, 38/152, 1910, 248–250.
46. Michael ROSENFELD, "Formes et figures de l'amour entre hommes dans le discours social, les écrits personnels et la littérature en France et en Belgique de 1870 à 1905," unpublished doctoral dissertation, Université catholique de Louvain and Université Sorbonne Nouvelle, 2020, 217–224.
47. Léon DE RODE, "[Review of the second edition of] Psychopathia sexualis mit besonderer Berücksichtigung der conträre Sexualempfindung: Étude médico-légale sur la psychopathie sexuelle et spécialement sur l'inversion sexuelle [by R. Von Krafft-Ebing]," *Bulletin de la Société de médecine mentale de Belgique*, 16/48, 1888, 37–47, 46.
48. On this collaboration, see OOSTERHUIS, *Stepchildren of Nature*, 96.
49. DE RODE, "[Review of the second edition of] Psychopathia sexualis," 38. The quotes in the following paragraph are from the same review.
50. OOSTERHUIS, *Stepchildren of Nature*, chap. 11.
51. The situation was complicated in Southeastern Europe. During the de facto rule of Alexandru Ioan Cuza from 1864 and after the country's independence in 1878, Romania – under French influence – did not criminalize homosexuality until the

Transylvanian penal code outlawed (only) homosexual rape later in the century. Independent Bulgaria criminalized homosexual acts in 1896. The Principality of Serbia recriminalized them in 1860.

52. Compared to Germany or Britain, there is far less scholarship available – certainly in English – on those countries where homosexual acts were not explicitly criminalized on the modern period before the Second World War. See CUROPOS, *L'Émergence de l'homosexualité*; Valeria P. BABINI and Chiara BECCALOSSI (eds.), *Italian Sexualities Uncovered, 1789–1914*, London: Palgrave Macmillan, 2015; Charlotte ROSS, *Eccentricity and Sameness: Discourses on Lesbianism and Desire between Women in Italy, 1860s–1930s*, Oxford: Peter Lang, 2015; BECCALOSSI, *Female Sexual Inversion*; Thierry DELESSERT and Michaël VOEGTLI, *Homosexualités masculines en Suisse: De l'invisibilté aux mobilisations*, Lausanne: Presses polytechniques et universitaires romandes, 2012; CLEMINSON and VÁZQUEZ GARCÍA, *Los Invisibles*; Alberto MIRA, *De Sodoma a Chueca: Una historia cultural de la homosexualidad en España en el siglo XX*, Barcelona: Egales, 2007; Natalia GERODETTI, *Modernising Sexualities: Towards a Socio-historical Understanding of Sexualities in the Swiss Nation*, Bern: Peter Lang, 2005.

53. Léon DE RODE, "[Review of the third edition of] Psychopathia Sexualis mit besonderer Berücksichtigung der conträren Sexualempfindung [by R. von Krafft-Ebing]," *Bulletin de la Société de médecine mentale de Belgique*, 16/50, 1888, 332–333; Léon DE RODE, "[Review of the fourth edition of] Psychopathia sexualis: Eine klinisch-forensische Studie [by R. von Krafft-Ebing]," *Bulletin de la Société de médecine mentale de Belgique*, 17/54, 1889, 388–389.

54. DE RODE, "[Review of the second edition of] Psychopathia sexualis," 44.

55. Léon DE RODE, "[Review of] Neue Forschungen auf dem Gebiet der Psychopathia sexualis [by R. von Krafft-Ebing]," *Bulletin de la Société de médecine mentale de Belgique*, 19/61, 1891, 217–221, 219.

56. Ibid., 221.

57. DE RODE, "[Review of the second edition of] Psychopathia sexualis," 44.

58. DE RODE, "[Review of the third edition of] Psychopathia Sexualis mit besonderer Berücksichtigung der conträren Sexualempfindung [by Richard von Krafft-Ebing]," 332.

59. DE RODE, "[Review of] Neue Forschungen," 220.

60. Ibid.

61. Ibid., 221.

62. DE RODE, "[Review of the fourth edition of] Psychopathia sexualis," 389.

63. DE RODE, "[Review of] Neue Forschungen," 221.

64. OOSTERHUIS, *Stepchildren of Nature*, part III.

65. FOUCAULT, *The History of Sexuality*, 100–102.

66. KRAFFT-EBING, *Psychopathia sexualis*, 1st ed., 1.

67. Ibid., 5.

68. On the emergence and the institutionalisation of psychiatry in Germany, see ENGSTROM, *Clinical Psychiatry in Imperial Germany*; Ann GOLDBERG, *Sex, Religion, and the Making of Modern Madness: The Eberbach Asylum and German Society, 1815–1849*, Oxford: Oxford University Press, 1999, chap. 2; BLASIUS, *Einfache Seelenstörung*, chaps. 2 and 3.

69. "Procès-verbal de la séance ordinaire tenue au Palais de l'Université à Bruxelles, le samedi 29 octobre 1887," *Bulletin de la Société de médecine mentale de Belgique*, 15/47, 1887, 6–8, 8.
70. Lesley HALL, *Sex, Gender and Social Change in Britain since 1880*, 2nd ed., Basingstoke: Macmillan, 2013, 35 and 42; Ivan CROZIER, "Nineteenth-Century British Psychiatric Writing about Homosexuality before Havelock Ellis: The Missing Story," *Journal of the History of Medicine and the Allied Sciences*, 63/1, 2008, 65–102; OOSTERHUIS, *Stepchildren of Nature*, 275–277; Lesley A. HALL, "Heroes or Villains? Reconsidering British fin de siècle Sexology and Its Impact," in: Lynne SEGAL (ed.), *New Sexual Agendas*, New York: New York University Press, 1997, 3–16.

5 Free Will Politics and the Avoidance of Inversion

1. Cesare LOMBROSO, *L'Uomo delinquente*, Milan: Hoepli, 1876.
2. Michele PIFFERI (ed.), *The Limits of Criminological Positivism: The Movement for Criminal Law Reform in the West, 1870–1940*, Abingdon: Routledge, 2022.
3. On international differences in the development of forensic cultures, see Willemijn RUBERG, Lara BERGERS, Pauline DIRVEN et al. (eds.), *Forensic Cultures in Modern Europe*, Manchester: Manchester University Press, 2023; Harry OOSTERHUIS and Arlie LOUGHAN, "Madness and Crime: Historical perspectives on Forensic Psychiatry," *International Journal of Law and Psychiatry*, 37/1, 2014, 1–16.
4. François SEMAL, "De la situation morale et légale et du placement des aliénés et dangereux," in: E. W. WARLOMONT, V. DUWEZ, and G. VERRIEST (eds.), *Congrès périodique international des sciences médicales: 4me session. Bruxelles. 1875. Compte-rendu*, Brussels: Manceaux and Baillière, 1876, 693–722.
5. *Parlementaire Handelingen: Kamer van Volksvertegenwoordigers*, 1889–1890, December 3, 1873, 99b.
6. Donald WEBER, *Homo criminalis: Belgische parlementsleden over misdaad en strafrecht, 1830–1940*, Brussels: VUBPress, 1996.
7. SEMAL, "De la situation morale," 716.
8. Jan VERPLAETSE, *Localising the Moral Sense: Neuroscience and the Search for the Cerebral Seat of Morality, 1800–1930*, Dordrecht: Springer, 2009. Much of free will's history remains to be written. Useful exceptions are Roger SMITH, *Free Will and the Human Sciences in Britain, 1870–1910*, London: Routledge, 2013; Martin J. WIENER, *Reconstructing the Criminal: Culture, Law and Policy in England, 1830–1914*, Cambridge: Cambridge University Press, 1990.
9. These physicians included Julien Offray de la Mettrie, Jean-Georges Cabanis, and François Broussais. See Anne THOMSON, *Bodies of Thought: Science, Religion and the Soul in the Early Enlightenment*, Oxford: Oxford University Press, 2008.
10. Leading materialistic physiologists and physicians in Germany included Karl Vogt, Jacob Moleschott, and Ludwig Büchner. See Marc RENNEVILLE, *Le langage des crânes: Histoire de la phrénologie*, 2nd ed., Paris: La Découverte, 2020; Kurt BAYERTZ, "Materialism," in: Michael N. FORSTER and Kristin GJESDAL (eds.), *The Oxford Handbook of German Philosophy in the Nineteenth Century*, New York: Oxford University Press, 2015, https://doi.org/10.1093/oxfordhb/9780199696543.001.0001; Frederick GREGORY, *Scientific Materialism in Nineteenth Century Germany*, Dordrecht: Reidel, 1977.

Notes to pages 72–75   169

11. GOLDSTEIN, *Console and Classify*.
12. SEMAL, "De la situation morale," 720.
13. Ibid., 694.
14. Comte was a student of Henri de Saint-Simon. His own disciple, Émile Littré, tirelessly popularized positivism in the 1850s and the 1860s. See Robert FOX, *The Savant and the State: Science and Cultural Politics in Nineteenth-Century France*, Baltimore, MD: Johns Hopkins University Press, 2012, chaps. 1 and 4.
15. Mary PICKERING, "Positivism in European Intellectual, Political, and Religious Life," in: Warren BRECKMAN and Peter E. GORDON (eds.), *The Cambridge History of Modern European Thought*, 2 vols., Cambridge: Cambridge University Press, 2019, vol. 1, 151–171; Mary GIBSON, *Born to Crime: Cesare Lombroso and the Origins of Biological Criminology*, Westport, CT: Praeger, 2002, 20 and 28.
16. These young progressives had been roused by the socialism of the French exile Pierre-Joseph Proudhon, who lived in Belgium between 1858 and 1862. On positivism in the Low Countries, see Kaat WILS, *De omweg van de wetenschap: Het positivisme en de Belgische en Nederlandse intellectuele cultuur*, Amsterdam: Amsterdam University Press, 2005.
17. Guillaume TIBERGHIEN, *Université libre de Bruxelles: Discours prononcé par G. Tiberghien, Recteur, le 7 octobre 1867. Athéisme, matérialisme et positivisme*, Brussels: Mayolez, 1867, 17. On the debate between spiritualists and materialists at the Free University of Brussels, see Pierre F. DALED, *Spiritualisme et matérialisme au XIXe siècle: L'Université de Bruxelles et la religion*, Brussels: Éditions de l'Université de Bruxelles, 1998.
18. From Paul Voituron's *Les causes du mouvement positiviste depuis 1848*. Quoted in WILS, *De omweg van de wetenschap*, 439, note 207.
19. Ibid., 176.
20. Sofie LACHAPELLE, "Between Miracle and Sickness: Louise Lateau and the Experience of Stigmata and Ecstasy," *Configurations*, 12/1, 2004, 77–105, 99.
21. Hubert BOËNS, *Louise Lateau ou les mystères de Bois-D'Haine dévoilés*, 2nd ed., Brussels: Manceaux, 1875, 7 and 71.
22. On France, see GOLDSTEIN, *Console and Classify*, chap. 9; GOLDSTEIN, "The Hysteria Diagnosis."
23. "Statuts," *Annales de la Société scientifique de Bruxelles*, 1, 1875–1876, 1–4, 3.
24. "Séance inaugurale du 18 novembre 1875," *Annales de la Société scientifique de Bruxelles*, 1, 1875–1876, 44–72, 69.
25. For more on Thomism, see Chapters 5 and 6. Emiel LAMBERTS, "Religious, Political and Social Settings of the Revival of Thomism, 1870–1960," in: Wim DECOCK, Bart RAYMAEKERS, and Peter HEYRMAN (eds.), *Neo-Thomism in Action: Law and Society Reshaped by Neo-Scholastic Philosophy, 1880–1960*, Leuven: Leuven University Press, 2021, 29–40.
26. BOËNS, *Louise Lateau*, 25.
27. Hubert BOËNS, "La criminalité au point de vue sociologique," *La philosophie positive: Deuxième série*, 12/23, 1879, 76–96, 83.
28. Leen BEYERS, "Rasdenken tussen geneeskunde en natuurwetenschap: Emile Houzé en de Société d'Anthropologie de Bruxelles, 1870–1940," in: Jo TOLLEBEEK, Geert VANPAEMEL, and Kaat WILS (eds.), *Degeneratie in België: Een geschiedenis van ideeën en praktijken*, Leuven: Leuven University Press, 2003, 43–77.

29. These notable members included the sociologist Guillaume De Greef, the historian Léon Vanderkindere, the political economist Hector Denis, and star barristers Paul Janson and Edmond Picard.
30. Paul HÉGER and Jules DALLEMAGNE, *Étude craniologique d'une série d'assassins excécutés en Belgique*, Brussels: Manceaux, 1881.
31. Benjamin-Constant INGELS, Jean CUYLITS, and Jules MOREL, *Congrès de phréniatrie et de neuropathologie tenu à Anvers du 7 au 9 septembre 1885: Compte-rendu*, Ghent: Vanderhaeghen, 1886.
32. "Procès-verbal de la séance extraordinaire qui a eu lieu à Bruxelles, au Palais de l'Université, le 8 août 1885," *Bulletin de la Société de médecine mentale de Belgique*, 13/38, 1885, 12–15, 13.
33. He drew specifically on the ideas of Henry Maudsley and Herbert Spencer. INGELS, CUYLITS, and MOREL, *Congrès de phréniatrie et de neuropathologie*, 279. On (social) Darwinism in Belgium, see Raf DE BONT, *Darwins kleinkinderen: De evolutieleer in België, 1865–1945*, Nijmegen: Vantilt, 2008.
34. INGELS, CUYLITS, and MOREL, *Congrès de phréniatrie et de neuropathologie*, 304.
35. Valentin MAGNAN, *Des anomalies, des abérrations et des perversions sexuelles: Communication faite à l'Académie de médecine dans la séance du 13 janvier 1885*, Paris: Delahaye and Lecrosnier, 1885, 4.
36. INGELS, CUYLITS, and MOREL, *Congrès de phréniatrie et de neuropathologie*, 286. See pages 287–288 for the following quotations.
37. Robert D. ANDERSON, *France 1870–1914: Politics and Society*, 2nd ed., London: Routledge and Kegan Paul, 1984, 12–13.
38. On Paris' long-standing association with progressivism and the city's perception by Belgian conservatives, see Raf DE BONT and Tom VERSCHAFFEL (eds.), *Het verderf van Parijs*, Leuven: Leuven University Press, 2004.
39. See GOLDSTEIN, "The Hysteria Diagnosis," 233.
40. Jean-Martin CHARCOT and Valentin MAGNAN, "Inversion du sens génital [part 1]," *Archives de neurologie*, 3/7, 1882, 53–60; Jean-Martin CHARCOT and Valentin MAGNAN, "Inversion du sens génital [part 2]," *Archives de neurologie*, 4/12, 1882, 296–322.
41. This was Daniel Hack Tuke. INGELS, CUYLITS, and MOREL, *Congrès de phréniatrie et de neuropathologie*, 326–327.
42. Ibid., 328.
43. Ibid., 318.
44. Els WITTE, "The Battle for Monasteries, Cemeteries and Schools: Belgium," in: Christopher CLARK and Wolfram KAISER (eds.), *Culture Wars: Secular-Catholic Conflict in Nineteenth-Century Europe*, Cambridge: Cambridge University Press, 2003, 102–128.
45. Emiel LAMBERTS and Jacques LORY (eds.), *1884: Un tournant politique en Belgique – De machtswisseling van 1884 in België*, Brussels: Presses de l'Université Saint-Louis, 1986.
46. DE SMAELE, "Politieke partijen in de Kamer."
47. Gita DENECKERE, "Vive le peuple! De arbeidsbeweging op het politieke toneel 1885–1890," in: Els WITTE, Jean-Pierre NANDRIN, Eliane GUBIN et al. (eds.), *Nieuwe geschiedenis van België*, 3 vols., Tielt: Lannoo, 2005, vol. 1, 500–518.
48. Stef CHRISTIAENSEN, *Tussen klassieke en moderne criminele politiek: Leven en beleid van Jules Lejeune*, Leuven: Leuven University Press, 2004; Lieven DUPONT,

"Jules Lejeune et la défense sociale," in: Françoise TULKENS (ed.), *Généalogie de la défense sociale en Belgique (1880–1914): Travaux du séminaire qui s'est tenu à l'Université Catholique de Louvain sous la direction de Michel Foucault*, Brussels: Story-Scientia, 1988, 77–86.

49. Yves CARTUYVELS, "Adolphe Prins and Social Defence in Belgium: The Reform in the Service of Maintaining Social Order," *GLOSSAE: European Journal of Legal History*, 17/1, 2020, 177–210; B. FRYDMAN, "Adolphe Prins et l'École de Bruxelles: La défense sociale dans la guerre d'idées," in: F. KUTTY and A. WEYEMBERGH (eds.), *La science pénale dans tous ses états: Liber amicorum Patrick Mandoux et Marc Preumont*, Brussels: Larcier, 2019, 559–585; Pierre VAN DER VORST and Philippe MARY (eds.), *Cent ans de criminologie à l'U.L.B.: Adolphe Prins, l'Union internationale de droit pénal, le Cercle universitaire pour les études criminologiques*, Brussels: Bruylant, 1990. On recidivism, also see WIENER, *Reconstructing the Criminal*, 342–358.

50. "Procès-verbal de la séance ordinaire tenue au Palais de l'Université à Bruxelles, le samedi 28 janvier 1888," *Bulletin de la Société de médecine mentale de Belgique*, 16/48, 1888, 9–22, 12–16. The quote is taken from page 13.

51. Paul HÉGER, "Les prisons-asiles," *Bulletin de la Société de médecine mentale de Belgique*, 99, 1900, 358–374, 365. See also Paul HÉGER, "Les prisons-asiles," *Revue de l'Université de Bruxelles*, 6, 1900–1901, 31–45, 37.

52. While in France the medical establishment was a parliamentary force to be reckoned with, especially with the rise of radical democrats under the Third Republic, in Belgium physician-legislators were relatively few and ideologically divided, even if medicalizing metaphors increasingly infused political language during the *fin de siècle*. See Anne MORELLI, "Les médecins parlementaires belges (XIXe–XXe siècles)," *Socialisme, hors série*, 2, 1993, 9–18, 15. Also see Karel VELLE, *De nieuwe biechtvaders: Sociale geschiedenis van de arts in België*, Leuven: Kritak, 1991, 177–185. Compare with Jack D. ELLIS, *The Physician-Legislators of France: Medicine and Politics in the Early Third Republic, 1870–1914*, Cambridge: Cambridge University Press, 1990. On medicalization in Belgium, see Jo TOLLEBEEK, Geert VANPAEMEL, and Kaat WILS (eds.), *Degeneratie in België, 1860–1940: Een geschiedenis van ideeën en praktijken*, Leuven: Leuven University Press, 2003; Liesbet NYS, Henk DE SMAELE, Jo TOLLEBEEK et al. (eds.), *De zieke natie: Over de medicalisering van de samenleving 1860–1914*, Groningen: Historische Uitgeverij, 2002.

53. "Discussion du rapport de la Commission chargée d'examiner les questions relatives aux aliénés dits criminels, soumises à l'Académie par M. le Ministre de la Justice," *Bulletin de l'Académie royale de médecine de Belgique: IVe série*, 3, 1889, 281–330, 362–395, 365–605 and 612–632, 567.

54. Ibid., 310.

55. The acknowledged leaders of the Lyon school were Gabriel Tarde and Alexandre Lacassagne. Martine KALUSZYNSKI, "The International Congresses of Criminal Anthropology: Shaping the French and International Criminological Movement, 1886–1914," in: Peter BECKER and Richard F. WETZELL (eds.), *Criminals and Their Scientists: The History of Criminology in International Perspective*, Cambridge: Cambridge University Press, 2006, 301–316; Marc RENNEVILLE, *Crime et folie: Deux siècles d'enquêtes médicales et judiciaires*, Paris: Fayard, 2003, chap. 8; NYE, *Crime, Madness, and Politics in Modern France*, chap. 4.

56. Total attendance at the second conference in Paris had not exceeded 184 participants from 22 countries. The fourth iteration at Geneva in 1896 was attended by 238 participants from 21 countries and the fifth at Amsterdam in 1901 by 379 participants from 23 countries.
57. Originally, the report was supposed to be presented by the German neuropsychiatrist Emanuel Mendel from the University of Berlin. We can safely speculate that both the topic and Mendel were selected because the forensic discussion of homosexuality had intensified more rapidly in Germany than anywhere else since the early 1870s, when the Prussian ban on 'unnatural fornication' became law throughout the newly unified German Empire. For reasons that remain unclear, however, Mendel withdrew and Léon De Rode was tapped to stand in for him. See "Programme du Congrès International d'Anthropologie criminelle qui se tiendra à Bruxelles du 8 au 14 août 1892," *Bulletin de la Société de médecine mentale de Belgique*, 20/64, 1892, 122–124, 123.
58. Léon DE RODE, "L'Inversion génitale et la législation," in: *Actes du troisième congrès international d'anthropologie criminelle tenu à Bruxelles en août 1892 sous le haut patronage du gouvernement: Biologie et sociologie*, Brussels: Hayez, 1893, 107–113, 107.
59. Ibid., 110–111.
60. Ibid., 111.
61. Ibid.
62. Ibid.
63. Capitalization in original. Ibid., 111–112.
64. Xavier FRANCOTTE, *De quelques points de morale sexuelle dans ses relations avec la médecine: Rapport présenté à la section de médecine de la Société scientifique de Bruxelles, séance du 10 avril 1907*, Leuven: Secrétariat de la Société scientifique, 1907, 36.
65. Xavier FRANCOTTE, *L'Anthropologie criminelle*, Paris: Baillière, 1891, 330.
66. Ibid., 350.
67. Louis DELATTRE, *Rapport de M. le Dr Louis Delattre, inspecteur d'hygiène, concernant un plan d'hygiène, d'éducation morale et hygiénique de la vie sexuelle*, Brussels: Nossent, 1922, 37.
68. Charles POTVIN, *Du gouvernement de soi-même: Les principes, le devoir, la vie privée, la patrie, le travail, les nations*, 6 vols., Paris: Hachette, 1877.
69. On Charles Potvin and his circle, see Christophe DE SPIEGELEER, *Een blauwe progressist: Charles Potvin (1818–1902) en het liberaal-sociale denken van zijn generatie*, Ghent: Liberaal Archief, 2011. Regarding Vanderkindere, see his presidential address Léon VANDERKINDERE, *Ligue de l'enseignement: Extrait du rapport présenté à l'Assemblée générale du 2 avril 1890*, Brussels: Weissenbruch, 1890.
70. Xavier FRANCOTTE, *Causeries sur des questions d'hygiène morale*, Liège: Imprimerie liégeoise, 1919, 7.
71. E.g. Vern L. BULLOUGH, *Science in the Bedroom: A History of Sex Research*, New York: Basic Books, 1994.
72. NYE, "The History of Sexuality in Context."
73. "Séance du 29 avril 1905 [Discours prononcé aux obsèques de M. Hubert]," *Bulletin de l'Académie royale de médecine de Belgique: IVe série*, 19, 1905, 209–212 (see also pages 201–202 of the same volume); Léopold DANDOIS, "Eugène Hubert,"

Revue médicale de Louvain, 7, 1905, 113; Ernest MASOIN, "Éloge funèbre de E. Hubert, prononcé le 19 juin 1905, en la salle des Promotions, par E. Masoin, professeur à la Faculté de Médecine," *Annuaire de l'Université Catholique de Louvain*, 70, 1906, lv–lxvii.

74. "L'Inversion génitale et la législation [Discussion]," in: *Actes du troisième congrès international d'anthropologie criminelle tenu à Bruxelles en Août 1892 sous le haut patronage du gouvernement: Biologie et sociologie*, Brussels: Hayez, 1893, 448–459, 448. Also published as Eugène HUBERT, "L'Inversion du sens génital," *Revue médicale*, 11, 1892, 359–363.
75. Emphasis in original. "L'Inversion génitale et la législation [Discussion]," 449.
76. Ibid.
77. Ibid., 451. This moralism reveals strong continuities with the classical, medieval, and early modern past, and it demonstrates the persistent relevance of the Christian tradition in particular. With varying points of emphasis across time and place, that tradition had long warned against temptation and excess, and against the stepping-stone effects of immoderation and indulgence. Theo van der Meer has called this a "psychology of excess." Theo VAN DER MEER, *Sodoms zaad in Nederland*, chap. 4, page 169 particularly. Compare with HOFMAN, "The End of Sodomy," chap. 6; COCKS, *Visions of Sodom*; Theo VAN DER MEER, "Sodomy and the Pursuit of a Third Sex in the Early Modern Period," in: Gilbert HERDT (ed.), *Third Sex, Third Gender: Beyond Sexual Dimorphism in Culture and History*, New York: Zone Books, 1993, 137–212.
78. "L'Inversion génitale et la législation [Discussion]," 452.
79. Ibid., 456. On Houzé and his scientific racism, see Maarten COUTTENIER, "'We Can't Help Laughing!': Physical Anthropology in Belgium and Congo (1882–1914)," in: Nicolas BANCEL, Thomas DAVID, and Dominic THOMAS (eds.), *The Invention of Race: Scientific and Popular Representations*, New York: Routledge, 2014, 100–116.
80. "L'Inversion génitale et la législation [Discussion]," 456.
81. René SEMELAIGNE, "Le troisième congrès international d'anthropologie criminelle," *Annales médico-psychologiques*, 16, 1892, 329–366, 353.
82. "Le troisième congrès d'anthropologie criminelle," *Journal des Tribunaux*, 11/909, 1892, 995–1001, 998.
83. Emile HOUZÉ and Léo WARNOTS, "Existe-t-il un type de criminel anatomiquement déterminé," in: *Actes du troisième congrès international d'anthropologie criminelle tenu à Bruxelles en Août 1892 sous le haut patronage du gouvernement: Biologie et sociologie*, Brussels: Hayez, 1893, 121–126, 122.
84. *Actes du troisième congrès international d'anthropologie criminelle tenu à Bruxelles en Août 1892 sous le haut patronage du gouvernement: Biologie et sociologie*, Brussels: Hayez, 1893, 259.
85. Ibid., 261. Also see Maurice DE BAETS, *Les bases de la morale et du droit*, Paris: Alcan and Siffer, 1892. On De Baets, see Ferdinand CLAEYS BOUUAERT, "M. le Chanoine Maurice De Baets: Professeur honoraire de la Faculté de Théologie," *Université catholique de Louvain. Katholieke Universiteit Leuven. Annuaire-Jaarboek*, 1930–1933, cxii–cxx; Ludo COLLIN, "Maurice de Baets et l'Institut Supérieur de Philosophie de Louvain," *Bulletin de l'Institut Historique Belge de Rome*, 55–56, 1985–1986, 253–285.
86. *Actes du troisième congrès*, 264.

87. Henk DE SMAELE, "Medische pathologie en juridische logica: Het politieke debat over de hervorming van het strafrecht," in: Liesbet NYS, Henk DE SMAELE, Jo TOLLEBEEK et al. (eds.), *De zieke natie: Over de medicalisering van de samenleving 1860–1914*, Groningen: Historische Uitgeverij, 2002, 356–369.
88. *Actes du troisième congrès*, 266.
89. Ibid., 284.
90. Albert BOURNET, "Troisième congrès d'anthropologie criminelle," *Archives de l'anthropologie criminelle et des sciences pénales*, 7/41, 1892, 465–591, 465 and 471–472. Also see "Le troisième congrès d'anthropologie criminelle," *Journal des Tribunaux*, 11/909, 1892, 995–1001, 997; "Anthropologie criminelle: 3ᵉ congrès," *L'Indépendance belge*, August 8–16, 1892; "[Anthropologie criminelle: 3ᵉ congrès]," *L'Indépendance belge*, August 18, 1892.
91. *Archives de l'anthropologie sexuelle*, 1886–1914.
92. *Jahrbuch für sexuelle Zwischenstufen mit besonderer Berücksichtigung der Homosexualität*, 1897–1923.
93. TARNOVSKII, *Izvrashchenie polovogo chuvstva*; Paolo MANTEGAZZA, *Gli Amori degli uomini: Saggio di una entnologia dell'amore*, Milan: Mantegazza, 1886; KRAFFT-EBING, *Psychopathia sexualis*.
94. Albert MOLL, *Die Conträre Sexualempfindung: Mit Benutzung amtlichen Materials*, Berlin: Fischer, 1891; Theodor RAMIEN (Magnus HIRSCHFELD), *Sappho und Sokrates oder wie erklärt sich die Liebe der Männer und Frauen zu Personen des eigenen Geschlechts?*, Leipzig: Spohr, 1896.
95. CHEVALIER, *De l'inversion de l'instinct sexuel*; Benjamin BALL, *La folie érotique*, Paris: Baillière, 1888; Paul GARNIER, *Les Fétichistes: Pervertis et invertis sexuels. Observations médico-légales*, Paris: Baillière, 1896.
96. Havelock ELLIS and John A. SYMONDS, *Sexual Inversion*, London: Wilson and Macmillan, 1897; Lucien S. A. M. VON RÖMER, *Het uranisch gezin: Wetenschappelijk onderzoek en conclusiën over homosexualiteit*, Amsterdam: Tierie, 1905.
97. Jules DALLEMAGNE, *Dégénérés et déséquilibrés*, Brussels: Lamertin, 1894, 495–537.
98. On Raffalovich, see Frederick S. RODEN (ed.), *Jewish, Christian, Queer: Crossroads and Identities*, 2nd ed., London: Routledge, 2016 [2009], chap. 7; Vernon A. ROSARIO, *The Erotic Imagination: French Histories of Perversity*, New York: Oxford University Press, 1997, 98–100; Vernon A. ROSARIO, "Pointy Penises, Fashion Crimes, and Hysterical Mollies," in: Jeffrey MERRICK and Bryant T. RAGAN Jr. (eds.), *Homosexuality in Modern France*, New York: Oxford University Press, 1996, 146–176, 161–162.
99. Marc-André RAFFALOVICH, "L'Uranisme: Inversion sexuelle congénitale. Observations et conseils," *Archives d'anthropologie criminelle, de médecine légale et de psychologie normale et pathologique*, 10/55, 1895, 99–127, 126. Also see Patrick CARDON, *Discours littéraires et scientifiques fin-de-siècle: La discussion sur les homosexualités dans la revue Archives d'anthropologie criminelle du Dr Lacassagne (1886–1914) autour de Marc-André Raffalovich*, Paris: Orizons, 2008.
100. [Marc-]André RAFFALOVICH, "Annales de l'unisexualité [1]," *Archives d'anthropologie criminelle, de médecine légale et de psychologie normale et pathologique*, 12/67, 1897, 87–102, 88.
101. RAFFALOVICH, "L'Uranisme," 122.

102. Paul NÄCKE, "Un cas de fétichisme de souliers avec remarques sur les perversions du sens génital," *Bulletin de la Société de médecine mentale de Belgique*, 22/74, 1894, 308–332.
103. For example, after his studies at the Salpêtrière in Paris the Belgian Paul Masoin published a short *Contribution to the Study of the Sexual Perversions in the Degenerate* in 1895, defending Magnan's materialism. J. A. Peeters also clung to degeneration in his review of Paul Garnier's book on sexual inversion, as did L. De Moor in his brief *Notes on a Case of Fetishism* of 1903. See Paul MASOIN, *Contribution à l'étude des perversions sexuelles chez les dégénérés*, Ghent: Vanderhaeghen, 1895, 15; J. A. PEETERS, "[Review of] Les fétichistes pervertis et invertis sexuels: Observations médico-légales [by P. Garnier]," *Bulletin de la Société de médecine mentale de Belgique*, 23/79, 1895, 421–423; L. DE MOOR, "Note sur un cas de fétichisme," *Bulletin de la Société de médecine mentale de Belgique*, 31/110–111, 1903, 189–194.
104. On the society, see Stephan DURVIAUX, "Le Cercle universitaire pour les études criminologiques," in: Pierre VAN DER VORST and Philippe MARY (eds.), *Cent ans de criminologie à l'U.L.B.*, Brussels: Bruylant, 1990, 21–44. On the development of criminology in Belgium and the importance of the criminological circle, also see Jean CONSTANT, "L'Enseignement de la criminologie en Belgique," in: *Cinquante ans de droit pénal et de criminologie: Publication jubilaire (1907–1957)*, Brussels: Revue de droit pénal et de criminologie, 1957, 197–210.
105. DALLEMAGNE, *Dégénérés et déséquilibrés*, 618.
106. Léon HENNEBICQ, "[Review of] Dégénérés et déséquilibrés [by J. Dallemagne]," *Journal des Tribunaux*, 14/1152, 1895, 737–748, 743.
107. Adolphe PRINS, "Conférence sur les doctrines nouvelles du droit pénal faite le 21 décembre 1895 au Palais de Justice de Bruxelles," *Revue de l'Université de Bruxelles*, 1, 1895–1896, 6–33, 10.
108. On Dallemagne, E. JAUQUET, "Notice sur la vie et les travaux de Jules Dallemagne," in: *Rapport de l'Université Libre de Bruxelles sur l'année académique 1922–1923*, Brussels: Université Libre, 1924, 27–31.
109. Raf DE BONT, "Meten en verzoenen: Louis Vervaeck en de Belgische criminele antropologie, circa 1900–1940," *Bijdragen tot de Eigentijdse Geschiedenis – Cahiers d'Histoire du Temps Présent*, 9, 2001, 63–104, 68.
110. On Vervaeck, see Raf DE BONT and Kaat WILS, "De meetbare misdadiger: Cesare Lombroso en de criminele antropologie in België," in: *Karakterkoppen: Over haviksneuzen en hamsterwangen*, Tielt: Lannoo, 2014, 115–135; Raf DE BONT, "Meten en verzoenen: Louis Vervaeck en de Belgische criminele antropologie, circa 1900–1940," in: Jo TOLLEBEEK, Geert VANPAEMEL, and Kaat WILS (eds.), *Degeneratie in België, 1860–1940: Een geschiedenis van ideeën en praktijken*, Leuven: Leuven University Press, 2003, 185–225.

6 Demographic Anxieties and Catholic Code

1. Richard TOGMAN, *Nationalizing Sex: Fertility, Fear, and Power*, New York: Oxford University Press, 2019.
2. Ian HACKING, "Biopower and the Avalanche of Printed Numbers," *Humanities in Society*, 5, 1982, 279–295.

3. Aliza S. WONG, *Race and the Nation in Liberal Italy, 1861–1911: Meridionalism, Empire, and Diaspora*, New York: Palgrave Macmillan, 2006.
4. Paulo J. FERNANDES, "The Press and Portuguese-British Relations at the Time of the British 'Ultimatum,'" in: José L. GARCIA, Chandrika KAUL, Filipa SUBTIL et al. (eds.), *Media and the Portuguese Empire*, s.l.: Palgrave Macmillan, 87–105.
5. Jeffrey WEEKS, *Sex, Politics and Society: The Regulation of Sex since 1800*, 3rd ed., London: Routledge, 2012 [1981], 162; Richard A. SOLOWAY, "Counting the Degenerates: The Statistics of Race Deterioration in Edwardian England," *Journal of Contemporary History*, 17/1, 1982, 138–164, 140. Also see Richard A. SOLOWAY, *Demography and Degeneration: Eugenics and the Declining Birthrate in Twentieth-Century Britain*, 2nd ed., Chapel Hill: University of North Carolina Press, 1995.
6. Francisco VÁZQUEZ GARCÍA, "Homosexualité et crise de 1898 en Espagne: L'Invention de Cadix comme la 'Sodome' moderne," in: Jean-Louis GUEREÑA (ed.), *Sexualités Occidentales, XVIIIe–XXIe siècles*, Tours: Presses Universitaires François Rabelais, 2014, 151–180; CLEMINSON and VÁZQUEZ GARCÍA, *Los Invisibles*, chap. 5.
7. There are as yet surprisingly few comparative histories of how 'biopolitical' anxiety inflected the concern with homosexuality. For useful introductions to the concept of biopolitics, which I do not elaborate on here for the sake of flow, see Sergei PROZOROV and Simona RENTEA (eds.), *The Routledge Handbook of Biopolitics*, London: Routledge, 2017; Thomas LEMKE, *Biopolitics: An Advanced Introduction*, translated by Eric F. TRUMP, New York: New York University Press, 2011.
8. On France, see Karen OFFEN, *Debating the Woman Question in the French Third Republic, 1870–1920*, Cambridge: Cambridge University Press, 2018; Joshua COLE, *The Power of Large Numbers: Population, Politics, and Gender in Nineteenth-Century France*, Ithaca, NY: Cornell University Press, 2000; Jean E. PEDERSEN, "Regulating Abortion and Birth Control: Gender, Medicine, and Republican Politics in France, 1870–1920," *French Historical Studies*, 19/3, 1996, 673–698; Richard TOMLINSON, "The 'Disappearance' of France, 1896–1940: French Politics and the Birth Rate," *The Historical Journal*, 28/2, 1985, 405–415; Karen OFFEN, "Depopulation, Nationalism, and Feminism in Fin-de-Siècle France," *American Historical Review*, 89/3, 1984, 648–676; Angus McLAREN, *Sexuality and Social Order: The Debate over the Fertility of Women and Workers in France, 1770–1920*, New York: Holmes and Meier, 1983.
9. Lucien-Anatole PRÉVOST-PARADOL, *La France nouvelle*, Paris: Lévy, 1868, 389.
10. Robert A. NYE, *Masculinity and Male Codes of Honor in Modern France*, New York: Oxford University Press, 1993, 78.
11. In 1880, Germany produced 2.7 million metric tons of pig iron to France's 1.35 million. By 1910, the figures were 14.8 million to 4 million tons respectively. Steel production and mercantile shipping show the same divergence. John H. CLAPHAM, *The Economic Development of France and Germany 1815–1914*, Cambridge: Cambridge University Press, 1921, 285 and 356.
12. These and further demographic data were drawn from Franz ROTHENBACHER, *The European Population, 1850–1945*, Basingstoke: Palgrave Macmillan, 2002.
13. On this commission and the wider pro-natal movement, see Virginie DE LUCA BARRUSSE, "Des liaisons avantageuses: L'Alliance nationale pour l'accroissement

de la population française et les fonctionnaires (1890–1914)," *Annales de démographie historique*, 116, 2008, 255–280; Jean E. PEDERSEN, "Regulating Abortion and Birth Control: Gender, Medicine, and Republican Politics in France, 1870–1920," *French Historical Studies*, 19/3, 1996, 673–698; Maria Sophia QUINE, *Population Politics in Twentieth-Century Europe: Fascist Dictatorships and Liberal Democracies*, London: Routledge, 1996, chap. 2; Alain BECCHIA, "Les milieux parlementaires et la dépopulation de 1900 à 1914," *Communications*, 44, 1986, 201–246, 202.

14. Daniel PICK, *Faces of Degeneration: A European Disorder, c.1848–c.1918*, Cambridge: Cambridge University Press, 1993, part 1.
15. Judith SURKIS, *Sexing the Citizen: Morality and Masculinity in France, 1870–1920*, Ithaca, NY: Cornell University Press, 2006; Alain CORBIN, "L'Hérédosyphilis ou l'impossible rédemption: Contribution à l'histoire de l'hérédité morbide," in: Alain CORBIN (ed.), *Le temps, le désir et l'horreur*, Paris: Aubier, 1991.
16. Emile ZOLA, *Fécondité*, Paris: Charpentier, 1899, 411. On Zola's pro-natalism, see Michael ROSENFELD, "Zola nataliste ou féministe? Pouvoir féminin et sexualités subversives dans 'Fécondité'," *Nineteenth-Century French Studies*, 51/1–2, 2022–2023, 103–120; Andrew J. COUNTER, "Zola's Fin-de-siècle Reproductive Politics," *French Studies*, 68/2, 2014, 193–208.
17. OFFEN, *Debating the Woman Question*, 86–93 and chap. 7.
18. COUNTER, "Zola's Fin-de-siècle Reproductive Politics," 207.
19. See NYE, *Masculinity and Male Codes of Honor*, chap. 6.
20. Joris-Karl HUYSMANS, *À Rebours*, Paris: Cent Bibliophiles, 1903 [1884], 110–111.
21. Ibid., 113. Also see ROSARIO, *The Erotic Imagination*, 142; NYE, *Masculinity and Male Codes of Honor*, 120.
22. SURKIS, *Sexing the Citizen*, 11 and 72; Martha HANNA, "Natalism, Homosexuality, and the Controversy over Corydon," in: Jeffrey MERRICK and Bryant T. RAGAN Jr. (eds.), *Homosexuality in Modern France*, New York: Oxford University Press, 1996, 202–224, 218.
23. Paul BUREAU, *La crise morale des temps nouveaux*, 9th ed., Paris: Bloud, 1908, 30.
24. CHEVALIER, *Une maladie de la personnalité*, 455. Also see VERHOEVEN, *Sexual Crime*, 48–51.
25. CARLIER, *Les deux prostitutions*, 280. Compare with Charles FÉRÉ, *L'Instinct sexuel: Évolution et dissolution*, Paris: Félix Alcan, 1899.
26. FÉRÉ, *L'Instinct sexuel*, 50 and 53. Also see Angus MCLAREN, *Impotence: A History*, Chicago: University of Chicago Press, 2007, 112; Robert A. NYE, "Honor, Impotence, and Male Sexuality in Nineteenth-Century French Medicine," *French Historical Studies*, 16/1, 1989, 48–71, 61. Even homosexuality's few French defenders, such as Marc-André Raffalovich and André Gide, were averse to effeminacy, favoring 'virile' friendships instead.
27. Régis REVENIN, "Homosexualité et virilité," in: Alain CORBIN, Jean-Jacques COURTINE, and Georges VIGARELLO (eds.), *Histoire de la virilité*, 3 vols., Paris: Seuil, 2011, vol. 2, 369–401, 376.
28. Saint-Paul wrote under the pseudonym Dr. Laupts. See DR. LAUPTS, *Tares et poisons: Perversion & perversité sexuelles. Une enquête médicale sur l'inversion. Notes et documents. Le roman d'un inverti-né. Le procès Wilde. La guérison et la*

prophylaxie de l'inversion, Paris: Georges Carré, 1896, 4. On Zola's engagement with homosexuality, see Michael ROSENFELD and William A. PENISTON (eds.), *The Italian Invert: A Gay Man's Intimate Confessions to Émile Zola*, New York: Columbia University Press, 2022; Michael ROSENFELD (ed.), *Confessions d'un homosexuel à Émile Zola*, Paris: Nouvelles Éditions Place, 2017.

29. NYE, "The History of Sexuality in Context," 398. See also Robert A. NYE, "Sex Difference and Male Homosexuality in French Medical Discourse 1830–1930," *Bulletin of the History of Medicine*, 63, 1989, 32–51.
30. DR. LAUPTS, *L'Homosexualité et les types homosexuels: Nouvelle édition de perversion et perversité sexuelles*, 2nd ed., Paris: Vigot Frères, 1910, 414.
31. Jean PUISSANT, "Le naturalisme en Belgique, expression littéraire de la crise ou de la prospérité?," in: Paul DELSEMME and Raymond TROUSSON (eds.), *Le naturalisme et les lettres françaises de Belgique*, Brussels: Éditions de l'Université de Bruxelles, 1984, 109–118, 111.
32. Overviews of the national and international turmoil that preoccupied continental Europe during the long nineteenth century can be found in John M. ROBERTS, *Europe 1880–1945*, 2nd ed., London: Longman, 1989, chaps. 1–8; Agatha RAMM, *Europe in the Nineteenth Century 1789–1905*, London: Longman, 1984; Anthony WOOD, *Europe 1815–1960*, 2nd ed., Harlow: Longman, 1984, parts 1–5.
33. On the history of Belgian neutrality, see Daniel H. THOMAS, *The Guarantee of Belgian Independence and Neutrality in European Diplomacy, 1830's–1930's*, Kingston: Thomas, 1983.
34. On the growing fear of a new Franco-German conflict and its consequences for Belgium, see Marie-Thérèse BITSCH, *La Belgique entre la France et l'Allemagne, 1905–1914*, Paris: Publications de la Sorbonne, 1994; Robert DEVLEESHOUWER, *Les Belges et le danger de guerre, 1910–1914*, Leuven: Nauwelaerts, 1958.
35. During this period, Belgium's annual economic growth averaged 5.2 percent, Britain's 3.1 percent, and Germany's 4.5 percent. See René LEBOUTTE, Jean PUISSANT, and Denis SCUTO, *Un siècle d'histoire industrielle (1873–1973): Belgique, Luxembourg, Pays-Bas. Industrialisation et sociétés*, Paris: SEDES, 1998, 31. Compare with Jean-Marie WAUTELET, *Structures industrielles et reproduction élargie du capital en Belgique (1850–1914)*, Louvain-la-Neuve: Academia and L'Harmattan, 1995, 17.
36. See CLAPHAM, *The Economic Development of France and Germany*, 280–285.
37. LEBOUTTE, PUISSANT, Denis SCUTO, *Un siècle d'histoire industrielle*, 31–33.
38. The Belgian state assumed colonial control over the formerly privately 'owned' Congo Free State of King Leopold II in 1908. Until the early 1920s, Belgium's hold over the much-coveted mineral-rich territory was tenuous in the face of French, German, and British imperialist expansionism. During the interwar period, however, Congo's colonization became a source of national pride. See Guy VANTHEMSCHE, *Belgium and the Congo, 1885–1980*, New York: Cambridge University Press, 2012, chaps. 3 and 4.
39. See REYNEBEAU, *Een geschiedenis van België*, 110–111.
40. Henri CHARRIAUT, *La Belgique moderne: Une terre d'expériences*, Paris: Ernest Flammarion, 1910, 2.
41. See Daniel LAQUA, *The Age of Internationalism and Belgium, 1880–1930: Peace, Progress and Prestige*, Manchester: Manchester University Press, 2013.

Notes to pages 93–95

42. They were held in 1885 (Antwerp), 1894 (Antwerp), 1897 (Brussels), 1905 (Liège), 1910 (Brussels), and 1913 (Ghent). See John E. FINDLING and Kimberley D. PELLE (eds.), *Encyclopedia of World's Fairs and Expositions*, Jefferson, NC: McFarland, 2008.
43. Katrien DIERCKX, *Pro Arte! Cui Bono? Kunst en expertise in laatnegentiende-eeuws Brussel (1860–1914)*, Brussels: University of Antwerp Press, 2021, 14.
44. Edmond PICARD, "Éloquence nouveau siècle," *Journal des Tribunaux*, 10/764, 1891, 1–5, 1.
45. Paul ARON, "Art nouveau in Belgium: A Laboratory of Modernity," in: Nathalie AUBERT, Pierre-Philippe FRAITURE, and Patrick MCGUINNESS (eds.), *La Belgique entre deux siècles: Laboratoire de la modernité, 1880–1914*, Bern: Peter Lang, 2007, 19–31, 30.
46. Ibid., 31.
47. See Jo DEFERME, *Uit de ketens van de vrijheid: Het debat over sociale politiek in België 1886–1914*, Leuven: Leuven University Press, 2007.
48. DE SMAELE, "Medische pathologie en juridische logica"; WEBER, *Homo criminalis*.
49. Liesbet NYS, "De grote school van de natie: Legerartsen over drankmisbruik en geslachtsziekten in het Belgisch leger (circa 1850–1950)," *Bijdragen en mededelingen betreffende de geschiedenis der Nederlanden*, 115/3, 2000, 365–391.
50. An VLEUGELS, *Narratives of Drunkenness: Belgium, 1830–1914*, London: Pickering and Chatto, 2013.
51. On the fight against syphilis, see Karel VELLE, "De syfiliskwestie in België in de 19de en het begin van de 20ste eeuw," *Tijdschrift voor Sociale Wetenschappen*, 32/4, 1987, 331–363.
52. Liesbet NYS, "Nationale plagen: Hygiënisten over het maatschappelijk lichaam," in: Liesbet NYS, Henk DE SMAELE, Jo TOLLEBEEK et al. (eds.), *De zieke natie: Over de medicalisering van de samenleving 1860–1914*, Groningen: Historische Uitgeverij, 2002, 220–241, 234.
53. ROTHENBACHER, *The European Population*, 117–143.
54. Charles PETITHAN, "La dégénérescence de la race belge, ses causes et ses remèdes [et rapports joints]," *Bulletin de la Société royale de médecine publique du royaume de Belgique*, 7, 1888, 62–95.
55. "Rapport de M. le Dr Schrevens (Tournai)," *Bulletin de l'Académie royale de médecine de Belgique*, 2, 1888, 89–94, 93.
56. Ibid., 92.
57. Charles PETITHAN, "Sur la position que doit prendre la gynécologie dans les questions sociales qui ont rapport à la procréation," in: GUYE, De PERROT, STOKVIS et al. (eds.), *Congrès périodique international des sciences médicales: 6me session. Amsterdam, septembre 1879. Compte-rendu*, Amsterdam: Van Rossen, 1880, 113–116, 114.
58. PETITHAN, "La dégénérescence de la race belge," 68. The White community in the Belgian Congo would always remain tiny in real terms and by comparison to other European colonizers. By 1938, for example, there were 260,000 Whites in the Dutch Indies compared to only 23,000 in the Belgian Congo. The populations of the Netherlands and Belgium were roughly equal at that time. See VANTHEMSCHE, *Belgium and the Congo*, 61–64. On the history of sexuality in the Congo Free

State and the Belgian Congo, which so far does not include homosexuality, see Amandine LAURO, "Violence, Anxieties, and the Making of Interracial Dangers: Colonial Surveillance and Interracial Sexuality in the Belgian Congo," in: Chelsea SHIELDS and Dagmar HERZOG (eds.), *The Routledge Companion to Sexuality and Colonialism*, New York: Routledge, 2021, 327–338; Amandine LAURO, *Coloniaux, ménagères et prostituées au Congo belge (1885–1930)*, Loverval: Labor, 2005.

59. Thomas Malthus, the father of modern demography, was opposed to contraception, which is partly why those in favor of and those opposed to birth control in the later nineteenth century added the 'neo' prefix. The reasons why people supported birth control varied widely, however, and the very vagueness of the term made it useful to critics who liked to paint all Malthusians with the same brush.
60. Nel DE MÛELENAERE, *Belgen, zijt gij ten strijde gereed? Militarisering in een neutrale natie, 1890–1914*, Leuven: Leuven University Press, 2019, 9.
61. *Parlementaire Handelingen: Kamer van Volksvertegenwoordigers*, January 16, 1904, 410–411.
62. *Parlementaire Handelingen: Kamer van Volksvertegenwoordigers*, October 11, 1901, 2465.
63. Camille JACQUART, "Le problème de la natalité en France," *Revue Sociale Catholique*, 8, 1903–1904, 39–52, 77–83 and 137–146.
64. Camille JACQUART, "Mouvement de l'état civil et de la population en Belgique pendant les années 1876 à 1900," *Bulletin de la commission centrale de statistique*, 19, 1906, 296–424, 354. The statistics that follow have been taken from this article.
65. JACQUART, "Le problème de la natalité en France," 81 and 144 respectively.
66. Jean STENGERS, "Les pratiques anticonceptionnelles dans le mariage au XIXe et au XXe siècles: Problèmes humains et attitudes religieuses," *Belgisch tijdschrift voor filologie en geschiedenis – Revue belge de philologie et d'histoire*, 49/2 and 4, 1971, 403–481 and 1119–1174, 1163.
67. Written by Vermeersch in a letter to Mercier on February 7, 1907. The letter is quoted by Stengers, in note two on page 1164 of his previously cited article.
68. Philippe VAN PRAAG, *Het bevolkingsvraagstuk in België: Ontwikkeling van standpunten en opvattingen (1900–1977)*, Antwerp: De Sikkel and De Nederlandsche Boekhandel, 1979, 20–22; Philippe VAN PRAAG, "De opkomst van het nieuw-malthusianisme in Vlaanderen," *Tijdschrift voor sociale geschiedenis*, 3/8, 1977, 197–220; STENGERS, "Les pratiques anticonceptionnelles," 1126–1154.
69. Ibid., 1130.
70. Désiré Joseph MERCIER, Henri DESPLATS, and Arthur VERMEERSCH, *Pour l'honnêteté conjugale: Nouvelle édition*, Leuven: Fonteyn, 1910, 2.
71. John T. NOONAN, *Contraception: A History of Its Treatment by the Catholic Theologians and Canonists. Enlarged Edition*, Cambridge, MA: Harvard University Press, 1986 [1965], 387–406. For an analysis of developments in French moral theology, see Claude LANGLOIS, *Le crime d'Onan: Le discours catholique sur la limitation des naissances (1816–1930)*, Paris: Les Belles Lettres, 2005.
72. Quoted in Paul SERVAIS, "The Church and the Family in Belgium, 1850–1914," *Belgisch Tijdschrift voor Nieuwste Geschiedenis – Revue Belge d'Histoire Contemporaine*, 31/3–4, 2001, 621–647, 627.
73. Hugh MCLEOD, "New Perspectives on the Religious History of Western and Northern Europe 1815–1960: Whatever Happened to Secularisation?," *Kyrkohistorisk årsskrift*, 100, 2000, 135–145, 135–136. On the alarmism

over men's growing truancy in late nineteenth-century Belgium, see Tine VAN OSSELAER, *The Pious Sex: Catholic Constructions of Masculinity and Femininity in Belgium, c1800–1940*, Leuven: Leuven University Press, 2013, part 2, chap. 2.
74. NOONAN, *Contraception*, 404.
75. Leon ROELANDTS, "Théologie pastorale," *Nouvelle Revue Théologique*, 38, 1906, 126–138, 126, 128, and 135 respectively.
76. Désiré-Joseph MERCIER, *Instructiones contra vitium onanismi, parochis et confessariis propositae*, Mechelen: s.e., 1909.
77. Robert Blair KAISER, *The Encyclical That Never Was: The Story of the Commission on Population, Family and Birth, 1964–1966*, London: Sheed and Ward, 1987, 116.
78. NOONAN, *Contraception*, 411.
79. While his moral theology inspired the encyclical, Vermeersch was not its actual author. See Lucia POZZI, *The Catholic Church and Modern Sexual Knowledge, 1850–1950*, Cham: Palgrave Macmillan, 2021, 111, note 21.
80. VAN PRAAG, *Het bevolkingsvraagstuk in België*, 14–17. Also see Raf DE BONT, "Un peuple qui s'en va: Ongerustheid over de kwaliteit en de kwantiteit van het Franse volk," in: Raf DE BONT and Tom VERSCHAFFEL (eds.), *Het verderf van Parijs*, Leuven: Leuven University Press, 2004, 131–147.
81. STENGERS, "Les pratiques anticonceptionnelles," 1142–1150; VAN PRAAG, *Het bevolkingsvraagstuk in België*, 17–20; Kathlijn PITTOMVILS, "Tussen repressie en permissiviteit: Socialisme, socialisten, prostitutie en geslachtsziekten (einde 19de eeuw-1997)," in: Denise DE WEERDT (ed.), *Begeerte heeft ons aangeraakt: Socialisten, sekse en seksualiteit*, Ghent: Provinciebestuur van Oost-Vlaanderen, 1999, 209–235.
82. There were also various attempts to criminalize inciting the use of contraceptives, which ultimately succeeded in 1923. DELBECKE, *De lange schaduw van de grondwetgever*, 385–396.
83. Thomas W. LAQUEUR, *Solitary Sex: A Cultural History of Masturbation*, New York: Zone Books, 2003, 152.
84. Arthur VERMEERSCH, *De castitate et de vitiis contrariis: Tractatus doctrinalis et moralis*, 2nd ed., Rome: Universita Gregoriana and Beyaert, 1921 [1919].
85. Auguste KNOCH, *L'Onanisme conjugal et le tribunal de la pénintence*, 4th ed., Arras: Brunet and Revue Ecclésiastique, 1914.
86. Emphasis in original. Auguste KNOCH, *L'Éducation de la chasteté*, 3rd ed., Paris: Pierre Téqui and Revue Ecclésiastique, 1914, 62.
87. On the culture of ascetic self-control and its deep historical roots, see Evert PEETERS, Leen VAN MOLLE, and Kaat WILS (eds.), *Beyond Pleasure: Cultures of Modern Asceticism*, New York: Berghahn Books, 2011; VAN DER MEER, "Sodomy and Its Discontents."
88. Auguste KNOCH, *Le Jeune Homme Chaste: L'Éducation de la pureté dans les collèges*, 2nd ed., Arras: Brunet and Revue Ecclésiastique, 1914, 62.
89. Ibid., 13. This sentiment was echoed in the conclusions of the Vatican's official inquiry on the education of purity during the late 1920s: "Ignorance provides more safety than science." Quoted in: POZZI, *The Catholic Church*, 105.
90. KNOCH, *Le Jeune Homme Chaste*, 52.
91. Ibid., 41 and 43.

92. FOUCAULT, *The History of Sexuality*, 19. While recognizing the value of Foucault's focus on confession to demonstrate how religious discourse simultaneously forms and subjugates subjectivity, Jeremy Carrette has, in line with others, criticized Foucault's reductionist "overdependency on confession as the central and most important tenet of the [Christian] religion." Christianity's and Catholicism's shaping power operated as much through forcing sexuality into (coded) speech as by disciplining it into a pregnant silence. See CARRETTE, *Foucault and Religion*, chap. 2.
93. Florence TAMAGNE, *A History of Homosexuality in Europe: Berlin, London, Paris 1919–1939*, New York: Algora, 2006, 389–392; Carolyn J. DEAN, *The Frail Social Body: Pornography, Homosexuality, and Other Fantasies in Interwar France*, Berkeley: University of California Press, 2000, chap. 4; HANNA, "Natalism."
94. VAN PRAAG, *Het bevolkingsvraagstuk in België*, chap. 2.
95. George M. MARSDEN, *Fundamentalism and American Culture*, 2nd ed., Oxford: Oxford University Press, 2006, 44; Nicholas HOPE, *German and Scandinavian Protestantism, 1700–1918*, Oxford: Oxford University Press, 1999; Elisabeth KLUIT, *Het protestantse Réveil in Nederland en daarbuiten, 1815–1865*, Amsterdam: Paris, 1970, chaps. 4, 9–10.
96. While rightly complicating the Eurocentric picture of global anti-vice movements, Jessica Pliley also acknowledges that often "the tenets of Christianity, particularly in its Protestant variety, infused anti-vice crusades." Jessica R. PLILEY, "Introduction: A Plea for a 'Vicious Turn' in Global History," in: Jessica R. PLILEY, Robert KRAMM, and Harald FISCHER-TINÉ (eds.), *Global Anti-vice Activism, 1850–1950: Fighting Drinks, Drugs, and Immorality*, Cambridge: Cambridge University Press, 2016, 1–29, 5.
97. Christine MACHIELS, *Les féminismes et la prostitution (1860–1960)*, Rennes: Presses universitaires de Rennes, 2016; LIMONCELLI, *The Politics of Trafficking*; BALDWIN (ed.), *Contagion and the State in Europe*, chap. 5, esp. 390–394.
98. Karin LÜTZEN, *Byen tæmmes: Kernefamilie, sociale reformer og velgørenhed i 1800-tallets København*, Copenhagen: Reitzels, 2014, 275–282; CARLSON, *Godly Seed*, 28–29; Natalia GERODETTI, "'Lay Experts': Women's Social Purity Groups and the Politics of Sexuality in Switzerland, 1890–1915," *Women's History Review*, 13/4, 2004, 585–610; LISBERG-HAAG, *Die Unzucht*; Pieter KOENDERS, *Tussen christelijk réveil en seksuele revolutie: Bestrijding van zedeloosheid in Nederland, met nadruk op de repressie van homoseksualiteit*, Amsterdam: Stichting beheer IISG, 1996, chap. 2; BRISTOW, *Vice and Vigilance*, 4.
99. DICKINSON, *Sex, Freedom and Power in Imperial Germany*, 15. On France, see Steven C. HAUSE, "Social Control in Late Nineteenth-Century France: Protestant Campaigns for Strict Public Morality," in: Christopher E. FORTH and Elinor ACCAMPO (eds.), *Confronting Modernity in Fin-de-Siècle France: Bodies, Minds and Gender*, Basingstoke: Palgrave Macmillan, 2010, 135–149.
100. Quoted in DICKINSON, *Sex, Freedom and Power in Imperial Germany*, 40.
101. NEEFS, *Between Sin and Disease*, 58–64 and 70–71; Christine MACHIELS, "Pour 'l'affranchissement des blanches,' contre la prostitution réglementée: La Société de moralité publique de Belgique (1875–1908)," in: Jean-Michel CHAUMONT and Christine MACHIELS (eds.), *Du sordide au mythe: L'Affaire de la traite des blanches (Bruxelles, 1880)*, Louvain-la-Neuve: Presses universitaires de Louvain, 2009, 133–149.

7 Literary Activism on Behalf of a Strange Love

1. FOUCAULT, *The History of Sexuality*, 101.
2. Alfred DOUGLAS, "Two Loves," *The Chameleon*, December 1994, www.bl.uk/collection-items/the-chameleon, last accessed on September 1, 2022, 26–28.
3. James KIRKUP, "The Love That Dares to Speak Its Name," *Gay News*, 96, June 16, 1976, 26.
4. Arnold ALETRINO, "La Situation sociale de l'Uraniste [+ Discussion]," in: J. K. A. WERTHEIM SALOMONSON (ed.), *Congrès international d'anthropologie criminelle: Compte rendu des travaux de la cinquième session tenue à Amsterdam du 9 au 14 Septembre 1901*, Amsterdam: De Bussy, 1901, 25–36 and 473–494. On Aletrino, see Kees JOOSSE, *Arnold Aletrino: Pessimist met perspectief*, Amsterdam: Rap, 1986.
5. ROSENFELD, *Formes et figures*, 665–675.
6. Clayton J. WHISNANT, *Queer Identities and Politics in Germany: A History, 1880–1945*, New York: Harrington Park, 2016; LAURITSEN and THORSTAD, *The Early Homosexual Rights Movement*; STEAKLEY, *The Homosexual Emancipation Movement in Germany*.
7. On the Dutch Scientific-Humanitarian Committee, see VAN DER MEER, *Jacob Anton Schorer*.
8. For an overview, Georges-Henri DUMONT, *La vie quotidienne en Belgique sous le règne de Léopold II (1867–1909)*, s.l.: Hachette, 1974, 140–164.
9. For biographical details, see Mirande LUCIEN, *Eekhoud le rauque*, Villeneuve d'Ascq: Presses Universitaires de Septentrion, 1999.
10. See DIERCKX, *Pro Arte!*
11. On artistic styles and politics in *fin-de-siècle* Belgium, see Christophe VERBRUGGEN, *Schrijverschap in de Belgische belle époque: Een sociaal-culturele geschiedenis*, Ghent: Academia Press and Vantilt, 2009; Paul ARON and Pierre-Yves SOUCY, *Les Revues littéraires belges de langue française de 1830 à nos jours: Essai de répertoire*, Brussels: Labor and Archives et Musée de la Littérature ASBL, 1993; Paul ARON, *Les écrivains belges et le socialisme (1880–1913): L'Expérience de l'art social, d'Edmond Picard à Émile Verhaeren*, Brussels: Labor, 1985.
12. Edmond PICARD, *La crise politique en Belgique: Extrait de la Revue Moderne*, Brussels: Mertens, 1883, 7.
13. Georges EEKHOUD, *La nouvelle Carthage*, Brussels: Kistemaeckers, 1888. On Eekhoud's esthetic anarchism, see Hans VANDEVOORDE, "'En ces temps de chevaleresque idéologie': Het 'erotisch anarchisme' van Georges Eekhoud," in: David GULLENTOPS and Hans VANDEVOORDE (eds.), *Anarchisten rond Emile Verhaeren*, Brussels: VUBPRESS, 2005, 125–152; Mirande LUCIEN, "Georges Eekhoud et l'anarchie: 'Les capiteuses tanières de la révolte!,'" *Littérature et nation*, 19, 1998, 97–116.
14. Georges-Henri DUMONT, "Quand le Coq rouge plantait ses ergots sur la Jeune Belgique (1895–1897): Communication de M. Georges-Henri Dumont à la séance mensuelle du 14 décembre 1991," *Bulletin de l'Académie royale de langue et de littérature françaises*, 69/3–4, 1991, 236–255, 238.
15. See, for example, Georges EEKHOUD, *Les milices de Saint François*, Brussels: Monnom, 1886; Georges EEKHOUD, *Kermesses*, Brussels: Kistemaeckers, 1884; Georges EEKHOUD, *Kees Doornik: Scènes du polder*, Brussels: Hochsteyn, 1883.

16. Georges EEKHOUD, *Personal diary*, AML, ML 2954/1, 307. Also see Mirande LUCIEN, *G. Eekhoud: Journal inédit. 1895–1905. Vol. 1 à 4*, AML, ML 02954, 25.
17. Ibid., 139.
18. Quoted in LUCIEN, *Eekhoud le rauque*, 33–34.
19. Georges EEKHOUD and Mirande LUCIEN, *Le quadrille du lancier et autres nouvelles*, Brussels: Gai-Kitsch-Camp, 1992, 25–26. Further quotes are also drawn from this publication.
20. Previously, homosexually inflected short stories, including the lancer's, had appeared in Georges EEKHOUD, *Mes Communions*, Brussels: Kistemaeckers, 1895 and Georges EEKHOUD, *Cycle patibulaire*, Brussels: Kistemaeckers, 1892. On two of those stories, see Michael ROSENFELD, "Subversion politique et sexuelle dans 'Appol et Brouscard' et 'Une mauvaise rencontre,'" *Textyles*, 58–59, 2020, 213–228.
21. This was the altered version of *Comte de la digue*, which had first appeared as a serial novel in *Mercure de France* in 1898. Georges EEKHOUD, *Escal-Vigor*, Paris: Mercure de France, 1899; Georges EEKHOUD, *A Strange Love: A Novel of Abnormal Passion*, New York: The Panurge Press, 1930. For the quotation, see Gretchen SCHULTZ, "French Literature: Nineteenth Century," *GLBTQ: An Encyclopedia of Gay, Lesbian, Bisexual, Transgender, and Queer Culture*, www.glbtq.com/literature/french_lit2_19c,5.html, last accessed on January 9, 2015. On the initial English translation, entitled *Escal Vigor*, see Michael ROSENFELD, "Escal-Vigor: 'A Novel from the French of Georges Eekhoud.' Comment traduire 'l'innomable,'" in: Béatrice COSTA and Catherine GRAVET (eds.), *Traduire la littérature belge francophone: Itinéraires des œuvres et des personnes*, Mons: Université de Mons, 2016.
22. Georges EEKHOUD, *Escal-Vigor*, Paris: Séguier, 1996 [1899], 194.
23. Ibid., 206.
24. Philippe CHAVASSE, "Martyrologe d'un genre nouveau: Le dénouement d'Escal-Vigor de Georges Eekhoud," *Nineteenth Century French Studies*, 34/3–4, 2006, 371–386.
25. EEKHOUD, *Escal-Vigor*, 212.
26. His book collection is preserved at the Hendrik Conscience Library in Antwerp. See Willem CLAESSENS, "Inventaris van de boeken uit de bibliotheek van Georges Eekhoud: Werken thans aanwezig in de Stadsbibliotheek Antwerpen," unpublished master's thesis, Stedelijke Technische Leergangen voor Bibliohteekwezen, 1975–1976.
27. Richard VON KRAFFT-EBING, *Psychopathia sexualis avec recherches spéciales sur l'inversion sexuelle: Traduit sur la huitième édition allemande*, translated by Émile LAURENT and Sigismond CSAPO, Paris: Masson, 1895.
28. The same kind of reading in and drawing on scientific works can be seen in the notes made by the journalist François Simonis whose court case was discussed in Chapter 3.
29. In an article for *La Réforme*, Eekhoud explained: "I have been profoundly touched, moved even, by imagining the atrocious fate suffered by these distinguished men because of ignorance, prejudice and hypocrisy, and I have drawn from their heart-rending confidences [in *Psychopathia sexualis*] a book of comprehension, compassion, yes even rehabilitation." Georges EEKHOUD, "A propos d'une polémique: Une lettre de Georges Eekhoud," *La Réforme*, March 5, 1900.

30. KRAFFT-EBING, *Psychopathia sexualis*, 360, 383, 392, and 333 and 334 respectively.
31. On the formative interplay between medical case studies, literary scripts, and sexual identities, see, among others, Birgit LANG, Joy DAMOUSI, and Alison LEWIS, *A History of the Case Study: Sexology, Psychoanalysis, Literature*, Manchester: Manchester University Press, 2017; Joy DAMOUSI, Birgit LANG, and Katie SUTTON (eds.), *Case Studies and the Dissemination of Knowledge*, New York: Routledge, 2015; Laurie MARHOEFER, "'The Book Was a Revelation, I Recognized Myself in It': Lesbian Sexuality, Censorship, and the Queer Press in Weimar-era Germany," *Journal of Women's History*, 27/2, 2015, 62–86.
32. See Chapters 4 and 5.
33. See Bart HELLINCK, "Inventaris van het archief van Suzanne De Pues (pseudoniem Suzan Daniel). Fondsnummer F/001," unpublished archive inventory, Fonds Suzan Daniel vzw and Amsab-Instituut voor Sociale Geschiedenis, 2003-2010.
34. Eekhoud to Pierron, dated April 28, 1900. Reproduced in Mirande LUCIEN, *Mon bien aimé petit Sander: Lettres de Georges Eekhoud à Sander Pierron (1892–1927). Suivis de six lettres de Sander Pierron à Georges Eekhoud*, Lille: Gai-Kitsch-Camp, 1993, 170–171.
35. SABr, HA WEST 0000, Assize Court of West-Flanders – Old series, file 898, report dated August 10, 1899.
36. "Comment le procès fut intenté: La pudibonderie en délire," *Pourquoi Pas?*, 22/943, 1932, 2161. On Bisthoven, see "Leon Janssens de Bisthoven," in: *Nationaal biografisch woordenboek*, vol. 7, Brussels: Paleis der Academiën, 1977, 415–419.
37. SABF, PGCAB, Series I: year III-1922, portfolio 191/B, map 1900: Publications immorales. 'L'homme en amour' de C. Lemonnier. 'Escal-Vigor' de G. Eekhoud."
38. On Picard, see Paul ARON and Cécile VANDERPELEN-DIAGRE, *Edmond Picard (1836–1924): Un bourgeois socialiste belge à la fin du dix-neuvième siècle. Essai d'histoire culturelle*, Brussels: Musées royaux des Beaux-Arts de Belgique, 2013.
39. Edmond PICARD, "Les Maladresses de la Justice: Eekhoud et son 'Escal-Vigor' poursuivies pour outrage aux mœurs," *L'Art moderne*, 20/10, 1900, 75–77, 76.
40. Ibid., 76–77.
41. The contemporary newspaper reports of the unminuted trial are partly reproduced in "L'Incorrigible M. Janssens de Bisthoven, Georges Eekhoud et Camille Lemonnier devant les assises de la Flandre Occidentale en octobre 1900," *Pourquoi Pas?*, 22/943, 1932, 2180–2189. Francotte has made an earlier appearance in Chapter 5.
42. On the active prosecution of pornography in Belgium under paragraph 383 of the penal code, see Leon JANSSENS, "Tussen angst, afkeer en wanhoop: Een emotionele geschiedenis van de strijd tegen pornografie in België (1880–1914)," unpublished doctoral dissertation, KU Leuven, 2023; Leon JANSSENS, "Pornography on Rails: Trains and Belgium's 'War on Pornography,' 1880–1891," *Journal of the History of Sexuality*, 32/3, 2023, 269–287.
43. For this quote and those to follow, see Jacques DETEMMERMAN, "Le procès d'Escal-Vigor," *Revue de l'Université de Bruxelles*, 4–5, 1984, 141–169, 158–163.
44. "M. Janssens de Bisthoven et Camille Lemonnier devant les assises de la Flandre Occidentale en octobre 1900," *Pourquoi Pas?*, 22/944, 1932, 2240–2243.

45. Mathieu VANHAELEWYN, "Homotrots op een heterotrottoir: Over holebi-monumenten in België," *Bijdragen tot de Eigentijdse Geschiedenis*, 20, 2008, 233–255, 240.
46. On the use of the pink triangle in gay, lesbian, and queer memory culture, see Sébastien TREMBLAY, *A Badge of Injury: The Pink Triangle as Global Symbol of Memory*, Oldenbourg: De Gruyter, 2024; NEWSOME, *Pink Triangle Legacies*; Erik N. JENSEN, "The Pink Triangle and Political Consciousness: Gays, Lesbians, and the Memory of Nazi Persecution," *Journal of the History of Sexuality*, 11/1–2, 2002, 319–349.
47. Auguste DEWINNE, "Escal-Vigor," *Le Peuple*, November 28, 1900, 1.
48. "Après les Procès de Bruges: Interviews littéraires. Émile Vandervelde," *Le Peuple*, December 17, 1900, 1; "Après les Procès de Bruges: Interviews littéraires. Jules Destrée," *Le Peuple*, December 3, 1900, 1. For more on this series of interviews in *Le Peuple*, see Michael ROSENFELD, "Gay Taboos in 1900 Brussels: The Literary, Journalistic and Private Debate Surrounding Georges Eekhoud's Novel Escal Vigor," *Dix-Neuf: Journal of the Society of Dix-Neuviémistes*, 22/1–2, 2018, 98–114.
49. "Après les Procès de Bruges: Interviews littéraires. Georges Eekhoud," *Le Peuple*, December 2, 1900, 1.
50. Ibid.
51. Louis DELMER, *L'Art en cour d'assises: Étude sur l'œuvre littéraire et sociale de Camille Lemonnier*, Paris: Savine and Rozez, 1893.
52. See the correspondence of Brussels' prosecutors in SABF, PGCAB, Series I: year III-1922, portfolio's 189/A to 193 concerning 'Mœurs publiques, publications licencieuses.'
53. DELBECKE, *De lange schaduw van de grondwetgever*, 345–385.
54. René FAYT, "Un éditeur des naturalistes: Henry Kistemaeckers," *Revue de l'Université de Bruxelles*, 4–5, 1984, 217–239, 238. Also see Colette BAUDET, *Grandeur et misères d'un éditeur belge: Henry Kistemaeckers (1851–1934)*, Brussels: Labor, 1986.
55. Referring to the prosecution, Kistemaeckers recalled the following when looking back on his trials in 1923: "[L]eur tâche était ingrate, le Jury prenant presque toujours position contre le Ministère public en matière de procès de presse. … J'y allais comme à une conférence ou à un spectacle." Henri KISTEMAECKERS, "Mes procès littéraires: Souvenirs d'un éditeur," *Mercure de France: Série Moderne*, 166/606, 1923, 670–692, 674.
56. See, Jane BLOCK, "The Art of the Law: Le Jeune Barreau, Patron of Arts and Letters," in: Jane BLOCK (ed.), *Belgium: The Golden Decades, 1880–1914*, New York: Peter Lang, 1997, 181–219.
57. DELMER, *L'Art en cour d'assises*, 26. Compare with Eugène DEMOLDER, *Sous la robe: Notes d'audience, de palais et d'ailleurs d'un juge de paix*, Paris: Mercure de France, 1897.
58. DIERCKX, *Pro Arte!*, chap. 3.
59. DETEMMERMAN, "Le procès d'Escal-Vigor," 168–169.
60. "Le procès Eekhoud," *Le Petit Bleu*, October 25, 1900. Also quoted in DETEMMERMAN, "Le procès d'Escal-Vigor," 151.
61. Edmond PICARD, "L'Uranisme," *Le Peuple*, November 19, 1900, 1.
62. Ibid.

63. Eekhoud to Pierron, July 6, 1900. Reproduced in LUCIEN, *Mon bien aimé petit Sander*, 177.
64. Eekhoud to Pierron, November 4, 1900. Reproduced in LUCIEN, *Mon bien aimé petit Sander*, 180–181. Sales were indeed good. By 1906, a seventh edition of *Escal-Vigor* appeared.
65. Reprinted as Georges EEKHOUD, "A propos d'Escal-Vigor," in: Mirande LUCIEN and Patrick CARDON (eds.), *Georges Eekhoud: Un illustre uraniste*, Lille: Gai-Kitsch-Camp, 1996 [1901], 51–55.
66. HIRSCHFELD, *Von einst bis jetzt*, 61.
67. NUMA PRAETORIUS, "Der Prozess von Georges Eekhoud wegen seines Romanes 'Escal-Vigor,'" *Jahrbuch für Sexuelle Zwischenstufen mit besonderer Berücksichtigung der Homosexualität*, 3, 1901, 520–525, 524–525.
68. Georges EEKHOUD, *Escal-Vigor*, translated by Richard MEIENREIS, Leipzig: Spohr, 1903.
69. Eekhoud's copy of Carpenter's *Homogenic Love* contains a letter from the author. The articles for *Akadémos* are reprinted in Georges EEKHOUD, "De la sensibilité dans la littérature moderne," in: Mirande LUCIEN and Patrick CARDON (eds.), *Georges Eekhoud: Un illustre uraniste 1854–1927*, Montpellier: GaiKitschCamp, 2012 [1909], 62–75; Georges EEKHOUD, "Saint-Sébastien dans la peinture," in: Mirande LUCIEN and Patrick CARDON (eds.), *Georges Eekhoud: Un illustre uraniste 1854–1927*, Montpellier: GaiKitschCamp, 2012 [1909], 57–61.
70. On *Ontwaking*, see Michael ROSENFELD, "Spreken over mannenliefde in 'Ontwaking': Sociale en discursieve netwerken rond Georges Eekhoud en Jacob Israël De Haan (1904–1910)," in: Maxime VAN STEEN and Jan LAMPAERT (eds.), *Vernieuwing in verstrengeling: Dynamische netwerken in artistieke tijdschriften*, Ghent: Academia Press, 2025, 33–58; Stijn VANCLOOSTER, Jan MOULAERT, and Erwin JOOS, *De Kapel tussen droom en daad: Anarchie en artistieke heropleving in Antwerpen rond 1900*, Antwerp: Van Mieghem, 2013, 63–105; Jan MOULAERT, *Rood en zwart*, 206 and 376; Ludo SIMONS, *Geschiedenis van de uitgeverij in Vlaanderen*, 2 vols., Tielt: Lannoo, 1984, vol. 2, 27–29. On De Haan's connection with Eekhoud, see Michael ROSENFELD, "'Je suis profondément heureux que vous soyez mon ami': L'Amitié de Georges Eekhoud et Jacob Israël de Haan," in: Régine BATTISON, Nikol DZIUB, and Augustin VOEGELE (eds.), *Amitiés vives: Littérature et amitié dans les correspondances d'écrivains*, Reims: Épure – Éditions et presses universitaires de Reims, 2022, 141–154; Rob DELVIGNE and Leo ROSS, "'Ik ben toch zoo innig blij dat u mijn vriend bent': De brieven van Jacob Israël de Haan aan Georges Eekhoud," *De Revisor*, 9/3, 1982, 61–72.
71. Cathérine GRAVET and Emile VAN BALBERGHE, "'Cher brutal abruti de mon cœur': Quelques notes à propos de trois lettres et de quatre envois inédits de Max Waller à Georges Eekhoud," *Francofonia: Studi e ricerche sulle letterature di lingua francese*, 10, 2001, 37–60, 51.
72. Georges EEKHOUD, *L'Autre Vue*, Paris: Mercure de France, 1904.
73. "Décidément, c'est ce que j'ai écrit de mieux." Quoted in LUCIEN, *Eekhoud le rauque*, 132. The English passage from Eekhoud's diary quoted earlier directly informed pages 56–59 of *L'Autre vue*.
74. Mirande LUCIEN, "'Un savoureux enfer': Naissance d'un roman. 'Voyous de velours' ou 'l'Autre Vue de Georges Eekhoud," *Textyles*, 8, 1991, 301–314, 313.

75. NUMA PRAETORIUS, "[Review of] L'Autre vue [by G. Eekhoud]," *Jahrbuch für Sexuelle Zwischenstufen mit besonderer Berücksichtigung der Homosexualität*, 7, 1905, 858–663, 860.
76. Eekhoud, *Personal diary*, AML, ML 2954/2, 72 (June 10, 1902).
77. Eekhoud to Pierron, February 17, 1902. Reproduced in LUCIEN, *Mon bien aimé petit Sander*, 191.
78. Precise date unclear. EEKHOUD, *Personal diary*, AML, ML 2954/8, 67.
79. Eekhoud to Pierron, December 6, 1901. Reproduced in LUCIEN, *Mon bien aimé petit Sander*, 189.
80. Mirande LUCIEN, *G. Eekhoud: Journal inédit. 1895–1905. Vol. 1 à 4*, AML, ML 02954, 80, 81, 88, 93, 102, 153, 157, and 164.
81. For example, EEKHOUD, *Personal diary*, AML, ML 2954/8, 170 and 192.
82. In the entry following that of December 17, the one that mentions the money given to Stan, Eekhoud notes this bit of news with emphasis on the fact that the elder of the two was sentenced to six months' imprisonment and the loss of his civil rights for six years on a charge of sexual assault. The proximity of these two entries clearly suggests Eekhoud's awareness of the dangers involved in cruising and of (paid) sex with youngsters. See EEKHOUD, *Personal diary*, AML, ML 2954/8, 170–171 (December 17 and 19, 1910).
83. For example, EEKHOUD, *Personal diary*, AML, ML 2954/3, 54; ML 2954/4, 9; and ML 2954/8, 73 and 170–171.
84. EEKHOUD, "De Oorsprong en de Evolutie van een Werk," 29.
85. From the 1909 volume of *Sexual-Probleme*, pages 208–209. Quoted in LUCIEN, *Eekhoud le rauque*, 153.
86. Georges EEKHOUD, *Le Cycle patibulaire*, Paris: Mercure de France, 1896, 191. The short story in question is *Le Tribunal au Chauffoir*, pages 191–230.
87. Maurice BLADEL, *L'Œuvre de Georges Eekhoud*, Brussels: Renaissance d'Occident, 1922, 55–60.
88. On the formative importance of scandal, see Didier ERIBON, *Insult and the Making of the Gay Self*, Durham, NC: Duke University Press, 2004, 143–152; Michael D. SIBALIS, "Defining Masculinity in Fin-de-Siécle France: Sexual Anxiety and the Emergence of the Homosexual," *Proceedings of the Annual Meeting of the Western Society for French History*, 25, 1998, 247–256.
89. Morris B. KAPLAN, *Sodom on the Thames: Sex, Love and Scandal in Wilde Times*, Ithaca, NY: Cornell University Press, 2005.
90. Robert BEACHY, "The German Invention of Homosexuality," *The Journal of Modern History*, 82/4, 2010, 801–838, 831.
91. Robert ALDRICH, *Colonialism and Homosexuality*, London: Routledge, 2003, 187–189.
92. On d'Adelswärd-Fersen, see Nancy ERBER, "Queer Follies: Effeminacy and Aestheticism in *fin-de-siècle* France, the Case of Baron d'Adelsward Fersen and Count de Warren," in: George ROBB and Nancy ERBER (eds.), *Disorder in the Court: Trials and Sexual Conflict at the Turn of the Century*, Basingstoke: Macmillan, 1999, 186–209. Regarding Denmark, see Wilhelm VON ROSEN, "Denmark 1866–1976: From Sodomy to Modernity," in: Jens RYDSTRÖM and Kati MUSTOLA (eds.), *Criminally Queer: Homosexuality and Criminal Law in Scandinavia*, Amsterdam: Aksant, 2004, 61–90.

93. Norman DOMEIER, *The Eulenburg Affair: A Cultural History of Politics in the German Empire*, translated by Deborah L. SCHNEIDER, Rochester, NY: Camden House, 2015.
94. SPECTOR, *Violent Sensations*, chap. 3; Scott SPECTOR, "Where Personal Fate Turns to Public Affair: Homosexual Scandal and Social Order in Vienna, 1900–1910," *Austrian History Yearbook*, 38, 2007, 15–24.
95. JOOSSE, *Arnold Aletrino*, 510–548; KOENDERS, *Tussen Christelijk réveil en seksuele revolutie*, 147–169.
96. See the Coda.

Coda

1. KOSSMANN, *The Low Countries*, 569.
2. As Hans Neefs writes: "In general, public discourse about sexual morality in the interwar period in both Catholic and secularist milieus centred on the hegemonic notions of chastity, sexual continence and martial fidelity. ... Alternative, more libertarian conceptions of sexuality existed in specific, small milieus but barely affected the public debate about VD in the interwar period." NEEFS, *Between Sin and Disease*, 180. On interwar Catholic morality, see Evert PEETERS, *De beloften van het lichaam: Een geschiedenis van de natuurlijke levenswijze in België, 1890–1940*, Amsterdam: Standaard Uitgeverij, 2008; Ria CHRISTENS, "De orthodoxie van het zaad: Seksualiteit en sekse-identiteit in de Rooms-katholieke traditie," in: Kaat WILS (ed.), *Het lichaam (m/v)*, Leuven: Leuven University Press, 2001, 231–249; Christian DE BORCHGRAVE, *God of Genot: Vlaanderen 1918–1940: Een kerk in strijd met de moderne zinnelijkheid*, Leuven: Van Halewyck, 1998, chap. 8. On libertarianism and *Körperkultur*, see PEETERS, *De beloften van het lichaam*, esp. chap. 9.
3. PEETERS, *De beloften van het lichaam*, 293–294; Anne GANZEVOORT, "Tussen norm, ideaal en politieke realiteit: 'Afwijkend' seksueel gedrag en Belgisch links," in: Denise DE WEERDT (ed.), *Begeerte heeft ons aangeraakt: Socialisten, sekse en seksualiteit*, Ghent: Provinciebestuur Oost-Vlaanderen, 1999, 239–277.
4. On interwar England and France, see Florence TAMAGNE, *A History of Homosexuality in Europe: Berlin, London, Paris 1919–1939*, 89–104 and 125–147.
5. Gaston-L. HUYSMANS, "À propos du monstrueux crime de la Citadelle de Liège." A copy is preserved in the GSA, Ministry of Justice, Public Security Service, Aliens Police General Files, Second Deposition, file 1433: 'Pédérastie 1930–1960.'
6. Jonathan FRYER, "'Alle bedenkingen' bij de dood van de schrijver Christopher Isherwood (1904–1986)," *Zonder Pardon*, 10/88, 1986, 5–11, 6.
7. Court files indicate that foreigners, particularly Brits, Germans, and Scandinavians, were often imbued with a false sense of safety while in Brussels owing to the absence of sodomy laws in Belgium. They were regularly caught soliciting sex with locals in public. As discussed in Chapter 3, Belgian judges interpreted the article on public indecency very expansively. See, among others, SABF, CAB, Series II: Sentenced Correctional Case Files 1885–1899, year 1897, file 3570, reg. 1138; SABF, CFIB, Series II: Sentenced Correctional Case Files 1893–1899, year 1895, port. 335, reg. 3678 and year 1897, port. 1084, reg. 96.

8. AJAX, "Autour du crime de Liège: Une lacune à combler," *La Nation belge*, September 1, 1931. A copy is preserved in the GSA, Ministry of Justice, Public Security Service, Aliens Police General Files, Second Deposition, file 1433: 'Pédérastie 1930–1960.'
9. HUYSMANS, "À propos du monstrueux crime de la Citadelle de Liège."
10. Dimitri RODEN, *Ondankbaar België: De Duitse Repressie in de Tweede Wereldoorlog*, Amsterdam: Amsterdam University Press, 2018, 18–19. The SS nevertheless made inroads into Belgium as well. See pages 29–30.
11. Ibid., 199–202. Much more research is needed, however, on the indirect and informal persecution of queer people in Belgium during this period, which cannot easily be derived from court records. On the issue, see Wannes DUPONT, "La 'déviance' sexuelle et la tolérance répressive dans la Belgique d'après-guerre," in: Jérôme COURTOY, Joachim SCHULTE, and Frédéric STROH (eds.), *Queeres Leben in der Großregion: Tagungsband Trier, 22 & 23.11.2023 – Vie queer en grande région: Actes du colloque, Trêves, 22 & 23.11.2023*, Sanem: Op der Lay, 2024, 173–184. For an example of indirect persecution, see Marc VERSCHOORIS, *Martha's labyrint: Een uitzonderlijke vrouwengeschiedenis, 1938–1944*, Gorredijk: Sterck and De Vreese, 2022.
12. See Régis SCHLAGDENHAUFFEN (ed.), *Queer in Europe during the Second World War*, Strasbourg: Council of Europe, 2018, chaps. 2 and 5; Anna TIJSSELING, "Schuldige seks: Homoseksuele zedendelinquenten rondom de Duitse bezettingstijd," unpublished doctoral dissertation, Utrecht University, 2009.
13. On this formative period, see Martin CONWAY, *The Sorrows of Belgium: Liberation and Political Reconstruction, 1944–1947*, Oxford: Oxford University Press, 2012.
14. Peter SCHRIJVERS, *Liberators: The Allies and Belgian Society, 1944–1945*, Cambridge: Cambridge University Press, 2009, 192–204.
15. Guillaume JACQUEMYNS, *La société belge sous l'occupation allemande 1940–1944: Privations et espoirs*, Brussels: Office de publicité, 1945, 110–111.
16. Luc HUYSE and Steven DHONDT (eds.), *Onverwerkt verleden: Collaboratie en repressie in België, 1942–1952. Een update na dertig jaar*, 2nd ed., Tielt: Kritak, 2020.
17. Tony JUDT, *Postwar: A History of Europe since 1945*, New York: Penguin, 2005, 6.
18. Georges HOORNAERT, "La loi devant la corruption de la jeunesse et l'excitation à la débauche," *Revue de droit pénal et de criminologie*, 27/6, 1946–1947, 491–520, 491–492.
19. Xavier RYCKMANS, "Une déclaration des droits de la famille," *Journal des Tribunaux*, 62/3709, 1947, 1–2.
20. LIGUE DES FAMILLES NOMBREUSES DE BELGIQUE, *Intérêts familiaux: Rapport général de la Commission Centrale des Intérêts Familiaux*, Brussels: Ligue des Familles Nombreuses, s.a. [c. 1944].
21. Maurice DUBOIS, "Enfance coupable, Enfance malheureuse: Problèmes d'après la guerre," *Revue de droit pénal et de criminologie*, 27/8, 1946–1947, 680–704, 681.
22. Stacy HUSHION, "Intimate Encounters and the Politics of German Occupation in Belgium, 1940–44/45," unpublished doctoral dissertation, University of Toronto, 2015; Carolien VAN LOON, "De geschorene en de scheerster: De vrouw in de straatrepressie na de Tweede Wereldoorlog," *Bijdragen tot de Eigentijdse Geschiedenis*, 19, 2008, 45–78.
23. SCHRIJVERS, *Liberators*, 206–220.

24. Paul DE CANT and Raymond SCREVENS, "Loi du 21 août 1948 supprimant la réglementation officielle de la prostitution," *Revue de droit pénal et de criminologie*, 29/2, 1948-1949, 160-171. On the postwar push to curb the spread of venereal disease and to abolish regulated prostitution, see NEEFS, *Between Sin and Disease*, chap. 7.
25. "Tandis que les filles qui ont besoin d'argent se laissent aller à la débauche, garçons, eux, recourent en vol" ("Whereas girls in search of money are tempted into debauchery, boys have recourse to theft"). HOORNAERT, "La loi devant la corruption de la jeunesse," 515. Compare with Aimée RACINE, *Les enfants traduits en justice: Étude d'après trois cents dossiers du tribunal pour enfants de l'arrondissement de Bruxelles*, Liège: Georges Thoné, 1935, 35 and 78-108. Also see Aurore FRANÇOIS, *Guerres et délinquance juvénile: Un demi-siècle de pratiques judiciaires et institutionelles envers des mineurs en difficulté (1912-1950)*, Brussels: La Charte, 2011. The same gendering was discernible in concurrent debates about maintaining the criminalization of adultery (which penalized women much more than men) and the harshening of the anti-abortion statute. See, for example, J. VAN PARYS, "Convient-il de maintenir les sanctions des délits d'adultère et d'entretien de concubine dans notre droit pénal?," *Revue de droit pénal et de criminologie*, 31/5, 1950-1951, 505-512; Louis GUYAUX, "Des modifications nécessaires à notre législation sur l'avortement, les moyens abortifs et les moyens anticonceptionnels," *Revue de droit pénal et de criminologie*, 27/4, 1946-1947, 314-346.
26. Raymond SCREVENS, "La loi supprimant la réglementation de la prostitution et son application," *Revue de droit pénal et de criminologie*, 33/6, 1952-1953, 567-582, 577-578.
27. DE CANT and SCREVENS, "Loi du 21 août 1948," 160.
28. "Corr. Bruxelles (21e ch.) 30 avril 1951: Prostitution. Racolage. Provocation au délit. Acquittement," *Journal des Tribunaux*, 66/3897, 1951, 322.
29. SCREVENS, "La loi supprimant la réglementation de la prostitution," 575-576.
30. For example, René STAS, "La délinquance contre les mœurs chez les mineurs justiciables du Juge des Enfants: Enquête portant sur les années 1948 et 1949 dans l'arrondissement de Liège," *Revue de droit pénal et de criminologie*, 33/1, 1952-1953, 35-56, 52.
31. RACINE, *Les enfants traduits en justice*, 81.
32. RACINE, *La délinquance juvénile en Belgique de 1939 à 1957*, Brussels: Centre d'étude de la délinquance juvénile, 1959, 93.
33. Ibid., 94.
34. Florimont LOX, "La rue, creuset de prédélinquance," *L'Enfant*, 7/2, 1954, 117-128, 119. Also see Raymond CHARLES, "Police et enfance inadaptée," *Revue de droit pénal et de criminologie*, 36/5, 1955-1956, 473-491.
35. Much of psychoanalysis' history in Belgium remains to be written. See Michel CODDENS, "La Belgique et la psychanalyse: Un rendez-vous manqué?," *Le Bulletin Freudien*, 51-52, April 2008, 17-51; Didier CROMPHOUT, "Les sentiers de la psychanalyse en Belgique," *Psychoanalytische Perspektieven*, 36, 1999, 9-24; Dany NOBUS and Katrien LIBBRECHT, "De Franse connectie: Een geschiedenis van de psychoanalyse in België," *Tijdschrift voor Psychoanalyse*, 3/3, 1997, 132-149. Specifically on the Catholic reception of psychoanalysis, see Agnès DESMAZIÈRES, *L'Inconscient au paradis: Comment les catholiques ont reçu la psychanalyse*, Paris: Payot and Rivages, 2011, chaps 1 and 3.

36. Joris CASSELMAN, *Etienne De Greeff, 1898–1961: Psychiater, criminoloog en romanschrijver. Leven, werk en huidige betekenis*, Antwerp: Maklu, 2010; Joris CASSELMAN, "Etienne de Greeff and His Contribution to Current Criminology," *International Annals of Criminology*, 48/1–2, 2010, 109–130.
37. On the various postwar strands of psychoanalysis in the United States, see Dagmar HERZOG, *Cold War Freud: Psychoanalysis in an Age of Catastrophes*, Cambridge: Cambridge University Press, 2017.
38. Florent Edouard LOUWAGE, *Psychologie et criminalité*, 2nd ed., Ninove: Anneessens, 1945 [1943], 7.
39. Cyrille J. C. F. FIJNAUT, "Florent Louwage 1888–1967," in: Cyrille FIJNAUT (ed.), *Gestalten uit het verleden: 32 voorgangers in de strafrechtwetenschap, de strafrechtpleging en de criminologie*, Deurne: Kluwer, 1993, 195–209, 207. Also see David SOMER, "Florent-Édouard Louwage: Une carrière hybride de policier, de technicien et d'homme du renseignement," in: Marc COOLS, Patrick LEROY, Marc LIBERT et al. (eds.), *1915–2015: Het verhaal van de Belgische militaire veligheidsdienst – 1915–2015: L'histoire du service de renseignement militaire et de sécurité belge*, Antwerp: Maklu, 2015, 315–333.
40. Freud's work was not the only one that nurtured the notion of homosexual seduction. On its history, see VENDRELL, *The Seduction of Youth*.
41. MASSION-VERNIORY and CHARLES, "Les aspects médico-psychologiques," 307–308.
42. LEY and MARCHAL, "L'Homosexualité," 324.
43. MASSION-VERNIORY and CHARLES, "Les aspects médico-psychologiques." Homosexual cases of venereal disease were also first reported in 1958 at Brussels' Saint Peter's hospital. See P. MEERTS, "Homosexualité masculine et endémie syphilitique: Constatations faites à Bruxelles," *Archives belges de dermatologie et de syphiligraphie*, 22/1, 1966, 9–20, 10. A little further along, Meerts notes: "En Belgique la fréquence de l'homosexualité semble n'avoir jamais été établie avec précision." Also see P. MEERTS., "Homosexualité masculine et syphilis," *Revue médicale de Bruxelles*, 21, 1965, 559–570 and 599–614.
44. Françoise TULKENS and Thierry MOREAU, *Droit de la jeunesse: Aide, assistance, protection*, Brussels: De Boeck and Larcier, 2000, 204–224.
45. Bart HELLINCK, *"Een droom waarvan we nooit konden vermoeden dat hij mogelijk zou zijn": Bijdrage tot de geschiedenis van 50 jaar homo- en lesbiennebeweging in Vlaanderen (1953–2003)*, 2nd ed., Ghent: Holebifederatie and Gelijke Kansen in Vlaanderen, 2003, 40–43.
46. On the difference, see Wannes DUPONT, "The Two-Faced Fifties: Homosexuality and Penal Policy in the International Forensic Community (1945–1965)," *Journal of the History of Sexuality*, 28/3, 2019, 357–395. Regarding the Lavender Scare, consult David K. JOHNSON, "America's Cold War Empire: Exporting the Lavender Scare," in: Meredith L. WEISS and Michael J. BOSIA (eds.), *Global Homophobia: States, Movements, and the Politics of Oppression*, Champaign: University of Illinois Press, 2013, 55–74; Gary KINSMAN and Patrizia GENTILE, *The Canadian War on Queers: National Security as Sexual Regulation*, Vancouver: UCB Press, 2010; David K. JOHNSON, *The Lavender Scare: The Cold War Persecution of Gays and Lesbians in the Federal Government*, Chicago: University of Chicago Press, 2004.
47. Florent E. LOUWAGE, "Delinquency in Europe after World War II," *Journal of Criminal Law and Criminology*, 42/1, 1951, 53–56, 55.

48. The French title from which other versions were translated was *Revue internationale de police criminelle*.
49. Florent E. LOUWAGE, "Perversions et névroses," *Revue internationale de police criminelle*, 3/15, 1948, 7–11, 8; Joseph Paul DE RIVER, *The Sexual Criminal: A Psychoanalytic Study*, 2nd ed., Burbank: Bloat, 2000 [1956]. Also see DUPONT, "The Two-Faced Fifties," 366–370.
50. "Sexual Offences," *International Criminal Police Review*, 7/60, 1952, 216–219.
51. Firmin FRANSSEN, "Miscellaneous Questions and Closing Session," *International Criminal Police Review*, 12/110, 1957, 237–239, 238.
52. SABF, Commissioner-General's Office of the Criminal Investigation Department, Ministry of Justice, portfolio 136: Homosexualité II, Interpol circular letter ICPO no. 4731 HOSEX, November 7, 1957.
53. SABF, Commissioner-General's Office of the Criminal Investigation Department, Ministry of Justice, portfolio, 135: Homosexualité I, Homosexualité. Législations pénales la concernant et ses incidences sur la criminalité.
54. HOME OFFICE. SCOTTISH HOME DEPARTMENT, *Report of the Committee on Homosexual Offences and Prostitution*, London: Her Majesty's Stationery Office, 1957.
55. See Chris WATERS, "The Homosexual as a Social Being in Britain, 1945–1968," *Journal of British Studies*, 51/3, 2012, 685–710.
56. Wannes DUPONT, "L'Homosexualité internationalisée: Politiques pénales, débats transnationaux et échanges transatlantiques à Interpol, l'OMS et l'ONU pendant les années 1950," *Sextant*, 36, 2020, 23–40; DUPONT, "The Two-Faced Fifties," 375–391.
57. Paul BORGHS, "In beweging," in: Wannes DUPONT, Elwin HOFMAN, and Jonas ROELENS (eds.), *Verzwegen Verlangen: Een geschiedenis van homoseksualiteit in België*, Antwerp: Vrijdag, 2017, 219–254, 222; Paul BORGHS, "The Gay and Lesbian Movement in Belgium from the 1950s to the Present," *QED: A Journal in GLBTQ Worldmaking*, 3/3, 2016, 29–70, 32; Bart HELLINCK, "Stammoeder," *Zizo*, 5/21, 1997, 14–15.
58. DUPONT, "Catholics and Sexual Change."
59. Wannes DUPONT, "Gay and Lesbian Liberation in the Low Countries: From Stonewall to Pink Pillar," *History Workshop Journal*, 92, 2021, 151–173.
60. Joke BAUWENS, "De openbare televisie en haar kijkers: Oude liefde roest niet?," in: Alexander DHOEST and Hilde VAN DEN BULCK (eds.), *Publieke televisie in Vlaanderen: Een geschiedenis*, Ghent: Academia, 2007, 91–126, 103–108.
61. Hans WARMERDAM and Pieter KOENDERS, *Cultuur en Ontspanning: Het COC, 1946–1966*, Utrecht: Rijksuniversiteit Utrecht, 1987, 179.
62. HELLINCK, *Een droom*, 95–106.
63. *Diagnose van het anders-zijn*, TV documentary directed by Piet De Valkeneer, first broadcast by Belgische Radio- en Televisieomroep on December 1, 1966.
64. Guy HOCQUENGHEM, *Le désir homosexuel*, Paris: Éditions universitaires, 1972.
65. On pillarization or consociationalism, see Harry H. G. POST, *Pillarization: An Analysis of Dutch and Belgian Society*, Aldershot: Avebury, 1989.
66. It was renamed Federation of Homosexual Working Groups in 1990, then GLB Federation (Holebifederatie) in 2002, and then çavaria in 2009 for reasons of inclusivity.
67. On these two scandals, see BORGHS, "The Gay and Lesbian Movement in Belgium," 47.

68. Wannes DUPONT, "Pas de Deux, Out of Step: Diverging Chronologies of Homosexuality's (De)Criminalization in the Low Countries," *Tijdschrift voor genderstudies – Journal for Gender Studies*, 22/4, 2019, 321–338, 331–332.
69. Bart HELLINCK, "Steven De Batselier (1932–2007)," *Het ondraaglijk besef. Nieuwsbrief van het Fonds Suzan Daniel*, 13, 2007, 7–8.
70. HELLINCK, *Een droom*, 106–108.
71. GEZONDHEIDSRAAD, "Advies inzake homoseksuele relaties met minderjarigen, in het bijzonder met betrekking tot artikel 248bis van het Wetboek van Strafrecht [Speijer-rapport]. 10347," in: *Handelingen der Staten-Generaal: Zitting 1969–1970. Bijlagen Tweede Kamer*, s'Gravenhage: Staatsdrukkerij en -uitgeverijbedrijf, 1969–1970, 5–22, 15.
72. IDIER, *Les alinéas au placard*; GUNTHER, *The Elastic Closet*, 62–65; Frédéric MARTEL, *The Pink and the Black: Homosexuals in France since 1968*, translated by Jane M. TODD, Stanford: Stanford University Press, 1999, chap. 7.
73. Raymond CHARLES, "Propos sur l'article 372bis du Code Pénal (article 87 de la loi du 8 avril 1965 sur la protection de la jeunesse)," *Revue de droit pénal et de criminologie*, 62/11, 1982, 809–835, 831.
74. The embarrassment surrounding the case of fellow party member Eliane Morissens had much to do with this. See HELLINCK, *Een droom*, 164 (note 150).
75. On the importance of *Dudgeon v. the United Kingdom*, see Paul JOHNSON, *Homosexuality and the European Court of Human Rights*, Abingdon: Routledge, 2013. The issue of consent is explicitly discussed in Chapter 5.
76. *Parlementaire Handelingen: Kamer van Volksvertegenwoordigers*, June 24, 1938, 3418–3419.
77. *Parlementaire Handelingen: Senaat*, June 5, 1985, *Plenaire vergadering*, 2806–2807 and *Parlementaire Handelingen: Senaat*, June 6, 1985, 2821.
78. On HIV/AIDS in Belgium, see NEEFS, *Between Sin and Disease*, part 3; Bart HELLINCK and Mark SERGEANT, *1981–2006: 25 jaar strijd tegen aids in Vlaanderen*, Ghent: Fonds Suzan Daniel, 2006.
79. A remaining discrimination was undone in 2015.
80. On the wave of legislative reform, see BORGHS, "The Gay and Lesbian Movement in Belgium"; Bart EECKHOUT and David PATERNOTTE, "A Paradise for LGBT Rights? The Paradox of Belgium," *Journal of Homosexuality*, 58/8, 2011, 1058–1084; David PATERNOTTE, "Belgium: The Paradoxical Strength of Disunion," in: Manon TREMBLAY, David PATERNOTTE, and Carol JOHNSON (eds.), *The Lesbian and Gay Movement and the State: Comparative Insights into a Transformed Relationship*, Farnham: Ashgate, 2011, 43–56; Paul BORGHS and Bart EECKHOUT, "LGB Rights in Belgium, 1999–2007: A Historical Survey of a Velvet Revolution," *International Journal of Law, Policy and the Family*, 24/1, 2010, 1–28.
81. I purposely do not add the "I" here to the acronym as intersex people have so far received less attention from policymakers. The francophone Free University of Brussels is co-founder of the INIA-network, which seeks to change that. See www.intersexnew.co.uk.
82. Alexander DHOEST, "LGBTs In, Muslims Out: Homonationalist Discourses and Counterdiscourses in the Flemish Press," *International Journal of Communication*, 14, 2020, 155–175; Wim PEUMANS, *Queer Muslims in Europe: Sexuality, Religion and Migration in Belgium*, London: I.B. Tauris, 2020; Phillip M. AYOUB and

David PATERNOTTE (eds.), *LGBT Activism and the Making of Europe: A Rainbow Europe?*, Basingstoke: Palgrave Macmillan, 2014; PUAR, *Terrorist Assemblages*.

83. The elections of June 2024 may have been a turning point in this respect. Emulating successful tactics from abroad, the far right successfully stirred public criticism of trans* issues and politics. Despite making big gains, however, the long-standing refusal of other major parties to cooperate with the Vlaams Belang is holding for now.
84. I am respectively referring to the francophone social-democrat Elio Di Rupo, who was prime minister from 2011 to 2014, and to Petra De Sutter, who served as deputy prime minister from 2020 to 2025 for the Green Party.
85. Phillip M. AYOUB, *When States Come Out: Europe's Sexual Minorities and the Politics of Visibility*, New York: Cambridge University Press, 2016.

Bibliography

For a full overview of the sources used for this research, see my dissertation *Free-Floating Evils: A Genealogy of Homosexuality in Belgium* at https://anet.be/record/uantwerpen/opacuantwerpen/c:lvd:14323687.

Unpublished Primary Sources

Institute for Social History, Ghent

Diagnose van het anders-zijn, TV documentary produced by the Belgische Radio- en Televisie-omroep (BRT), broadcast on December 1, 1966.

Archives and Museum of Literature, Brussels

LUCIEN Mirande, *G. Eekhoud. Journal inédit. 1895–1905. Vol. 1 à 4*, unpublished partial transcript of Georges Eekhoud's personal diary, Brussels: Archives et Musée de la Littérature, ML 7355/0001-0003, s.a.
Personal diary of Georges Eekhoud, unpublished manuscript, ML 2954 (29 maps in 8 portfolios), 1895–1927.

Brussels City Archives, Brussels

Police records, Twentieth century, Series D, no D59-104: 'Pédérastes'

General State Archives, Brussels

Ministry of Justice, Public security administration, Aliens police, General files 1794–1914, finding aid I160.
Ministry of Justice, Public security administration, Aliens police, General files, conveyance of 2003, finding aid I417.

State Archives of Bruges, Bruges

HA WEST 0000: Assize court of West-Flanders, Old series, finding aid R82.

State Archives of Brussels at Forest

When I consulted them, the archives of the Brussels courts were still housed in the now defunct repository at Anderlecht.

> Assize Court of Brabant and precursors, Series I, 1794–1923, files 632–1389, finding aid T35.
> Assize Court of Brabant and precursors, Series I, 1794–1923, files 1391–2369, finding aid T56.
> Court of Appeal of Brussels, Correctional case files 1885–1949, finding aids I23, I27 and I968.
> Court of Appeal of Brussels, Series II, Sentenced correctional case files 1811–1884, finding aid I38.
> Court of First Instance of Brussels, Civil chambers, Minutes of court sessions and rulings 1871–1939, finding aid I024.
> Court of First Instance of Brussels, Correctional chambers, Dismissed case files from the interwar period, finding aid I996.
> Court of First Instance of Brussels, Correctional chambers, Sentenced case files 1892–1939 [unsorted series], finding aid I995.
> Court of First Instance of Brussels, Correctional chambers, Sentenced and dismissed correctional case files, Series II, 1893–1899, finding aid I994.
> Court of First Instance of Brussels, Correctional chambers, Series I, year-IV-1896, finding aid I993.
> Court of First Instance of Brussels, Juvenile court, Sentenced case files 1917–1920 and 1954–1959, finding aid I1008.
> Ministry of Justice, Commissioner general's office of the criminal investigaton department, finding aid I31.
> Ministry of Justice, Prison of Vorst/Forest, Archives of the anthropological service 1918–1940, finding aid I950.
> Procurator-General's office attached to the Court of Appeal of Brussels, Series I, year III-1922, finding aid T58.

Periodicals and Serial Reference Works

Annales de l'Université de Bruxelles: Faculté de médecine.
Annales de la Société de médecine légale de Belgique.
Annales de la Société scientifique de Bruxelles.
Annales médico-psychologiques.
Annuaire de l'Université Catholique de Louvain.
Archiv für Psychiatrie und Nervenkrankheiten.
Archives de l'anthropologie criminelle.
Archives de neurologie.
Bulletin de l'Académie royale de médecine de Belgique.
Bulletin de la Commission centrale de statistique.
Bulletin de la Société d'anthropologie de Bruxelles.
Bulletin de la Société de médecine mentale de Belgique.
Bulletin de la Société royale de médecine publique du royaume de Belgique.
International Criminal Police Review.

Jahrbuch für Sexuelle Zwischenstufen mit besonderer Berücksichtigung der Homosexualität.
Journal des Tribunaux.
Journal médical de Bruxelles.
L'Art moderne.
L'Étoile belge. (newspaper)
L'Indépendance belge. (newspaper)
La Belgique judicaire.
La Gazette. (newspaper)
La philosophie positive.
Le Coq rouge.
Le Petit Belge. (newspaper)
Le Petit Bleu. (newspaper)
Le Peuple. (newspaper)
Mercure de France: Série Moderne.
Nouvelle Revue Théologique.
Ontwaking.
Pandectes belges.
Pandectes périodiques.
Parlementaire Handelingen: Kamer van Volksvertegenwoordigers
Pasicrisie belge.
Pourquoi Pas?
Répertoire général de la jurisprudence belge.
Revue belge de la police administrative et judiciaire.
Revue de droit pénal et de criminologie.
Revue de l'Université de Bruxelles.
Revue ecclésiastique de Liège.
Revue internationale de police criminelle.
Revue médicale [de Louvain].
Revue Sociale Catholique.
Statistique de la Belgique. Population.
Ville de Bruxelles: Bulletin communal.

Published Primary Sources

"Adresse de la Société au ministre de la Justice, relative aux réformes à inscrire dans la loi sur le régime des aliénés," *Bulletin de la Société de médecine mentale de Belgique*, 1/1, 1872, 79–83.
"Anthropologie criminelle: 3e congrès," *L'Indépendance belge*, August 8–16, 1892.
"[Anthropologie criminelle: 3e congrès]," *L'Indépendance belge*, August 18, 1892.
"Après les Procès de Bruges: Interviews littéraires. Émile Vandervelde," *Le Peuple*, December 17, 1900, 1.
"Civ. Anvers (1er ch.), 26 mai 1888: Divorce. Injures graves. Pédérastie. Adultère hors du domicile conjugal. Recevabilité," *Pandectes périodiques: Recueil de jurisprudence, de législation et de doctrine*, 1, 1888, 1544–1545.
"Comment le procès fut intenté: La pudibonderie en délire," *Pourquoi Pas?*, 22/943, 1932, 2161.

"Corr. Bruxelles (21e ch.) 30 avril 1951: Prostitution. Racolage. Provocation au délit. Acquittement," *Journal des Tribunaux*, 66/3897, 1951, 322.

"Cour d'appel de Bruxelles: Huitième chambre. Présidence de M. Hayoit de Termicourt, cons. 26 février 1910. Outrage public aux mœurs. Dessins obscènes. Conférence sur le néo-malthusianisme," *La Belgique judicaire*, 68/45, 1910, 713–719.

"Discussion du rapport de la Commission chargée d'examiner les questions relatives aux aliénés dits criminels, soumises à l'Académie par M. le Ministre de la Justice," *Bulletin de l'Académie royale de médecine de Belgique: IVe série*, 3, 1889, 281–330, 362–395, 365–605 and 612–632.

"Double délit: Intention. Juge du fond. Appréciation," in: *Pasicrisie belge*, 3 vols., vol. 3, Brussels: Bruylant, 1863, 343–346.

"Gand, 19 mars 1909: Outrages aux mœurs. Articles 383 et 385 du code pénal. Application. Interprétation des faits et gestes. Règles à suivre," in: *Pandectes périodiques*, vol. 22, Brussels: Larcier, 1909, 776–777.

"L'Incorrigible M. Janssens de Bisthoven, Georges Eekhoud et Camille Lemonnier devant les assises de la Flandre Occidentale en octobre 1900," *Pourquoi Pas?*, 22/943, 1932, 2180–2189.

"L'Instruction du crime de la Place royale," *Le Petit Bleu*, June 13, 1899.

"L'Inversion génitale et la législation [Discussion]," in: *Actes du troisième congrès international d'anthropologie criminelle tenu à Bruxelles en Août 1892 sous le haut patronage du gouvernement: Biologie et sociologie*, Brussels: Hayez, 1893, 448–459.

"Le crime de la place Royale à Bruxelles," *Le Petit belge*, June 9, 10, 13 and 15, 1899.

"Le crime de la place Royale," *L'Indépendance belge*, June 11, 1899.

"Le mystère de l'hôtel Osy," *Le Petit Bleu*, June 14, 1899.

"Le procès Eekhoud," *Le Petit Bleu*, October 25, 1900.

"Le troisième congrès d'anthropologie criminelle," *Journal des Tribunaux*, 11/909, 1892, 995–1001.

"M. Janssens de Bisthoven et Camille Lemonnier devant les assises de la Flandre Occidentale en octobre 1900," *Pourquoi Pas?*, 22/944, 1932, 2240–2243.

"Outrage public aux mœurs," in: Edmond PICARD, Napoléon D'HOFFSCHMIDT, and Jules DE LE COURT (eds.), *Pandectes belges*, vol. 72, Brussels: Larcier, 1902, 512–554.

"Procès-verbal de la séance extraordinaire qui a eu lieu à Bruxelles, au Palais de l'Université, le 8 août 1885," *Bulletin de la Société de médecine mentale de Belgique*, 13/38, 1885, 12–15.

"Procès-verbal de la séance ordinaire du 4 mai 1875, tenue à Bruxelles au Palais de l'Université," *Bulletin de la Société de médecine mentale de Belgique*, 3/6, 1875, 5–10.

"Procès-verbal de la séance ordinaire tenue à Bruxelles, le 31 janvier 1885," *Bulletin de la Société de médecine mentale de Belgique*, 13/36, 1885, 9–12.

"Procès-verbal de la séance ordinaire tenue au Palais de l'Université à Bruxelles, le samedi 29 octobre 1887," *Bulletin de la Société de médecine mentale de Belgique*, 15/47, 1887, 6–8.

"Procès-verbal de la séance ordinaire tenue au Palais de l'Université à Bruxelles, le samedi 28 janvier 1888," *Bulletin de la Société de médecine mentale de Belgique*, 16/48, 1888, 9–22.

"Procès-verbal de la séance ordinaire tenue au Palais de l'Université à Bruxelles, le samedi 30 juillet 1887," *Bulletin de la Société de médecine mentale de Belgique*, 15/47, 1887, 3–5.
"Programme du Congrès International d'Anthropologie criminelle qui se tiendra à Bruxelles du 8 au 14 août 1892," *Bulletin de la Société de médecine mentale de Belgique*, 20/64, 1892, 122–124.
"Rapport de M. le Dr Schrevens (Tournai)," *Bulletin de l'Académie royale de médecine de Belgique*, 2, 1888, 89–94.
"Séance du 29 avril 1905 [Discours prononcé aux obsèques de M. Hubert]," *Bulletin de l'Académie royale de médecine de Belgique: IVe série*, 19, 1905, 209–212.
"Séance inaugurale du 18 novembre 1875," *Annales de la Société scientifique de Bruxelles*, 1, 1875–1876, 44–72.
"Sexual Offences," *International Criminal Police Review*, 7/60, 1952, 216–219.
"Statuts," *Annales de la Société scientifique de Bruxelles*, 1, 1875–1876, 1–4.
"Tribunal civil d'Anvers (1re ch.): Présidence de M. Op de Beeck. 26 mai 1888. Droit civil. Divorce. Injures graves. Pédérastie. Adultère hors du domicile conjugal. Recevabilité," *Journal des Tribunaux*, 7/538, 1888, 840–842.
"Un peu gras, ce que nous avons à vous conter," *L'Indépendance belge*, September 3, 1890, 1–2.
Actes du troisième congrès international d'anthropologie criminelle tenu à Bruxelles en Août 1892 sous le haut patronage du gouvernement: Biologie et sociologie, Brussels: Hayez, 1893.
Ajax, "Autour du crime de Liège: Une lacune à combler," *La Nation belge*, September 1, 1931.
ALETRINO Arnold, "La Situation sociale de l'Uraniste [+ Discussion]," in: J. K. A. Wertheim SALOMONSON (ed.), *Congrès international d'anthropologie criminelle: Compte rendu des travaux de la cinquième session tenue à Amsterdam du 9 au 14 Septembre 1901*, Amsterdam: De Bussy, 1901, 25–36 and 473–494.
AUERBACH Berthold, "Dans les bas-fonds de Bruxelles: Choses vues," *Journal des Tribunaux*, 12/1019, 1893, 1457–1468.
BALL Benjamin, *La folie érotique*, Paris: Baillière, 1888.
BELTJENS Gustave, *Le code d'instruction criminelle belge et les lois spéciales annotés d'après 1° Les principes juridiques, 2° La doctrine des auteurs belges et français 3° Les décisions des cours et tribunaux*, 2 vols., vol. 1, Brussels: Bruylant and Maresq, 1903.
BELYM Léon, "Aspects actuels de la criminalité sexuelle et perspectives de son traitement pénitentiaire," *Revue de droit pénal et de criminologie et archives internationales de médecine légale*, 1927, 1015–1044 and 1174–1195.
BELYM Léon, "Considérations sur la criminalité érotique," *Bulletin de la Société d'anthropologie de Bruxelles*, 41/2, 1927, 132–150.
BILTRIS Norbert, "L'Attentat à la pudeur et le viol," *Revue de droit pénal et de criminologie*, 1925, 1002–1046 and 1161–1199.
BLADEL Maurice, *L'Œuvre de Georges Eekhoud*, Brussels: Renaissance d'Occident, 1922.
BOËNS Hubert, "La criminalité au point de vue sociologique," *La philosophie positive. Deuxième série*, 12/23, 1879, 76–96.
BOËNS Hubert, *Louise Lateau ou les mystères de Bois-D'Haine dévoilés*, 2nd ed., Brussels: Manceaux, 1875.

BORMANS Théophile, *Répertoire belge de législation, d'instructions, de doctrine et de jurisprudence concernant la médecine légale, l'exercice de l'art de guérir et la police sanitaire*, Brussels: Larcier, 1882.

BOUÉ Ariste, *Commentaire sur la loi des aliénés du 30 juin 1838*, s.l.: s.e., s.a.

BOULENGER Max, "Quelques appréciations étrangères sur l'assistance des aliénés en Belgique," *Journal médical de Bruxelles*, 14/47, 1909, 737–742.

BOURNET Albert, "Troisième congrès d'anthropologie criminelle," *Archives de l'anthropologie criminelle et des sciences pénales*, 7/41, 1892, 465–591.

BUREAU Paul, *La crise morale des temps nouveaux*, 9th ed., Paris: Bloud, 1908.

CARLIER Félix, *Les deux prostitutions*, Paris: Dentu, 1887.

CHARCOT Jean-Martin and Valentin MAGNAN, "Inversion du sens génital [part 1]," *Archives de neurologie*, 3/7, 1882, 53–60.

CHARCOT Jean-Martin and Valentin MAGNAN, "Inversion du sens génital [part 2]," *Archives de neurologie*, 4/12, 1882, 296–322.

CHARRIAUT Henri, *La Belgique moderne: Une terre d'expériences*, Paris: Ernest Flammarion, 1910.

CHAUVEAU Adolphe and Hélie FAUSTIN, *Théorie du code pénal*, 2 vols., vol. 2, Brussels: Wahlen, 1840.

CHEVALIER Julien, *De l'inversion de l'instinct sexuel au point de vue médico-légal*, Lyon: Imprimerie nouvelle, 1885.

CHEVALIER Julien, *Une maladie de la personnalité: L'Inversion sexuelle*, Lyon: Storck and Masson, 1893.

CLAEYS BOUUAERT Ferdinand, "M. le Chanoine Maurice De Baets: Professeur honoraire de la Faculté de Théologie," *Université catholique de Louvain. Katholieke Universiteit Leuven. Annuaire-Jaarboek*, 1930–1933, cxii–cxx.

CLAPHAM John H., *The Economic Development of France and Germany 1815–1914*, Cambridge: Cambridge University Press, 1921.

Commission chargée de préparer un Projet de Loi sur la Police des mœurs instituée par arrêté royal du 13 octobre 1887: Procès-verbaux des séances de la section de législation, des séances de la section d'hygiène et des séances plénières, Brussels: Joseph Goemaere, 1891.

CROCQ Jean, *La situation du médecin d'asile en Belgique*, Brussels: Severeyns, 1907.

DALLEMAGNE Jules, *Dégénérés et déséquilibrés*, Brussels: Lamertin, 1894.

DAMBRE Ange-Louis, *Traité de médecine légale et de jurisprudence de la médecine*, 3 vols., Ghent: Hoste, 1859–1867.

DE BAETS Maurice, *Les bases de la morale et du droit*, Paris: Alcan and Siffer, 1892.

DE BUSSCHERE Alphonse, "Le viol et l'attentat à la pudeur [part 1]," *Annales de la Société de médecine légale de Belgique*, 5/1, 1893, 14–31.

DE MOOR L., "Note sur un cas de fétichisme," *Bulletin de la Société de médecine mentale de Belgique*, 31/110–111, 1903, 189–194.

DE RODE Léon, "L'Inversion génitale et la législation," in: *Actes du troisième congrès international d'anthropologie criminelle tenu à Bruxelles en août 1892 sous le haut patronage du gouvernement: Biologie et sociologie*, Brussels: Hayez, 1893, 107–113.

DE RODE Léon, "[Review of] Neue Forschungen auf dem Gebiet der Psychopathia sexualis [by R. von Krafft-Ebing]," *Bulletin de la Société de médecine mentale de Belgique*, 19/61, 1891, 217–221.

DE RODE Léon, "[Review of the fourth edition of] Psychopathia sexualis: Eine klinisch-forensische Studie [by R. von Krafft-Ebing]," *Bulletin de la Société de médecine mentale de Belgique*, 17/54, 1889, 388–389.

DE RODE Léon, "[Review of the second edition of] Psychopathia sexualis mit besonderer Berücksichtigung der conträre Sexualempfindung: Étude médico-légale sur la psychopathie sexuelle et spécialement sur l'inversion sexuelle [by R. Von Krafft-Ebing]," *Bulletin de la Société de médecine mentale de Belgique*, 16/48, 1888, 37–47.

DE RODE Léon, "[Review of the third edition of] Psychopathia Sexualis mit besonderer Berücksichtigung der conträren Sexualempfindung [by R. von Krafft-Ebing]," *Bulletin de la Société de médecine mentale de Belgique*, 16/50, 1888, 332–333.

DEFFERNEZ Edmond, *Des maisons de logement pour ouvriers célibataires: Rapport présenté au Congrès contre l'alcoolisme, tenu à Bruxelles en septembre 1897*, Brecht: Braeckmans, 1898.

DELATTRE Louis, *Rapport de M. le Dr Louis Delattre, inspecteur d'hygiène, concernant un plan d'hygiène, d'éducation morale et hygiénique de la vie sexuelle*, Brussels: Nossent, 1922.

DELMER Louis, *L'Art en cour d'assises: Étude sur l'œuvre littéraire et sociale de Camille Lemonnier*, Paris: Savine and Rozez, 1893.

DEMOLDER Eugène, *Sous la robe: Notes d'audience, de palais et d'ailleurs d'un juge de paix*, Paris: Mercure de France, 1897.

DESOER Emmanuel, *Code pratique de police judiciaire et administrative à l'usage des bourgmestres, des commissaires et agents de police, des officiers de gendarmerie, des gendarmes et des gardes champêtres*, 2nd ed., Brussels: Larcier and Lauriel, 1882.

DEWINNE Auguste, "Escal-Vigor," *Le Peuple*, November 28, 1900, 1.

DOUGLAS Alfred, "Two Loves," *The Chameleon*, December, 1994, www.bl.uk/collection-items/the-chameleon, last accessed on September 1, 2022, 26–28.

DR. LAUPTS, *L'Homosexualité et les types homosexuels: Nouvelle édition de perversion et perversité sexuelles*, 2nd ed., Paris: Vigot Frères, 1910.

DR. LAUPTS, *Tares et poisons: Perversion & perversité sexuelles. Une enquête médicale sur l'inversion. Notes et documents. Le roman d'un inverti-né. Le procès Wilde. La guérison et la prophylaxie de l'inversion*, Paris: Georges Carré, 1896.

EEKHOUD Georges, "À propos d'Escal-Vigor," in: Mirande LUCIEN and Patrick CARDON (eds.), *Georges Eekhoud: Un illustre uraniste*, Lille: Gai-Kitsch-Camp, 1996 [1901], 51–55.

EEKHOUD Georges, "A propos d'une polémique: Une lettre de Georges Eekhoud," *La Réforme*, March 5, 1900.

EEKHOUD Georges, *A Strange Love: A Novel of Abnormal Passion*, New York: The Panurge Press, 1930.

EEKHOUD Georges, *Cycle patibulaire*, Brussels: Kistemaeckers, 1892.

EEKHOUD Georges, "De la sensibilité dans la littérature moderne," in: Mirande LUCIEN and Patrick CARDON (eds.), *Georges Eekhoud: Un illustre uraniste 1854–1927*, Montpellier: GaiKitschCamp, 2012 [1909], 62–75.

EEKHOUD Georges, "De Oorsprong en de Evolutie van een Werk," *Ontwaking*, 4, 1904, 15–31.

EEKHOUD Georges, *Escal-Vigor*, Paris: Mercure de France, 1899.

EEKHOUD Georges, *Escal-Vigor*, Paris: Séguier, 1996 [1899].

EEKHOUD Georges, *Escal-Vigor*, translated by Richard MEIENREIS, Leipzig: Spohr, 1903.
EEKHOUD Georges, *Kees Doornik: Scènes du polder*, Brussels: Hochsteyn, 1883.
EEKHOUD Georges, *Kermesses*, Brussels: Kistemaeckers, 1884.
EEKHOUD Georges, *L'Autre vue*, Paris: Mercure de France, 1904.
EEKHOUD Georges, *La nouvelle Carthage*, Brussels: Kistemaeckers, 1888.
EEKHOUD Georges, *Le Cycle patibulaire*, Paris: Mercure de France, 1896.
EEKHOUD Georges, *Les milices de Saint François*, Brussels: Monnom, 1886.
EEKHOUD Georges, *Mes Communions*, Brussels: Kistemaeckers, 1895.
EEKHOUD Georges, "Saint-Sébastien dans la peinture," in: Mirande LUCIEN and Patrick CARDON (eds.), *Georges Eekhoud: Un illustre uraniste 1854–1927*, Montpellier: GaiKitschCamp, 2012 [1909], 57–61.
EEKHOUD Georges and Mirande LUCIEN, *Le quadrille du lancier et autres nouvelles*, Brussels: Gai-Kitsch-Camp, 1992.
ELLIS Havelock and John A. SYMONDS, *Sexual Inversion*, London: Wilson and Macmillan, 1897.
FÉRÉ Charles, *L'Instinct sexuel: Évolution et dissolution*, Paris: Félix Alcan, 1899.
FIAUX Louis, *La prostitution en Belgique*, Paris, 1892.
FLEXNER Abraham, *Prostitution in Europe*, New York: The Century, 1919 [1914].
FOSDICK Raymond B., *European Police Systems*, New York: The Century, 1915.
FRANCOTTE Xavier, *Aperçu du développement et de l'état actuel de l'enseignement de la médecine mentale en Belgique*, Ghent: Vanderhaeghen, 1894.
FRANCOTTE Xavier, *Causeries sur des questions d'hygiène morale*, Liège: Imprimerie liégeoise, 1919.
FRANCOTTE Xavier, *De quelques points de morale sexuelle dans ses relations avec la médecine: Rapport présenté à la section de médecine de la Société scientifique de Bruxelles, séance du 10 avril 1907*, Leuven: Secrétariat de la Société scientifique, 1907.
FRANCOTTE Xavier, *L'Anthropologie criminelle*, Paris: Baillière, 1891.
FRANK Louis, *Le crime de la Rue des Hirondelles: L'Affaire Van Calck à Bruxelles. Étude de police criminelle*, Paris: Frank, 1909.
GALET O., "Essai de détermination de quelques caractères de la délinquance contre les mœurs," *Bulletin de la Société d'anthropologie de Bruxelles*, 41/2, 1927, 167–198 and 200–234.
GARNIER Paul, *Les fétichistes: Pervertis et invertis sexuels. Observations médico-légales*, Paris: Baillière, 1896.
GLORIEUX Zénon, "La psychiatrie et l'assistance aux malades mentaux (1830–1930)," in: *Cent ans de médecine en Belgique 1830–1930: Numéro spécial publié à l'occasion du centenaire de l'indépendance*, Ixelles-Brussels: Vromans, 1931, 123–145.
HAESAERT Jean-Polydore, "Évolution de la jurisprudence belge en matière d'outrages publics aux mœurs (art. 385 du code Pénal)," *Revue de droit pénal et de criminologie*, 1927, 1155–1173.
HÉGER Paul, "Les prisons-asiles," *Bulletin de la Société de médecine mentale de Belgique*, 99, 1900, 358–374.
HÉGER Paul, "Les prisons-asiles," *Revue de l'Université de Bruxelles*, 6, 1900–1901, 31–45.
HÉGER Paul and Jules DALLEMAGNE, *Étude craniologique d'une série d'assassins excécutés en Belgique*, Brussels: Manceaux, 1881.

HENNEBICQ Léon, "[Review of] Dégénérés et déséquilibrés [by J. Dallemagne]," *Journal des Tribunaux*, 14/1152, 1895, 737–748.

HIRSCHFELD Magnus, *Die Homosexualität des Mannes und des Weibes*, Berlin: Marcus, 1914.

HIRSCHFELD Magnus, *Memoir Celebrating 25 Years of the First LGBT Organization*, translated by Michael A. LOMBARDI-NASH, s.l.: Urania Manuscripts, 2019.

HIRSCHFELD Magnus, "Urteile römisch-katholischer Priester über die Stellung des Christentums zur staatl: Bestrafung der gleichgeschlechtlichen Liebe," *Jahrbuch für sexuelle Zwischenstufen mit besonderer Berücksichtigung der Homosexualität*, 2, 1900, 161–203.

HIRSCHFELD Magnus, *Von einst bis jetzt: Geschichte einer homosexuellen Bewegung 1897–1922. Herausgegeben und mit einem Nachwort versehen von Manfred Herzer und James Steakley*, Berlin: Rosa Winkel, 1986 [1922–1923].

HOUZÉ Emile and Léo WARNOTS, "Existe-t-il un type de criminel anatomiquement déterminé," in: *Actes du troisième congrès international d'anthropologie criminelle tenu à Bruxelles en Août 1892 sous le haut patronage du gouvernement: Biologie et sociologie*, Brussels: Hayez, 1893, 121–126.

HUBERT Eugène, "L'Inversion du sens génital," *Revue médicale*, 11, 1892, 359–363.

Huitième rapport de la Commission permanente d'inspection des établissements d'aliénés instituée par arrêté royal du 17 mars 1853: 1862, Brussels: Hayez, 1864.

HUYSMANS Gaston-L., "À propos du monstrueux crime de la Citadelle de Liège," *L'Étoile belge*, August 19, 1931.

HUYSMANS Joris K., *À Rebours*, Paris: Cent Bibliophiles, 1903 [1884].

Indicateur des urinoirs de Bruxelles contenant un Tableau officiel des Urinoirs et des chroniques, articles et nouvelles littéraires se rapportant à l'urinoir et à son histoire ainsi qu'à l'Art de bien uriner, Brussels: s.e., s.a.

INGELS Benjamin-Constant, Jean CUYLITS, and Jules MOREL, *Congrès de phréniatrie et de neuropathologie tenu à Anvers du 7 au 9 septembre 1885: Compte-rendu*, Ghent: Vanderhaeghen, 1886.

JACQUART Camille, "Le problème de la natalité en France," *Revue Sociale Catholique*, 8, 1903–1904, 39–52, 77–83 and 137–146.

JACQUART Camille, "Mouvement de l'état civil et de la population en Belgique pendant les années 1876 à 1900," *Bulletin de la Commission centrale de statistique*, 19, 1906, 296–424.

JAMAR Lucien (ed.), *1814 à 1880: Répertoire général de la jurisprudence belge contenant l'analyse de toutes les décisions rendues en Belgique depuis 1814 jusqu'à 1880 inclusivement en matière civile, commerciale, criminelle, de droit public et administratif*, 11 vols., Brussels: Bruylant-Christophe, 1882–1884.

JAUQUET E., "Notice sur la vie et les travaux de Jules Dallemagne," in: *Rapport de l'Université Libre de Bruxelles sur l'année académique 1922–1923*, Brussels: Université Libre, 1924, 27–31.

JOLY Henri, *La Belgique criminelle*, Paris: Lecoffre, 1907.

KISTEMAECKERS Henri, "Mes procès littéraires: Souvenirs d'un éditeur," *Mercure de France: Série Moderne*, 166/606, 1923, 670–692.

KNOCH Auguste, *L'Éducation de la chasteté*, 3rd ed., Paris: Pierre Téqui and Revue Ecclésiastique, 1914.

KNOCH Auguste, *Le Jeune Homme Chaste: L'Éducation de la pureté dans les collèges*, 2nd ed., Arras: Brunet and Revue Ecclésiastique, 1914.

KNOCH Auguste, *L'Onanisme conjugal et le tribunal de la pénintence*, 4th ed., Arras: Brunet and Revue Ecclésiastique, 1914.

LAGASSSE Charles and Charles DE QUÉKER, *Enquête sur les habitations ouvrières en 1890: Rapport présenté au Comité de Patronage de la Ville de Bruxelles*, Brussels: De Bremaeker-Wauts, 1890.

LE JEUNE Jules, "Circulaire ministérielle: Outrage aux mœurs. Intention. Pissoirs. Autorité communale," *La Belgique judiciaire*, 48/68, 1890, 1087.

LENTZ François, "Attentat aux mœurs: Rapport médico-légal," *Bulletin de la Société de médecine mentale de Belgique*, 9/21, 1881, 67–71.

LENTZ François, "[Review of] Des divers états de trouble intellectuel devant la juridiction civile [by R. Von Krafft-Ebing]," *Bulletin de la Société de médecine mentale de Belgique*, 4/8, 1876, 44–57.

LENTZ François, "[Review of] Traité de psycho-pathologie légale [by R. Von Krafft-Ebing]," *Bulletin de la Société de médecine mentale de Belgique*, 4/8, 1876, 67–75.

LENTZ François, "[Review of] Ueber Geistestörungen durch Zwangvorstellungen [by R. von Krafft-Ebing]," *Bulletin de la Société de médecine mentale de Belgique*, 7/13, 1879, 38–41.

Ligue des Familles Nombreuses de Belgique, *Intérêts familiaux: Rapport général de la Commission Centrale des Intérêts Familiaux*, Brussels: Ligue des Familles Nombreuses, s.a. [c. 1944].

Loi et règlements sur le régime des aliénés, Brussels: Deltombe, 1851.

LOMBROSO Cesare, *L'Uomo delinquente*, Milan: Hoepli, 1876.

LOUWAGE Florent Edouard, *Psychologie et criminalité*, 2nd ed., Ninove: Anneessens, 1945 [1943].

LUCIEN Mirande, *Mon bien aimé petit Sander: Lettres de Georges Eekhoud à Sander Pierron (1892–1927). Suivis de six lettres de Sander Pierron à Georges Eekhoud*, Lille: Cahiers Gai-Kitsch-Camp, 1993.

MAGNAN Valentin, *Des anomalies, des abérrations et des perversions sexuelles: Communication faite à l'Académie de médecine dans la séance du 13 janvier 1885*, Paris: Delahaye and Lecrosnier, 1885.

MAHAIM Ernest, *Les abonnements d'ouvriers sur les lignes des chemins de fer belges et leurs effets sociaux*, Brussels: Misch and Thron, 1910.

MANTEGAZZA Paolo, *Gli amori degli uomini: Saggio di una entnologia dell'amore*, Milan: Mantegazza, 1886.

MASOIN Paul, *Contribution à l'étude des perversions sexuelles chez les dégénérés*, Ghent: Vanderhaeghen, 1895.

MASOIN Ernest, "Éloge funèbre de E. Hubert, prononcé le 19 juin 1905, en la salle des Promotions, par E. Masoin, professeur à la Faculté de Médecine," *Annuaire de l'Université Catholique de Louvain*, 70, 1906, lv–lxvii.

MASOIN Ernest, "Le docteur Léon De Rode," *Bulletin de la Société de médecine mentale de Belgique*, 38/152, 1910, 248–250.

MERCIER Désiré-Joseph, *Instructiones contra vitium onanismi, parochis et confessariis propositae*, Mechelen: s.e., 1909.

MERCIER Désiré-Joseph, Henri DESPLATS, and Arthur VERMEERSCH, *Pour l'honnêteté conjugale: Nouvelle édition*, Leuven: Fonteyn, 1910.

MERCIER J., *De la loi du 27 novembre 1891 sur la répression du vagabondage et de la mendicité*, Brussels: Larcier, 1891.

MOLL Albert, *Die Conträre Sexualempfindung: Mit Benutzung amtlichen Materials*, Berlin: Fischer, 1891.
NÄCKE Paul, "Un cas de fétichisme de souliers avec remarques sur les perversions du sens génital," *Bulletin de la Société de médecine mentale de Belgique*, 22/74, 1894, 308–332.
Neuvième rapport de la Commission permanente d'inspection des établissements d'aliénés instituée par arrêté royale du 18 mars 1853: 1863, 1864 et 1865, Brussels: Gobbaerts, 1866.
NUMA PRAETORIUS, "Die Bibliographie der Homosexualität für das Jahr 1901 mit Ausschluss der Belletristik," *Jahrbuch für sexuelle Zwischenstufen mit besonderer Berücksichtigung der Homosexualität*, 4, 1902, 775–920.
NUMA PRAETORIUS, "Der Prozess von Georges Eekhoud wegen seines Romanes 'Escal-Vigor,'" *Jahrbuch für Sexuelle Zwischenstufen mit besonderer Berücksichtigung der Homosexualität*, 3, 1901, 520–525.
NUMA PRAETORIUS, "[Review of] L'Autre vue [by G. Eekhoud]," *Jahrbuch für Sexuelle Zwischenstufen mit besonderer Berücksichtigung der Homosexualität*, 7, 1905, 858–663.
NYPELS Jean Servais Guillaume and Jean SERVAIS, *Le code pénal belge interprété, principalement au point de vue de la pratique*, 2nd ed., 4 vols., vol. 1, Brussels: Bruylant, 1896–1899.
PEETERS J. A., "[Review of] Les fétichistes pervertis et invertis sexuels: Observations médico-légales [by P. Garnier]," *Bulletin de la Société de médecine mentale de Belgique*, 23/79, 1895, 421–423.
PEETERS J. A., "[Review of] Zur conträren sexual Empfindung in klinische forensisches Hinsicht [by R. Von Krafft-Ebing]," *Bulletin de la Société de médecine mentale de Belgique*, 10/25, 1882, 68–71.
PETITHAN Charles, "La dégénérescence de la race belge, ses causes et ses remèdes [et rapports joints]," *Bulletin de la Société royale de médecine publique du royaume de Belgique*, 7, 1888, 62–95.
PETITHAN Charles, "Sur la position que doit prendre la gynécologie dans les questions sociales qui ont rapport à la procréation," in: Guye, De Perrot, Stokvis et al. (eds.), *Congrès périodique international des sciences médicales: 6me session. Amsterdam, septembre 1879. Compte-rendu*, Amsterdam: Van Rossen, 1880, 113–116.
PICARD Edmond, "Éloquence nouveau siècle," *Journal des Tribunaux*, 10/764, 1891, 1–5.
PICARD Edmond, *La crise politique en Belgique: Extrait de la Revue Moderne*, Brussels: Mertens, 1883.
PICARD Edmond, "Les Maladresses de la Justice: Eekhoud et son 'Escal-Vigor' poursuivies pour outrage aux mœurs," *L'Art moderne*, 20/10, 1900, 75–77.
PICARD Edmond, "L'Uranisme," *Le Peuple*, November 19, 1900, 1.
POTVIN Charles, *Du gouvernement de soi-même: Les principes, le devoir, la vie privée, la patrie, le travail, les nations*, 6 vols., Paris: Hachette, 1877.
PRÉVOST-PARADOL Lucien-Anatole, *La France nouvelle*, Paris: Lévy, 1868.
PRINS Adolphe, "Conférence sur les doctrines nouvelles du droit pénal faite le 21 décembre 1895 au Palais de Justice de Bruxelles," *Revue de l'Université de Bruxelles*, 1, 1895–1896, 6–33.
QUANTER Rudolf, *Die Sittlichkeitsverbrechen im Laufe der Jahrhundert und ihre strafrechtliche Beurteilung*, 2nd ed., Berlin: Bermühler, 1904.

QUANTER Rudolf, *Die Sittlichkeitsverbrechen im Laufe der Jahrhundert und ihre strafrechtliche Beurteilung*, 8th ed., Berlin: Scientia, 1970 [1925].

RACINE Aimée, *Les enfants traduits en justice: Étude d'après trois cents dossiers du tribunal pour enfants de l'arrondissement de Bruxelles*, Liège: Georges Thoné, 1935.

RAFFALOVICH [Marc-]André, "Annales de l'unisexualité [1]," *Archives d'anthropologie criminelle, de médecine légale et de psychologie normale et pathologique*, 12/67, 1897, 87–102.

RAFFALOVICH Marc-André, "L'Uranisme: Inversion sexuelle congénitale. Observations et conseils," *Archives d'anthropologie criminelle, de médecine légale et de psychologie normale et pathologique*, 10/55, 1895, 99–127.

RAMIEN Theodor, *Sappho und Sokrates oder wie erklärt sich die Liebe der Männer und Frauen zu Personen des eigenen Geschlechts?*, Leipzig: Spohr, 1896.

Rapport de la Commission supérieure d'inspection des établissements d'aliénés instituée par arrêté royale du 18 novembre 1851, Brussels: Hayez, 1853.

ROELANDTS Leon, "Théologie pastorale," *Nouvelle Revue Théologique*, 38, 1906, 126–138.

ROSENFELD Michael (ed.), *Confessions d'un homosexuel à Émile Zola*, Paris: Nouvelles Éditions Place, 2017.

ROSENFELD Michael and William A. PENISTON (eds.), *The Italian Invert: A Gay Man's Intimate Confessions to Émile Zola*, New York: Columbia University Press, 2022.

SAEY Maurice, *Les dessous de Bruxelles*, Brussels: Dujardin, 1908.

SEMAL François, *De la loi sur les aliénés et des réformes à y apporter: Rapport lu en Séance extraordinaire de la Fédération médicale belge le 20 novembre 1872*, Brussels: Manceaux, 1872.

SEMAL François, "De la situation morale et légale et du placement des aliénés et dangereux," in: E. W. WARLOMONT, V. DUWEZ, and G. VERRIEST (eds.), *Congrès périodique international des sciences médicales: 4me session. Bruxelles. 1875. Compte-rendu*, Brussels: Manceaux and Baillière, 1876, 693–722.

SEMAL François, "Rapport sur l'organisation du service des aliénés en Belgique," *Bulletin de la Société de médecine mentale de Belgique*, 1/1, 1873, 29–41.

SEMELAIGNE René, "Le troisième congrès international d'anthropologie criminelle," *Annales médico-psychologiques*, 16, 1892, 329–366.

Statistique de la Belgique: Population. Recensement général du 31 décembre 1890, 2 vols., vol. 2, Brussels: Lesigne, 1893.

Statistique de la Belgique: Population. Recensement général du 31 décembre 1910, 5 vols., vol. 4, Brussels: Weissenbruch, 1915.

TARNOVSKII Veniamin M., *Izvrashchenie polovogo chuvstva: Sudebno-psikhiatricheskii ocherk dlia vrachei i iuristov*, Saint Petersburg: s.e., 1885.

TARNOWSKY Benjamin, *Die krankhaften Erscheinungen des Geschlechtsinnes: Eine forensisch-psychiatrische Studie*, Berlin: Hirschwald, 1886.

TAYART DE BORMS Victor, "La prostitution masculine: Les homosexuels devant la loi," *Revue belge de la police administrative et judiciaire*, 52/136, 1931, 50–77.

TIBERGHIEN Guillaume, *Université libre de Bruxelles: Discours prononcé par G. Tiberghien, Recteur, le 7 octobre 1867. Athéisme, matérialisme et positivisme*, Brussels: Mayolez, 1867.

Treizième rapport sur la situation des asiles d'aliénés du royaume: Années 1883 à 1892, Brussels: Goemaere, 1895.

VANDERKINDERE Léon, *Ligue de l'enseignement: Extrait du rapport présenté à l'Assemblée générale du 2 avril 1890*, Brussels: Weissenbruch, 1890.
VANDERVELDE Émile, *L'Exode rural et le retour aux champs*, Paris: Alcan, 1903.
VERMEERSCH Arthur, *De castitate et de vitiis contrariis: Tractatus doctrinalis et moralis*, 2nd ed., Rome: Universita Gregoriana and Beyaert, 1921 [1919].
Ville de Bruxelles: Bulletin communal. Année 1881, 2 vols., vol. 1, Brussels: Baertsoen, 1881.
Ville de Bruxelles: Les recensements de 1910, Brussels: Guyot, 1912.
VON KRAFFT-EBING Richard, *Lehrbuch der gerichtlichen Psychopathologie mit Berücksichtigung der Gesetzgebung von Österreich, Deutschland und Frankreich*, Stuttgart: Enke, 1875.
VON KRAFFT-EBING Richard, *Psychopathia sexualis avec recherches spéciales sur l'inversion sexuelle: Traduit sur la huitième édition allemande*, translated by Émile LAURENT and Sigismond CSAPO, Paris: Masson, 1895.
VON KRAFFT-EBING Richard, *Psychopathia sexualis mit besonderer Berücksichtigung der conträren Sexualempfindung: Eine klinisch-forensische Studie*, Stuttgart: Enke, 1887.
VON KRAFFT-EBING Richard, *Psychopathia sexualis: Eine klinisch-forensische Studie*, Stuttgart: Enke, 1886.
VON KRAFFT-EBING Richard, "Ueber gewisse Anomalien des Geschlechtstriebs und die klinisch-forensische Verwerthung derselben als eines wahrscheinlich functionellen Degenerationszeichens des centralen Nervensystems," *Archiv für Psychiatrie und Nervenkrankheiten*, 7, 1877, 291–312.
VON RÖMER Lucien S. A. M., *Het uranisch gezin: Wetenschappelijk onderzoek en conclusiën over homosexualiteit*, Amsterdam: Tierie, 1905.
WESTPHAL Carl, "Die conträre Sexualempfindung: Symptom eines neuropatischen (psychopathischen) Zustandes," *Archiv für Psychiatrie und Nervenkrankheiten*, 2, 1869, 83–108.
ZOLA Emile, *Fécondité*, Paris: Charpentier, 1899.

Secondary Literature

ABRAHAM Julie, *Metropolitan Lovers: The Homosexuality of Cities*, Minneapolis: University of Minnesota Press, 2009.
AFARY Janet and Kevin B. ANDERSON, *Foucault and the Iranian Revolution: Gender and the Seductions of Islam*, London: University of Chicago Press, 2005.
AFKEN Janin and Bendikt WOLF (eds.), *Sexual Culture in Germany in the 1970s: A Golden Age for Queers?* Basingstoke: Palgrave Macmillan, 2019.
ALDRICH Robert, *Colonialism and Homosexuality*, London: Routledge, 2003.
ALDRICH Robert, "Homosexuality and the City: An Historical Overview," *Urban Studies*, 41/9, 2004, 1719–1737.
ALEXANDER Rustam, *Regulating Homosexuality in Soviet Russia, 1956–91: A Different History*, Manchester: Manchester University Press, 2021.
ANDERSON Malcolm, *In Thrall to Political Change: Police and Gendarmerie in France*, Oxford: Oxford University Press, 2011.
ANDERSON Robert D., *France 1870–1914: Politics and Society*, 2nd ed. London: Routledge and Kegan Paul, 1984.

ARON Paul, "Art nouveau in Belgium: A Laboratory of Modernity," in: Nathalie AUBERT, Pierre-Philippe FRAITURE, and Patrick McGUINNESS (eds.), *La Belgique entre deux siècles: Laboratoire de la modernité, 1880–1914*, Bern: Peter Lang, 2007, 19–31.

ARON Paul, *Les écrivains belges et le socialisme (1880–1913): L'Expérience de l'art social, d'Edmond Picard à Émile Verhaeren*, Brussels: Labor, 1985.

ARON Paul and Cécile VANDERPELEN-DIAGRE, *Edmond Picard (1836–1924): Un bourgeois socialiste belge à la fin du dix-neuvième siècle. Essai d'histoire culturelle*, Brussels: Musées royaux des Beaux-Arts de Belgique, 2013.

ARON Paul and Pierre-Yves SOUCY, *Les Revues littéraires belges de langue française de 1830 à nos jours: Essai de répertoire*, Brussels: Labor and Archives et Musée de la Littérature ASBL, 1993.

ARONDEKAR Anjali, *For the Record: On Sexuality and the Colonial Archive in India*, Durham, NC : Duke University Press, 2009.

AYOUB Phillip M., *When States Come Out: Europe's Sexual Minorities and the Politics of Visibility*, New York: Cambridge University Press, 2016.

AYOUB Phillip M. and David PATERNOTTE (eds.), *LGBT Activism and the Making of Europe: A Rainbow Europe?* Basingstoke: Palgrave Macmillan, 2014.

BABINI Valeria P. and Chiara BECCALOSSI (eds.), *Italian Sexualities Uncovered, 1789–1914*, London: Palgrave Macmillan, 2015.

BALDWIN Peter (ed.), *Contagion and the State in Europe, 1830–1930*, Cambridge: Cambridge University Press, 2004.

BAUDET Colette, *Grandeur et misères d'un éditeur belge: Henry Kistemaeckers (1851–1934)*, Brussels: Labor, 1986.

BAUER Heike and Matt COOK (eds.), *Queer 1950s: Rethinking Sexuality in the Postwar Years*, Basingstoke: Palgrave Macmillan, 2012.

BAUWENS Joke, "De openbare televisie en haar kijkers: Oude liefde roest niet?," in: Alexander DHOEST and Hilde VAN DEN BULCK (eds.), *Publieke televisie in Vlaanderen: Een geschiedenis*, Ghent: Academia Press, 2007, 91–126.

BAYERTZ Kurt, "Materialism," in: Michael N. FORSTER and Kristin GJESDAL (eds.), *The Oxford Handbook of German Philosophy in the Nineteenth Century*, New York: Oxford University Press, 2015. https://doi.org/10.1093/oxfordhb/9780199696543.001.0001.

BEACHY Robert, *Gay Berlin: Birthplace of a Modern Identity*, New York: Knopf Publishing Group, 2014.

BEACHY Robert, "The German Invention of Homosexuality," *The Journal of Modern History*, 82/4, 2010, 801–838.

BEACHY Robert, "To Police and Protect: The Surveillance of Homosexuality in Imperial Berlin," in: Scott SPECTOR, Helmut PUFF, and Dagmar HERZOG (eds.), *After the History of Sexuality: German Genealogies with and beyond Foucault*, New York: Berghahn Books, 2012, 109–123.

BECCALOSSI Chiara, *Female Sexual Inversion: Same-Sex Desires in Italian and British Sexology, ca. 1870–1920*, Basingstoke: Palgrave Macmillan, 2012.

BECCHIA Alain, "Les milieux parlementaires et la dépopulation de 1900 à 1914," *Communications*, 44, 1986, 201–246.

BEKE Wouter, *De ziel van een zuil: De Christelijke Volkspartij 1945–1968*, Leuven: Leuven University Press, 2005.

BENNETT Judith M., "'Lesbian-Like' and the Social History of Lesbians," *Journal of the History of Sexuality*, 9/1–2, 2000, 1–24.

BERGER Daniel, Didier COLARD, Michel DE REYMAEKER et al., *Nachtraven*, s.l.: Gemeentekrediet, 1987.
BERGERS Lara, "A Culture of Testimony: The Importance of 'Speaking Witnesses' in Dutch Sexual Crimes Investigations, 1930–1960," in: Willemijn RUBERG, Lara BERGERS, and Pauline DIRVEN et al. (eds.), *Forensic Cultures in Modern Europe*, Manchester: Manchester University Press, 2023, 49–70.
BERLIÈRE Jean-Marc, *La police des mœurs sous la IIIe république*, Paris: Seuil, 1992.
BERLIÈRE Jean-Marc, "La professionalisation de la police en France: Un phénomène nouveau au début du XXème siècle," *Déviance et société*, 11/1, 1987, 67–104.
BEYEN Marnix, Judith POLLMANN and Henk TE VELDE, *De Lage Landen: Een geschiedenis voor vandaag*, Rekkem: Ons Erfdeel, 2021.
BEYERS Leen, "Rasdenken tussen geneeskunde en natuurwetenschap: Emile Houzé en de Société d'Anthropologie de Bruxelles, 1870–1940," in: Jo TOLLEBEEK, Geert VANPAEMEL, and Kaat WILS (eds.), *Degeneratie in België: Een geschiedenis van ideeën en praktijken*, Leuven: Leuven University Press, 2003, 43–77.
BILLEN Claire and Jean-Michel DECROLY, *De kleinste kamertjes in de grootstad: Openbaar sanitair in Brussel van de Middeleeuwen tot vandaag*, Brussels: Musea van de Stad Brussel, 2003.
BINKLEY Sam, Paddy DOLAN, Stefanie ERNST et al., "The Planned and the Unplanned: A Roundtable Discussion on the Legacies of Michel Foucault and Norbert Elias," *Foucault Studies*, 8, 2010, 53–77.
BITSCH Marie-Thérèse, *La Belgique entre la France et l'Allemagne, 1905–1914*, Paris: Publications de la Sorbonne, 1994.
BLAND Lucy, *Banishing the Beast: English Feminism and Sexual Morality, 1885–1914*, London: Penguin, 1995.
BLASIUS Dirk, *"Einfache Seelenstörung": Geschichte der deutschen Psychiatrie 1800–1945*, Frankfurt am Main: Fischer, 1994.
BLOCK Jane, "The Art of the Law: Le Jeune Barreau, Patron of Arts and Letters," in: Jane BLOCK (ed.), *Belgium: The Golden Decades, 1880–1914*, New York: Peter Lang, 1997, 181–219.
BORGHS Paul, "In beweging," in: Wannes DUPONT, Elwin HOFMAN, and Jonas ROELENS (eds.), *Verzwegen Verlangen: Een geschiedenis van homoseksualiteit in België*, Antwerp: Vrijdag, 2017, 219–254.
BORGHS Paul, "The Gay and Lesbian Movement in Belgium from the 1950s to the Present," *QED: A Journal in GLBTQ Worldmaking*, 3/3, 2016, 29–70.
BORGHS Paul and Bart EECKHOUT, "LGB Rights in Belgium, 1999–2007: A Historical Survey of a Velvet Revolution," *International Journal of Law, Policy and the Family*, 24/1, 2010, 1–28.
BOSWELL John, "Revolutions, Universals, and Sexual Categories," in: Martin DUBERMAN, Martha VICINUS, and George CHAUNCEY (eds.), *Hidden from History: Reclaiming the Gay and Lesbian Past*, New York: Meridian, 1990, 17–36.
BRADY Sean, *Masculinity and Male Homosexuality in Britain, 1861–1913*, London: Palgrave Macmillan, 2005.
BRISTOW Joseph, "Remapping the Sites of Modern Gay History: Legal Reform, Medico-Legal Thought, Homosexual Scandal, Erotic Geography," *Journal of British Studies*, 46/1, 2007, 116–142.
BRISTOW Edward J., *Vice and Vigilance: Purity Movements in Britain since 1700*, Dublin: Gill-Macmillan and Rowman and Littlefield, 1977.

BRUNDAGE James A., *Law, Sex, and Christian Society in Medieval Europe*, Chicago: University of Chicago Press, 1987.

Brussel, geplande geschiedenis: Stedenbouw in de 19e en 20e eeuw, Brussels: Meert, 2017.

BULLOUGH Vern L., *Science in the Bedroom: A History of Sex Research*, New York: BasicBooks, 1994.

BUOT François, *Gay Paris: Une histoire du Paris interlope entre 1900 et 1940*, Paris: Fayard, 2013.

BURNS Christine (ed.), *Trans Britain: Our Journey from the Shadows*, London: Unbound, 2019.

CARDON Patrick, *Discours littéraires et scientifiques fin-de-siècle: La discussion sur les homosexualités dans la revue Archives d'anthropologie criminelle du Dr Lacassagne (1886–1914) autour de Marc-André Raffalovich*, Paris: Orizons, 2008.

CARLSON Allan C., *Godly Seed: American Evangelicals Confront Birth Control, 1873–1973*, New Brunswick: Transaction, 2012.

CARRETTE Jeremy R., *Foucault and Religion: Spiritual Corporality and Political Spirituality*, London: Routledge, 2000.

CARTUYVELS Yves, "Adolphe Prins and Social Defence in Belgium: The Reform in the Service of Maintaining Social Order," *GLOSSAE: European Journal of Legal History*, 17/1, 2020, 177–210.

CASSELMAN Joris, *Etienne De Greeff, 1898–1961: Psychiater, criminoloog en romanschrijver. Leven, werk en huidige betekenis*, Antwerp: Maklu, 2010.

CASSELMAN Joris, "Etienne de Greeff and His Contribution to Current Criminology," *International Annals of Criminology*, 48/1–2, 2010, 109–130.

CHARLES Raymond, "Police et enfance inadaptée," *Revue de droit pénal et de criminologie*, 36/5, 1955–1956, 473–491.

CHARLES Raymond, "Propos sur l'article 372bis du Code Pénal (article 87 de la loi du 8 avril 1965 sur la protection de la jeunesse)," *Revue de droit pénal et de criminologie*, 62/11, 1982, 809–835.

CHARTIER Nicolas, "De onderbuik van Brussel: De mannelijke homoseksuele subcultuur in Brussel tijdens de negentiende eeuw," *Belgisch Tijdschrift voor Nieuwste Geschiedenis – Revue Belge d'Histoire Contemporaine*, 38/3–4, 2008, 407–435.

CHAUMONT Jean-Michel and Christine MACHIELS (eds.), *Du sordide au mythe: L'Affaire de la traite des blanches (Bruxelles, 1880)*, Louvain-la-Neuve: Presses universitaires de Louvain, 2009.

CHAUNCEY George, "Christian Brotherhood or Sexual Perversion? Homosexual Identity and the Construction of Sexual Boundaries in the World War One Era," *Journal of Social History*, 19/2, 1985, 189–211.

CHAUNCEY George, "From Sexual Inversion to Homosexuality: Medicine and the Changing Conceptualization of Female Deviance," *Salmagundi: A Quarterly of the Humanities and Social Sciences*, 58–59, 1982–1983, 114–146.

CHAUNCEY George, *Gay New York: Gender, Urban Culture and the Making of the Gay Male World, 1890–1940*, New York: BasicBooks, 1994.

CHAUVAUD Frédéric, *Experts et expertise judiciaire: France, XIXe et XXe siècles*, Rennes: Presses universitaires de Rennes, 2003.

CHAVASSE Philippe, "Martyrologe d'un genre nouveau: Le dénouement d'Escal-Vigor de Georges Eekhoud," *Nineteenth-Century French Studies*, 34/3–4, 2006, 371–386.

CHIANG Howard H., "Liberating Sex, Knowing Desire: 'Scientia Sexualis' and Epistemic Turning Points in the History of Sexuality," *History of the Human Sciences*, 23/5, 2010, 42–69.

CHRISTENS Ria, "De orthodoxie van het zaad: Seksualiteit en sekse-identiteit in de Rooms-katholieke traditie," in: Kaat WILS (ed.), *Het lichaam (m/v)*, Leuven: Leuven University Press, 2001, 231–249.

CHRISTIAENSEN Stef, *Tussen klassieke en moderne criminele politiek: Leven en beleid van Jules Lejeune*, Leuven: Leuven University Press, 2004.

CLAESSENS Willem, "Inventaris van de boeken uit de bibliotheek van Georges Eekhoud: Werken thans aanwezig in de Stadsbibliotheek Antwerpen," unpublished master's thesis, Stedelijke Technische Leergangen voor Bibliohteekwezen, 1975–1976.

CLEMINSON Richard M. and Francisco VÁZQUEZ GARCÍA, *"Los Invisibles": A History of Male Homosexuality in Spain, 1850–1940*, Cardiff: University of Wales Press, 2007.

COCKS Harry G., *Nameless Offences: Homosexual Desire in the Nineteenth Century*, 2nd ed., London: I.B. Tauris, 2010 [2003].

COCKS Harry G., *Visions of Sodom: Religion, Homoerotic Desire, and the End of the World in England, c. 1550–1850*, Chicago: University of Chicago Press, 2017.

CODDENS Michel, "La Belgique et la psychanalyse: Un rendez-vous manqué?," *Le Bulletin Freudien*, 51–52/April, 2008, 17–51.

COLE Joshua, *The Power of Large Numbers: Population, Politics, and Gender in Nineteenth-Century France*, Ithaca, NY: Cornell University Press, 2000.

COLLIN Ludo, "Maurice de Baets et l'Institut Supérieur de Philosophie de Louvain," *Bulletin de l'Institut Historique Belge de Rome*, 55–56, 1985–1986, 253–285.

CONSTANT Jean, "L'Enseignement de la criminologie en Belgique," in: *Cinquante ans de droit pénal et de criminologie: Publication jubilaire (1907–1957)*, Brussels: Revue de droit pénal et de criminologie, 1957, 197–210.

CONWAY Martin, *The Sorrows of Belgium: Liberation and Political Reconstruction, 1944–1947*, Oxford: Oxford University Press, 2012.

COOK Bernard A., *Belgium: A History*, New York: Peter Lang, 2002.

COOK Matt, *London and the Culture of Homosexuality, 1885–1914*, Cambridge: Cambridge University Press, 2003.

COOK Matt, "Urban Desires," *History Workshop Journal*, 62/1, 2006, 292–300.

CORBIN Alain, "L'Hérédosyphilis ou l'impossible rédemption: Contribution à l'histoire de l'hérédité morbide," in: Alain CORBIN (ed.), *Le temps, le désir et l'horreur*, Paris: Aubier, 1991.

CORBIN Alain, *Women for Hire: Prostitution and Sexuality in France after 1850*, translated by Alan SHERIDAN, Cambridge, MA: Harvard University Press, 1990.

COUNTER Andrew J., "Zola's Fin-de-siècle Reproductive Politics," *French Studies*, 68/2, 2014, 193–208.

COUTTENIER Maarten, "'We Can't Help Laughing!' Physical Anthropology in Belgium and Congo (1882–1914)," in: Nicolas BANCEL, Thomas DAVID, and Dominic THOMAS (eds.), *The Invention of Race: Scientific and Popular Representations*, New York: Routledge, 2014, 100–116.

CRAWFORD Katherine, *European Sexualities, 1400–1800*, Cambridge: Cambridge University Press, 2007.

CROMPHOUT Didier, "Les sentiers de la psychanalyse en Belgique," *Psychoanalytische Perspektieven*, 36, 1999, 9–24.

CROZIER Ivan, "Nineteenth-Century British Psychiatric Writing about Homosexuality before Havelock Ellis: The Missing Story," *Journal of the History of Medicine and the Allied Sciences*, 63/1, 2008, 65–102.

CUROPOS Fernando, *L'Émergence de l'homosexualité dans la littérature portugaise (1875–1910)*, Paris: L'Harmattan, 2016.

CUYLITS Jean, "[Review of] Des appétits sexuels contre nature devant le forum ou même devant la justice [by R. von Krafft-Ebing]," *Bulletin de la Société de médecine mentale de Belgique*, 13/39, 1885, 89–90.

D'EMILIO John, "Capitalism and Gay Identity," in: Ann SNITOW, Christine STANSELL, and Sharon THOMPSON (eds.), *Powers of Desire: The Politics of Sexuality*, New York: Monthly Review Press, 1983, 100–113.

DA AGRA Candido, "Dangerosité et dégénérescence: La médecine mentale en Belgique à la fin du XIXe siècle et au début du XXe siècle," in: Françoise TULKENS (ed.), *Généalogie de la défense sociale en Belgique (1880–1914)*, Brussels: Story-Scientia, 1988, 89–111.

DAGGERS Jenny and Diana NEAL (eds.), *Sex, Gender, and Religion: Josephine Butler Revisited*, New York: Peter Lang, 2006.

DALED Pierre F., *Spiritualisme et matérialisme au XIXe siècle: L'Université de Bruxelles et la religion*, Brussels: Éditions de l'Université de Bruxelles, 1998.

DAMOUSI Joy, Birgit LANG, and Katie SUTTON (eds.), *Case Studies and the Dissemination of Knowledge*, New York: Routledge, 2015.

DANDOIS Léopold, "Eugène Hubert," *Revue médicale de Louvain*, 7, 1905, 113.

DE BENS Els, *De pers in België: Het verhaal van de Belgische dagbladpers gisteren, vandaag en morgen*, Tielt: Lannoo, 1997.

DE BONT Raf, *Darwins kleinkinderen: De evolutieleer in België, 1865–1945*, Nijmegen: Vantilt, 2008.

DE BONT Raf, "Meten en verzoenen: Louis Vervaeck en de Belgische criminele antropologie, circa 1900–1940," *Bijdragen tot de Eigentijdse Geschiedenis – Cahiers d'Histoire du Temps Présent*, 9, 2001, 63–104.

DE BONT Raf, "Un peuple qui s'en va: Ongerustheid over de kwaliteit en de kwantiteit van het Franse volk," in: Raf DE BONT and Tom VERSCHAFFEL (eds.), *Het verderf van Parijs*, Leuven: Leuven University Press, 2004, 131–147.

DE BONT Raf and Tom VERSCHAFFEL (eds.), *Het verderf van Parijs*, Leuven: Leuven University Press, 2004.

DE BONT Raf and Kaat WILS, "De meetbare misdadiger: Cesare Lombroso en de criminele antropologie in België," in: *Karakterkoppen: Over haviksneuzen en hamsterwangen*, Tielt: Lannoo, 2014, 115–135.

DE BORCHGRAVE Christian, *God of genot: Vlaanderen 1918–1940. Een kerk in strijd met de moderne zinnelijkheid*, Leuven: Van Halewyck, 1998.

DE CANT Paul and Raymond SCREVENS, "Loi du 21 août 1948 supprimant la réglementation officielle de la prostitution," *Revue de droit pénal et de criminologie*, 29/2, 1948–1949, 160–171.

DE CONINCK Herman, "Humo sprak met Jos Van Ussel," *Humo*, 2858, 1976, 28–41.

DE GANCK Tommy, *Le sexe, une invention moderne? Réactions face aux anomalies sexuelles et à l'hermaphrodisme en Belgique contemporaine, 1830–1914*, Brussels: Université des Femmes, 2013.

DE LUCA BARRUSSE Virginie, "Des liaisons avantageuses: L'Alliance nationale pour l'accroissement de la population française et les fonctionnaires (1890–1914)," *Annales de démographie historique*, 116, 2008, 255–280.

DE MÛELENAERE Nel, *Belgen, zijt gij ten strijde gereed? Militarisering in een neutrale natie, 1890–1914*, Leuven: Leuven University Press, 2019.

DE RIVER Joseph Paul, *The Sexual Criminal: A Psychoanalytic Study*, 2nd ed., Burbank: Bloat, 2000 [1956].

DE RUYVER Brice and Johan GOETHALS, "Auguste Ley 1873–1956," in: Cyrille FIJNAUT (ed.), *Gestalten uit het verleden: 32 voorgangers in de strafrechtwetenschap, de strafrechtpleging en de criminologie*, Deurne: Kluwer, 1993, 185–193.

DE SCHAEPDRIJVER Sophie, "De reglementering van prostitutie, 1844–1877. Opkomst en ondergang van een experiment," *Belgisch Tijdschrift voor Nieuwste Geschiedenis – Revue belge d'histoire contemporaine*, 16/3–4, 1985, 476–506.

DE SCHAEPDRIJVER Sophie, "Regulering van prostitutie in de negentiende eeuw: Een concreet voorbeeld. Brussel, 1844–1877," in: *Het openbaar initiatief van de gemeenten in België 1795–1940: Handelingen van het 12de internationaal colloquium, Spa 4–7 september 1984*, vol. 2, Brussels: Gemeentekrediet, 1986, 537–558.

DE SMAELE Henk, "Medische pathologie en juridische logica: Het politieke debat over de hervorming van het strafrecht," in: Liesbet NYS, Henk DE SMAELE, Jo TOLLEBEEK et al. (eds.), *De zieke natie: Over de medicalisering van de samenleving 1860–1914*, Groningen: Historische Uitgeverij, 2002, 356–369.

DE SMAELE Henk, "Politieke partijen in de Kamer, 1830–1914," in: Emmanuel GERARD, Els WITTE, Eliane GUBIN et al. (eds.), *Geschiedenis van de Belgische Kamer van Volksvertegenwoordigers 1830–2002*, Brussels: Kamer van Volksvertegenwoordigers, 2003, 131–157.

DE SPIEGELEER Christophe, *Een blauwe progressist: Charles Potvin (1818–1902) en het liberaal-sociale denken van zijn generatie*, Ghent: Liberaal Archief, 2011.

DEAN Carolyn J., *The Frail Social Body: Pornography, Homosexuality, and Other Fantasies in Interwar France*, Berkeley: University of California Press, 2000.

DEAN Mitchell, "Foucault's Obsession with Western Modernity," in: Barry SMART (ed.), *Michel Foucault: Critical Assessments*, 7 vols., vol. 5, London: Routledge, 1994–1995, 285–299.

DEFERME Jo, *Uit de ketens van de vrijheid: Het debat over sociale politiek in België 1886–1914*, Leuven: Leuven University Press, 2007.

DELBECKE Bram, *De lange schaduw van de grondwetgever: Perswetgeving en persmisdrijven in België (1831–1914)*, Ghent: Academia Press, 2012.

DELESSERT Thierry and Michaël VOEGTLI, *Homosexualités masculines en Suisse: De l'invisibilté aux mobilisations*, Lausanne: Presses polytechniques et universitaires romandes, 2012.

DELVIGNE Rob and Leo ROSS, "'Ik ben toch zoo innig blij dat u mijn vriend bent': De brieven van Jacob Israël de Haan aan Georges Eekhoud," *De Revisor*, 9/3, 1982, 61–72.

DELWIT Pascal and José GOTOVITCH (eds.), *La peur du rouge*, Brussels: Éditions de l'Université de Bruxelles, 1996.

DEMOLDER J., "Ontwerp van een juridisch kader," in: Patrick VANDERMEERSCH (ed.), *Psychiatrie, godsdienst en gezag: De ontstaansgeschiedenis van de psychiatrie in België als paradigma*, Leuven: Acco, 1984, 153–160.

DENECKERE Gita, *Sire, het volk mort: Sociaal protest in België 1831–1918*, Antwerp: Hadewijch and AMSAB, 1997.

DENECKERE Gita, "'Van scholen zonder God verlos ons, Heer': Hoe de liberalen de Schoolstrijd wonnen dankzij een schandaal van kindermisbruik in de kerk," in: Maarten VAN GINDERACHTER, Koen AERTS, and Antoon VRINTS (eds.), *Het*

land dat nooit was: Een tegenfeitelijke geschiedenis van België, Antwerp: Bezige Bij, 2014, 126–167.
DENECKERE Gita, "Vive le peuple! De arbeidsbeweging op het politieke toneel 1885–1890," in: Els WITTE, Jean-Pierre NANDRIN, Eliane GUBIN et al. (eds.), *Nieuwe geschiedenis van België*, 3 vols., vol. 1, Tielt: Lannoo, 2005, 500–518.
DESMAZIÈRES Agnès, *L'Inconscient au paradis: Comment les catholiques ont reçu la psychanalyse*, Paris: Payot and Rivages, 2011.
DETEMMERMAN Jacques, "Le procès d'Escal-Vigor," *Revue de l'Université de Bruxelles*, 4–5, 1984, 141–169.
DEVLEESHOUWER Robert, *Les Belges et le danger de guerre, 1910–1914*, Leuven: Nauwelaerts, 1958.
DHOEST Alexander, "LGBTs In, Muslims Out: Homonationalist Discourses and Counterdiscourses in the Flemish Press," *International Journal of Communication*, 14, 2020, 155–175.
DICKINSON Edward R., *Sex, Freedom and Power in Imperial Germany 1880–1914*, Cambridge: Cambridge University Press, 2014.
DIERCKX Katrien, *Pro Arte! Cui Bono? Kunst en expertise in laatnegentiende-eeuws Brussel (1860–1914)*, Brussels: University Press Antwerp, 2021.
DINSHAW Carolyn, *Getting Medieval: Sexualities and Communities, Pre- and Postmodern*, Durham, NC: Duke University Press, 1999.
DOAN Laura, *Disturbing Practices: History, Sexuality, and Women's Experience of Modern War*, Chicago: University of Chicago Press, 2013.
DOBLER Jens, *Zwischen Duldungspolitik und Verbrechensbekämpfung: Homosexuellenverfolgung durch die Berliner Polizei von 1848 bis 1933*, Frankfurt am Main: Verlag für Polizeiwissenschaft, 2008.
DOMEIER Norman, *The Eulenburg Affair: A Cultural History of Politics in the German Empire*, translated by Deborah L. SCHNEIDER, Rochester: Camden House, 2015.
DOWBIGGIN Ian, *Inheriting Madness: Professionalisation and Psychiatric Knowledge in Nineteenth-Century France*, Berkeley: University of California Press, 1991.
DUBERMAN Martin, Martha VINCUS, and George CHAUNCEY (eds.), *Hidden from History: Reclaiming the Gay and Lesbian Past*, New York: Meridian, 1990.
DUBOIS Maurice, "Enfance coupable. Enfance malheureuse: Problèmes d'après la guerre," *Revue de droit pénal et de criminologie*, 27/8, 1946–1947, 680–704.
DUBOUT Kevin, *Der Richter und Sein Tagebuch: Eugen Wilhelm als Elsässer und homosexueller Aktivist im Deutschen Kaiserreich*, Frankfurt am Main: Campus, 2018.
DUGGAN Lisa, "Down There: The Queer South and the Future of History Writing," *GLQ: A Journal of Lesbian and Gay Studies*, 8/3, 2002, 379–387.
DUMONT Georges-Henri, *La vie quotidienne en Belgique sous le règne de Léopold II (1867–1909)*, s.l.: Hachette, 1974.
DUMONT Georges-Henri, "Quand le Coq rouge plantait ses ergots sur la Jeune Belgique (1895–1897): Communication de M. Georges-Henri Dumont à la séance mensuelle du 14 décembre 1991," *Bulletin de l'Académie royale de langue et de littérature françaises*, 69/3–4, 1991, 236–255.
DUPONT Lieven, "Jules Lejeune et la défense sociale," in: Françoise TULKENS (ed.), *Généalogie de la défense sociale en Belgique (1880–1914): Travaux du séminaire qui s'est tenu à l'Université Catholique de Louvain sous la direction de Michel Foucault*, Brussels: Story-Scientia, 1988, 77–86.

DUPONT Wannes, "Catholics and Sexual Change in Flanders," in: Gert HEKMA and Alain GIAMI (eds.), *Sexual Revolutions*, Basingstoke: Palgrave Macmillan, 2014, 81–98.

DUPONT Wannes, "Gay and Lesbian Liberation in the Low Countries: From Stonewall to Pink Pillar," *History Workshop Journal*, 92/Autumn, 2021, 151–173.

DUPONT Wannes, "Global Catholicism and the Population Bomb," in: Barbara KLICH-KLUCZEWSKA, Joachim VON PUTTKAMER, and Immo REBITSCHEK (eds.), *Biopolitics in Central and Eastern Europe in the 20th Century: Fearing for the Nation*, Abingdon: Routledge, 2023, 121–134.

DUPONT Wannes, "In Good Faith: Belgian Catholics' Attempts to Overturn the Ban on Contraception (1945–1968)," in: Cécile VANDERPELEN and Caroline SÄGESSER (eds.), *La Sainte Famille: Sexualité et parentalité dans l'Église catholique*, Brussels: Éditions de l'Université de Bruxelles, 2017, 67–76.

DUPONT Wannes, "L'Homosexualité internationalisée: Politiques pénales, débats transnationaux et échanges transatlantiques à Interpol, l'OMS et l'ONU pendant les années 1950," *Sextant*, 36, 2020, 23–40.

DUPONT Wannes, "Modernités et homosexualités belges," *Cahiers d'histoire: Revue d'histoire critique*, 119, 2012, 19–34.

DUPONT Wannes, "Of Human Love: Catholics Campaigning for Sexual Aggiornamento in Postwar Belgium," in: Alana HARRIS (ed.), *The Schism of '68: Catholicism, Contraception and "Humanae Vitae" in Europe, 1945–1975*, Basingstoke: Palgrave Macmillan, 2018, 49–71.

DUPONT Wannes, "Pas de Deux, Out of Step: Diverging Chronologies of Homosexuality's (De)Criminalization in the Low Countries," *Tijdschrift voor genderstudies – Journal for Gender Studies*, 22/4, 2019, 321–338.

DUPONT Wannes, "Pederasten op de Place royale: Een fragment uit het vergeten verleden van Brussel," *Leidschrift: Historisch tijdschrift*, 26/1, 2011, 79–91.

DUPONT Wannes, "The Case for Contraception: Medicine, Morality and Sexology at the Catholic University of Leuven (1930–1968)," *Histoire, médecine et santé*, 13, 2018, 49–65.

DUPONT Wannes, "The Two-faced Fifties: Homosexuality and Penal Policy in the International Forensic Community (1945–1965)," *Journal of the History of Sexuality*, 28/3, 2019, 357–395.

DUPONT Wannes and Henk DE SMAELE, "Orakelen over de heimelijkheid: Seksualiteit in de Belgische historiografie," *Belgisch Tijdschrift voor Nieuwste Geschiedenis – Revue Belge d'Histoire Contemporaine*, 38/3–4, 2008, 273–296.

DURVIAUX Stephan, "Le Cercle universitaire pour les études criminologiques," in: Pierre VAN DER VORST and Philippe MARY (eds.), *Cent ans de criminologie à l'U.L.B.*, Brussels: Bruylant, 1990, 21–44.

EARLS Averill E., "Unnatural Offenses of English Import: The Political Association of Englishness and Same-Sex Desire in Nineteenth-Century Irish Nationalist Media," *Journal of the History of Sexuality*, 28/3, 2019, 396–424.

EECKHOUT Bart and David PATERNOTTE, "A Paradise for LGBT Rights? The Paradox of Belgium," *Journal of Homosexuality*, 58/8, 2011, 1058–1084.

ELEWA BADAR Mohamed, *The Concept of Mens Rea in International Criminal Law: The Case for a Unified Approach*, Oxford: Hart, 2013.

ELIAS Norbert, *Het civilisatieproces: Sociogenetische en psychogenetische onderzoekingen*, Utrecht: Het Spectrum, 1990.

ELLIS Jack D., *The Physician-Legislators of France: Medicine and Politics in the Early Third Republic, 1870–1914*, Cambridge: Cambridge University Press, 1990.

ENGSTROM Eric J., *Clinical Psychiatry in Imperial Germany: A History of Psychiatric Practice*, Ithaca, NY: Cornell University Press, 2003.

ERBER Nancy, "Queer Follies: Effeminacy and Aestheticism in fin-de-siècle France, the Case of Baron d'Adelsward Fersen and Count de Warren," in: George ROBB and Nancy ERBER (eds.), *Disorder in the Court: Trials and Sexual Conflict at the Turn of the Century*, Basingstoke: Macmillan, 1999, 186–209.

ERIBON Didier, *Insult and the Making of the Gay Self*, Durham, NC: Duke University Press, 2004.

EVANS Jennifer, *Life among the Ruins: Cityscape and Sexuality in Cold War Berlin*, Basingstoke: Palgrave Macmillan, 2011.

EVANS Jennifer and Matt COOK (eds.), *Queer Cities, Queer Cultures: Europe since 1945*, London: Bloomsbury Academic, 2014.

EWING Christopher, *The Color of Desire: The Queer Politics of Race in the Federal Republic of Germany after 1970*, Ithaca, NY: Cornell University Press, 2024.

FAUVEL Aude and Wannes DUPONT, "Gheel, la 'ville des fous': Un mythe séculaire, une pratique méconnue (1860–2010)," in: Alexandre KLEIN, Hervé GUILLEMAIN, and Marie-Claude THIFAULT (eds.), *La fin de l'asile? Histoire de la déshospitalisation psychiatrique dans l'espace francophone au XXe siècle*, Rennes: Presses Universitaires de Rennes, 2018, 25–37.

FAYT René, "Un éditeur des naturalistes: Henry Kistemaeckers," *Revue de l'Université de Bruxelles*, 4–5, 1984, 217–239.

FÉRAY Jean-Claude, *Grecques, les mœurs du hanneton? Histoire du mot pédéraste et de ses dérivés en langue française*, Paris: Quintes-feuilles, 2004.

FERNANDES Paulo J., "The Press and Portuguese-British Relations at the Time of the British 'Ultimatum,'" in: José L. GARCIA, Chandrika KAUL, Filipa SUBTIL et al. (eds.), *Media and the Portuguese Empire*, s.l.: Palgrave Macmillan, 87–105.

FERNÁNDEZ GALEANO Javier, *Maricas: Queer Cultures and State Violence in Argentina and Spain, 1942–1982*, Lincoln: Nebraska University Press, 2024.

FERRITER Diarmaid, *Occasions of Sin: Sex and Society in Modern Ireland*, London: Profile, 2010.

FIJNAUT Cyrille J. C. F., "Florent Louwage 1888–1967," in: Cyrille FIJNAUT (ed.), *Gestalten uit het verleden: 32 voorgangers in de strafrechtwetenschap, de strafrechtpleging en de criminologie*, Deurne: Kluwer, 1993, 195–209.

FINDLING John E. and Kimberley D. PELLE (eds.), *Encyclopedia of World's Fairs and Expositions*, Jefferson, NC: McFarland, 2008.

FOUCAULT Michel, "Nietzsche, Genealogy, History," in: Donald F. BOUCHARD (ed.), *Language, Couter-Memory, Practice: Selected Essays and Interviews*, Ithaca, NY: Cornell University Press, 1977, 139–164.

FOUCAULT Michel, "Polemics, Politics, and Problematizations," in: Paul RABINOW (ed.), *Michel Foucault: Ethics, Subjectivity and Truth*, translated by Robert HURLEY, New York: The New Press, 1994, 111–119.

FOUCAULT Michel, *The History of Sexuality, Volume 1: An Introduction*, translated by Robert HURLEY, New York: Pantheon Books, 1978.

FOUCAULT Michel, Valerio MARCHETTI, and Antonella SALOMONI (eds.), *Abnormal: Lectures at the Collège de France, 1974–1975*, New York: Picador, 2003.

Fox Robert, *The Savant and the State: Science and Cultural Politics in Nineteenth-Century France*, Baltimore, MD: Johns Hopkins University Press, 2012.

François Aurore, *Guerres et délinquance juvénile: Un demi-siècle de pratiques judiciaires et institutionelles envers des mineurs en difficulté (1912–1950)*, Brussels: La Charte, 2011.

François Aurore and Christine Machiels, "Une guerre de chiffres: L'Usage des statistiques par les discours abolitionniste et réglementariste sur la prostitution à Bruxelles (1844–1948)," *Histoire & mesure*, 22/2, 2007, https://doi.org/10.4000/histoiremesure.2523, last accessed on August 12, 2024, 103–1034.

Franssen Firmin, "Miscellaneous Questions and Closing Session," *International Criminal Police Review*, 12/110, 1957, 237–239.

Fremdling Rainer, "De Europese spoorwegen 1825–2001, een overzicht," in: Bart Van der Herten, Michelangelo Van Meerten, and Greta Verbeurgt (eds.), *Sporen in België: 175 jaar spoorwegen, 75 jaar NMBS*, Leuven: Leuven University Press, 2001, 20–63.

Frydman B., "Adolphe Prins et l'École de Bruxelles: La défense sociale dans la guerre d'idées," in: F. Kutty and A. Weyembergh (eds.), *La science pénale dans tous ses états: Liber amicorum Patrick Mandoux et Marc Preumont*, Brussels: Larcier, 2019, 559–585.

Fryer Jonathan, "'Alle bedenkingen' bij de dood van de schrijver Christopher Isherwood (1904–1986)," *Zonder Pardon*, 10/88, 1986, 5–11.

Fryer Jonathan, *Isherwood*, London: New English Library, 1977.

Gallagher Lowell, Frederick S. Roden, and Patricia J. Smith (eds.), *Catholic Figures, Queer Narratives*, Basingstoke: Palgrave Macmillan, 2006.

Ganzevoort Anne, "Tussen norm, ideaal en politieke realiteit: 'Afwijkend' seksueel gedrag en Belgisch links," in: Denise De Weerdt (ed.), *Begeerte heeft ons aangeraakt: Socialisten, sekse en seksualiteit*, Ghent: Provinciebestuur Oost-Vlaanderen, 1999, 239–277.

Garber Linda, "Where in the World Are the Lesbians?," *Journal of the History of Sexuality*, 14/1–2, 2005, 28–50.

Gerodetti Natalia, "'Lay Experts': Women's Social Purity Groups and the Politics of Sexuality in Switzerland, 1890–1915," *Women's History Review*, 13/4, 2004, 585–610.

Gerodetti Natalia, *Modernising Sexualities: Towards a Socio-Historical Understanding of Sexualities in the Swiss Nation*, Bern: Peter Lang, 2005.

Gezondheidsraad, "Advies inzake homoseksuele relaties met minderjarigen, in het bijzonder met betrekking tot artikel 248bis van het Wetboek van Strafrecht [Speijer-rapport]. 10347," in: *Handelingen der Staten-Generaal. Zitting 1969–1970. Bijlagen Tweede Kamer*, s'Gravenhage: Staatsrukkerij en -uitgeverijbedrijf, 1969–1970, 5–22.

Gibson Mary, *Born to Crime: Cesare Lombroso and the Origins of Biological Criminology*, Westport, CT: Praeger, 2002.

Gill-Peterson Jules, *A Short History of Trans Misogyny*, London: Verso, 2024.

Godart Gauthier, *L'asile en procès: Le scandale d'Evere (1871–1872) et la prise en charge de la folie en Belgique*, Louvain-la-Neuve: Presses universitaires de Louvain, 2019.

Godart Gauthier, "'Un drame dans une maison des fous': L'Affaire d'Evere (Bruxelles, 1871–1872), ce qu'elle révèle du régime des aliénés en Belgique, ses effets dans un contexte propice à la réforme," *Journal of Belgian History*, 47/4, 2017, 112–143.

GOLDBERG Ann, *Sex, Religion, and the Making of Modern Madness: The Eberbach Asylum and German Society, 1815–1849*, Oxford: Oxford University Press, 1999.
GOLDSTEIN Jan E., *Console and Classify: The French Psychiatric Profession in the Nineteenth Century*, 2nd ed., Chicago: University of Chicago Press, 2001.
GOLDSTEIN Jan E., "The Hysteria Diagnosis and the Politics of Anticlericalism in Late Nineteenth-Century France," *The Journal of Modern History*, 54/2, 1982, 209–239.
GOULD Andrew C., *Origins of Liberal Dominance: State, Church, and Party in Nineteenth-Century Europe*, Ann Arbor: University of Michigan Press, 1999.
GRAVET Cathérine and Emile VAN BALBERGHE, "'Cher brutal abruti de mon cœur': Quelques notes à propos de trois lettres et de quatre envois inédits de Max Waller à Georges Eekhoud," *Francofonia: Studi e ricerche sulle letterature di lingua francese*, 10, 2001, 37–60.
GREGORY Frederick, *Scientific Materialism in Nineteenth Century Germany*, Dordrecht: Reidel, 1977.
GRIFFITHS Craig, *The Ambivalence of Gay Liberation: Male Homosexual Politics in 1970s West Germany*, Oxford: Oxford University Press, 2021.
GUILLEMAIN Hervé, *Diriger les consciences, guérir les âmes: Une histoire comparée des pratiques thérapeutiques et religieuses (1830–1939)*, Paris: La découverte, 2006.
GUNTHER Scott, *The Elastic Closet: A History of Homosexuality in France, 1942-present*, Basingstoke: Palgrave Macmillan, 2009.
GUYAUX Louis, "Des modifications nécessaires à notre législation sur l'avortement, les moyens abortifs et les moyens anticonceptionnels," *Revue de droit pénal et de criminologie*, 27/4, 1946–1947, 314–346.
HACKING Ian, "Biopower and the Avalanche of Printed Numbers," *Humanities in Society*, 5, 1982, 279–295.
HACKING Ian, *The Social Construction of What?*, Cambridge, MA: Harvard University Press, 1999.
HALBERSTAM Jack, *Female Masculinity*, Durham, NC: Duke University Press, 1998.
HALL Lesley A., "Heroes or Villains? Reconsidering British fin de siècle Sexology and Its Impact," in: Lynne SEGAL (ed.), *New Sexual Agendas*, New York: New York University Press, 1997, 3–16.
HALL Lesley, *Sex, Gender and Social Change in Britain since 1880*, 2nd ed., Basingstoke: Macmillan, 2013.
HALPERIN David M., *How to Do the History of Homosexuality*, Chicago: University of Chicago Press, 2002.
HANNA Martha, "Natalism, Homosexuality, and the Controversy over Corydon," in: Jeffrey MERRICK and Bryant T.Jr. RAGAN (eds.), *Homosexuality in Modern France*, New York: Oxford University Press, 1996, 202–224.
HAUSE Steven C., "Social Control in Late Nineteenth-Century France: Protestant Campaigns for Strict Public Morality," in: Christopher E. FORTH and Elinor ACCAMPO (eds.), *Confronting Modernity in Fin-de-Siècle France: Bodies, Minds and Gender*, Basigstoke: Palgrave Macmillan, 2010, 135–149.
HAUSER Renate I., "Sexuality, Neurasthenia and the Law: Richard von Krafft-Ebing (1840–1902)," unpublished doctoral dissertation, University College of the University of London, 1992.

HEALEY Dan, *Homosexual Desire in Revolutionary Russia: The Regulation of Sexual and Gender Dissent*, Chicago: University of Chicago Press, 2001.

HEALEY Dan, *Russian Homophobia from Stalin to Sochi*, London: Bloomsbury Academic, 2018.

HEKMA Gert, *Homoseksualiteit, een medische reputatie: De uitdoktering van de homoseksueel in negentiende-eeuws Nederland*, Amsterdam: Sua, 1987.

HELLINCK Bart, "*Een droom waarvan we nooit konden vermoeden dat hij mogelijk zou zijn*": *Bijdrage tot de geschiedenis van 50 jaar homo- en lesbiennebeweging in Vlaanderen (1953–2003)*, 2nd ed., Ghent and Brussels: Holebifederatie and Gelijke Kansen in Vlaanderen, 2003.

HELLINCK Bart, "Inventaris van het archief van Suzanne De Pues (pseudoniem Suzan Daniel). Fondsnummer F/001," unpublished archive inventory, Fonds Suzan Daniel vzw and Amsab-Instituut voor Sociale Geschiedenis, 2003–2010.

HELLINCK Bart, "Stammoeder," *Zizo*, 5/21, 1997, 14–15.

HELLINCK Bart, "Steven De Batselier (1932–2007)," *Het ondraaglijk besef: Nieuwsbrief van het Fonds Suzan Daniel*, 13, 2007, 7–8.

HELLINCK Bart and Mark SERGEANT, *1981–2006: 25 jaar strijd tegen aids in Vlaanderen*, Ghent: Fonds Suzan Daniel, 2006.

HERGEMÖLLER Bernd-Ulrich, *Einführung in die Historiographie der Homosexualitäten*, Tübingen: Dition Diskord, 1999.

HERZOG Dagmar, *Cold War Freud: Psychoanalysis in an Age of Catastrophes*, Cambridge: Cambridge University Press, 2017.

HERZOG Dagmar, "The Reception of the Kinsey Reports in Europe," *Sexuality and Culture*, 10/1, 2006, 39–48.

HEWITT Jessie, *Institutionalizing Gender: Madness, the Family, and Psychiatric Power in Nineteenth-Century France*, Ithaca, NY: Cornell University Press, 2020.

HIGGS David, *Queer Sites: Gay Urban Histories since 1600*, London: Routledge, 1999.

HOCQUENGHEM Guy, *Le désir homosexuel*, Paris: Éditions universitaires, 1972.

HOEGAERTS Josephine, *Masculinity and Nationhood, 1830–1910: Constructions of Identity and Citizenship in Belgium*, Basingstoke: Palgrave Macmillan, 2014.

HOEGAERTS Josephine, "Trust and Temptation: Adultery and Masculinity in the Nineteenth-Century Divorce Court," *Sextant: Revue du groupe interdisciplinaire d'études sur les femmes et le genre*, 27, 2009, 15–28.

HOFMAN Elwin, "The End of Sodomy: Law, Prosecution Patterns, and the Evanescent Will to Knowledge in Belgium, France, and the Netherlands, 1770–1830," *Journal of Social History*, 54/2, 2020, 480–502.

HOME OFFICE. SCOTTISH HOME DEPARTMENT, *Report of the Committee on Homosexual Offences and Prostitution*, London: Her Majesty's Stationery Office, 1957.

HOORNAERT Georges, "La loi devant la corruption de la jeunesse et l'excitation à la débauche," *Revue de droit pénal et de criminologie*, 27/6, 1946–1947, 491–520.

HOPE Nicholas, *German and Scandinavian Protestantism, 1700–1918*, Oxford: Oxford University Press, 1999.

HOULBROOK Matt, *Queer London: Perils and Pleasures in the Sexual Metropolis, 1918–1957*, Chicago: University of Chicago Press, 2005.

HOWARD John, *Men Like That: A Southern Queer History*, Chicago: University of Chicago Press, 1999.

HOWELL Phillip, *Geographies of Regulation: Policing Prostitution in Nintetheenth-Century Britain and the Empire*, Cambridge: Cambridge University Press, 2009.

HUARD Geoffroy, *Los antisociales: Historia de la homosexualidad en Barcelona y París, 1945–1975*, Madrid: Marcial Pons, 2014.

HUBBARD Phil, "Queering the City: Homosociality and Homosexuality in the Modern Metropolis," *Journal of Urban History*, 33/2, 2007, 310–319.

HUNEKE Samuel C., *States of Liberation: Gay Men between Dictatorship and Democracy in Cold War Germany*, Toronto: University of Toronto Press, 2022.

HUSHION Stacy, "Intimate Encounters and the Politics of German Occupation in Belgium, 1940–44/45," unpublished doctoral dissertation, University of Toronto, 2015.

HUTTER Jörg, *Die gesellschaftliche Kontrolle des homosexuellen Begehrens. Medizinische Definitionen und juristische Sanktionen im 19. Jahrhundert*, Frankfurt am Main: Campus, 1992.

HUYSE Luc and Steven DHONDT (eds.), *Onverwerkt verleden: Collaboratie en repressie in België, 1942–1952. Een update na dertig jaar*, 2nd ed., Tielt: Kritak, 2020.

IACUB Marcela, *Through the Keyhole: A History of Sex, Space and Public Modesty in Modern France*, translated by Vinay SWAMY, Manchester: Manchester University Press, 2016.

IDIER Antoine, *Les alinéas au placard: L'Abrogation du délit d'homosexualité, 1977–1982*, Paris: Cartouche, 2013.

JACKSON Julian, *Living in Arcadia: Homosexuality, Politics, and Morality in France from the Liberation to Aids*, Chicago: University of Chicago Press, 2009.

JACQUEMYNS Guillaume, *La société belge sous l'occupation allemande 1940–1944: Privations et espoirs*, Brussels: Office de publicité, 1945.

JANSSENS Leon, "Pornography on Rails: Trains and Belgium's 'War on Pornography,' 1880–1891," *Journal of the History of Sexuality*, 32/3, 2023, 269–287.

JANSSENS Leon, "Tussen angst, afkeer en wanhoop: Een emotionele geschiedenis van de strijd tegen pornografie in België (1880–1914)," unpublished doctoral dissertation, KU Leuven, 2023.

JENNINGS Rebecca, *Tomboys and Bachelor Girls: A Lesbian History of Post-War Britain*, Manchester: Manchester University Press, 2017.

JENSEN Erik N., "The Pink Triangle and Political Consciousness: Gays, Lesbians, and the Memory of Nazi Persecution," *Journal of the History of Sexuality*, 11/1–2, 2002, 319–349.

JOHNSON David K., "America's Cold War Empire: Exporting the Lavender Scare," in: Meredith L. WEISS and Michael J. BOSIA (eds.), *Global Homophobia: States, Movements, and the Politics of Oppression*, Champaign: University of Illinois Press, 2013, 55–74.

JOHNSON David K., *The Lavender Scare: The Cold War Persecution of Gays and Lesbians in the Federal Government*, Chicago: University of Chicago Press, 2004.

JOHNSON Paul, *Homosexuality and the European Court of Human Rights*, Abingdon: Routledge, 2013.

JOOSSE Kees, *Arnold Aletrino: Pessimist met perspectief*, Amsterdam: Rap, 1986.

JORDAN Mark D., *The Invention of Sodomy*, Chicago: University of Chicago Press, 1997.

JUDT Tony, *Postwar: A History of Europe Since 1945*, New York: Penguin, 2005.

KAHAN Benjamin, *The Book of Minor Perverts: Sexology, Etiology, and the Emergences of Sexuality*, Chicago: University of Chicago Press, 2019.

KAISER Robert Blair, *The Encyclical That Never Was: The Story of the Commission on Population, Family and Birth, 1964–1966*, London: Sheed and Ward, 1987.

KALUSZYNSKI Martine, "The International Congresses of Criminal Anthropology: Shaping the French and International Criminological Movement, 1886–1914," in: Peter BECKER and Richard F. WETZELL (eds.), *Criminals and Their Scientists: The History of Criminology in International Perspective*, Cambridge: Cambridge University Press, 2006, 301–316.

KAPLAN Morris B., *Sodom on the Thames: Sex, Love and Scandal in Wilde Times*, Ithaca: Cornell University Press, 2005.

KARCZEWSKI Kamil, "Transnational Flows of Knowledge and the Legislation of Homosexuality in Interwar Poland," *Contemporary European History*, 2022, DOI: 10.1017/S0960777322000108, last accessed on July 29, 2023, 1–18.

KENNY Nicolas, *The Feel of the City: Experiences of Urban Transformation*, Toronto: University of Toronto Press, 2014.

KEUNINGS Luc, "De geschiedenis van het Brusselse politiekorps (van 1830 tot 1914)," *Gemeentekrediet van België: Driemaandelijks tijdschrift*, 37/145, 1983, 149–184.

KEUNINGS Luc, *Des polices si tranquilles: Une histoire de l'appareil policier belge au XIXe siècle*, s.l.: Presses universitaires de Louvain, 2009.

KEUNINGS Luc, "Du garde-ville à l'agent de police: Les débuts de la professionalisation de la police en Belgique (1880–1914)," *L'Officier de police – De politieofficier*, 7, 1988, 1–96.

KEUNINGS Luc, "Les 'bras armés' de Thémis: Les policiers bruxellois à la Belle-Époque," *Les Cahiers de la Fonderie: Revue d'Histoire Sociale et Industrielle de la Région Bruxelloise*, 27, 2003, 17–24.

KEUNINGS Luc, "Ordre public et peur du rouge au XIXème siècle: La police, les socialistes et les anarchistes à Bruxelles (1886–1914)," *Belgisch Tijdschrift voor Nieuwste Geschiedenis – Revue belge d'histoire contemporaine*, 25/3–4, 1994–1995, 329–396.

KINSMAN Gary and Patrizia GENTILE, *The Canadian War on Queers: National Security as Sexual Regulation*, Vancouver: UCB Press, 2010.

KIRKUP James, "The Love That Dares To Speak Its Name," *Gay New*, 96, June 16, 1976, 26.

KLUIT Elisabeth, *Het protestantse Réveil in Nederland en daarbuiten, 1815–1865*, Amsterdam: Paris, 1970.

KNEPPER Paul, *The Invention of International Crime: A Global Issue in the Making, 1881–1914*, Basingstoke: Palgrave Macmillan, 2010.

KOENDERS Pieter, *Tussen christelijk réveil en seksuele revolutie: Bestrijding van zedeloosheid in Nederland, met nadruk op de repressie van homoseksualiteit*, Amsterdam: Stichting beheer IISG, 1996.

KOŚCIAŃSKA Agnieszka, *Gender, Pleasure and Violence: The Construction of Expert Knowledge of Sexuality in Poland*, Bloomington: Indiana University Press, 2021.

KOŚCIAŃSKA Agnieszka, *To See a Moose: The History of Polish Sex Education*, New York: Berghahn Books, 2021.

Kościańska Agnieszka, Kateřina LIŠKOVÁ, and Hadley Z. RENKIN (eds.), *The Routledge Handbook of Sexuality in East Central Europe*, London: Routledge, 2025.

KOSOFSKY SEDGWICK Eve, *Epistemology of the Closet*, Berkeley: University of California Press, 1990.

KOSS Stephen, *The Rise and Fall of the Political Press in Britain*, 2 vols., Chapel Hill: University of North Carolina Press, 1981–1984.

KOSSMANN Ernst H., *The Low Countries, 1870–1940*, Oxford: Clarendon Press and Oxford University Press, 1978.
KOVEN Seth, *Slumming: Sexual and Social Politics in Victorian London*, Princeton: Princeton University Press, 2004.
KRUITHOF Jaap, "Leven, persoon en werk van Jos Van Ussel," in: Jaap KRUITHOF and Ignace GEURTS (eds.), *De seksualiteit herzien: Het werk van Jos Van Ussel*, Deventer: Van Loghum Slaterus, 1979, 9–37.
KRUITHOF Jaap and Ignace GEURTS (eds.), *De seksualiteit herzien: Het werk van Jos Van Ussel*, Deventer: Van Loghum Slaterus, 1979.
KRUITHOF Jaap and Jos VAN USSEL, *Jeugd voor de muur: Vlaamse studenten over hun seksuele problematiek*, Antwerp: Ontwikkeling, 1962.
KUNZEL Regina, *Criminal Intimacy: Prison and the Uneven History of Modern American Sexuality*, Chicago: University of Chicago Press, 2008.
KUNZEL Regina, "The Power of Queer History," *American Historical Review*, 123/5, 2018, 1560–1582.
KUNZEL Regina, "The Uneven History of Modern American Sexuality," *Modern American History*, 1/1, 2018, 97–100.
KURGAN-VAN HENTENRYK Ginette, "Economie en vervoer," in: Jean STENGERS (ed.), *Brussel: Groei van een hoofdstad*, Antwerp: Mercatorfonds, 1986, 216–226.
KURIMAY Anita, *Queer Budapest, 1873–1961*, Chicago: University of Chicago Press, 2020.
LACHAPELLE Sofie, "Between Miracle and Sickness: Louise Lateau and the Experience of Stigmata and Ecstasy," *Configurations*, 12/1, 2004, 77–105.
LAMBERTS Emiel, "Religious, Political and Social Settings of the Revival of Thomism, 1870–1960," in: Wim DECOCK, Bart RAYMAEKERS, and Peter HEYRMAN (eds.), *Neo-Thomism in Action: Law and Society Reshaped by Neo-Scholastic Philosophy, 1880–1960*, Leuven: Leuven University Press, 2021, 29–40.
LAMBERTS Emiel and Jacques LORY (eds.), *1884: Un tournant politique en Belgique – De machtswisseling van 1884 in België*, Brussels: Presses de l'Université Saint-Louis, 1986.
LANG Birgit, Joy DAMOUSI, and Alison LEWIS, *A History of the Case Study: Sexology, Psychoanalysis, Literature*, Manchester: Manchester University Press, 2017.
LANGLOIS Claude, *Le crime d'Onan: Le discours catholique sur la limitation des naissances (1816–1930)*, Paris: Les Belles Lettres, 2005.
LANSER Susan S., *The Sexuality of History: Modernity and the Sapphic, 1565–1830*, Chicago: University of Chicago Press, 2014.
LAQUA Daniel, *The Age of Internationalism and Belgium, 1880–1930: Peace, Progress and Prestige*, Manchester: Manchester University Press, 2013.
LAQUEUR Thomas W., *Solitary Sex: A Cultural History of Masturbation*, New York: Zone Books, 2003.
LAURITSEN John and David THORSTAD, *The Early Homosexual Rights Movement, 1864–1935*, New York: Times Change Press, 1995.
LAURO Amandine, *Coloniaux, ménagères et prostituées au Congo belge (1885–1930)*, Loverval: Labor, 2005.
LAURO Amandine, "Violence, Anxieties, and the Making of Interracial Dangers: Colonial Surveillance and Interracial Sexuality in the Belgian Congo," in: Chelsea SHIELDS and Dagmar HERZOG (eds.), *The Routledge Companion to Sexuality and Colonialism*, New York: Routledge, 2021, 327–338.

LE CLERCQ Geoffroy, "La perception des violences sexuelles en Belgique (1830–1867): Construction juridique, pratique répressive et réactions sociales," in: Ginette KURGAN-VAN HENTENRYK (ed.), *Un pays si tranquille: La violence en Belgique au XIXe siècle*, Brussels: Éditions de l'Université de Bruxelles, 1999, 107–129.

LE CLERCQ Geoffroy, "Violences sexuelles, scandale et ordre public: Le regard du législateur, de la justice et des autres acteurs sociaux au 19ème siècle," *Belgisch Tijdschrift voor Nieuwste Geschiedenis – Revue Belge d'Histoire Contemporaine*, 28/1–2, 1999, 5–53.

LEBOUTTE René, Jean PUISSANT, and Denis SCUTO, *Un siècle d'histoire industrielle (1873–1973): Belgique, Luxembourg, Pays-Bas. Industrialisation et sociétés*, Paris: SEDES, 1998.

LECK Ralph M., *Vita Sexualis: Karl Ulrichs and the Origins of Sexual Science*, Urbana: University of Illinois Press, 2016.

LEES Andrew and Lynn H. LEES, *Cities and the Making of Modern Europe, 1750–1914*, Cambridge: Cambridge University Press, 2010.

LEMKE Thomas, *Biopolitics: An Advanced Introduction*, translated by Eric F. TRUMP, New York: New York University Press, 2011.

"Leon Janssens de Bisthoven," in: *Nationaal biografisch woordenboek*, vol. 7, Brussels: Paleis der Academiën, 1977, 415–419.

LEROY-FORGEOT Flora, *Histoire juridique de l'homosexualité en Europe*, Paris: Presses universitaires de France, 1997.

LEWIS Brian, *Wolfenden's Witnesses: Homosexuality in Postwar Britain*, Basingstoke: Palgrave Macmillan, 2016.

LEY Auguste and André MARCHAL, "L'Homosexualité: Étude médico-juridique," *Revue de droit pénal et de criminologie*, 36/1, 1955, 323–341.

LIMONCELLI Stephanie, *The Politics of Trafficking: The First International Movement to Combat the Sexual Exploitation of Women*, Stanford: Stanford University Press, 2010.

LISBERG-HAAG Isabell, *"Die Unzucht – das Grab der Völker": Die Evangelische Sittlichkeitsbewegung und die "sexuelle Moderne" (1870–1918)*, Münster: Lit, 2002.

LIŠKOVÁ Kateřina, *Sexual Liberation, Socialist Style: Communist Czechoslovakia and the Science of Desire*, Cambridge: Cambridge University Press, 2018.

LOFTON Kathryn, "Why Religion Is Hard for Historians (and How It Can Be Easier)," *Modern American History*, 3/1, 2020, 69–86.

LOUWAGE Florent E., "Delinquency in Europe after World War II," *Journal of Criminal Law and Criminology*, 42/1, 1951, 53–56.

LOUWAGE Florent E., "Perversions et névroses," *Revue internationale de police criminelle*, 3/15, 1948, 7–11.

LOX Florimont, "La rue, creuset de prédélinquance," *L'Enfant*, 7/2, 1954, 117–128.

LUCIEN Mirande, *Eekhoud le rauque*, Villeneuve d'Ascq: Presses Universitaires de Septentrion, 1999.

LUCIEN Mirande, "Georges Eekhoud et l'anarchie: 'Le capiteuses tanières de la révolte!,'" *Littérature et nation*, 19, 1998, 97–116.

LUCIEN Mirande, "'Un savoureux enfer': Naissance d'un roman. 'Voyous de velours' ou 'l'Autre Vue' de Georges Eekhoud," *Textyles*, 8, 1991, 301–314.

LÜCKE Martin, *Männlichkeit in Unordnung: Homosexualität und männliche Prostitution in Kaiserreich und Weimarer Republik*, Frankfurt am Main: Campus, 2008.

LÜTZEN Karin, *Byen tæmmes: Kernefamilie, sociale reformer og velgørenhed i 1800-tallets København*, Copenhagen: Reitzels, 2014.
MACHIELS Christine, *Les féminismes et la prostitution (1860–1960)*, Rennes: Presses universitaires de Rennes, 2016.
MACHIELS Christine, "Pour 'l'affranchissement des blanches,' contre la prostitution réglementée. La Société de moralité publique de Belgique (1875–1908)," in: Jean-Michel CHAUMONT and Christine MACHIELS (eds.), *Du sordide au mythe: L'Affaire de la traite des blanches (Bruxelles, 1880)*, Louvain-la-Neuve: Presses universitaires de Louvain, 2009, 133–149.
MARCUSE Herbert, *Eros and Civilization*, New York: Springer Nature, 1955.
MARHOEFER Laurie, *Sex and the Weimar Republic: German Homosexual Emancipation and the Rise of the Nazis*, Toronto: University of Toronto Press, 2015.
MARHOEFER Laurie, "'The Book Was a Revelation, I Recognized Myself in It': Lesbian Sexuality, Censorship, and the Queer Press in Weimar-era Germany," *Journal of Women's History*, 27/2, 2015, 62–86.
MARSDEN George M., *Fundamentalism and American Culture*, 2nd ed, Oxford: Oxford University Press, 2006.
MARTEL Frédéric, *The Pink and the Black: Homosexuals in France since 1968*, translated by Jane M. TODD, Stanford: Stanford University Press, 1999.
MASSION-VERNIORY Léon and Raymond CHARLES, "Les aspects médico-psychologiques, sociaux et juridiques de l'homophilie," *Revue de droit pénal et de criminologie*, 38/3, 1957, 241–327.
MAYNARD Steven, "Through a Hole in the Lavatory Wall: Homosexual Subcultures, Police Surveillance, and the Dialectics of Discovery, Toronto, 1890–1930," *Journal of the History of Sexuality*, 5/2, 1994, 207–242.
MAYNARD Steven, "'Without Working?' Capitalism, Urban Culture, and Gay History," *Journal of Urban History*, 30/3, 2004, 378–398.
MCINTOSH Mary, "The Homosexual Role," *Social Problems*, 16/2, 1968, 182–192.
MCLAREN Angus, *Impotence: A History*, Chicago: University of Chicago Press, 2007.
MCLAREN Angus, *Sexual Blackmail: A Modern History*, Cambridge: Harvard University Press, 2002.
MCLAREN Angus, *Sexuality and Social Order: The Debate over the Fertility of Women and Workers in France, 1770–1920*, New York: Holmes and Meier, 1983.
MCLAREN Angus, *The Trials of Masculinity: Policing Sexual Boundaries, 1870–1930*, Chicago: University of Chicago Press, 1997.
MCLELLAN Joise, *Love in the Time of Communism: Intimacy and Sexuality in the GDR*, Cambridge: Cambridge University Press, 2011.
MCLEOD Hugh, "New Perspectives on the Religious History of Western and Northern Europe 1815–1960: Whatever Happened to Secularisation?," *Kyrkohistorisk årsskrift*, 100, 2000, 135–145.
MEERTS P., "Homosexualité masculine et endémie syphilitique: Constatations faites à Bruxelles," *Archives belges de dermatologie et de syphiligraphie*, 22/1, 1966, 9–20.
MEERTS P., "Homosexualité masculine et syphilis," *Revue médicale de Bruxelles*, 21, 1965, 559–570 and 599–614.
MERRICK Jeffrey, "'Nocturnal Birds' in the Champs-Elysées: Police and Pederasty in Prerevolutionary Paris," *GLQ: A Journal of Lesbian and Gay Studies*, 8/3, 2001, 425–432.

MIRA Alberto, *De Sodoma a Chueca: Una historia cultural de la homosexualidad en España en el siglo XX*, Barcelona: Egales, 2007.

MOLE Richard C. M. (ed.), *Soviet and Post-Soviet Sexualities*, Abingdon: Routledge, 2019.

MORELLI Anne, "Les médecins parlementaires belges (XIXe–XXe siècles)," *Socialisme, hors série*, 2, 1993, 9–18.

MOSS Michael and David THOMAS (eds.), *Archival Silences: Missing, Lost and, Uncreated Archives*, London: Routledge, 2021.

MOULAERT Jan, *Rood en zwart: De anarchistische beweging in België 1880–1914*, Leuven: Davidsfonds, 1995.

MUYS Eva and Karel VELLE, "Seksuele delinquentie in het onderwijsmilieu: Pedofiele onderwijzers in de 19de eeuw," *Belgisch Tijdschrift voor Nieuwste Geschiedenis – Revue belge d'histoire contemporaine*, 18/3–4, 1998, 293–337.

Neefs Hans, *Between Sin and Disease: The Social Fight against Syphilis and AIDS in Belgium (1880–2000)*, Saarbrücken: LAP Lambert, 2010.

NEWSOME W. Jake, *Pink Triangle Legacies: Coming Out in the Shadow of the Holocaust*, Ithaca, NY: Cornell University Press, 2022.

NOBUS Dany and Katrien LIBBRECHT, "De Franse connectie: Een geschiedenis van de psychoanalyse in België," *Tijdschrift voor Psychoanalyse*, 3/3, 1997, 132–149.

NOONAN John T., *Contraception: A History of Its Treatment by the Catholic Theologians and Canonists. Enlarged Edition*, Cambridge, MA: Harvard University Press, 1986 [1965].

NYE Robert A., *Crime, Madness, and Politics in Modern France: The Medical Concept of National Decline*, Princeton: Princeton University Press, 1984.

NYE Robert A., "Honor, Impotence, and Male Sexuality in Nineteenth-Century French Medicine," *French Historical Studies*, 16/1, 1989, 48–71.

NYE Robert A., *Masculinity and Male Codes of Honor in Modern France*, New York: Oxford University Press, 1993.

NYE Robert A., "Sex Difference and Male Homsexuality in French Medical Discourse 1830–1930," *Bulletin of the History of Medicine*, 63, 1989, 32–51.

NYE Robert A., "The History of Sexuality in Context: National Sexological Traditions," *Science in Context*, 4/2, 1991, 387–406.

NYS Liesbet, "De grote school van de natie: Legerartsen over drankmisbruik en geslachtsziekten in het Belgisch leger (circa 1850–1950)," *Bijdragen en mededelingen betreffende de geschiedenis der Nederlanden*, 115/3, 2000, 365–391.

NYS Liesbet, "Nationale plagen: Hygiënisten over het maatschappelijk lichaam," in: Liesbet NYS, Henk DE SMAELE, Jo TOLLEBEEK et al. (eds.), *De zieke natie: Over de medicalisering van de samenleving 1860–1914*, Groningen: Historische Uitgeverij, 2002, 220–241.

NYS Liesbet, Henk DE SMAELE, Jo TOLLEBEEK et al. (eds.), *De zieke natie: Over de medicalisering van de samenleving 1860–1914*, Groningen: Historische Uitgeverij, 2002.

O'DWYER Conor, *Coming Out of Communism: The Emergence of LGBT Activism in Eastern Europe*, New York: New York University Press, 2018.

OFFEN Karen, *Debating the Woman Question in the French Third Republic, 1870–1920*, Cambridge: Cambridge University Press, 2018.

OFFEN Karen, "Depopulation, Nationalism, and Feminism in Fin-de-Siècle France," *American Historical Review*, 89/3, 1984, 648–676.

OLSON Kevin, *Subaltern Silence: A Postcolonial Genealogy*, New York: Columbia University Press, 2024.
OOSTERHUIS Harry, *De smalle marges van de katholieke moraal: Homoseksualiteit in katholiek Nederland 1900–1970*, Amsterdam: s.e., 1992.
OOSTERHUIS Harry, *Stepchildren of Nature: Krafft-Ebing, Psychiatry and the Making of Sexual Identity*, Chicago: University of Chicago Press, 2000.
OOSTERHUIS Harry and Arlie LOUGHAN, "Madness and Crime: Historical Perspectives on Forensic Psychiatry," *International Journal of Law and Psychiatry*, 37/1, 2014, 1–16.
OOSTERHUIS Harry and Jessica SLIJKHUIS, *Verziekte zenuwen en zeden: De opkomst van de psychiatrie in Nederland (1870–1920)*, Rotterdam: Erasmus Publishing, 2012.
OUKHOW Michel, "Herinneringen," in: Jacques KRUITHOF and Ignace GEURTS (eds.), *De seksualiteit herzien: Het werk van Jos van Ussel*, Deventer: Van Loghum Slaterus, 1979, 154–162.
PASTORELLO Thierry, "L'Abolition du crime de sodomie en 1791: Un long processus social, répressif et pénal," *Cahiers d'histoire: Revue d'histoire critique*, 112–113, 2010, 197–208.
PASTORELLO Thierry, *Sodome à Paris, fin XVIIIème-milieu XIXème: L'Homosexualité masculine en construction*, Paris: Creaphis, 2011.
PATERNOTTE David, "Belgium: The Paradoxical Strength of Disunion," in: Manon TREMBLAY, David PATERNOTTE, and Carol JOHNSON (eds.), *The Lesbian and Gay Movement and the State: Comparative Insights into a Transformed Relationship*, Farnham: Ashgate, 2011, 43–56.
PEDERSEN Jean E., "Regulating Abortion and Birth Control: Gender, Medicine, and Republican Politics in France, 1870–1920," *French Historical Studies*, 19/3, 1996, 673–698.
PEETERS Evert, *De beloften van het lichaam: Een geschiedenis van de natuurlijke levenswijze in België, 1890–1940*, Amsterdam: Standaard Uitgeverij, 2008.
PEETERS Evert, Leen VAN MOLLE, and Kaat WILS (eds.), *Beyond Pleasure: Cultures of Modern Asceticism*, New York: Berghahn Books, 2011.
PENISTON William A., "A Public Offense against Decency: The Trial of the Count de Germiny and the 'Moral Order' of the Third Republic," in: George ROBB and Nancy ERBER (eds.), *Disorder in the Court: Trials and Sexual Conflict at the Turn of the Century*, London: Macmillan, 1999, 12–32.
PENISTON William A., *Pederasts and Others: Urban Culture and Sexual Identity in Nineteenth-Century Paris*, New York: Routledge, 2004.
PEUMANS Wim, *Queer Muslims in Europe: Sexuality, Religion and Migration in Belgium*, London: I.B. Tauris, 2020.
PICK Daniel, *Faces of Degeneration: A European Disorder, c.1848–c.1918*, Cambridge: Cambridge University Press, 1993.
PICKERING Mary, "Positivism in European Intellectual, Political, and Religious Life," in: Warren BRECKMAN and Peter E. GORDON (eds.), *The Cambridge History of Modern European Thought*, 2 vols., vol. 1, Cambridge: Cambridge University Press, 2019, 151–171.
PIETTE Valérie, *Domestiques et servantes: Des vies sous condition. Essai sur le travail domestique en Belgique au 19e siècle*, Brussels: Académie royale de Belgique, 2000.

PIFFERI Michele (ed.), *The Limits of Criminological Positivism: The Movement for Criminal Law Reform in the West, 1870–1940*, Abingdon: Routledge, 2022.

PITTOMVILS Kathlijn, "Tussen repressie en permissiviteit: Socialisme, socialisten, prostitutie en geslachtsziekten (einde 19de eeuw-1997)," in: Denise DE WEERDT (ed.), *Begeerte heeft ons aangeraak: Socialisten, sekse en seksualiteit*, Ghent: Provinciebestuur van Oost-Vlaanderen, 1999, 209–235.

PLILEY Jessica R., "Introduction: A Plea For a 'Vicious Turn' In Global History," in: Jessica R. PLILEY, Robert KRAMM, and Harald FISCHER-TINÉ (eds.), *Global Anti-Vice Activism, 1850–1950: Fighting Drinks, Drugs, and Immorality*, Cambridge: Cambridge University Press, 2016, 1–29.

PLUMMER Kenneth (ed.), *The Making of the Modern Homosexual*, London: Hutchinson, 1981.

POLASKY Janet L., *Reforming Urban Labor: Routes to the City, Roots in the Country*, Ithaca, NY: Cornell University Press, 2010.

POST Harry H. G., *Pillarization: An Analysis of Dutch and Belgian Society*, Aldershot: Avebury, 1989.

POZZI Lucia, *The Catholic Church and Modern Sexual Knowledge, 1850–1950*, Cham: Palgrave Macmillan, 2021.

PRAERO Massimo, *Le moment politique de l'homosexualité: Mouvements, identités et communautés en France*, Lyon: Presses universitaires de Lyon, 2014.

PRETSELL Douglas O., *The Correspondence of Karl Heinrich Ulrichs, 1846–1894*, Basingstoke: Palgrave Macmillan, 2020.

PRETZEL Andreas, *Homosexuellenpolitik in der frühen Bundesrepublik*, Hamburg: Männerschwarm, 2010.

PRETZEL Andreas and Volker WEISS (eds.), *Rosa Radikale: Die Schwulenbewegung der 70er Jahre*, Hamburg: Männerschwarm, 2012.

PROZOROV Sergei and Simona RENTEA (eds.), *The Routledge Handbook of Biopolitics*, London: Routledge, 2017.

PUAR Jasbir, *Terrorist Assemblages: Homonationalism in Queer Times*, Durham, NC: Duke University Press, 2007.

PUFF Helmut, "After the History of (Male) Homosexuality," in: Scott SPECTOR, Helmut PUFF, and Dagmar HERZOG (eds.), *After the History of Sexuality: German Genealogies with and beyond Foucault*, New York: Berghahn Books, 2012, 18–30.

PUISSANT Jean, "Le naturalisme en Belgique, expression littéraire de la crise ou de la prospérité?," in: Paul DELSEMME and Raymond TROUSSON (eds.), *Le naturalisme et les lettres françaises de Belgique*, Brussels: Éditions de l'Université de Bruxelles, 1984, 109–118.

QUINE Maria Sophia, *Population Politics in Twentieth-Century Europe: Fascist Dictatorships and Liberal Democracies*, London: Routledge, 1996.

RACINE Aimée, *La délinquance juvénile en Belgique de 1939 à 1957*, Brussels: Centre d'étude de la délinquance juvénile, 1959.

RAGAN Bryant T. Jr., "Same-Sex Sexual Relations and the French Revolution: The Decriminalization of Sodomy in 1791," in: Sean BRADY and Mark SEYMOUR (eds.), *From Sodomy Laws to Same-Sex Marriage: International Perspectives since 1789*, London: Bloomsbury Academic, 2019, 15–30.

RAMM Agatha, *Europe in the Nineteenth Century 1789–1905*, London: Longman, 1984.

RAMSAY Laura M., *Sexuality and the Church of England, 1918–1980*, Cham: Palgrave Macmillan, 2024.

REINKE Herbert and Margo DE KOSTER, "History of the Police Profession," in: Gerben BRUINSMA and David WEISBURD (eds.), *Encyclopedia of Criminology and Criminal Justice*, New York: Springer, 2014, 2296–2309.

RENNEVILLE Marc, *Crime et folie: Deux siècles d'enquêtes médicales et judiciaires*, Paris: Fayard, 2003.

RENNEVILLE Marc, *Le langage des crânes: Histoire de la phrénologie*, 2nd ed., Paris: La Découverte, 2020.

REVENIN Régis, *Homosexualité et prostitution masculines à Paris 1870–1918*, Paris: L'Harmattan, 2005.

REVENIN Régis, "Homosexualité et virilité," in: Alain CORBIN, Jean-Jacques COURTINE, and Georges VIGARELLO (eds.), *Histoire de la virilité*, 3 vols., vol. 2, Paris: Seuil, 2011, 369–401.

REVENIN Régis, "L'Émergence d'un monde homosexuel moderne dans le Paris de la Belle Époque," *Revue d'histoire moderne et contemporaine*, 53/4, 2006, 74–86.

REYNEBEAU Marc, *Een geschiedenis van België*, 2nd ed., Tielt: Lannoo, 2009 [2003].

ROBERTS John M., *Europe 1880–1945*, 2nd ed., London: Longman, 1989.

ROBINSON Lucy, *Gay Men and the Left in Post-War Britain: How the Personal Got Political*, Mancheser: Manchester University Press, 2007.

RODEN Dimitri, *Ondankbaar België: De Duitse Repressie in de Tweede Wereldoorlog*, Amsterdam: Amsterdam University Press, 2018.

RODEN Frederick S. (ed.), *Jewish, Christian, Queer: Crossroads and Identities*, 2nd ed., London: Routledge, 2016 [2009].

RODEN Frederick S., *Same-Sex Desire in Victorian Religious Culture*, Basingstoke: Palgrave Macmillan, 2002.

ROELENS Jonas, *Citizens and Sodomites: Persecution and Perception of Sodomy in the Southern Low Countries (1400–1700)*, Leiden: Brill, 2024.

ROSARIO Vernon A., "Pointy Penises, Fashion Crimes, and Hysterical Mollies," in: Jeffrey MERRICK and Bryant T.Jr. RAGAN (eds.), *Homosexuality in Modern France*, New York: Oxford University Press, 1996, 146–176.

ROSARIO Vernon A., *The Erotic Imagination: French Histories of Perversity*, New York: Oxford University Press, 1997.

ROSENFELD Michael, "Escal-Vigor: 'A Novel From the French of Georges Eekhoud.' Comment traduire 'l'innomable,'" in: Béatrice COSTA and Catherine GRAVET (eds.), *Traduire la littérature belge francophone: Itinéraires des œuvres et des personnes*, Mons: Université de Mons, 2016.

ROSENFELD Michael, "Formes et figures de l'amour entre hommes dans le discours social, les écrits personnels et la littérature en France et en Belgique de 1870 à 1905," unpublished doctoral dissertation, Université catholique de Louvain and Université Sorbonne Nouvelle, 2020.

ROSENFELD Michael, "Gay Taboos in 1900 Brussels: The Literary, Journalistic and Private Debate Surrounding Georges Eekhoud's Novel Escal Vigor," *Dix-Neuf: Journal of the Society of Dix-Neuviémistes*, 22/1–2, 2018, 98–114.

ROSENFELD Michael, "'Je suis profondément heureux que vous soyez mon ami': L'Amitié de Georges Eekhoud et Jacob Israël de Haan," in: Régine BATTISON, Nikol DZIUB, and Augustin VOEGELE (eds.), *Amitiés vives: Littérature et amitié dans les correspondances d'écrivains*, Reims: Épure – Éditions et presses universitaires de Reims, 2022, 141–154.

ROSENFELD Michael, "Spreken over mannenliefde in 'Ontwaking': Sociale en discursieve netwerken rond Georges Eekhoud en Jacob Israël De Haan (1904–1910)," in: Maxime VAN STEEN and Jan LAMPAERT (eds.), *Vernieuwing in verstrengeling: Dynamische netwerken in artistieke tijdschriften*, Ghent: Academia Press, 2025, 33–58.

ROSENFELD Michael, "Subversion politique et sexuelle dans 'Appol et Brouscard' et 'Une mauvaise rencontre,'" *Textyles*, 58–59, 2020, 213–228.

ROSENFELD Michael, "Zola nataliste ou féministe? Pouvoir féminin et sexualités subversives dans 'Fécondité'," *Nineteenth-Century French Studies*, 51/1–2, 2022–2023, 103–120.

ROSS Andrew I., *Public City/Public Sex: Homosexuality, Prostitution, and Urban Culture in Nineteenth-Century Paris*, Philadelphia: Temple University Press, 2019.

ROSS Charlotte, *Eccentricity and Sameness: Discourses on Lesbianism and Desire between Women in Italy, 1860s–1930s*, Oxford: Peter Lang, 2015.

ROTHENBACHER Franz, *The European Population, 1850–1945*, Basingstoke: Palgrave Macmillan, 2002.

RUBERG Willemijn, "Onzekere kennis: De rol van forensische geneeskunde en psychiatrie in Nederlandse verkrachtingszaken (1811–1920)," *Tijdschrift voor sociale en economische geschiedenis*, 9/1, 2012, 87–110.

RUBERG Willemijn, "Travelling Knowledge and Forensic Medicine: Infanticide, Body and Mind in the Netherlands, 1811–1911," *Medical History*, 57/3, 2013, 359–376.

RUBERG Willemijn, Lara BERGERS, Pauline DIRVEN et al. (eds.), *Forensic Cultures in Modern Europe*, Manchester: Manchester University Press, 2023.

RUBERG Willemijn and Nathanje DIJKSTRA, "De forensische wetenschap in Nederland (1800–1930): Een terreinverkenning," *Studium: Tijdschrift voor Wetenschaps- en Universiteitsgeschiedenis*, 9/3, 2016, 121–143.

RYCKMANS Xavier, "Une déclaration des droits de la famille," *Journal des Tribunaux*, 62/3709, 1947, 1–2.

RYDSTRÖM Jens, *Sinners and Citizens: Bestiality and Homosexuality in Sweden, 1880–1950*, Chicago: University of Chicago Press, 2003.

SAID Edward W., *Orientalism*, New York: Vintage Books, 1979.

SAMPER VENDRELL Javier, *The Seduction of Youth: Print Culture and Homosexual Rights in the Weimar Republic*, Toronto: University of Toronto Press, 2020.

SCHLAGDENHAUFFEN Régis (ed.), *Queer in Europe During the Second World War*, Strasbourg: Council of Europe, 2018.

SCHRIJVERS Peter, *Liberators: The Allies and Belgian Society, 1944–1945*, Cambridge: Cambridge University Press, 2009.

SCHULTZ Gretchen, *French Literature: Nineteenth Century*, GLBTQ. An Encyclopedia of Gay, Lesbian, Bisexual, Transgender, and Queer culture, www.glbtq.com/literature/french_lit2_19c,5.html, last accessed on January 9, 2015.

SCOTT Joan W., "History-Writing as Critique," in: Keith JENKINS, Sue MORGAN, and Alun MUNSLOW (eds.), *Manifestos for History*, London: Routledge, 2007, 19–38.

SCREVENS Raymond, "La loi supprimant la réglementation de la prostitution et son application," *Revue de droit pénal et de criminologie*, 33/6, 1952–1953, 567–582.

SEGERS Yves and Leen VAN MOLLE, *Leven van het land: Boeren in België, 1750–2000*, Leuven: Davidsfonds, 2004.

SERVAIS Paul, "The Church and the Family in Belgium, 1850–1914," *Belgisch Tijdschrift voor Nieuwste Geschiedenis – Revue Belge d'Histoire Contemporaine*, 31/3–4, 2001, 621–647.

SHAPIRA Michal, "Indecently Exposed: The Male Body and Vagrancy in Metropolitan London before the Fin de Siècle," *Gender & History*, 30/1, 2018, 52–69.

SHEPPARD Todd, *Sex, France, and Arab Men, 1962–1979*, Chicago: University of Chicago Press, 2017.

SIBALIS Michael D., "Defining Masculinity in Fin-de-Siécle France: Sexual Anxiety and the Emergence of the Homosexual," *Proceedings of the Annual Meeting of the Western Society for French History*, 25, 1998, 247–256.

SIBALIS Michael D., "Homosexuality in Early Modern France," in: Katherine O'DONNELL and Michael O'ROURKE (eds.), *Queer Masculinities*, Basingstoke: Palgrave Macmillan, 2006, 211–231.

SIBALIS Michael D., "Male Homosexuality in the Age of Enlightenment and Revolution, 1680–1850," in: Robert ALDRICH (ed.), *Gay Life and Culture: A World History*, London: Thames and Hudson, 2006, 103–123.

SIBALIS Michael D., "The Regulation of Male Homosexuality in Revolutionary and Napoleonic France, 1789–1815," in: Jeffrey MERRICK and Bryant T.Jr. RAGAN (eds.), *Homosexuality in Modern France*, New York: Oxford University Press, 1996, 80–101.

SIMONS Ludo, *Geschiedenis van de uitgeverij in Vlaanderen*, 2 vols., vol. 2, Tielt: Lannoo, 1984.

SMITH Dennis, "The 'Civilizing Process' and 'The History of Sexuality': Comparing Norbert Elias and Michel Foucault," *Theory and Society*, 28/1, 1999, 79–100.

SMITH Helen, *Masculinity, Class and Same-Sex Desire in Industrial England, 1895–1957*, Basingstoke: Palgrave Macmillan, 2015.

SMITH Roger, *Free Will and the Human Sciences in Britain, 1870–1910*, London: Routledge, 2013.

SOLOWAY Richard A., "Counting the Degenerates: The Statistics of Race Deterioration in Edwardian England," *Journal of Contemporary History*, 17/1, 1982, 138–164.

SOLOWAY Richard A., *Demography and Degeneration: Eugenics and the Declining Birthrate in Twentieth-Century Britain*, 2nd ed., Chapel Hill: University of North Carolina Press, 1995.

SOMER David, "Florent-Édouard Louwage: Une carrière hybride de policier, de technicien et d'homme du renseignement," in: Marc COOLS, Patrick LEROY, Marc LIBERT et al. (eds.), *1915–2015. Het verhaal van de Belgische militaire veligheidsdienst – 1915–2015: L'histoire du service de renseignement militaire et de sécurité belge*, Antwerp: Maklu, 2015, 315–333.

SPECTOR Scott, *Violent Sensations: Sex, Crime, and Utopia in Vienna and Berlin, 1860–1914*, Chicago: University of Chicago Press, 2016.

SPECTOR Scott, "Where Personal Fate Turns to Public Affair: Homosexual Scandal and Social Order in Vienna, 1900–1910," *Austrian History Yearbook*, 38, 2007, 15–24.

STAS René, "La délinquance contre les mœurs chez les mineurs justiciables du Juge des Enfants: Enquête portant sur les années 1948 et 1949 dans l'arrondissement de Liège," *Revue de droit pénal et de criminologie*, 33/1, 1952–1953, 35–56.

STEAKLEY James, *The Homosexual Emancipation Movement in Germany*, New York: Arno, 1975.

STENGERS Jean, "Les pratiques anticonceptionnelles dans le mariage au XIXe et au XXe siècles: Problèmes humains et attitudes religieuses," *Belgisch tijdschrift voor filologie en geschiedenis – Revue belge de philologie et d'histoire*, 49/2 and 4, 1971, 403–481 and 1119–1174.

STEVENS Liesbet, *Strafrecht en seksualiteit: De misdrijven inzake aanranding van de eerbaarheid, verkrachting, ontucht, prostitutie, seksreclame, zedenschennis en overspel*, Antwerp: Intersentia, 2002.

STRIKWERDA Carl, *A House Divided: Catholics, Socialists, and Flemish Nationalists in Nineteenth-Century Belgium*, Lanham, MD: Rowman and Littlefield, 1997.

SURKIS Judith, *Sexing the Citizen: Morality and Masculinity in France, 1870–1920*, Ithaca, NY: Cornell University Press, 2006.

SUTTON Katie, *Sexuality in Modern German History*, London: Bloomsbury Academic, 2023.

SZULC Łukasz, "Histories of Sexualities in Central and Eastern Europe," *Notches*, November 24, 2015, https://notchesblog.com/2015/11/24/histories-of-sexualities-in-central-and-eastern-europe, last accessed on July 18, 2023.

SZULC Łukasz, *Transnational Homosexuals in Communist Poland Cross-Border Flows in Gay and Lesbian Magazine*, Cham: Springer, 2019.

TAMAGNE Florence, *A History of Homosexuality in Europe: Berlin, London, Paris 1919–1939*, New York: Algora, 2006.

TERRY Jennifer, "Theorizing Deviant Historiography," *Differences: A Journal of Feminist Cultural Studies*, 3/2, 1991, 55–73.

THOMAS Daniel H., *The Guarantee of Belgian Independence and Neutrality in European Diplomacy, 1830's–1930's*, Kingston: Thomas, 1983.

THOMAS David, Simon FOWLER, and Valerie JOHNSON, *The Silence of the Archive*, London: Facet, 2017.

THOMSON Anne, *Bodies of Thought: Science, Religion and the Soul in the Early Enlightenment*, Oxford: Oxford University Press, 2008.

TIJSSELING Anna, "Schuldige seks: Homoseksuele zedendelinquenten rondom de Duitse bezettingstijd," unpublished doctoral dissertation, Utrecht University, 2009.

TOBIN Robert D., *Peripheral Desires: The German Discovery of Sex*, Philadelphia: University of Philadelphia Press, 2015.

TOGMAN Richard, *Nationalizing Sex: Fertility, Fear, and Power*, New York: Oxford University Press, 2019.

TOLLEBEEK Jo, Geert VANPAEMEL, and Kaat WILS (eds.), *Degeneratie in België, 1860–1940: Een geschiedenis van ideeën en praktijken*, Leuven: Leuven University Press, 2003.

TOMLINSON Richard, "The 'Disappearance' of France, 1896–1940: French Politics and the Birth Rate," *The Historical Journal*, 28/2, 1985, 405–415.

TRAUB Valerie, "The New Unhistoricism in Queer Studies," *PMLA*, 128/1, 2013, 21–39.

TRAUB Valerie, *Thinking Sex with the Early Moderns*, Philadelphia: University of Pennsylvania Press, 2016.

TREMBLAY Sébastien, *A Badge of Injury: The Pink Triangle as Global Symbol of Memory*, Oldenbourg: De Gruyter, 2024.

TROUILLOT Michel-Rolph, *Silencing the Past: Power and the Production of History*, Boston: Beacon, 2015 [1995].

TULKENS Françoise and Thierry MOREAU, *Droit de la jeunesse: Aide, assistance, protection*, Brussels: De Boeck and Larcier, 2000.
TURNER William B., *A Genealogy of Queer Theory*, Philadelphia: Temple University Press, 2000.
UPCHURCH Charles, *Before Wilde: Sex between Men in Britain's Age of Reform*, Berkeley: University of California Press, 2009.
VAN DEN DUNGEN Pierre, *Milieux de presse et journalistes en Belgique (1828–1914)*, Brussel: Académie royale de Belgique, 2005.
VAN DER HERTEN Bart, *België onder stoom: Transport en communicatie tijdens de 19de eeuw*, Leuven: Leuven University Press, 2004.
VAN DER MEER Theo, *Jonkheer mr. Jacob Anton Schorer (1866–1957): Een biografie van homoseksualiteit*, Amsterdam: Schorer Boeken, 2007.
VAN DER MEER Theo, "Private Acts, Public Space: Defining Boundaries in Nineteenth-Century Holland," in: William M. LEAP (ed.), *Public Sex, Gay Space*, New York: Columbia University Press, 1999, 223–245.
VAN DER MEER Theo, *Sodoms zaad in Nederland: Het ontstaan van homoseksualiteit in de vroegmoderne tijd*, Nijmegen: SUN, 1995.
VAN DER MEER Theo, "Sodomy and Its Discontents: Discourse, Desire, and the Rise of a Same-Sex Proto-Something in the Early Modern Republic," *Historical Reflections/Réflexions Historiques*, 33/1, 2007, 41–67.
VAN DER MEER Theo, "Sodomy and the Pursuit of a Third Sex in the Early Modern Period," in: Gilbert HERDT (ed.), *Third Sex, Third Gender: Beyond Sexual Dimorphism in Culture and History*, New York: Zone Books, 1993, 137–212.
VAN DER VORST Pierre and Philippe MARY (eds.), *Cent ans de criminologie à l'U.L.B.: Adolphe Prins, l'Union internationale de droit pénal, le Cercle universitaire pour les études criminologiques*, Brussels: Bruylant, 1990.
VAN KRIEKEN Robert, *Norbert Elias*, London: Routledge, 1998.
VAN KRIEKEN Robert, "The Organization of the Soul: Elias and Foucault on Discipline and the Self," *Archives européennes de sociologie – European journal of sociology – Europäisches Archiv für Soziologie*, 31, 1990, 353–371.
VAN LOON Carolien, "De geschorene en de scheerster: De vrouw in de straatrepressie na de Tweede Wereldoorlog," *Bijdragen tot de Eigentijdse Geschiedenis*, 19, 2008, 45–78.
VAN NAERSSEN Lex, *Zoeken naar warmte: De werken van Jos van Ussel*, Deventer: Van Loghum Slaterus, 1978.
VAN OSSELAER Tine, *The Pious Sex: Catholic Constructions of Masculinity and Femininity in Belgium, c1800–1940*, Leuven: Leuven University Press, 2013.
VAN OUTRIVE Lode, Yves CARTUYVELS, and Paul PONSAERS, *Sire, ik ben ongerust: Geschiedenis van de Belgische politie 1794–1991*, Leuven: Kritak, 1992.
VAN PARYS J., "Convient-il de maintenir les sanctions des délits d'adultère et d'entretien de concubine dans notre droit pénal?," *Revue de droit pénal et de criminologie*, 31/5, 1950–1951, 505–512.
VAN PRAAG Philippe, "De opkomst van het nieuw-malthusianisme in Vlaanderen," *Tijdschrift voor sociale geschiedenis*, 3/8, 1977, 197–220.
VAN PRAAG Philippe, *Het bevolkingsvraagstuk in België: Ontwikkeling van standpunten en opvattingen (1900–1977)*, Antwerp: De Sikkel and De Nederlandsche Boekhandel, 1979.

VAN USSEL Jos, *Afscheid van de seksualiteit*, 5th ed., Deventer: Van Loghum Slaterus, 1978 [1970].
VAN USSEL Jos, *Geschiedenis van het seksuele probleem*, Meppel: Boom, 1968.
VAN USSEL Jos, *Histoire de la répression sexuelle*, translated by Catherine CHEVALOT, Paris: Laffont, 1972.
VAN USSEL Jos, *História da repressão sexual*, translated by Ramiro DA FONSECA, Lisbon: Europa-América, 1975.
VAN USSEL Jos, *La represion sexual*, Mexico City: Roca, 1974.
VAN USSEL Jos, *La repressione sessuale: Storia e cause del condizionamento borghese*, translated by Milli GRAFFI, Milan: Bompiani, 1971.
VAN USSEL Jos, *Seksualundertrykkelsens historie*, translated by Inge BERTHELSEN, Copenhagen: Medusa, 1978.
VAN USSEL Jos, *Sexualunterdrückung: Geschichte der Sexualfeindschaft*, translated by Hubertus MARTIN, Reinbeck bei Hamburg: Rowohlt, 1970.
VAN USSEL Jos M. W., "Sociogenese en evolutie van het probleem der seksuele propaedeuse tussen de 16de en de 18de eeuw, vooral in Frankrijk en Duitsland: Bijdrage tot de studie van de burgerlijke seksuele moraal," unpublished doctoral dissertation, 2 vols., University of Amsterdam, 1967.
VANCLOOSTER Stijn, Jan MOULAERT, and Erwin JOOS, *De Kapel tussen droom en daad: Anarchie en artistieke heropleving in Antwerpen rond 1900*, Antwerp: Van Mieghem, 2013.
VANDENDRIESSCHE Joris, *Medical Societies and Scientific Culture in Nineteenth-Century Belgium*, Oxford: Oxford University Press, 2018.
VANDEVOORDE Hans, "'En ces temps de chevaleresque idéologie' Het 'erotisch anarchisme' van Georges Eekhoud," in: David GULLENTOPS and Hans VANDEVOORDE (eds.), *Anarchisten rond Emile Verhaeren*, Brussels: VUBPRESS, 2005, 125–152.
VANHAELEWYN Mathieu, "Homotrots op een heterotrottoir: Over holebimonumenten in België," *Bijdragen tot de Eigentijdse Geschiedenis*, 20, 2008, 233–255.
VANTHEMSCHE Guy, *Belgium and the Congo, 1885–1980*, New York: Cambridge University Press, 2012.
VÁZQUEZ GARCÍA Francisco, "Homosexualité et crise de 1898 en Espagne: L'Invention de Cadix comme la 'Sodome' moderne," in: Jean-Louis GUEREÑA (ed.), *Sexualités Occidentales, XVIIIe–XXIe siècles*, Tours: Presses Universitaires François Rabelais, 2014, 151–180.
VEKEMAN Famke, "De seponeringspolitiek van gerechtelijke strafdossiers betreffende seksueel geweld doorgelicht: Een bijdrage tot de geschiedenis van de seksuele mentaliteit en het strafrechtelijk discours tijdens de eerste helft van de twintigste eeuw," *Van mensen en dingen*, 3/3, 2005, 269–286.
VELLE Karel, *De nieuwe biechtvaders: Sociale geschiedenis van de arts in België*, Leuven: Kritak, 1991.
VELLE Karel, "De syfiliskwestie in België in de 19de en het begin van de 20ste eeuw," *Tijdschrift voor Sociale Wetenschappen*, 32/4, 1987, 331–363.
VERBRUGGEN Christophe, *Schrijverschap in de Belgische belle époque: Een sociaal-culturele geschiedenis*, Ghent: Academia Press and Vantilt, 2009.
VERCAMMEN Rik and Vicky VANRUYSSEVELDT, "Van centraal beleid naar lokale praktijk: Het 'probleem' van landloperij in België (1890–1910)," *Journal of Belgian History*, 45/1, 2015, 120–161.

VĒRDIŅŠ Kārlis and Jānis OZOLIŅŠ (eds.), *Queer Stories of Europe*, Newcastle upon Tyne: Cambridge Scholars, 2016.

VERHOEVEN Timothy, *Sexual Crime, Religion and Masculinity in Fin-de-siècle France: The Flamidien Affair*, Basingstoke: Palgrave Macmillan, 2019.

VERPLAETSE Jan, *Localising the Moral Sense: Neuroscience and the Search for the Cerebral Seat of Morality, 1800–1930*, Dordrecht: Springer, 2009.

VERSCHOORIS Marc, *Martha's labyrint: Een uitzonderlijke vrouwengeschiedenis, 1938–1944*, Gorredijk: Sterck and De Vreese, 2022.

VLEUGELS An, *Narratives of Drunkenness: Belgium, 1830–1914*, London: Pickering and Chatto, 2013.

VON ROSEN Wilhelm, "Denmark 1866–1976: From Sodomy to Modernity," in: Jens RYDSTRÖM and Kati MUSTOLA (eds.), *Criminally Queer: Homosexuality and Criminal Law in Scandinavia*, Amsterdam: Aksant, 2004, 61–90.

WAALDIJK Kees, *Legal Recognition of Homosexual Orientation in the Countries of the World: A Chronological Overview with Footnotes*, Leiden University, https://openaccess.leidenuniv.nl/bitstream/handle/1887/14543/Waaldijk+2009+-+Legal+Recogniton+of+Homosexual+Orientation+-+Chronological+Overview.pdf?sequence=1, last accessed on August 10, 2022.

WAKEMAN Rosemary, *A Modern History of European Cities, 1815 to the Present*, London: Bloomsbury Academic, 2020.

WALKOWITZ Judith R., *City of Dreadful Delight: Narratives of Sexual Danger in Late-Victorian London*, Chicago: University of Chicago Press, 1992.

WALSHE Eibhear, *Oscar's Shadow: Wilde, Homosexuality and Modern Ireland*, Cork: Cork University Press, 2011.

WARMERDAM Hans and Pieter KOENDERS, *Cultuur en Ontspanning: Het COC, 1946–1966*, Utrecht: Rijksuniversiteit Utrecht, 1987.

WATERS Chris, "Distance and Desire in the New British Queer History," *GLQ: A Journal of Lesbian and Gay Studies*, 14/1, 2008, 139–155.

WATERS Chris, "The Homosexual as a Social Being in Britain, 1945–1968," *Journal of British Studies*, 51/3, 2012, 685–710.

WAUTELET Jean-Marie, *Structures industrielles et reproduction élargie du capital en Belgique (1850–1914)*, Louvain-la-Neuve: Academia and L'Harmattan, 1995.

WEBER Donald, *Homo criminalis: Belgische parlementsleden over misdaad en strafrecht, 1830–1940*, Brussels: VUB Press, 1996.

WEBER Donald, "Werkmanstreinen en de geboorte van de moderne pendelaar, 1870–1914," *Brood & Rozen*, 15/4, 2009, https://doi.org/10.21825/br.v14i5.3406, last accessed on August 12, 2024, 131–148.

WEBER Philippe, *Der Trieb zum Erzählen: Sexualpathologie und Homosexualität, 1852–1914*, Bielefeld: transcript Verlag, 2008.

WEEKS Jeffrey, "Queer(y)ing the 'Modern Homosexual,'" *The Journal of British Studies*, 51/3, 2012, 523–539.

WEEKS Jeffrey, *Sex, Politics and Society: The Regulation of Sex since 1800*, 3rd ed., London: Routledge, 2012 [1981].

WEEKS Jeffrey, "The 'Homosexual Role' after 30 Years: An Appreciation of the Work of Mary McIntosh," *Sexualities*, 1/2, 1998, 131–152.

WELTER François, "Quand l'intérêt public se heurte aux obstacles institutionnels et matériels: Une police judiciaire près des parquets, solution aux défis de la police

judiciaire en Belgique (1830–1922)," *Bijdragen tot de Eigentijdse Geschiedenis*, 24, 2011, 35–63.
WHISNANT Clayton J., *Male Homosexuality in West Germany: Between Persecution and Freedom, 1945–1969*, Basingstoke: Palgrave Macmillan, 2012.
WHISNANT Clayton J., *Queer Identities and Politics in Germany: A History, 1880–1945*, New York: Harrington Park, 2016.
WIENER Joel H. (ed.), *Papers for the Millions: The New Journalism in Britain, 1850s to 1914*, New York: Greenwood Press, 1986.
WIENER Martin J., *Reconstructing the Criminal: Culture, Law and Policy in England, 1830–1914*, Cambridge: Cambridge University Press, 1990.
WILS Kaat, *De omweg van de wetenschap: Het positivisme en de Belgische en Nederlandse intellectuele cultuur*, Amsterdam: Amsterdam University Press, 2005.
WITTE Els, "The Battle for Monasteries, Cemeteries and Schools: Belgium," in: Christopher CLARK and Wolfram KAISER (eds.), *Culture Wars: Secular-Catholic Conflict in Nineteenth-Century Europe*, Cambridge: Cambridge University Press, 2003, 102–128.
WITTE Els, Jean-Pierre NANDRIN, Eliane GUBIN et al. (eds.), *Nieuwe geschiedenis van België*, 3 vols., vol. 1, Tielt: Lannoo, 2005.
WOLFFRAM Heather, *Forensic Psychology in Germany: Witnessing Crime, 1880–1939*, s.l.: Palgrave Macmillan, 2018.
WOLFFRAM Heather, "Teaching Grossian Criminalistics in Imperial Germany," in: Willemijn RUBERG, Lara BERGERS, Pauline DIRVEN et al. (eds.), *Forensic Cultures in Modern Europe*, Manchester: Manchester University Press, 2023, 92–116.
WONG Aliza S., *Race and the Nation in Liberal Italy, 1861–1911: Meridionalism, Empire, and Diaspora*, New York: Palgrave Macmillan, 2006.
WOOD Anthony, *Europe 1815–1960*, 2nd ed., Harlow: Longman, 1984.

Index

accidental exposure, 49, 53
adoption rights, 133
adultery, tolerance and pragmatism, 37, 98
age of consent, 42, 120, 126, 128, 132
    Franco-Danish model, 127–128
aggravated assault, 53
Aletrino, Arnold, 105, 117, 119
anatomo-deterministic model of sexual perversion, 62, 74, 76–77, 83, 85. *See also* Krafft-Ebing, Richard von; Magnan, Valentin; Semal, François
Anthropological Society of Brussels, 75, 79, 81
anti-discrimination legislation, 132
anti-slavery and abolitionist movements, 103
Aquinas, Thomas, 74
    contraception, 98
    sex and marriage, 98
ars erotica, 7
article 372bis of the Belgian Penal Code, 126, 128–129
    demonstrations against, 130
    repeal, 130–132
Auden, W.H., 122

Ball, Benjamin, 85
Belgian Cultural Center (Centre Culturel Belge-Cultuur Centrum België), 129
Belgian independence (1830), 4, 22, 36, 46, 59, 92
Belgian League of Education, 81
Belgian penal code, 47
    article 372bis, 126, 128–129
    demonstrations against, 130
    repeal, 130–132
    indecent proposals, 124
    moral liberalism, 50, 52
    outrage aux mœurs publics (Art. 385), 47
Belgian Revolution. *See* Belgian independence (1830)
Belgian Society for Sexual Education, 1
Belgian Society of Mental Medicine (BSMM), 75. *See also* Semal, François
    professionalization of psychiatry, 60

Belgian Workers Party, 37, 79, 93, 107, 115
Belgium. *See also* Brussels
    cultural and intellectual diversity, 93
    demographic slump, regional differences, 96–98
    history of homosexuality, 4
    Catholicism, 6. *See also* Catholicism
    criminalization, lack of, 4, 11, 45, 50
    psychiatrization of homosexuality, 51–53. *See also* medicalization and pathologization of 'perversion'
    sex in society, 10
    silence and the historiography of sexuality, 4–6, 10–11. *See also* silence and the historiography of sexuality
    industrial strength, 92
    modernity, embrace of, 93
    neutrality, 92–93
    population, 93
    demographic slump, 96–98
Belgium's liberation (Sept 1944), 123
Benedikt, Moritz, 75, 77
birth control and contraception, 90, 96, 100. *See also* fertility and birth rates
    Catholic church, 97–99
    fertility decline and birth rates, 13, 88
birth rates. *See* fertility and birth rates
blackmail, 118
    false accusations, 24, 26, 39
    law enforcement, 39, 41
Bladel, Maurice, 119
Bloch, Iwan, 118
Boeykens, Jackie, 131
Bonaparte, Napoleon, 46
born criminal concept, 70, 80, 83, 85. *See also* Lombroso, Cesare
bourgeois sexual morality, 1–2, 23, 69
Brussels. *See also* Belgium
    cruising, 23
    demographic growth, 17
    fin-de-siècle Brussels, 15–16, 19–21
    queer culture, 19–21
    urban bachelor culture, 19

Brussels (cont.)
    industrialization, 16, 22
    migrant workers, 17, 20
        family status, 19–21
    queer space, 22
        downtown areas, 23
        historical city centre, 23–24
        public toilets and urinals, 22, 24, 34–35, 48
        urban wastelands, 22–23
Butler, Josephine, 103

Calvinism, 119
capitalism and sex-negativity in the West, 1–2, 89
Carpenter, Edward, 111, 117
Casti Connubii (Chaste Union), 99
Catholicism
    Aquinian doctrine, 74
    contraception, 98
    sex and marriage, 98
    Casti Connubii (Chaste Union), 99
    civilizationising of individuals and of society, 68
    discretion of the confessional, 101
    fertility rates, impact on, 96
    mental institutions, control of, 57
    psychiatrization of 'perversion,' 12, 57, 69
    removal of Christian Democrats from government, 132
    sex-negativity in the West, impact on, 1, 8–9
        culture of silence, 9, 13
    sodomy as *crimen nefandum*, 8
censorship, 2, 32, 114–116, 119
Center for Leisure and Culture (COC) (NL), 129
Charcot, Jean-Martin, 61, 76–77
Charles, Raymond, 126, 131–132
Chevalier, Julien, 21, 85, 91
class and social status, 20, 26–27, 57, 110
    bourgeois sexual morality, 1–2, 23, 69
    voyous de velours, 117–118
colonialism, 88–89, 92, 95
communism, 121, 123
    red scare, 37
community, sense of, 16, 29, 43
comparative law, Belgian and German jurisprudence, 12
Comte, Auguste, 61, 73
Concert of Europe, 92
Congress of Vienna (1814-15), 58
consociationalism, 130
corruption of law enforcement, 37, 39–40
crime and responsibility, 70–71, 86
    anatomo-deterministic model of sexual perversion, 76–77
    free will, 72, 74, 84
    medicalization and pathologization of 'perversion,' 45–46, 51, 55, 63
    spiritualism, 73
crime de la Place Royale, 44
    newspaper reporting, 32–34
        anecdote and hearsay, 34
        salacious interest, 33–34
criminal anthropology, 70–71, 75, 78, 81–83, 87
criminal investigations
    crime de la Place Royale, 32–35, 44
    silence and solidarity, 42–43
    trial of Bruges (Lemonnier and Eekhoud), 112–114
criminal law, 12
    Belgian penal code, 47
        article 372bis, 126, 128–132
        indecent proposals, 124
        moral liberalism, 50, 52
        outrage aux mœurs publics (Art. 385), 47
    Dutch penal code, 120
    Enlightenment, penal code reforms, 72
    French penal codes, introduction in Belgium, 46
    German penal code
        öffentliche Ärgerniss (Para. 183), 47
        prosecutorial practice, 122
        sodomy law, 65
    Napoleonic penal code, 46
    penal code of Wilhelmine Germany, 46
Criminal Man (Lombroso), 70
criminalization of homosexual acts, 4, 11, 45, 132
    national differences, 46–48
cruising, 22–24, 34, 42, 108, 121–122
Cuylits, Jean, 63, 77

d'Ädelsward-Fersen, Jacques, 117, 119
Dallemagne, Jules, 85–87
de Batselier, Steven, 131
de Bont, Raf, 87
De Greeff, Etienne, 125
de jaren stillekes (the silent years), 1
De Pues, Suzanne, 111, 129
De Rode, Léon, 63–65, 111
    gratuitous medicalizing of homosexuality, 65–67
    homosexuality as unchecked hedonism, 66–68, 79–81
decentralization and local autonomy, 31, 59
    mental hospitals, 59–60
dechristianization, 76–77, 89, 97, 102. *See also* secularism
decriminalization of homosexuality, 13, 46, 69, 120, 128, 132

Index

degeneration theory, 61–65, 79–80, 86–87, 90, 95–96
  protean nature, 64, 91
demographic anxieties, 88–89
  Belgium, 17, 92–96
    Catholicism, 99–104
    regional differences, 96–99
  fertility and birth rates, 13, 88–89, 94–96
    Belgian regional differences, 96–98
    birth control and contraception, 13, 88, 90, 96, 100
    Catholic church, 97–99
    France, 90
    Germany, 90
    homosexuality's association with, 91
    post-WWII Belgium, 123
  France, 89–91
  neo-Malthusianism, 95, 97, 99
    contraceptive information, 99
Denmark, 120
  Franco-Danish model (age of consent), 128
  Great Morality Scandal, 119
Descartes, René, 72
determinism, 12
  anatomo-deterministic model of sexual perversion, 62, 74, 76–77, 83, 85
  determinism/free will debate, 82–85
  radical materialism and determinism, 73–75
  sexual roots, 75–78
Dewinne, Auguste, 114–115
dichotomies within historiography of sexuality
  innocence versus corruption, 3, 64, 68, 89
  pursuit of pleasure versus duty of procreation, 3, 45, 80, 90, 102
discrimination scandals, 132
Doan, Laura, 7
Douglas, Lord Alfred, 105
downtown areas, 17, 19, 40
  as queer space, 15, 23–24, 50, 105, 121, 126
Dutch penal code, 120

economic laissez-faire, 17, 60, 71, 77, 88, 92
Eekhoud, Georges, 13, 27, 106
  anarchist sympathies, 107
  Escal-Vigor, 106, 110–113
    success, 117
  intellectual literary and artistic movement, involvement in, 106–107
  The Lancer's Quadrille, 108–110
  working class, erotic longing for, 107–108
Elias, Norbert, 1. *See also* shame and self-restraint, relationship between
Ellis, Havelock, 81, 85–86, 111
Enlightenment, 46, 103
  penal code reforms, 72

Eros and Civilization (Marcuse), 2
Escal-Vigor (Eekhoud), 106, 110–113
  success, 117
eugenics, 95
Eulenburg affair (1907–1909) (D), 8, 119
European Court of Human Rights, 132
exhibitionism, 35, 50

fascism, 99, 121
Féré, Charles, 91
fertility and birth rates, 13, 88–89
  Belgium, 94–96
    post-WWII, 123
    regional differences, 96–98
  birth control and contraception, 88
  Catholicism, 96
  demographic anxieties, 13, 88–89, 94–96
    Belgian regional differences, 96–98
    birth control and contraception, 13, 88, 90, 96, 100
    Catholic church, 97–99
    France, 90
    Germany, 90
    homosexuality's association with, 91
    post-WWII Belgium, 123
  France, 90
  Germany, 90
  homosexuality's association with, 91
  marriage, 123
Feuerbach, Ludwig, 72
Fifth International Conference on Criminal Anthropology (1901), 105
First Moroccan Crisis (1905), 92
Forster, E.M., 122
Foucault, Michel
  historiography of sexuality, impact on, 3–4, 67, 105
    Catholicism, 8–9, 102
    reverse discourse, 105
    scientia sexualis, 6
    Van Ussel, criticisms of, 2–4, 6
France
  demograpic anxieties, 90
  European dominance, 89
  homosexuality, 6
    criminalization of homosexual acts, 46
    psychiatrization of 'perversion,' 12
Franco-Prussian War (1870-1871), 89, 92
Francotte, Xavier, 80, 113
Franssen, Firmin, 128
free will, 12, 70–75, 82
  crime and responsibility, 72, 74, 84
  determinism/free will debate, 51, 62, 77, 81–85
  freedom of art and ideas, 116. *See also* censorship

Index

French penal codes (1791)
  introduction in Belgium, 46
Freud, Sigmund, 81, 113, 125–126
  influence, 1–2
Front Homosexuel d'Action Révolutionnaire (B), 129
Fryer, Jonathan, 121

Gall, Franz-Joseph, 72
Garnier, Paul, 85
gender bending, 130
gender identity, 133. *See also* sexual identity
General Conference of German Morality Associations, 103
German occupation of Belgium, 121
German penal code
  öffentliche Ärgerniss (Para. 183), 47
  prosecutorial practice, 122
  sodomy law, 65
Germany
  homosexuality, 6
    criminalization of homosexual acts, 47
    medicalization and pathologization of 'perversion,' 46, 50–52
    psychiatrization of 'perversion,' 51–52
    public indecency, 49–51
    rising strength and power, 89
Great Awakening, 103
Great Morality Scandal (1906) (DK), 119
Griesinger, Wilhelm, 61

Haene, Piet de, 131
heterosexual age of consent, 120, 128
heterosexual indecencies or assault, 50, 53
heterosexual prostitution, 5, 35, 37, 126
Hirschfeld, Magnus, 27–28, 85, 111, 117
historical city centres as queer space, 23–24
The History of Sexuality (Foucault), 2–4, 105
History of the Sexual Problem (Van Ussel), 2–3
  Foucault's influence, 2–4
HIV/AIDS, 132
Hocquenghem, Guy, 130
homogenization of modern homosexual identity, 6–7
'homonationalism,' 133
homosexual movement, emergence of, 114, 126, 128–131
  Germany, 47, 67
homosexual relations between consenting adults, 31, 46, 51, 65, 128
homosexual seduction theory, 124–126
  rejection, 131
homosexuality in the public discourse, 57, 129–130, 132–134. *See also* silence and the historiography of sexuality

honor, 26–27
Houzé, Émile, 82
Howard, John, 7
Hubert, Eugène, 81–82

idealism, 72
ideological resistance to pathologization of perversion, 12, 70–71, 87
indecent assault, 52
  Germany, 49
indecent proposals, 124
infringement of adults' personal integrity, 46, 51
innocence and virtue, 3, 101
  purity in boarding schools, 101–102
insanity laws
  Belgium, 59
  France, 59
insanity pleas, 54
  skepticism of legal profession, 54–56
intentionality, 47–48
  public indecency
    Belgian law, 12
    German courts, 49
International Abolitionist Federation, 103
Interpol, 13, 127
interwar years, 33, 121–122
  demographic anxieties, 102
  law enforcement, 39, 44
Isherwood, Christopher, 25, 121
Israël De Haan, Jacob, 117

Jacquart, Camille, 96–98
Janssens de Bisthoven, Léon, 112–114
John Paul II (Pope), 9
journalism. *See* newspaper reporting

Kinsey, Alfred, 1, 128
Kistemaeckers, Henry, 115
Knoch, Auguste, 100–102
Krafft-Ebing, Richard von, 61–63, 85, 111
Krupp, Alfred Friedrich, 119
Kuyper, Abraham, 119

L'Homme en Amour (Lemonnier), 112
La Jeune Belgique, 107, 116
Lacan, Jacques, 125
laissez-faire liberalism, 17, 60, 71, 77, 88, 92
Lamarck, Jean-Baptiste
  influence, 62
language of sex and sexuality, 58
  analytical and prescriptive discourse, 3, 67–68, 90
  Catholicism and sex-negativity, 9
  onanism, 13

Index

reverse discourse, 67–68, 105–106, 111
secularization, 57, 101
Lateau, Louise, 74, 76
law enforcement, 11, 13
  Belgium, 31
    corruption, 37, 39
    police records and court files, 34–35
    post-WWII, 125
    silence and solidarity, 42–43
    vice squad, 34–35, 37–38
  Berlin, 31
  comparison of European policing systems, 36
  heterosexual prostitution versus homosexual 'deviance,' 125–126
  insanity pleas, 54
  Paris, 31
  police priorities, 36–38
  pre-professionalization, 36
  prosecution of homosexual acts, 38–39
    bribery and corruption, 39
    revenge and settling personal scores, 40–42
Law on the Administration of the Insane (1850) (B), 59
law/biology debate, 83–84
  anatomo-deterministic model of sexual perversion, 62, 74, 76–77, 83, 85
  insanity pleas, 54–56
Lefèbvre, Ferdinand, 74, 82
Lejeune, Jules, 77, 87, 104
Leo XIII (Pope), 74, 98
Leopold II (King of Belgium), 22, 79
Leopold III (King of Belgium), 123
lesbianism, 126, 129–131
libertarianism, 121
Liguori, Alphonsus de, 98–99
local autonomy principle, 36, 59
Lombroso, Cesare, 70, 73, 83
Louwage, Florent, 125–128

MacDonald, Hector, 119
Magnan, Valentin, 61, 75–77, 85
male homosexuality as sexual deviation, 3–4, 7
Mantegazza, Paolo, 85
Marcuse, Herbert, 1–2. *See also* sexual shame in Western society
marriage, 19, 90
  Catholicism, 97–98
  of convenience, 84
  fertility and birth rates, 123
  same-sex marriage, 133
Marx, Karl, 2, 37
Marxism, 9
materialism, 12, 71–72
  monistic materialists, 72
  radical materialism and determinism, 73–75
    sexual roots, 75–78

reductive, 3
scientific, 72
Maudsley, Henry, 83
medicalization and pathologization of 'perversion,' 45–46, 55, 69–70, 100. *See also* moral and legal responsibility for homosexual acts
  Belgium
    reluctance to accept, 54–56
  Catholicism, 9
  Germany, 46, 50–52
  ideological resistance, 12, 70–71
  impact on reverse discourse and legitimacy narrative, 67–68
  overmedicalization, 66–67
  theories against, 63–65
mental hospitals
  Belgian decentralist policy, 59
  neglect and lack of proper medical care, 60
  French state-funded hospitals, 59
Mercier, Cardinal Désiré-Joseph, 97–99
National League Against Depopulation, 99
Mill, John Stuart, 73
minors. *See* moral corruption of minors; sexual molestation of children
mitigation, homosexual desires as, 54
modern homosexual identity, homogenization, 6–7
Moll, Albert, 85, 111, 115
moral and legal responsibility for homosexual acts, 45–46, 51, 63, 70. *See also* medicalization and pathologization of 'perversion'
moral contagion threat, 127
moral corruption of minors, 46, 52, 124–126
Moral Order (F), 76
Morality Law (1911) (NL), 119
morality movements, 103–104
Morel, Bénédict, 61
Morel, Jules, 77
Morissens, Eliane, 131
Mouvement Homosexuel d'Action Révolutionnaire (B), 129

Näcke, Paul, 86
Napoleon III, 73
Napoleon, Bonaparte
  defeat at Waterloo, 58
Napoleonic law, 47, 62
Napoleonic penal code, 46
Napoleonic wars, 59, 89
National League Against Depopulation, 99
Nazi persecution of homosexuals, 114, 122, 127
neo-Malthusianism, 95, 97–100

neo-Thomism, 99
Netherlands, 65, 120–121
  Belgian independence (1830), 4, 22, 36, 46, 59, 92
  Calvinism, 119
  consociationalism, 130
  criminalization of homosexual acts, 47
  Franco-Danish model (age of consent), 128
  professionalization of psychiatry, 69
  Protestantism, 13
  recriminalization of homosexuality, 120
newspaper reporting
  crime de la Place Royale, 32–34
  anecdote and hearsay, 34
  salacious interest, 33–34
Nihil volitum, nisi praecognitum, 101
Nordau, Max, 64

offences against public decency. *See* public decency laws
onanism, language of, 13, 89, 99–101, 114
Oosterhuis, Harry, 67

pathologization of 'perversion.' *See* medicalization and pathologization of 'perversion'
'pederasty,' 4, 35
penal code of Wilhelmine Germany, 46
Petithan, Charles, 94–96
pillarization, 130
'pinkwashing,' 133
police judiciaire, 38
police records and court files, 34–35, 38–39. *See also* law enforcement
positivism, 12, 61, 73–76, 81, 84
  positivist secularism, 57
postcolonial studies, 7
post-WWII Belgium, 123–124
power and sexual repression, relationship between, 2–4
pragmatism, 32, 47, 83, 86–87, 98
preoccupation with sex and sexual deviation, 3–4, 45, 62, 91
Prévost-Paradol, Lucien-Anatole, 89
Prins, Adolphe, 78
prison-asylums, 71, 78
private bathhouses, safe spaces, 25
professionalization (lack of) of law enforcement, 36
professionalization (lack of) of psychiatry, 60–61, 68, 73
promiscuity, 20–21
prosecution of homosexual acts, 38–39
  Belgium under Nazi rule, 122
  bribery and corruption, 39
  German courts, public indecency, 49–51
  homosexual desires as mitigation, 54
  silence and solidarity, 42–43
prostitution, 125
  heterosexual prostitution, 5, 35, 37, 126
  regulated prostitution, 85
  abolition, 124
  abolition campaigns, 37, 103–104
  law enforcement monitoring of, 37
Protestantism, 9, 58, 89, 101
  Great Awakening, 103
  Netherlands, 13
  Protestant morality movements, 103
  rationalism, 103
  regulated prostitution, abolition of, 37
  Wilde and Protestant virtue, 8, 118
psychiatric assessment, 54
psychiatrization of 'perversion,' 12, 57–58
  Belgium, 12, 51–53
  Catholicism, 12, 57, 69
  France, 12
  Germany, 51–53
psychiatry as a profession, 59–61
Psychopathia Sexualis (Krafft-Ebing), 63–66, 68, 111
psychopathological nature of homosexuality, 55–57, 80
  Belgium, 58, 62, 128
  France, 57–58
  professionalization of psychology, 60
psychosociological approach to homosexuality, 86
public decency laws, 22, 38, 40, 46, 49–50, 52, 97
  censorship, 114–116
  interpretations, 48
  Trial of Bruges, 112–114
public indecency
  Germany, 49–51
  policing of public decency, 49–51
public interest, 46
public toilets and urinals as queer space, 22, 24, 34–35, 48
punishment, 38, 79. *See also* criminal law; insanity laws; law enforcement; public decency laws; sodomy laws
  public acts, 27
  punishable acts, 46, 53, 116, 124
  social defense doctrine, 78
  whether morally/legally/criminally responsible homosexual acts, 62–63, 65, 70

'queer dives,' safe spaces, 25–26, 34–35
queer rights, 133
queer space, Brussels, 22, 105
  downtown areas, 23

Index

fin-de-siècle Brussels, 35
   historical city centre, 23–24
   public toilets and urinals, 22, 24, 34–35, 48
   safe spaces, 24–26
   urban wastelands, 22–23
queer theory, 6–7

Raffalovich, Marc-André, 86, 111, 113
rationalism, 70, 72–73, 103
recriminalization of homosexuality, 4, 13, 120, 126, 128
reductive materialism, 3
Regout, Robert, 119
regulated prostitution, 85
   abolition, 124
   campaigns, 37, 103–104
   law enforcement monitoring of, 37
repression
   police enforcement, 31
   self-censorship, 33
responsible man concept, 72
reverse discourse, 67–68, 105–106, 111
right to free speech, 114–116
rooming houses, safe spaces, 24–25

safe spaces
   private bathhouses, 25
   'queer dives,' 25–26
   rooming houses, 24–25
Saint-Paul, Georges, 91
same-sex marriage, 133
Schouten, Hubertus Johannes, 118
scientia sexualis (science of sex), 6. *See also* Foucault, Michel
secession. *See* Belgian independence (1830)
secularism, 9, 46, 76, 89, 96, 133
   demographic anxieties, 102
   positivist, 57–58
   secular psychiatry, 57–58, 69
Semal, François, 69, 71, 75
sex tourism, 11, 122
sexual assault, 52
sexual identity, 3, 7
   pathologized identity, 66
sexual molestation of children, 54
sexual repression, 2–4
sexual restraint and civilizing impact, 1–2
sexual shame in Western society, 2. *See also* Marcuse, Herbert
sexual transgression, 46
shame and self-restraint, relationship between, 1, 27. *See also* Elias, Norbert
silence and solidarity, 42–43, 105
silence and the historiography of sexuality, 1, 8, 13. *See also* homosexuality in the public discourse

Catholicism, 8–9
homosexuality as a social problem, 8
lack of sources, 4–6, 10–11
national difference, 8
social reform, 93–94, 132
socialism, 73, 75, 93, 100, 107, 112, 130
socio-political tensions
   Belgian Workers Party, 37, 79, 93, 107, 115
   law enforcement, 37–38, 93
sodomy laws
   abolition in France, 31
   Belgium, 46
   Germany, 62, 65
Spencer, Herbert, 73
spiritualism, 72–74
   self-control and strength of character, 80–81
   spiritualist-materialist divisions, 75
   determinism, 82
strikes (1886 and 1887), 95
subcultures, 16, 29, 43
subsidiarity principle, 36
suppression versus will to know, 2–3. *See also* silence and the historiography of sexuality
surveillance, 31, 35
   failures, 39, 42

Tarnowsky, Benjamin, 65, 85
terminology, 10–11. *See also* language of sex and sexuality
pédérastie/pédéraste, 26
Third International Conference on Criminal Anthropology (1892), 13, 71, 78
Thomism, 74, 99
transgender, 133
Treaty of London (1839), 92
trial of Bruges (Lemonnier and Eekhoud), 112–114
   freedom of the artist, 115
Tuke, Daniel Hack, 77

Ulrichs, Karl Heinrich, 46, 62, 65, 67
'underworld' of vice and exploitation, 25–26, 29, 33, 122
Union of Opposites, 59
United Kingdom of the Netherlands
   Belgian secession, 36
   creation, 58
'Uranism,' 62, 105, 111–113
urban bachelor culture of Brussels, 19–21, 29
urban wastelands as queer space, 22–23
urbanized nature of homosexuality, 16

Van Ussel, Jos
   death, 4
   History of the Sexual Problem, 2–4
   PhD, 1–2

Vandervelde, Émile, 100, 115
Vermeersch, Arthur, 97, 99–100
Vervaeck, Louis, 87
vice squad, 37
  corruption, 37
  police records, 34–35
  socio-political tensions, 37
  White Slave Trade Affair, 37
Vincineau, Michel, 131
von Römer, Lucien, 85, 117
voyous de velours (velvet street urchins), 117–118

Western anti-sexual syndrome, 6. *See also* Van Ussel, Jos

Westernization of sexuality, 6–7
Westphal, Carl, 61–62, 79
White Slave Trade Affair (1880), 37
Wilde, Oscar, 8, 110, 118
  conviction, 119
  trial, 8, 25, 111, 118
Woeste, Charles, 95–96, 115
women's rights, 103
World War I, 89, 100, 106, 121
World War II, 121–122, 127
  wartime collaboration, 123–124

Zola, Émile, 90–91, 111, 116

Printed in the United Kingdom by TJ Clays Ltd.